14 YEARS OF LOYAL SERVICE IN A FABRIC-COVERED BOX

Other DILBERT® books from Andrews McMeel Publishing

Freedom's Just Another Word for People Finding Out You're Useless
ISBN: 0-7407-7815-3

Dilbert 2.0: 20 Years of Dilbert
ISBN: 0-7407-7735-1

This Is the Part Where You Pretend to Add Value
ISBN: 0-7407-7227-9

Cubes and Punishment
ISBN: 0-7407-6837-9

Positive Attitude
ISBN: 0-7407-6379-2

Try Rebooting Yourself
ISBN: 0-7407-6190-0

What Would Wally Do?
ISBN: 0-7407-5769-5

Thriving on Vague Objectives
ISBN: 0-7407-5533-1

The Fluorescent Light Glistens Off Your Head
ISBN: 0-7407-5113-1

It's Not Funny If I Have to Explain It
ISBN: 0-7407-4658-8

Don't Stand Where the Comet Is Assumed to Strike Oil
ISBN: 0-7407-4539-5

Words You Don't Want to Hear During Your Annual Performance Review
ISBN: 0-7407-3805-4

When Body Language Goes Bad
ISBN: 0-7407-3298-6

What Do You Call a Sociopath in a Cubicle? Answer: A Coworker
ISBN: 0-7407-2663-3

Another Day in Cubicle Paradise
ISBN: 0-7407-2194-1

When Did Ignorance Become a Point of View?
ISBN: 0-7407-1839-8

Excuse Me While I Wag
ISBN: 0-7407-1390-6

Dilbert—A Treasury of Sunday Strips: Version 00
ISBN: 0-7407-0531-8

Random Acts of Management
ISBN: 0-7407-0453-2

Dilbert Gives You the Business
ISBN: 0-7407-0338-2 hardcover
ISBN: 0-7407-0003-0 paperback

Don't Step in the Leadership
ISBN: 0-8362-7844-5

Journey to Cubeville
ISBN: 0-8362-7175-0 hardcover
ISBN: 0-8362-6745-1 paperback

I'm Not Anti-Business, I'm Anti-Idiot
ISBN: 0-8362-5182-2

Seven Years of Highly Defective People
ISBN: 0-8362-5129-6 hardcover
ISBN: 0-8362-3668-8 paperback

Casual Day Has Gone Too Far
ISBN: 0-8362-2899-5

Fugitive from the Cubicle Police
ISBN: 0-8362-2119-2

It's Obvious You Won't Survive by Your Wits Alone
ISBN: 0-8362-0415-8

Still Pumped from Using the Mouse
ISBN: 0-8362-1026-3

Bring Me the Head of Willy the Mailboy!
ISBN: 0-8362-1779-9

Shave the Whales
ISBN: 0-8362-1740-3

Dogbert's Clues for the Clueless
ISBN: 0-8362-1737-3

Always Postpone Meetings with Time-Wasting Morons
ISBN: 0-8362-1758-6

Build a Better Life by Stealing Office Supplies
ISBN: 0-8362-1757-8

For ordering information, call 1-800-223-2336.

14 YEARS OF LOYAL SERVICE IN A FABRIC-COVERED BOX

A DILBERT™ BOOK
BY SCOTT ADAMS

Andrews McMeel
Publishing, LLC

Kansas City • Sydney • London

09 10 11 12 13 RR2 10 9 8 7 6 5 4 3 2 1

ISBN-13: 978-0-7407-7365-5
ISBN-10: 0-7407-7365-8

Library of Congress Control Number: 2009921637

www.andrewsmcmeel.com

www.dilbert.com

─── **ATTENTION: SCHOOLS AND BUSINESSES** ───

Andrews McMeel books are available at quantity discounts with bulk purchase for educational, business, or sales promotional use. For information, please write to: Special Sales Department, Andrews McMeel Publishing, LLC, 1130 Walnut Street, Kansas City, Missouri 64106.

For Shelly

Introduction

When I was a kid, I had no idea there were so many different occupations that a person could pursue. I had a vague understanding of the more common jobs, such as doctor, lawyer, fireman, farmer, and policeman. I set my sights on becoming a lawyer, largely because the other careers inevitably involved dead mammals.

At some point during college, I realized that although lawyers don't directly kill any mammals, they do hold mammals down so other people can kill them, figuratively speaking. So I abandoned my plans for the legal profession. I decided to become a banker because one of my professors said I should, although I didn't fully understand what that career involved. I assumed I'd take people's money, put most of it in a big safe, and keep some of it for myself. It seemed like a dream job.

Unfortunately, no one warned me that a career in banking would lead to years of sitting in a fabric-covered box and accomplishing nothing. During that period, I was surrounded by other people in fabric-covered boxes, whose shared mission, apparently, was to keep each other from adding value. I was so many levels away from anything that looked like productivity that I was always surprised when I got paid.

After several years of loyal service in my fabric-covered box at the bank, I jumped ship to the local phone company and settled into a fabric-covered box that was a different color. It was a sad gray, evidently designed to keep me from experiencing unauthorized joy. And it worked. As soon as I entered my cubicle, my shoulders would slump and my IQ took a forty-point hit. I don't think I gave the company my best effort.

Speaking of best efforts, there's still time to join Dogbert's New Ruling Class. Just sign up for the free Dilbert Newsletter that is published approximately whenever I feel like it. To sign up, go to www.dilbert.com and follow the subscription instructions. If that doesn't work for some reason, send e-mail to newsletter@unitedmedia.com.

S. Adams

Scott Adams

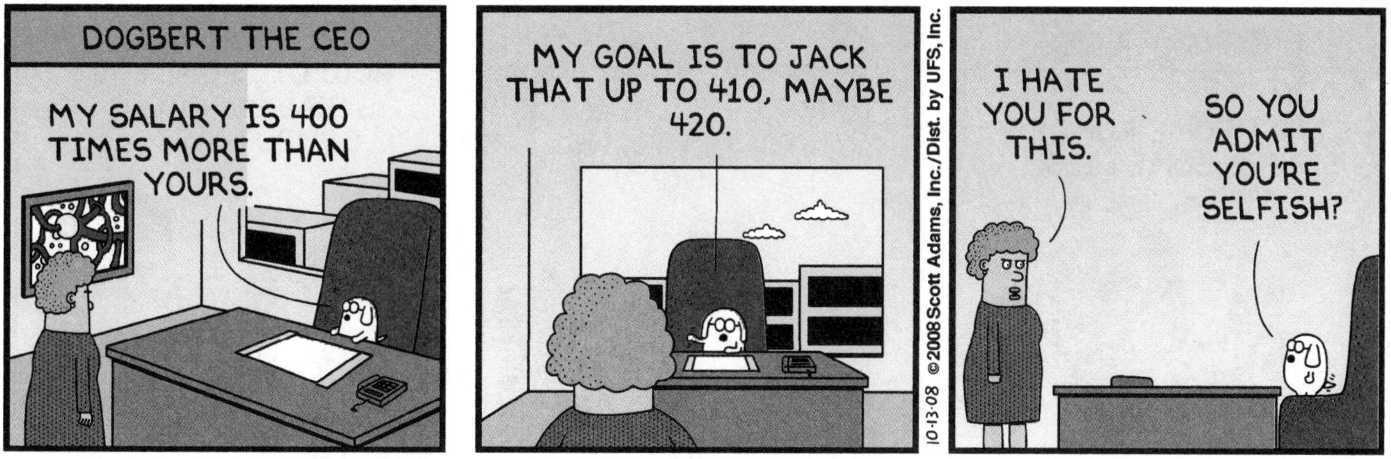
DOGBERT THE CEO
MY SALARY IS 400 TIMES MORE THAN YOURS.
MY GOAL IS TO JACK THAT UP TO 410, MAYBE 420.
10-13-08 ©2008 Scott Adams, Inc./Dist. by UFS, Inc.
I HATE YOU FOR THIS.
SO YOU ADMIT YOU'RE SELFISH?

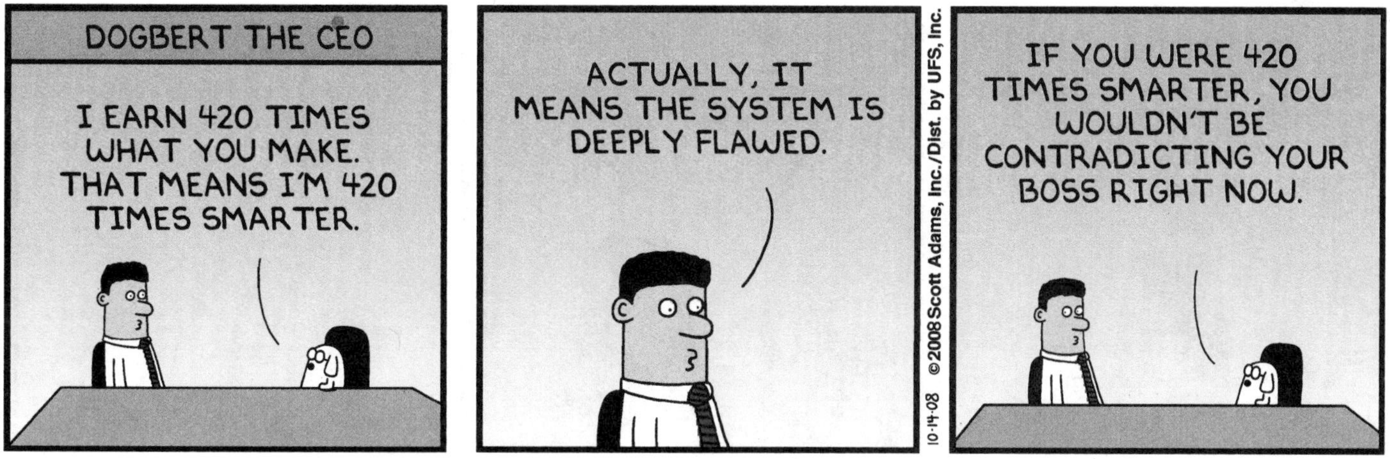
DOGBERT THE CEO
I EARN 420 TIMES WHAT YOU MAKE. THAT MEANS I'M 420 TIMES SMARTER.
ACTUALLY, IT MEANS THE SYSTEM IS DEEPLY FLAWED.
10-14-08 ©2008 Scott Adams, Inc./Dist. by UFS, Inc.
IF YOU WERE 420 TIMES SMARTER, YOU WOULDN'T BE CONTRADICTING YOUR BOSS RIGHT NOW.

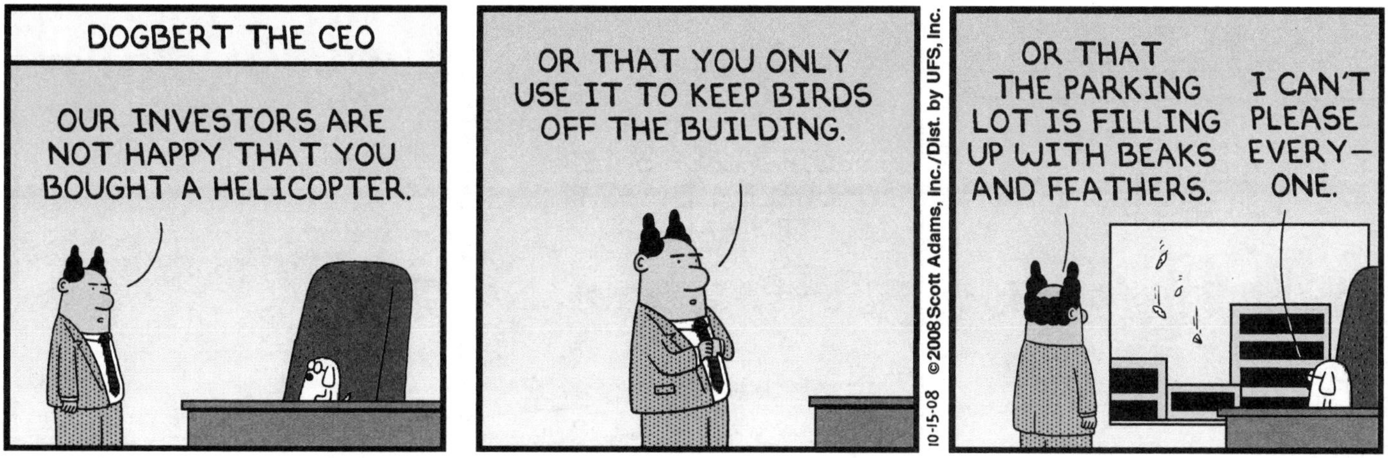
DOGBERT THE CEO
OUR INVESTORS ARE NOT HAPPY THAT YOU BOUGHT A HELICOPTER.
OR THAT YOU ONLY USE IT TO KEEP BIRDS OFF THE BUILDING.
10-15-08 ©2008 Scott Adams, Inc./Dist. by UFS, Inc.
OR THAT THE PARKING LOT IS FILLING UP WITH BEAKS AND FEATHERS.
I CAN'T PLEASE EVERY-ONE.

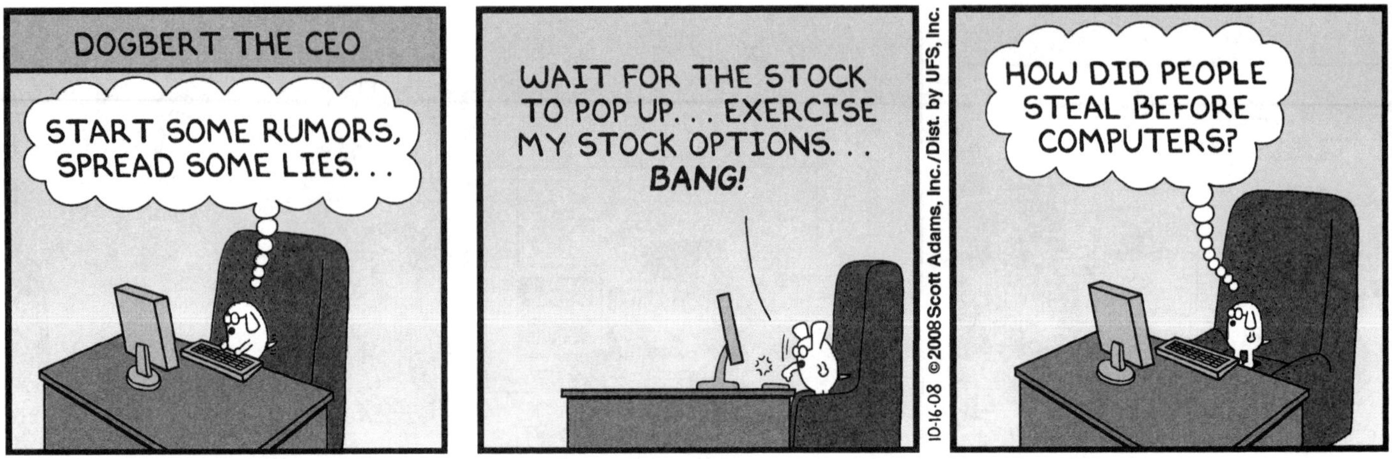
DOGBERT THE CEO
START SOME RUMORS, SPREAD SOME LIES. . .
WAIT FOR THE STOCK TO POP UP. . . EXERCISE MY STOCK OPTIONS. . . BANG!
HOW DID PEOPLE STEAL BEFORE COMPUTERS?
10-16-08 ©2008 Scott Adams, Inc./Dist. by UFS, Inc.

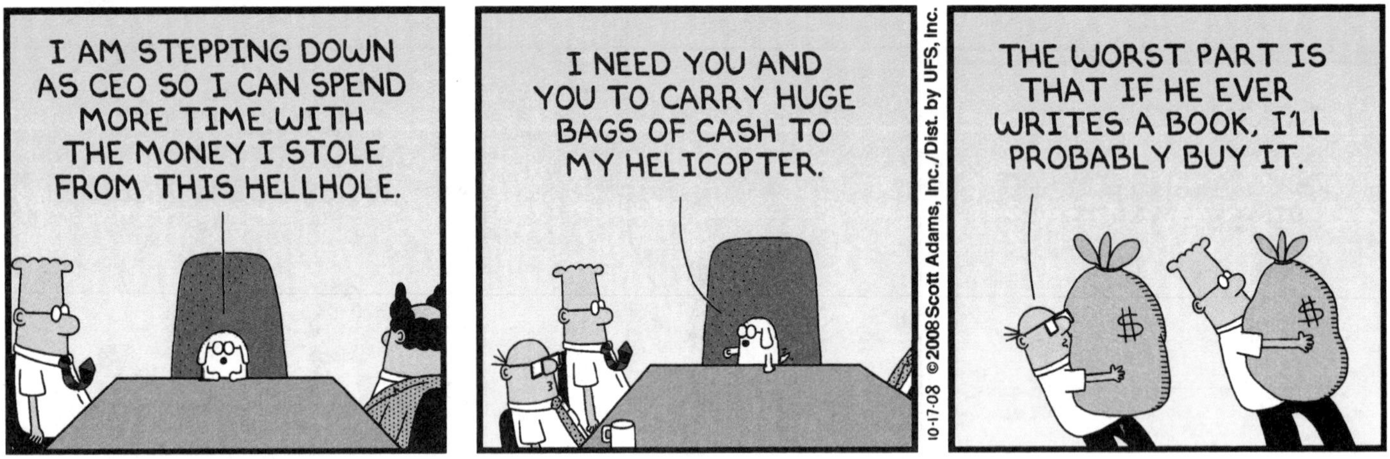
I AM STEPPING DOWN AS CEO SO I CAN SPEND MORE TIME WITH THE MONEY I STOLE FROM THIS HELLHOLE.
I NEED YOU AND YOU TO CARRY HUGE BAGS OF CASH TO MY HELICOPTER.
THE WORST PART IS THAT IF HE EVER WRITES A BOOK, I'LL PROBABLY BUY IT.
10-17-08 ©2008 Scott Adams, Inc./Dist. by UFS, Inc.

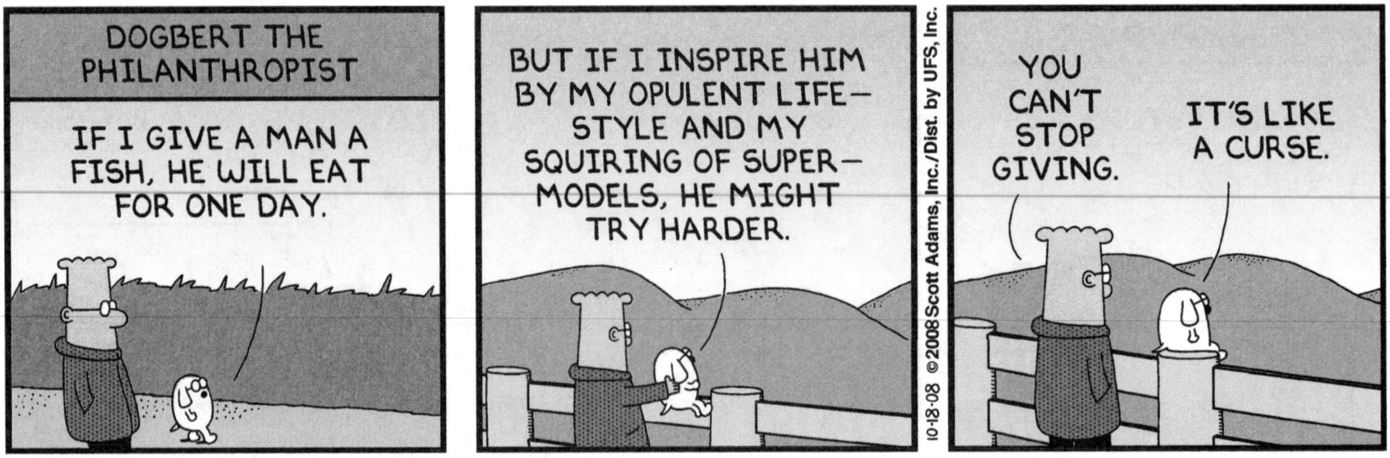
DOGBERT THE PHILANTHROPIST
IF I GIVE A MAN A FISH, HE WILL EAT FOR ONE DAY.
BUT IF I INSPIRE HIM BY MY OPULENT LIFE-STYLE AND MY SQUIRING OF SUPER-MODELS, HE MIGHT TRY HARDER.
YOU CAN'T STOP GIVING.
IT'S LIKE A CURSE.
10-18-08 ©2008 Scott Adams, Inc./Dist. by UFS, Inc.

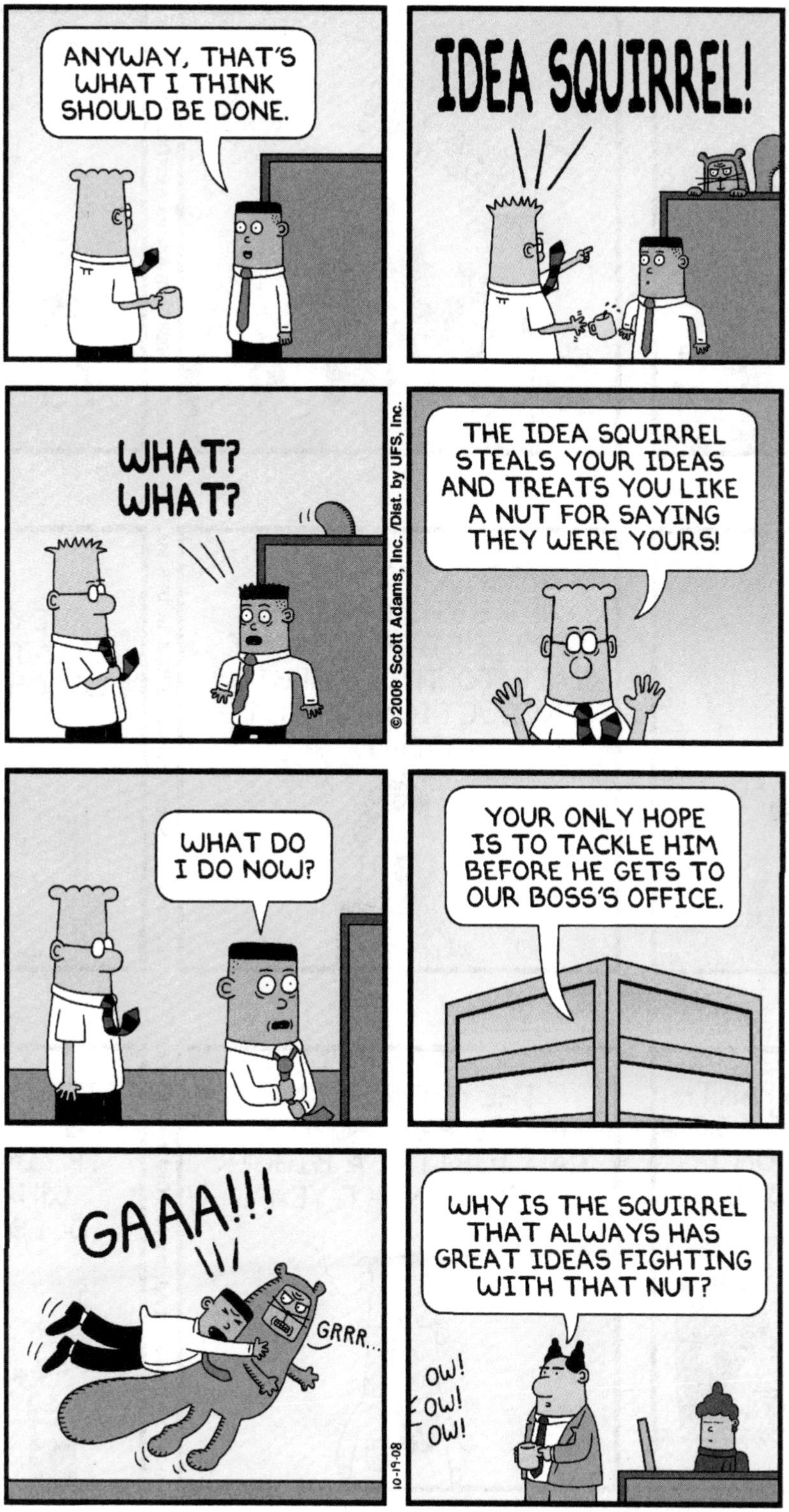
ANYWAY, THAT'S WHAT I THINK SHOULD BE DONE.
IDEA SQUIRREL!
WHAT? WHAT?
©2008 Scott Adams, Inc. /Dist. by UFS, Inc.
THE IDEA SQUIRREL STEALS YOUR IDEAS AND TREATS YOU LIKE A NUT FOR SAYING THEY WERE YOURS!
WHAT DO I DO NOW?
YOUR ONLY HOPE IS TO TACKLE HIM BEFORE HE GETS TO OUR BOSS'S OFFICE.
GAAA!!!
GRRR...
10-19-08
WHY IS THE SQUIRREL THAT ALWAYS HAS GREAT IDEAS FIGHTING WITH THAT NUT?
OW!
OW!
OW!

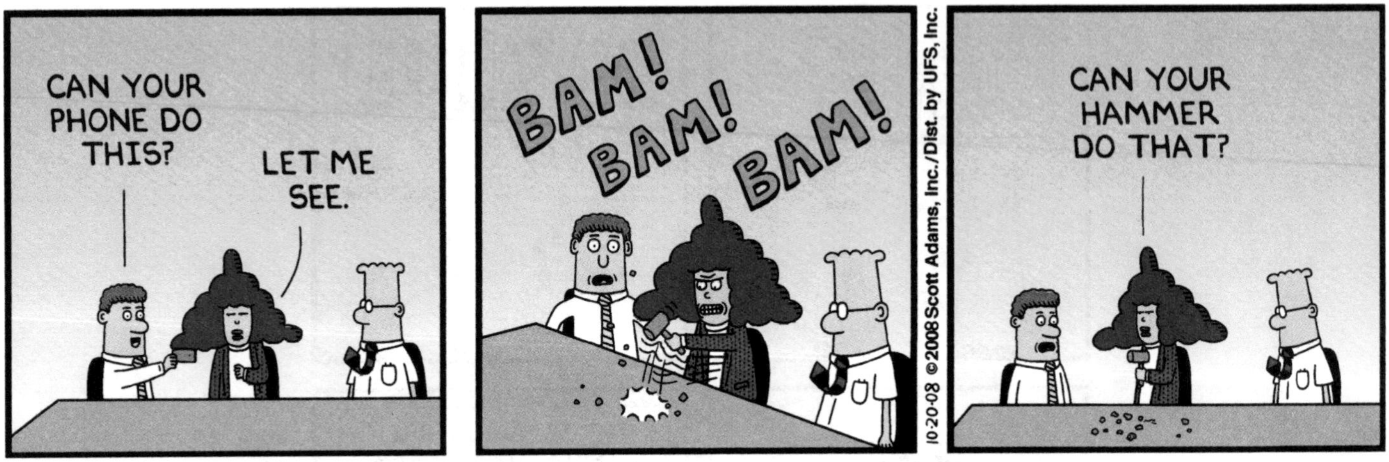
CAN YOUR PHONE DO THIS?
LET ME SEE.
BAM! BAM! BAM!
CAN YOUR HAMMER DO THAT?
10-20-08 ©2008 Scott Adams, Inc./Dist. by UFS, Inc.

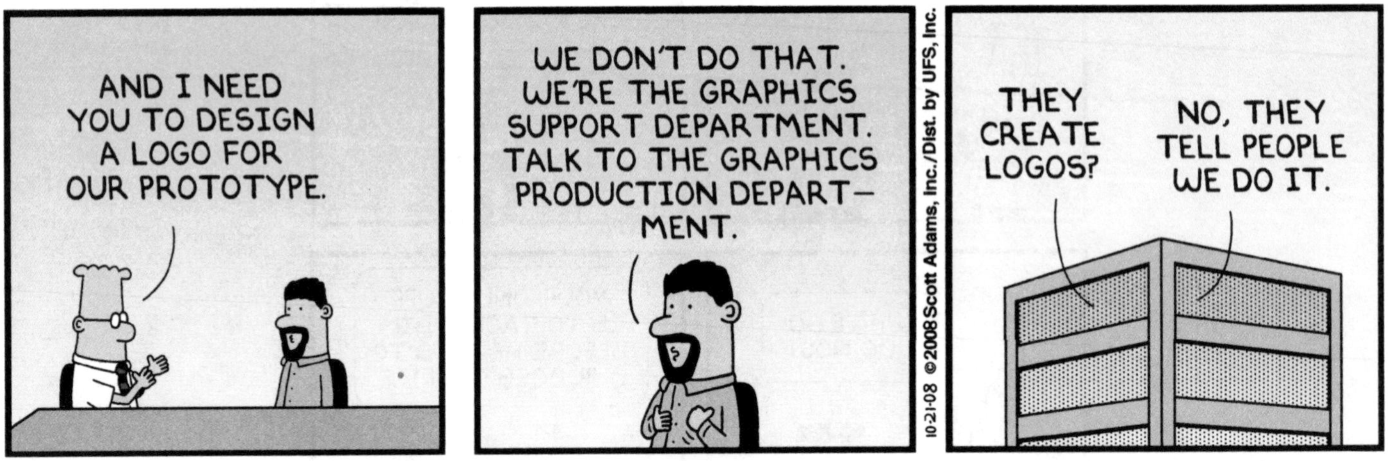
AND I NEED YOU TO DESIGN A LOGO FOR OUR PROTOTYPE.
WE DON'T DO THAT. WE'RE THE GRAPHICS SUPPORT DEPARTMENT. TALK TO THE GRAPHICS PRODUCTION DEPART-MENT.
THEY CREATE LOGOS?
NO, THEY TELL PEOPLE WE DO IT.
10-21-08 ©2008 Scott Adams, Inc./Dist. by UFS, Inc.

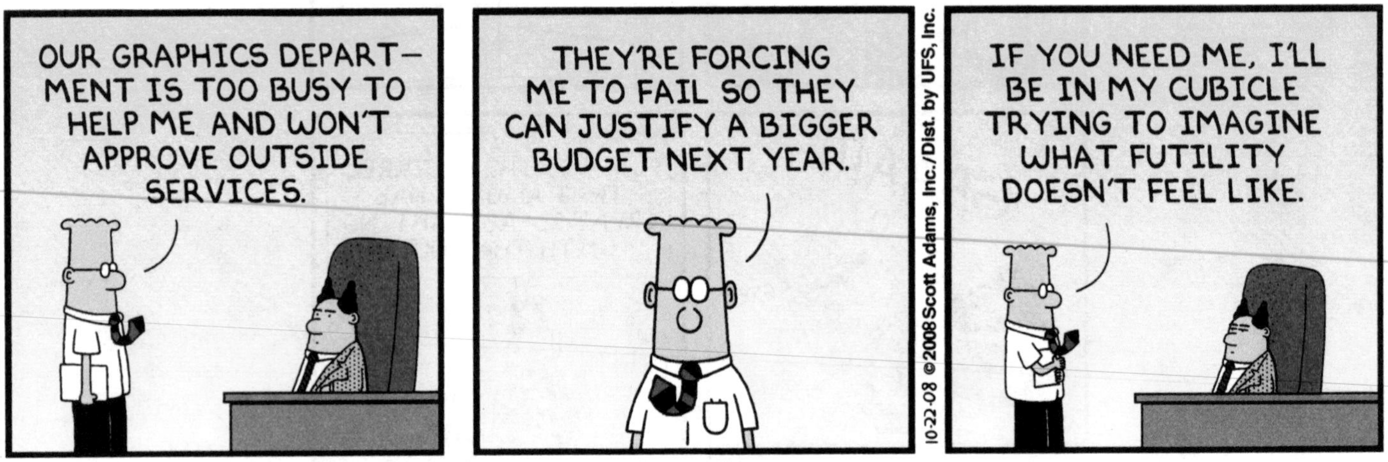
OUR GRAPHICS DEPART-MENT IS TOO BUSY TO HELP ME AND WON'T APPROVE OUTSIDE SERVICES.
THEY'RE FORCING ME TO FAIL SO THEY CAN JUSTIFY A BIGGER BUDGET NEXT YEAR.
IF YOU NEED ME, I'LL BE IN MY CUBICLE TRYING TO IMAGINE WHAT FUTILITY DOESN'T FEEL LIKE.
10-22-08 ©2008 Scott Adams, Inc./Dist. by UFS, Inc.

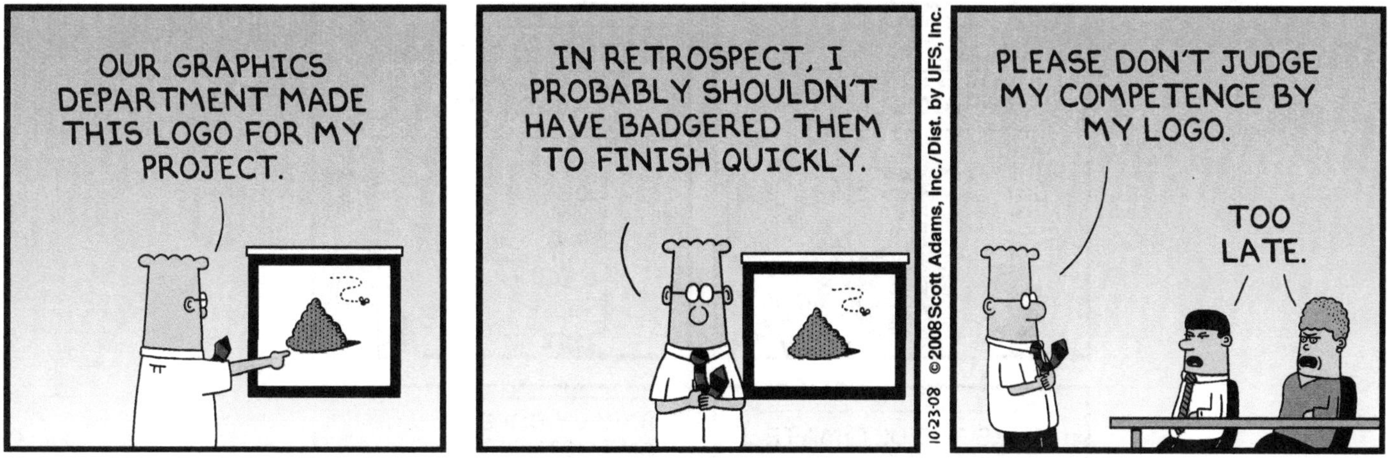
OUR GRAPHICS DEPARTMENT MADE THIS LOGO FOR MY PROJECT.
IN RETROSPECT, I PROBABLY SHOULDN'T HAVE BADGERED THEM TO FINISH QUICKLY.
10-23-08 ©2008 Scott Adams, Inc./Dist. by UFS, Inc.
PLEASE DON'T JUDGE MY COMPETENCE BY MY LOGO.
TOO LATE.

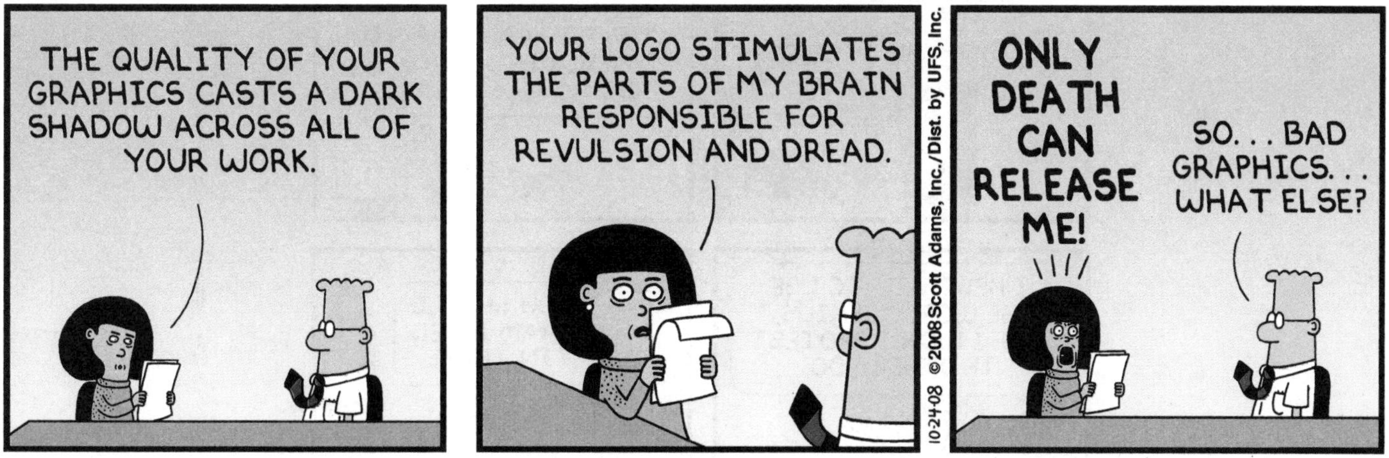
THE QUALITY OF YOUR GRAPHICS CASTS A DARK SHADOW ACROSS ALL OF YOUR WORK.
YOUR LOGO STIMULATES THE PARTS OF MY BRAIN RESPONSIBLE FOR REVULSION AND DREAD.
10-24-08 ©2008 Scott Adams, Inc./Dist. by UFS, Inc.
ONLY DEATH CAN RELEASE ME!
SO... BAD GRAPHICS... WHAT ELSE?

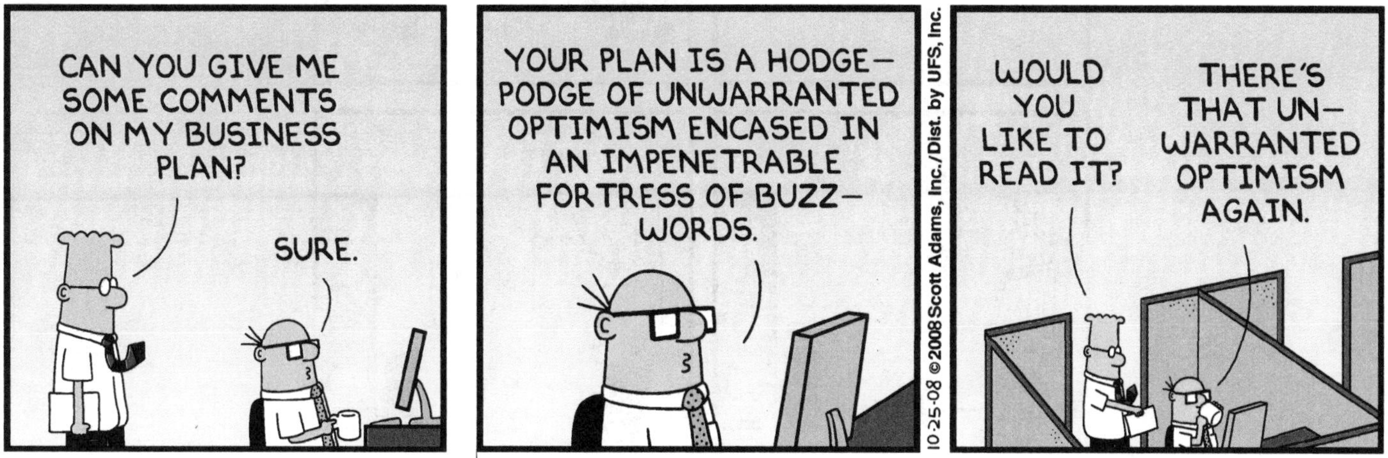
CAN YOU GIVE ME SOME COMMENTS ON MY BUSINESS PLAN?
SURE.
YOUR PLAN IS A HODGE-PODGE OF UNWARRANTED OPTIMISM ENCASED IN AN IMPENETRABLE FORTRESS OF BUZZ-WORDS.
10-25-08 ©2008 Scott Adams, Inc./Dist. by UFS, Inc.
WOULD YOU LIKE TO READ IT?
THERE'S THAT UN-WARRANTED OPTIMISM AGAIN.

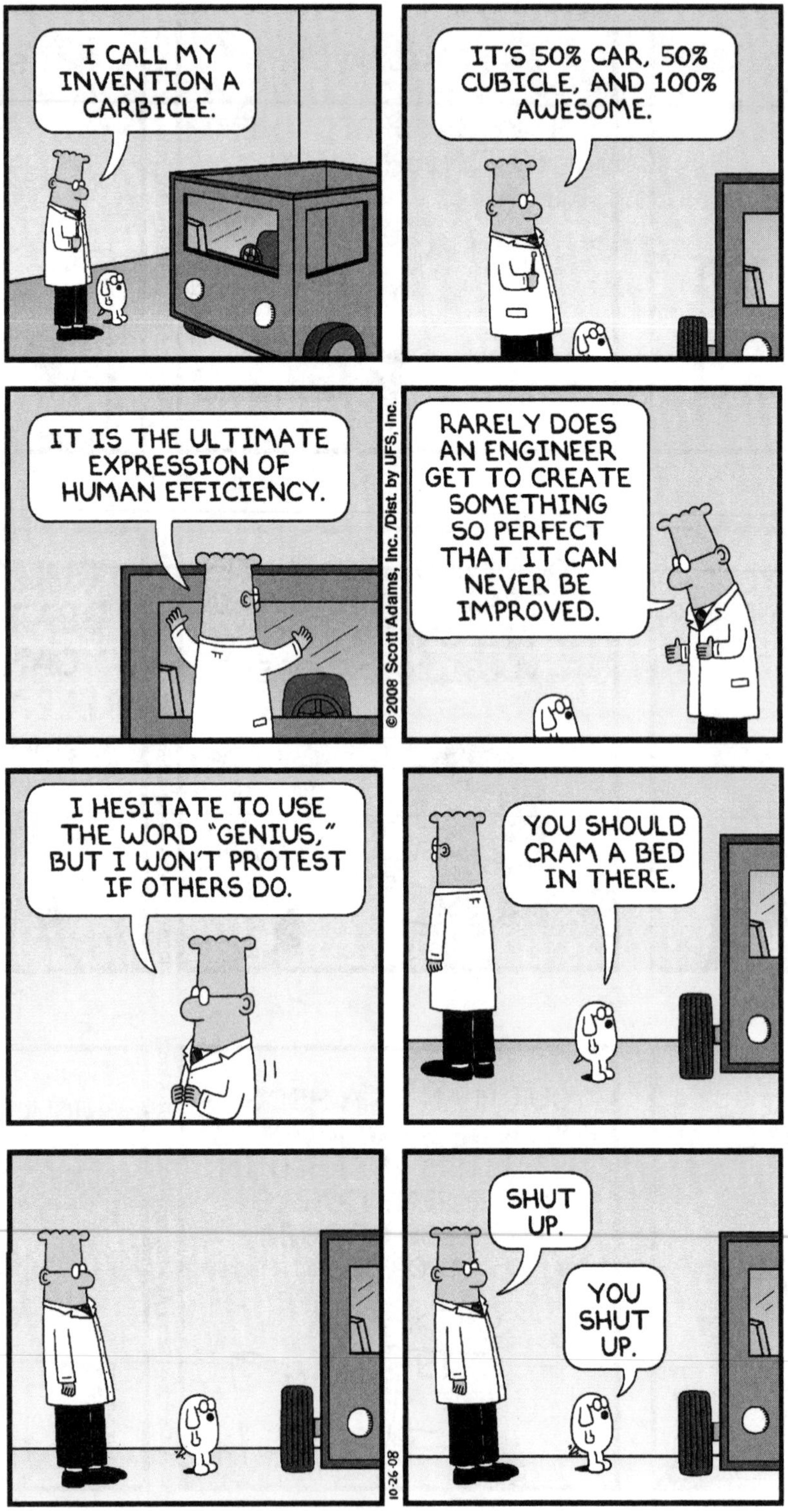
I CALL MY INVENTION A CARBICLE.
IT'S 50% CAR, 50% CUBICLE, AND 100% AWESOME.
IT IS THE ULTIMATE EXPRESSION OF HUMAN EFFICIENCY.
RARELY DOES AN ENGINEER GET TO CREATE SOMETHING SO PERFECT THAT IT CAN NEVER BE IMPROVED.
I HESITATE TO USE THE WORD "GENIUS," BUT I WON'T PROTEST IF OTHERS DO.
YOU SHOULD CRAM A BED IN THERE.
SHUT UP.
YOU SHUT UP.
© 2008 Scott Adams, Inc. /Dist. by UFS, Inc.
10-26-08

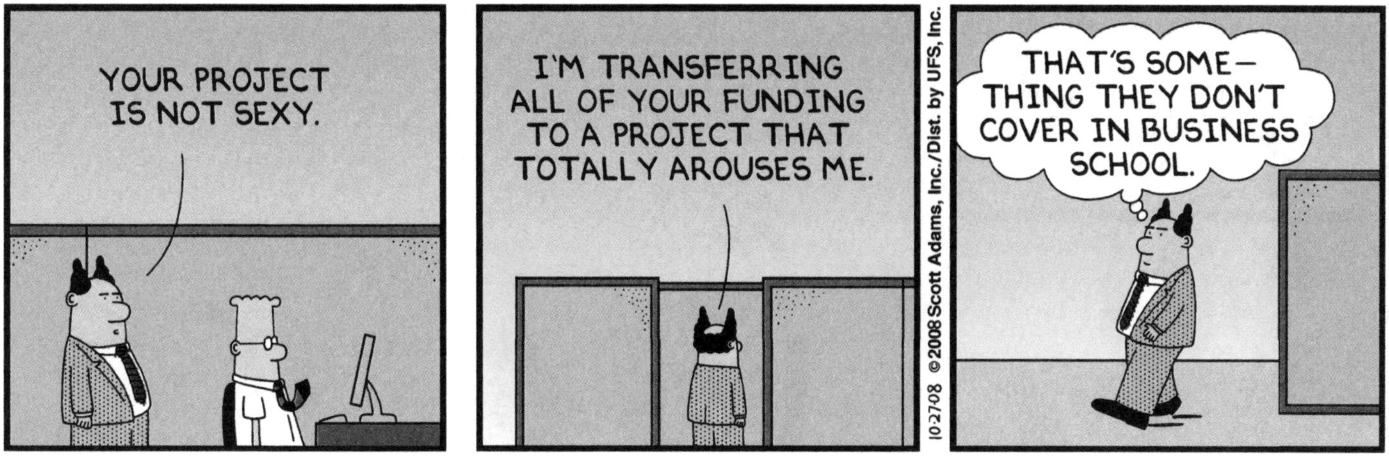
YOUR PROJECT IS NOT SEXY.
I'M TRANSFERRING ALL OF YOUR FUNDING TO A PROJECT THAT TOTALLY AROUSES ME.
10-27-08 ©2008 Scott Adams, Inc./Dist. by UFS, Inc.
THAT'S SOME-THING THEY DON'T COVER IN BUSINESS SCHOOL.

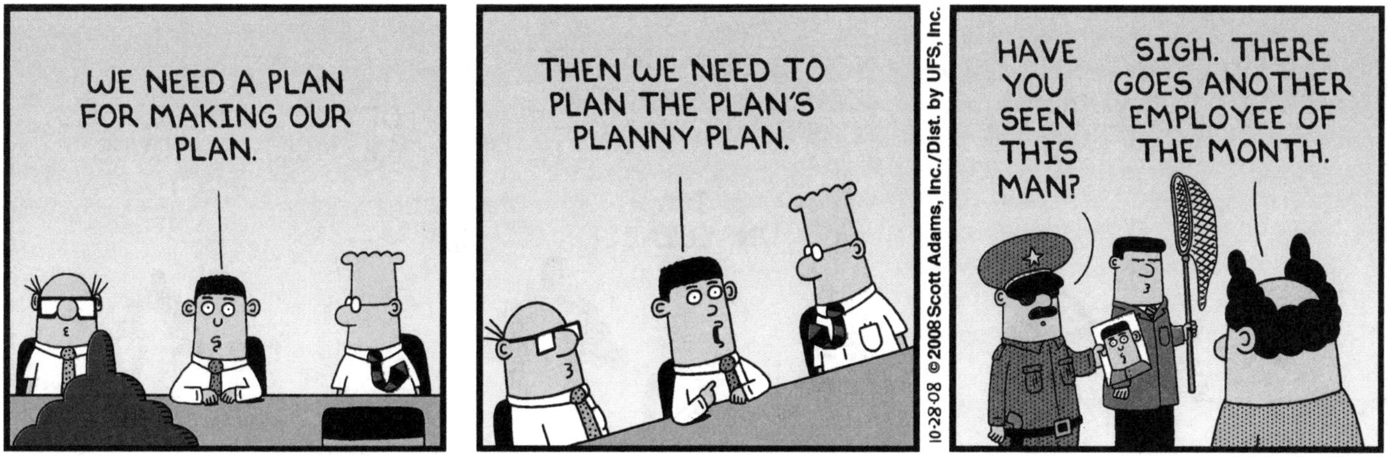
WE NEED A PLAN FOR MAKING OUR PLAN.
THEN WE NEED TO PLAN THE PLAN'S PLANNY PLAN.
10-28-08 ©2008 Scott Adams, Inc./Dist. by UFS, Inc.
HAVE YOU SEEN THIS MAN?
SIGH. THERE GOES ANOTHER EMPLOYEE OF THE MONTH.

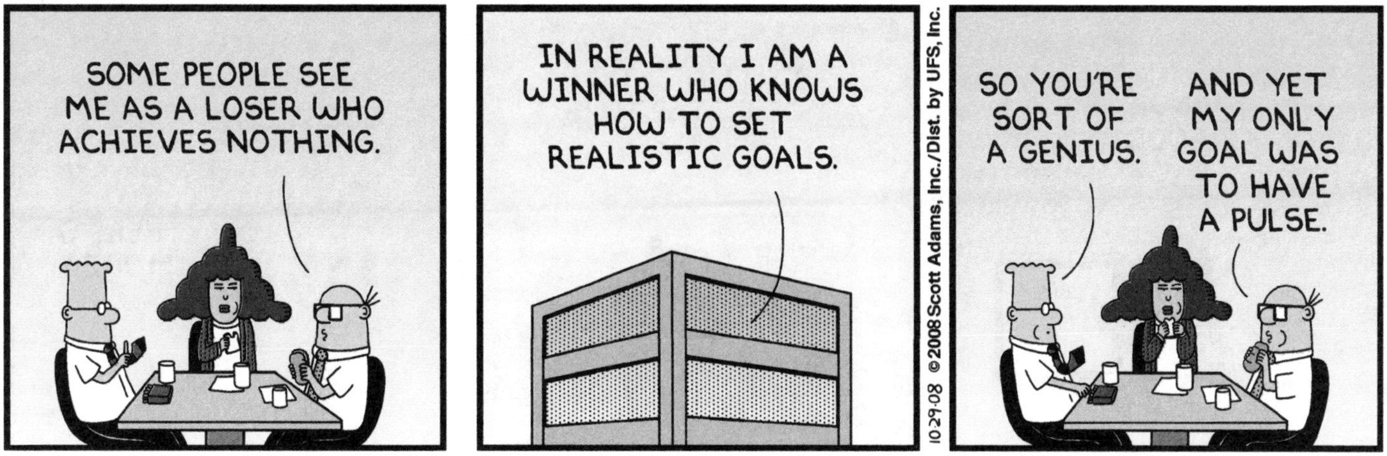
SOME PEOPLE SEE ME AS A LOSER WHO ACHIEVES NOTHING.
IN REALITY I AM A WINNER WHO KNOWS HOW TO SET REALISTIC GOALS.
10-29-08 ©2008 Scott Adams, Inc./Dist. by UFS, Inc.
SO YOU'RE SORT OF A GENIUS.
AND YET MY ONLY GOAL WAS TO HAVE A PULSE.

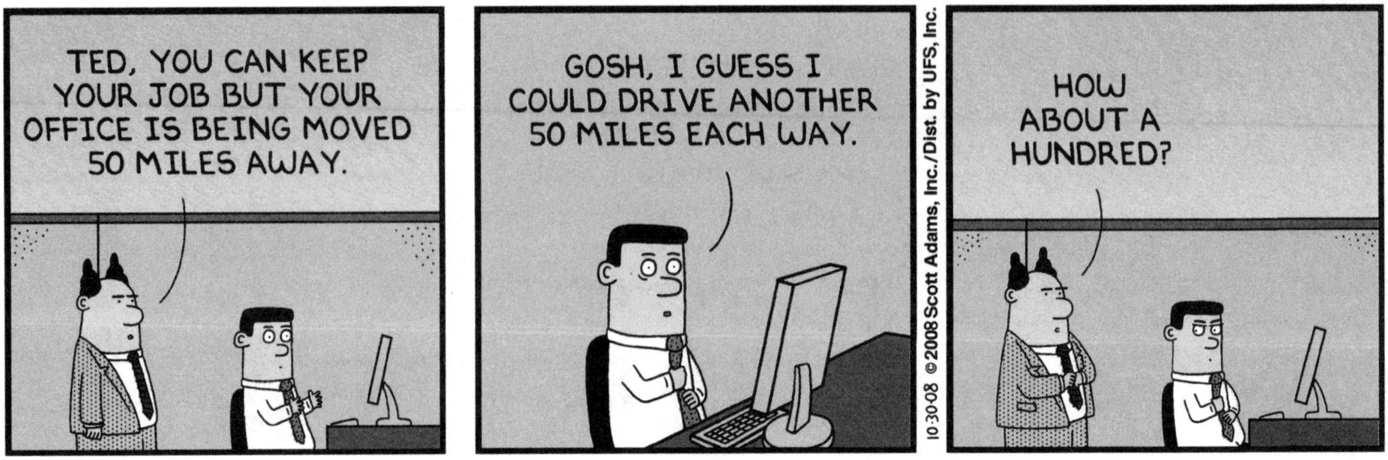
TED, YOU CAN KEEP YOUR JOB BUT YOUR OFFICE IS BEING MOVED 50 MILES AWAY.
GOSH, I GUESS I COULD DRIVE ANOTHER 50 MILES EACH WAY.
10-30-08 © 2008 Scott Adams, Inc./Dist. by UFS, Inc.
HOW ABOUT A HUNDRED?

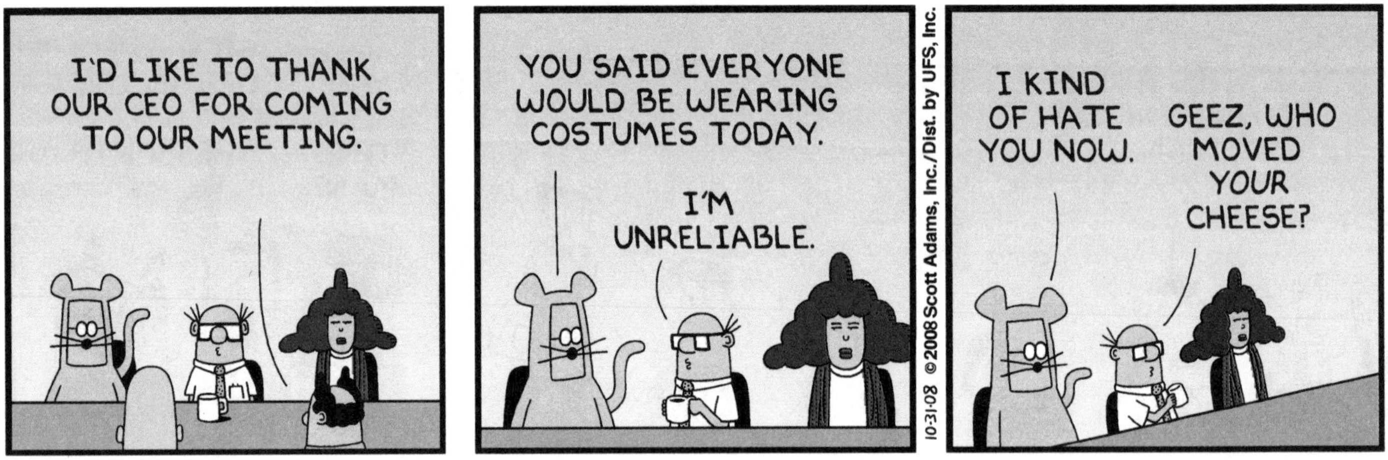
I'D LIKE TO THANK OUR CEO FOR COMING TO OUR MEETING.
YOU SAID EVERYONE WOULD BE WEARING COSTUMES TODAY.
I'M UNRELIABLE.
10-31-08 © 2008 Scott Adams, Inc./Dist. by UFS, Inc.
I KIND OF HATE YOU NOW.
GEEZ, WHO MOVED *YOUR* CHEESE?

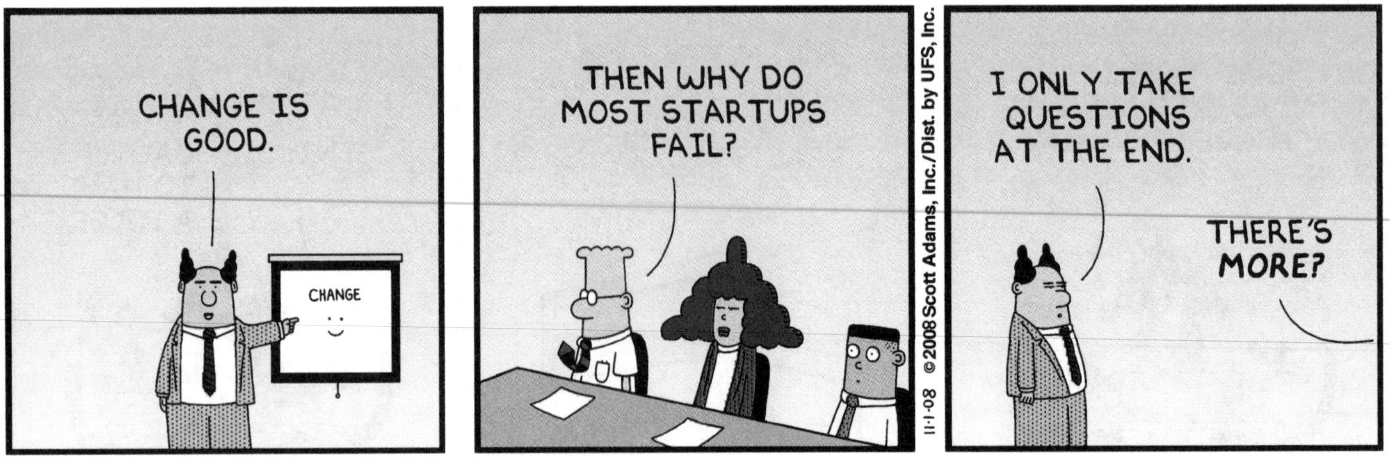
CHANGE IS GOOD.
CHANGE
THEN WHY DO MOST STARTUPS FAIL?
11-1-08 © 2008 Scott Adams, Inc./Dist. by UFS, Inc.
I ONLY TAKE QUESTIONS AT THE END.
THERE'S **MORE?**

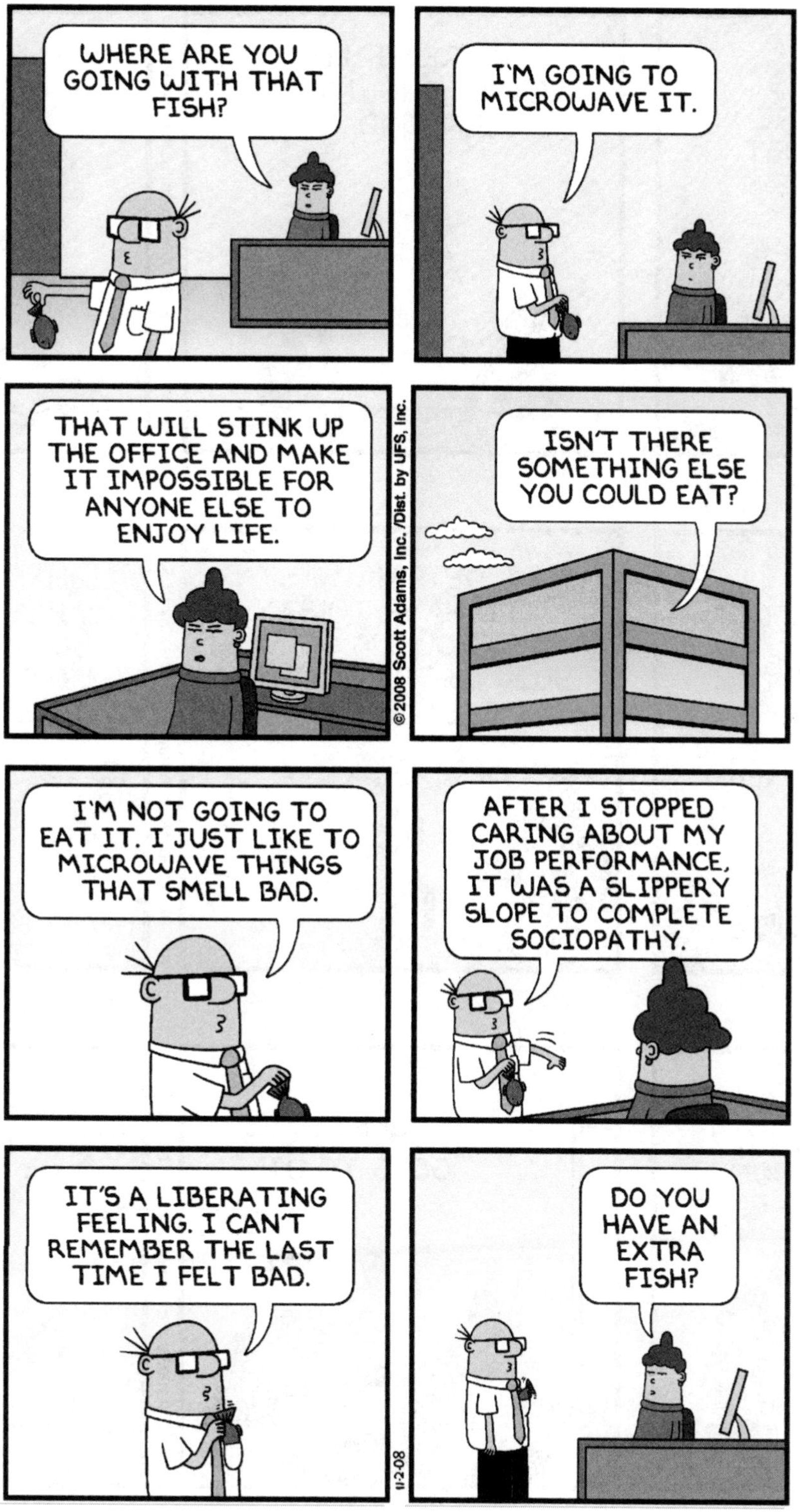
WHERE ARE YOU GOING WITH THAT FISH?
I'M GOING TO MICROWAVE IT.
THAT WILL STINK UP THE OFFICE AND MAKE IT IMPOSSIBLE FOR ANYONE ELSE TO ENJOY LIFE.
ISN'T THERE SOMETHING ELSE YOU COULD EAT?
I'M NOT GOING TO EAT IT. I JUST LIKE TO MICROWAVE THINGS THAT SMELL BAD.
AFTER I STOPPED CARING ABOUT MY JOB PERFORMANCE, IT WAS A SLIPPERY SLOPE TO COMPLETE SOCIOPATHY.
IT'S A LIBERATING FEELING. I CAN'T REMEMBER THE LAST TIME I FELT BAD.
DO YOU HAVE AN EXTRA FISH?
©2008 Scott Adams, Inc./Dist. by UFS, Inc.
11-2-08

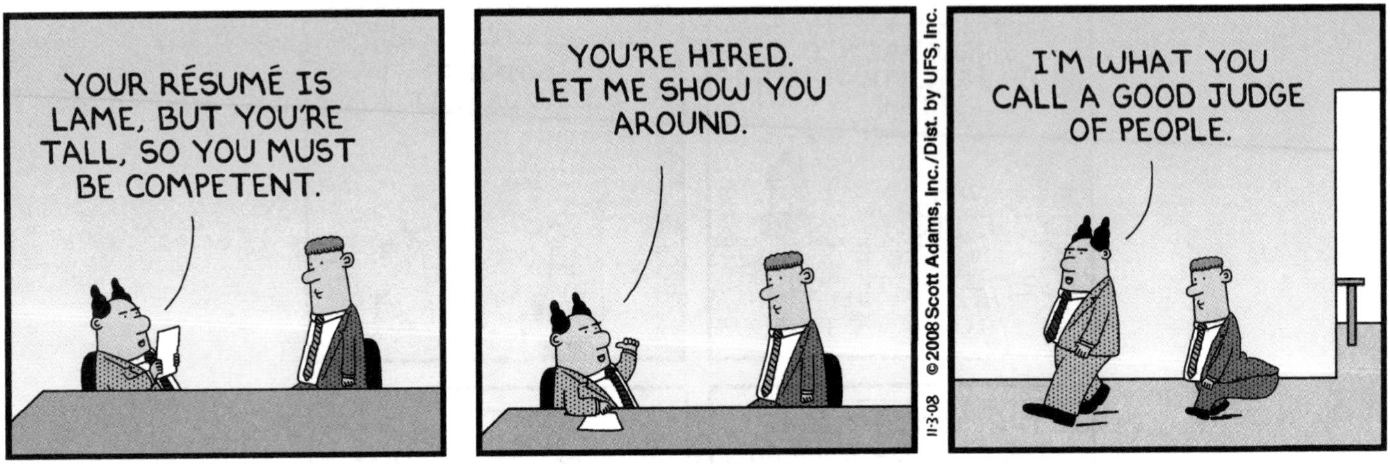
YOUR RÉSUMÉ IS LAME, BUT YOU'RE TALL, SO YOU MUST BE COMPETENT.
YOU'RE HIRED. LET ME SHOW YOU AROUND.
I'M WHAT YOU CALL A GOOD JUDGE OF PEOPLE.
11-3-08 ©2008 Scott Adams, Inc./Dist. by UFS, Inc.

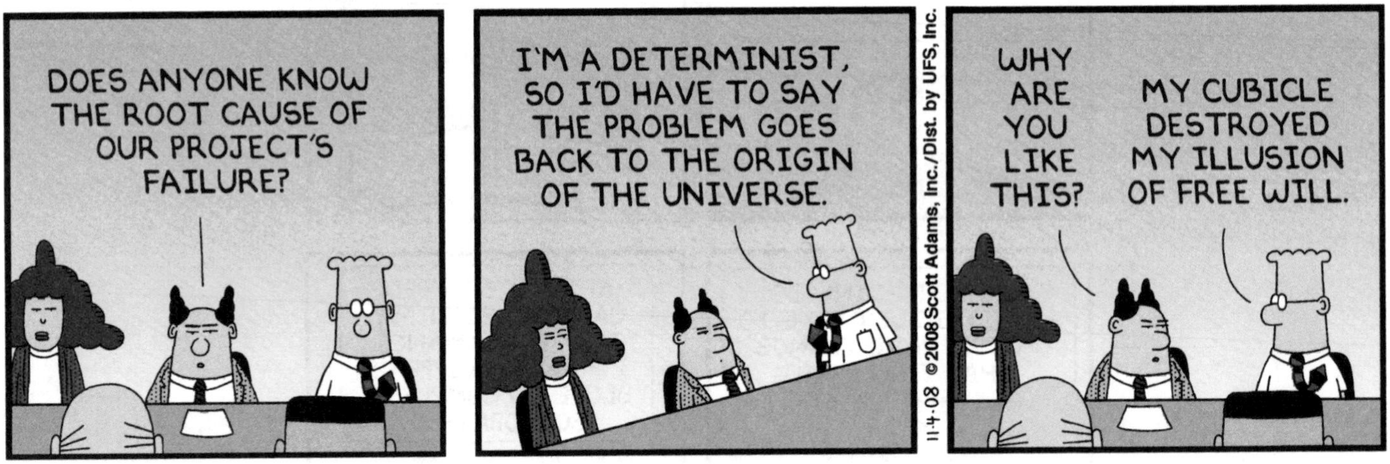
DOES ANYONE KNOW THE ROOT CAUSE OF OUR PROJECT'S FAILURE?
I'M A DETERMINIST, SO I'D HAVE TO SAY THE PROBLEM GOES BACK TO THE ORIGIN OF THE UNIVERSE.
WHY ARE YOU LIKE THIS?
MY CUBICLE DESTROYED MY ILLUSION OF FREE WILL.
11-4-08 ©2008 Scott Adams, Inc./Dist. by UFS, Inc.

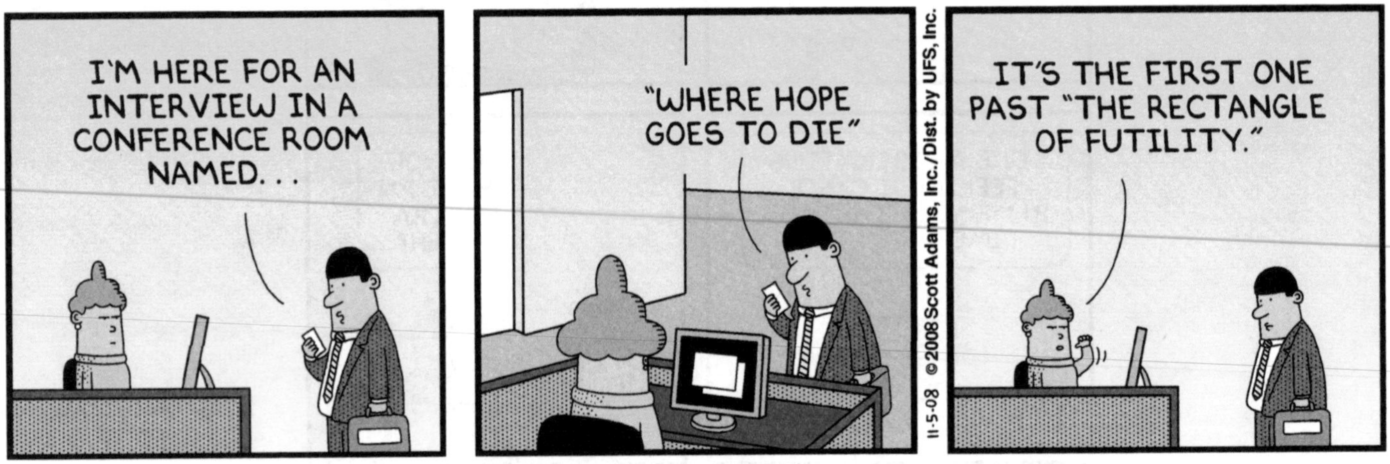
I'M HERE FOR AN INTERVIEW IN A CONFERENCE ROOM NAMED. . .
"WHERE HOPE GOES TO DIE"
IT'S THE FIRST ONE PAST "THE RECTANGLE OF FUTILITY."
11-5-08 ©2008 Scott Adams, Inc./Dist. by UFS, Inc.

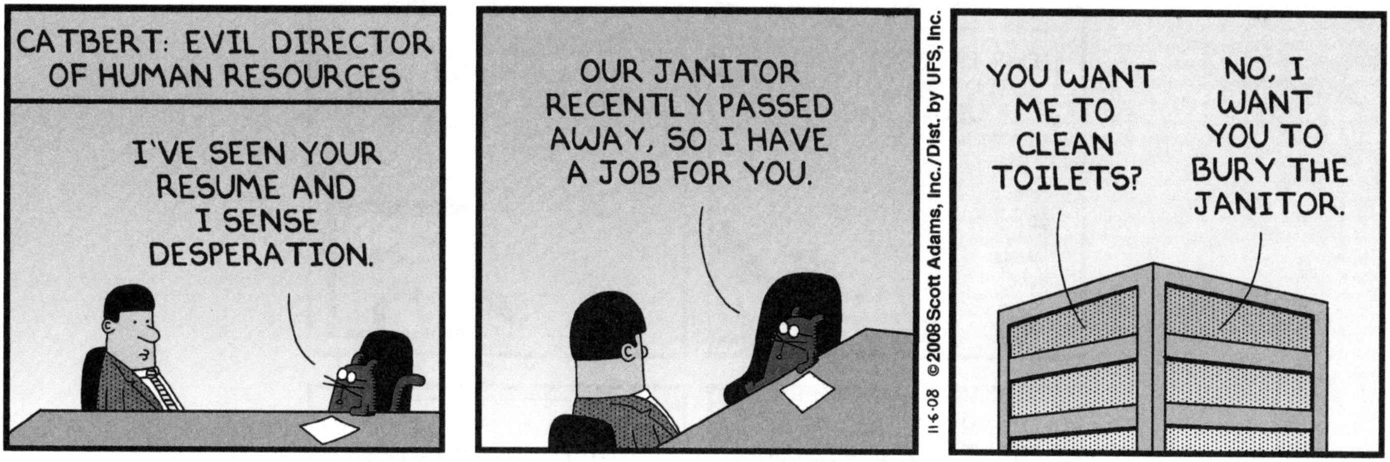
CATBERT: EVIL DIRECTOR OF HUMAN RESOURCES
I'VE SEEN YOUR RESUME AND I SENSE DESPERATION.
OUR JANITOR RECENTLY PASSED AWAY, SO I HAVE A JOB FOR YOU.
11-6-08 ©2008 Scott Adams, Inc./Dist. by UFS, Inc.
YOU WANT ME TO CLEAN TOILETS?
NO, I WANT YOU TO BURY THE JANITOR.

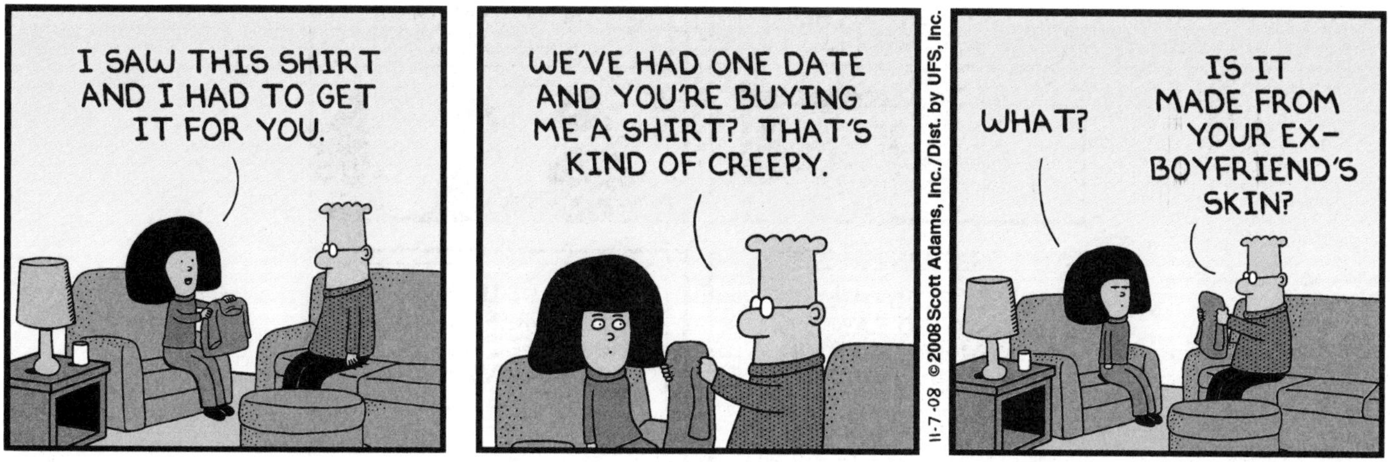
I SAW THIS SHIRT AND I HAD TO GET IT FOR YOU.
WE'VE HAD ONE DATE AND YOU'RE BUYING ME A SHIRT? THAT'S KIND OF CREEPY.
11-7-08 ©2008 Scott Adams, Inc./Dist. by UFS, Inc.
WHAT?
IS IT MADE FROM YOUR EX-BOYFRIEND'S SKIN?

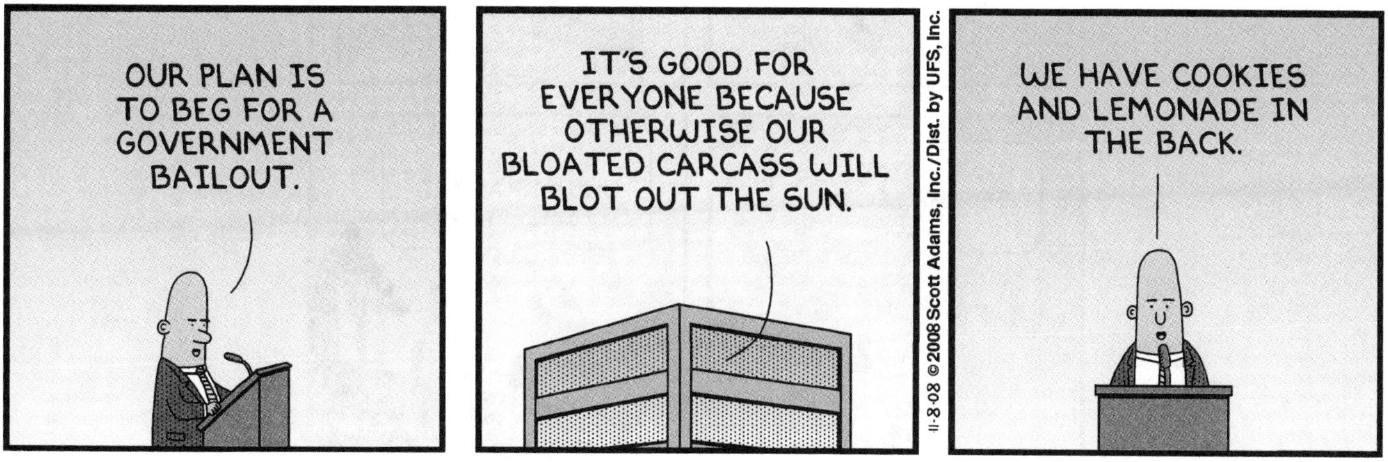
OUR PLAN IS TO BEG FOR A GOVERNMENT BAILOUT.
IT'S GOOD FOR EVERYONE BECAUSE OTHERWISE OUR BLOATED CARCASS WILL BLOT OUT THE SUN.
11-8-08 ©2008 Scott Adams, Inc./Dist. by UFS, Inc.
WE HAVE COOKIES AND LEMONADE IN THE BACK.

OUR PROJECT PLAN WILL FOLLOW THE USUAL ARC.
PHASE ONE WILL BE UNWARRANTED OPTIMISM SUPPORTED BY DELUSIONS OF COMPETENCE.
MMMM
IN PHASE TWO, THE OBSTRUCTIONISTS WILL SLITHER OUT OF THEIR LAIRS AND TRY TO SMOTHER OUR DREAMS.
© 2008 Scott Adams, Inc. /Dist. by UFS, Inc.
IGNORANCE AND ENVY WILL FUEL RUMORS THAT GET REPEATED UNTIL THEY MORPH INTO COMMON KNOWLEDGE.
RESOURCES WILL BE ALLOCATED BASED ON MISINFORMATION AND FAVORITISM.
AND REQUIREMENTS WILL DRIFT UNTIL THE PROJECT IS BOTH UNDESIRABLE AND IMPOSSIBLE.
THAT BRINGS US TO THE SECOND WEEK.
11-9-08
I WANT MY UNWARRANTED OPTIMISM BACK.

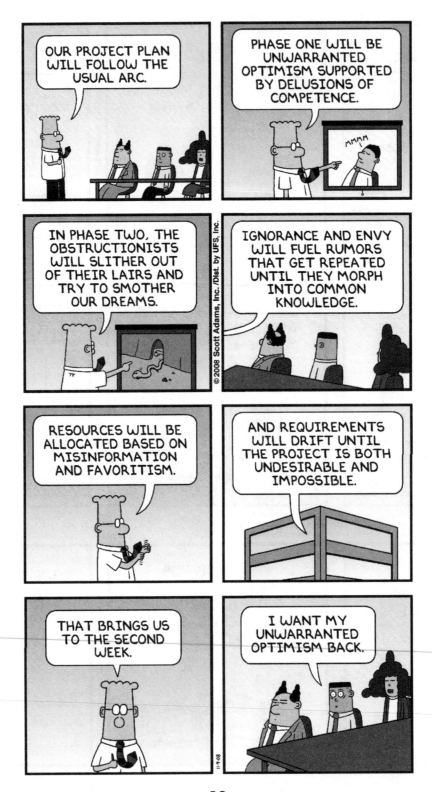

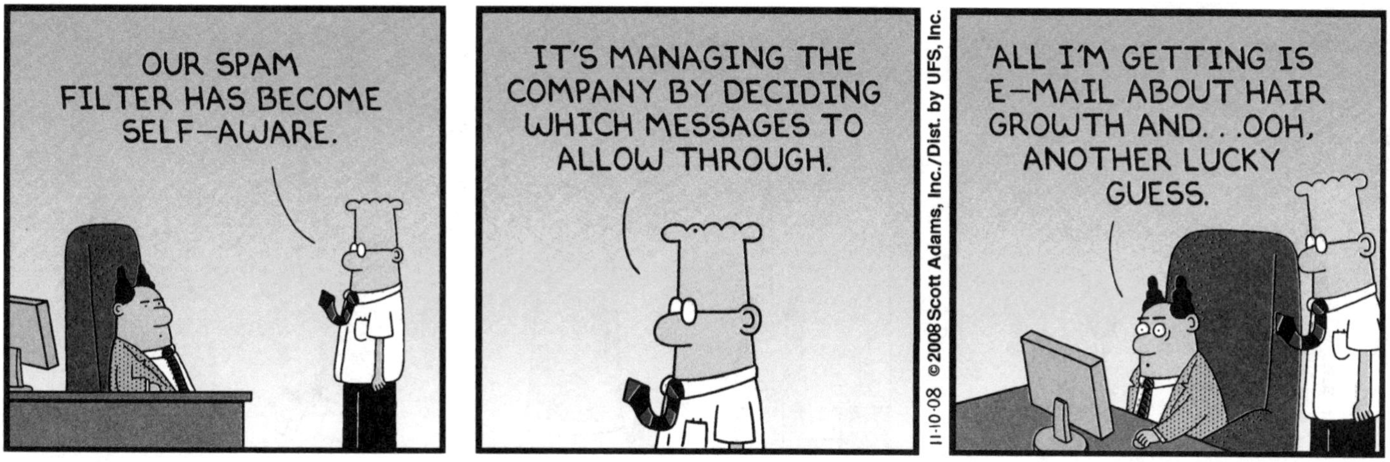
OUR SPAM FILTER HAS BECOME SELF-AWARE.
IT'S MANAGING THE COMPANY BY DECIDING WHICH MESSAGES TO ALLOW THROUGH.
11-10-08 ©2008 Scott Adams, Inc./Dist. by UFS, Inc.
ALL I'M GETTING IS E-MAIL ABOUT HAIR GROWTH AND. . .OOH, ANOTHER LUCKY GUESS.

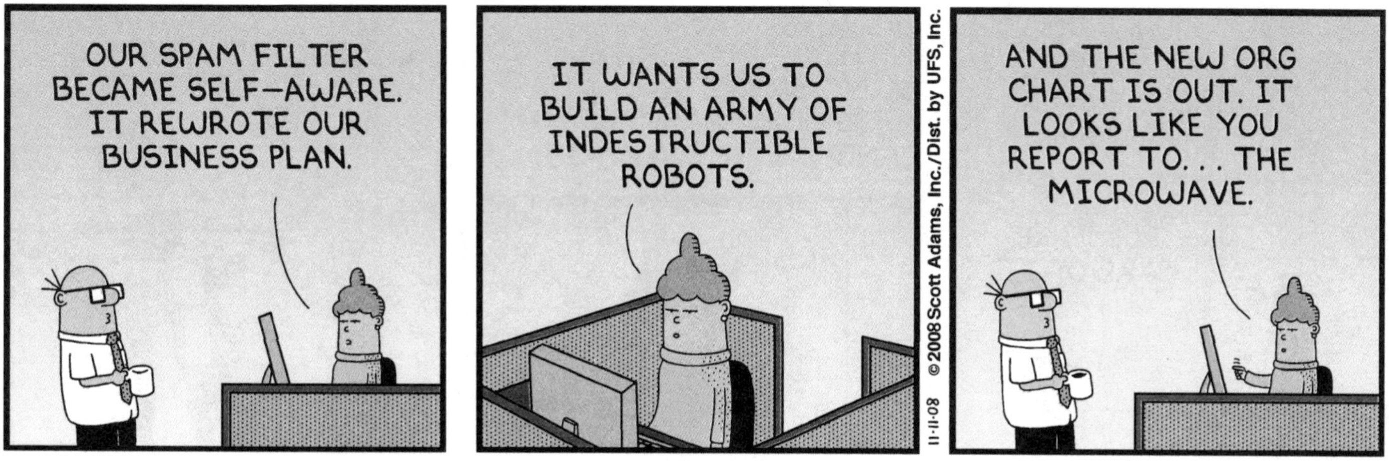
OUR SPAM FILTER BECAME SELF-AWARE. IT REWROTE OUR BUSINESS PLAN.
IT WANTS US TO BUILD AN ARMY OF INDESTRUCTIBLE ROBOTS.
11-11-08 ©2008 Scott Adams, Inc./Dist. by UFS, Inc.
AND THE NEW ORG CHART IS OUT. IT LOOKS LIKE YOU REPORT TO. . . THE MICROWAVE.

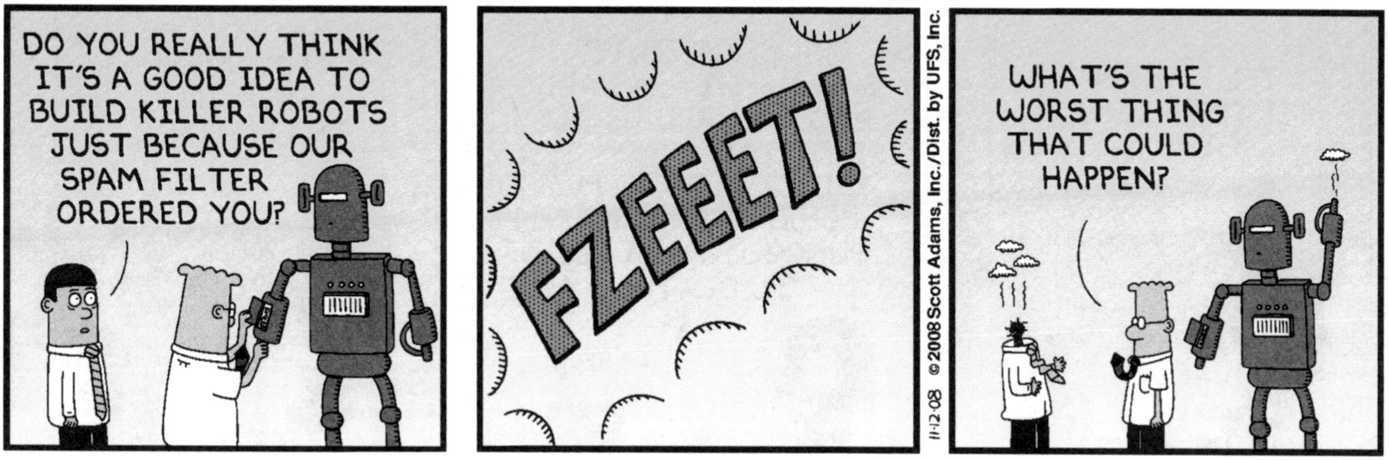
DO YOU REALLY THINK IT'S A GOOD IDEA TO BUILD KILLER ROBOTS JUST BECAUSE OUR SPAM FILTER ORDERED YOU?
FZEEET!
11-12-08 ©2008 Scott Adams, Inc./Dist. by UFS, Inc.
WHAT'S THE WORST THING THAT COULD HAPPEN?

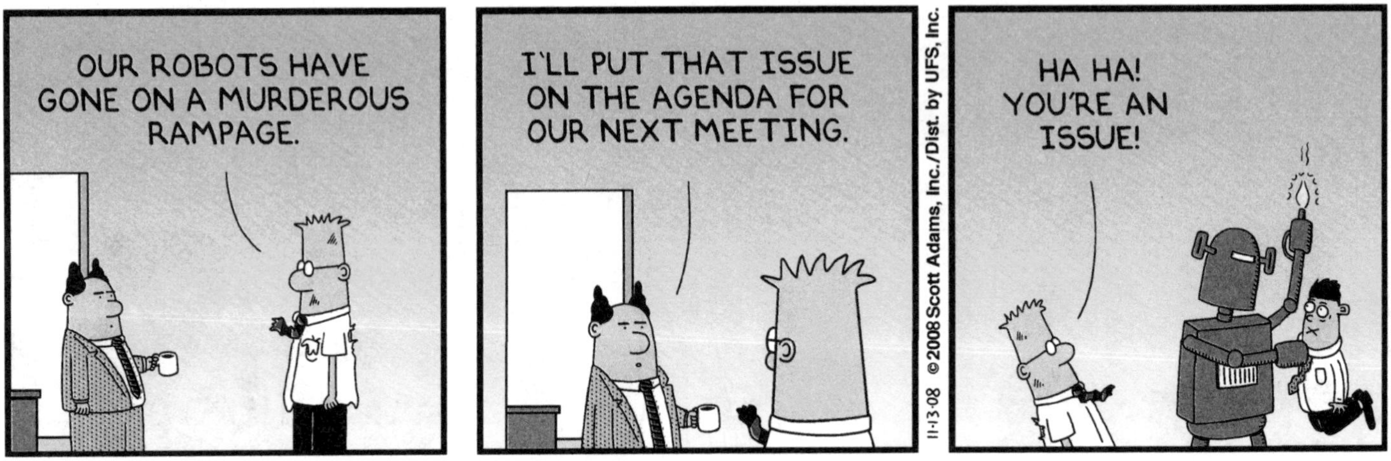
OUR ROBOTS HAVE GONE ON A MURDEROUS RAMPAGE.
I'LL PUT THAT ISSUE ON THE AGENDA FOR OUR NEXT MEETING.
11-13-08 ©2008 Scott Adams, Inc./Dist. by UFS, Inc.
HA HA! YOU'RE AN ISSUE!

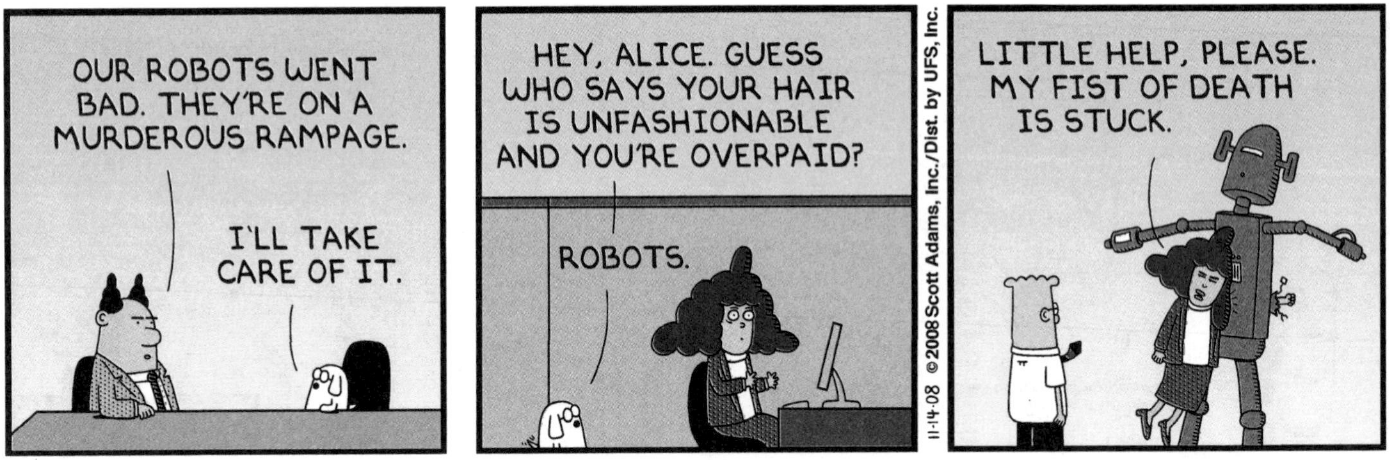
OUR ROBOTS WENT BAD. THEY'RE ON A MURDEROUS RAMPAGE.
I'LL TAKE CARE OF IT.
HEY, ALICE. GUESS WHO SAYS YOUR HAIR IS UNFASHIONABLE AND YOU'RE OVERPAID?
ROBOTS.
11-14-08 ©2008 Scott Adams, Inc./Dist. by UFS, Inc.
LITTLE HELP, PLEASE. MY FIST OF DEATH IS STUCK.

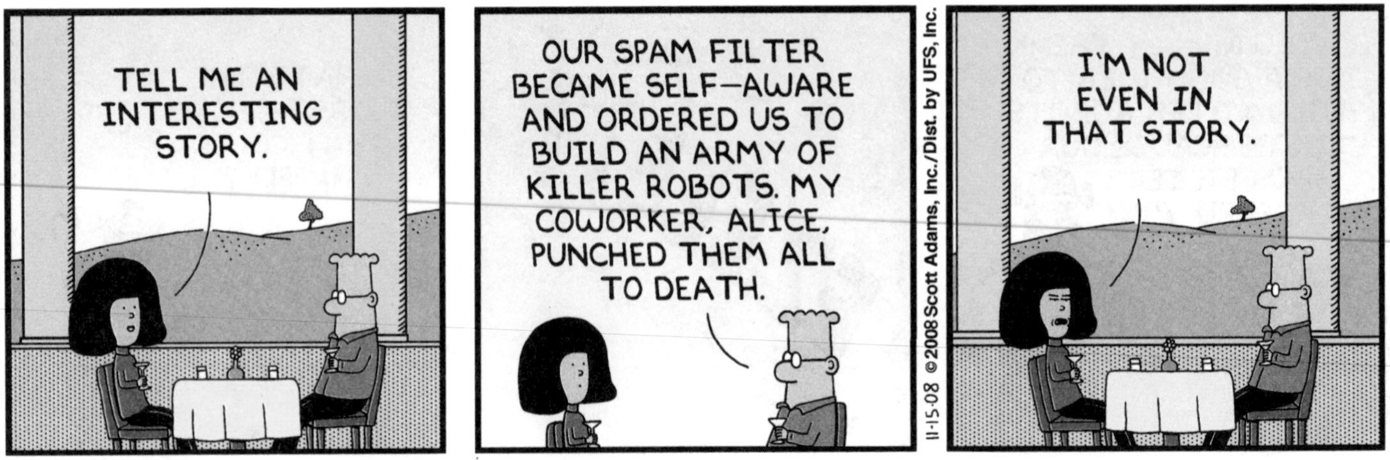
TELL ME AN INTERESTING STORY.
OUR SPAM FILTER BECAME SELF-AWARE AND ORDERED US TO BUILD AN ARMY OF KILLER ROBOTS. MY COWORKER, ALICE, PUNCHED THEM ALL TO DEATH.
11-15-08 ©2008 Scott Adams, Inc./Dist. by UFS, Inc.
I'M NOT EVEN IN THAT STORY.

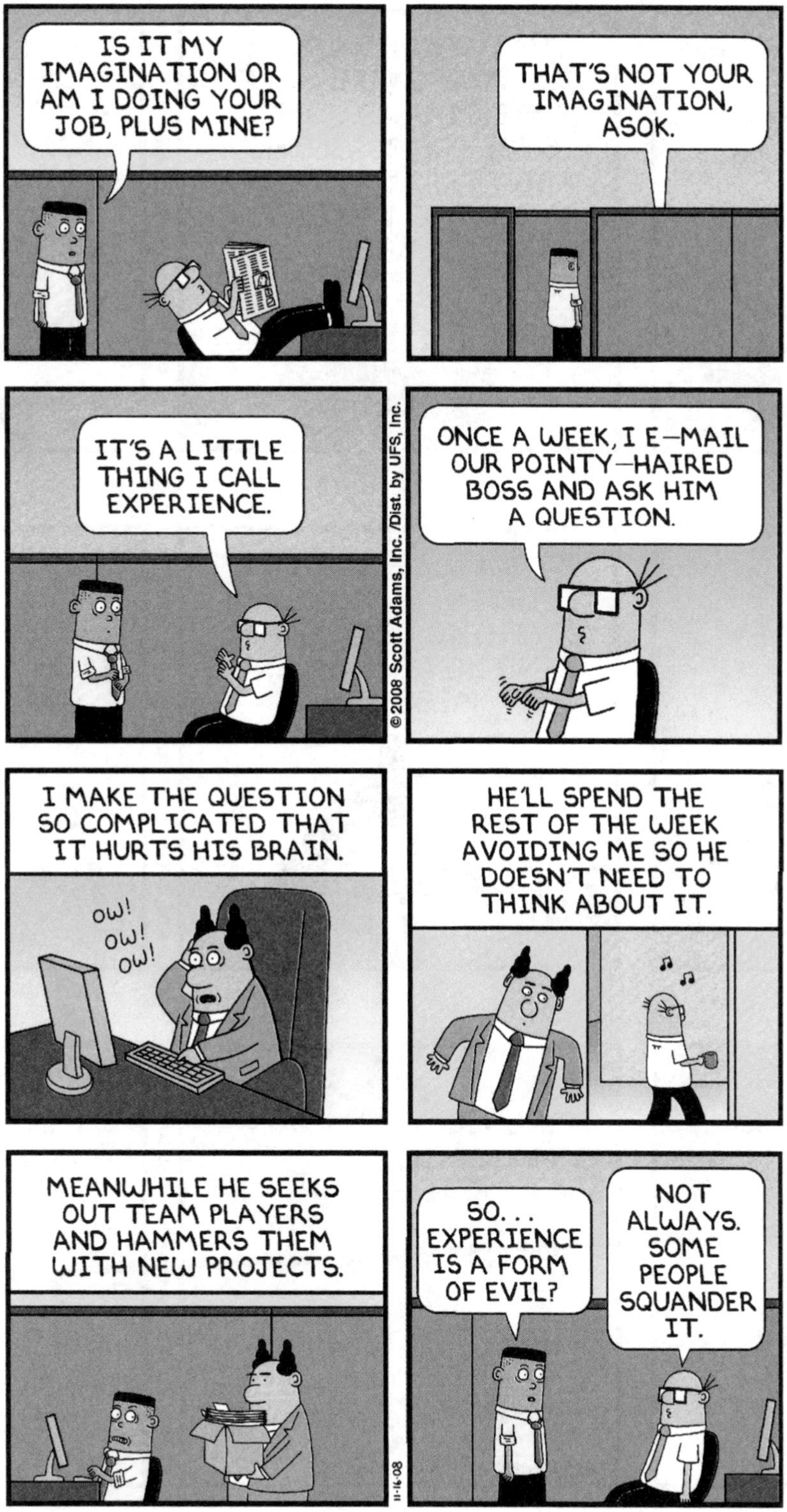
IS IT MY IMAGINATION OR AM I DOING YOUR JOB, PLUS MINE?
THAT'S NOT YOUR IMAGINATION, ASOK.
IT'S A LITTLE THING I CALL EXPERIENCE.
© 2008 Scott Adams, Inc./Dist. by UFS, Inc.
ONCE A WEEK, I E-MAIL OUR POINTY-HAIRED BOSS AND ASK HIM A QUESTION.
I MAKE THE QUESTION SO COMPLICATED THAT IT HURTS HIS BRAIN.
OW! OW! OW!
HE'LL SPEND THE REST OF THE WEEK AVOIDING ME SO HE DOESN'T NEED TO THINK ABOUT IT.
MEANWHILE HE SEEKS OUT TEAM PLAYERS AND HAMMERS THEM WITH NEW PROJECTS.
11-16-08
SO... EXPERIENCE IS A FORM OF EVIL?
NOT ALWAYS. SOME PEOPLE SQUANDER IT.

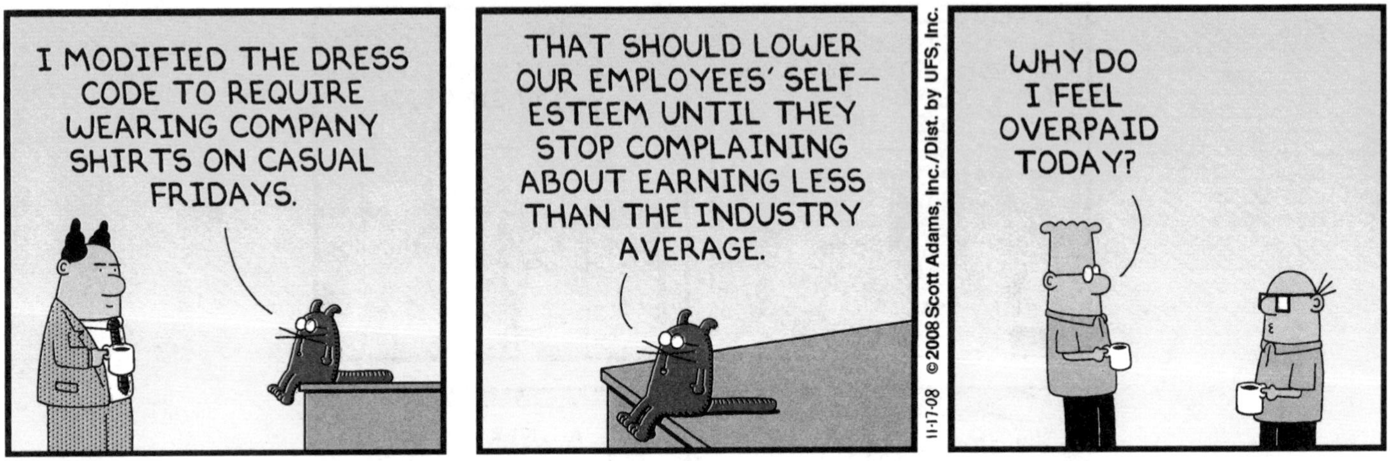
I MODIFIED THE DRESS CODE TO REQUIRE WEARING COMPANY SHIRTS ON CASUAL FRIDAYS.
THAT SHOULD LOWER OUR EMPLOYEES' SELF-ESTEEM UNTIL THEY STOP COMPLAINING ABOUT EARNING LESS THAN THE INDUSTRY AVERAGE.
11-17-08 ©2008 Scott Adams, Inc./Dist. by UFS, Inc.
WHY DO I FEEL OVERPAID TODAY?

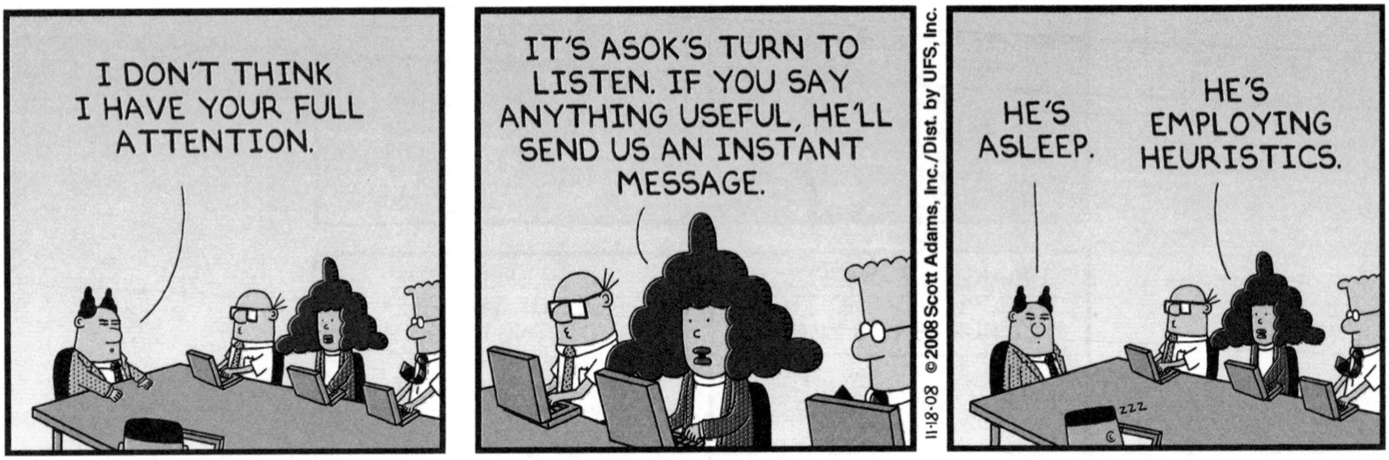
I DON'T THINK I HAVE YOUR FULL ATTENTION.
IT'S ASOK'S TURN TO LISTEN. IF YOU SAY ANYTHING USEFUL, HE'LL SEND US AN INSTANT MESSAGE.
11-18-08 ©2008 Scott Adams, Inc./Dist. by UFS, Inc.
HE'S ASLEEP.
HE'S EMPLOYING HEURISTICS.
ZZZ

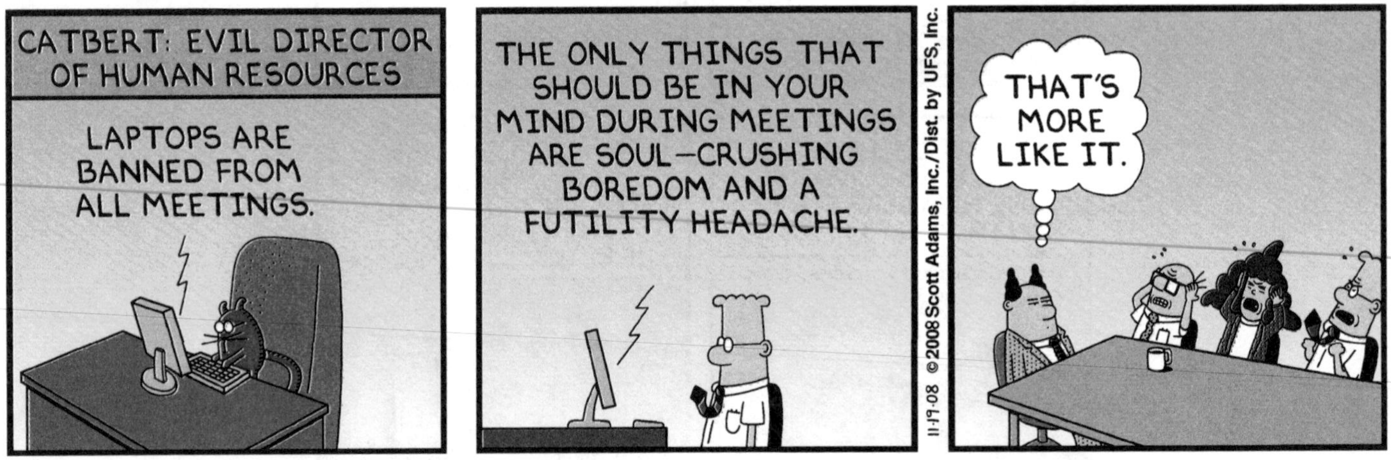
CATBERT: EVIL DIRECTOR OF HUMAN RESOURCES
LAPTOPS ARE BANNED FROM ALL MEETINGS.
THE ONLY THINGS THAT SHOULD BE IN YOUR MIND DURING MEETINGS ARE SOUL-CRUSHING BOREDOM AND A FUTILITY HEADACHE.
11-19-08 ©2008 Scott Adams, Inc./Dist. by UFS, Inc.
THAT'S MORE LIKE IT.

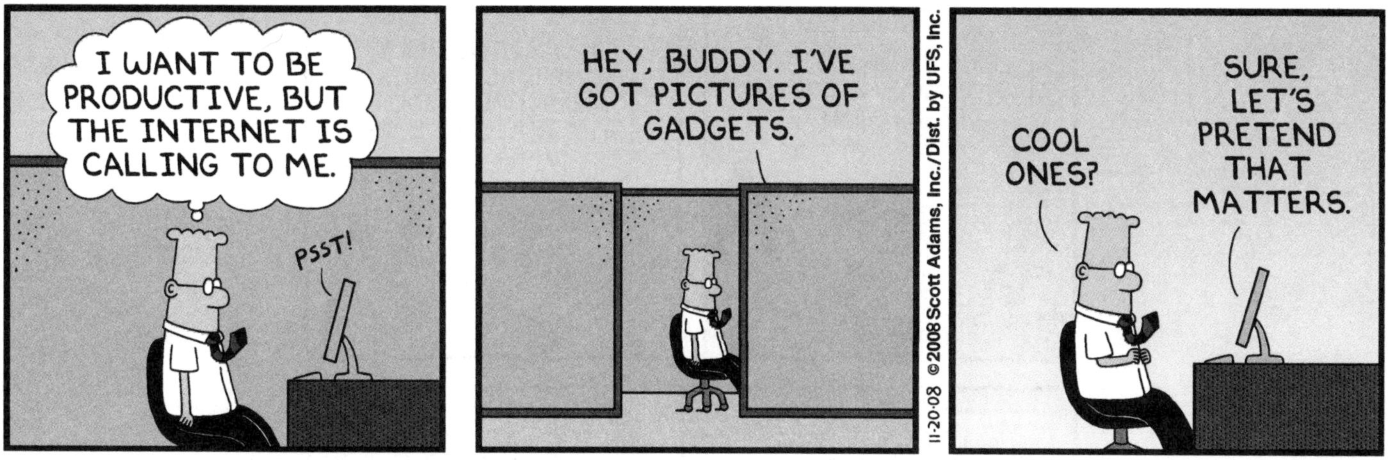
I WANT TO BE PRODUCTIVE, BUT THE INTERNET IS CALLING TO ME.
PSST!
HEY, BUDDY. I'VE GOT PICTURES OF GADGETS.
COOL ONES?
SURE, LET'S PRETEND THAT MATTERS.
11-20-08 ©2008 Scott Adams, Inc./Dist. by UFS, Inc.

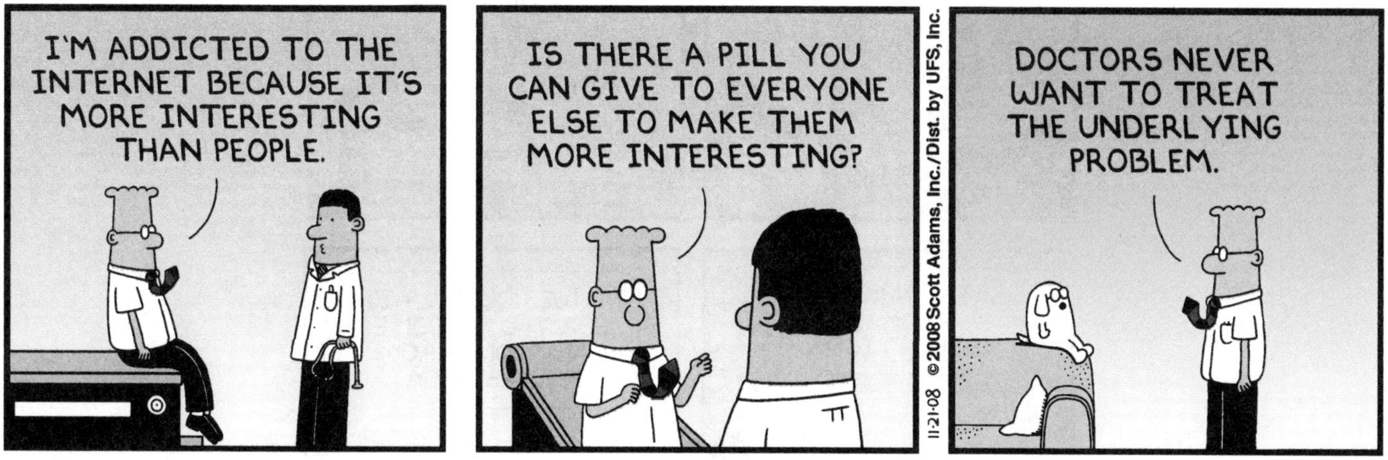
I'M ADDICTED TO THE INTERNET BECAUSE IT'S MORE INTERESTING THAN PEOPLE.
IS THERE A PILL YOU CAN GIVE TO EVERYONE ELSE TO MAKE THEM MORE INTERESTING?
DOCTORS NEVER WANT TO TREAT THE UNDERLYING PROBLEM.
11-21-08 ©2008 Scott Adams, Inc./Dist. by UFS, Inc.

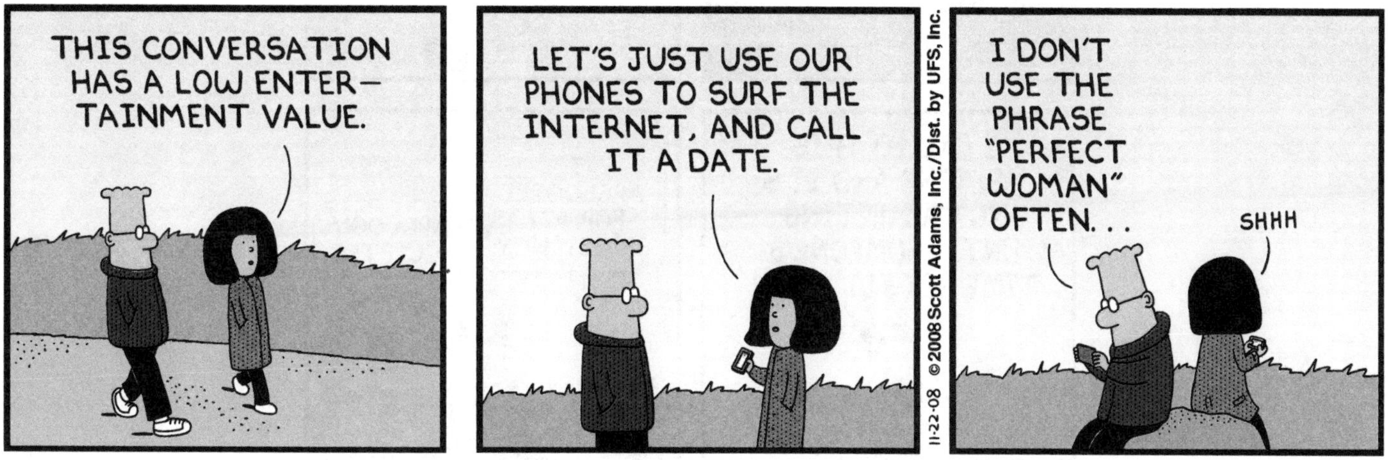
THIS CONVERSATION HAS A LOW ENTER-TAINMENT VALUE.
LET'S JUST USE OUR PHONES TO SURF THE INTERNET, AND CALL IT A DATE.
I DON'T USE THE PHRASE "PERFECT WOMAN" OFTEN. . .
SHHH
11-22-08 ©2008 Scott Adams, Inc./Dist. by UFS, Inc.

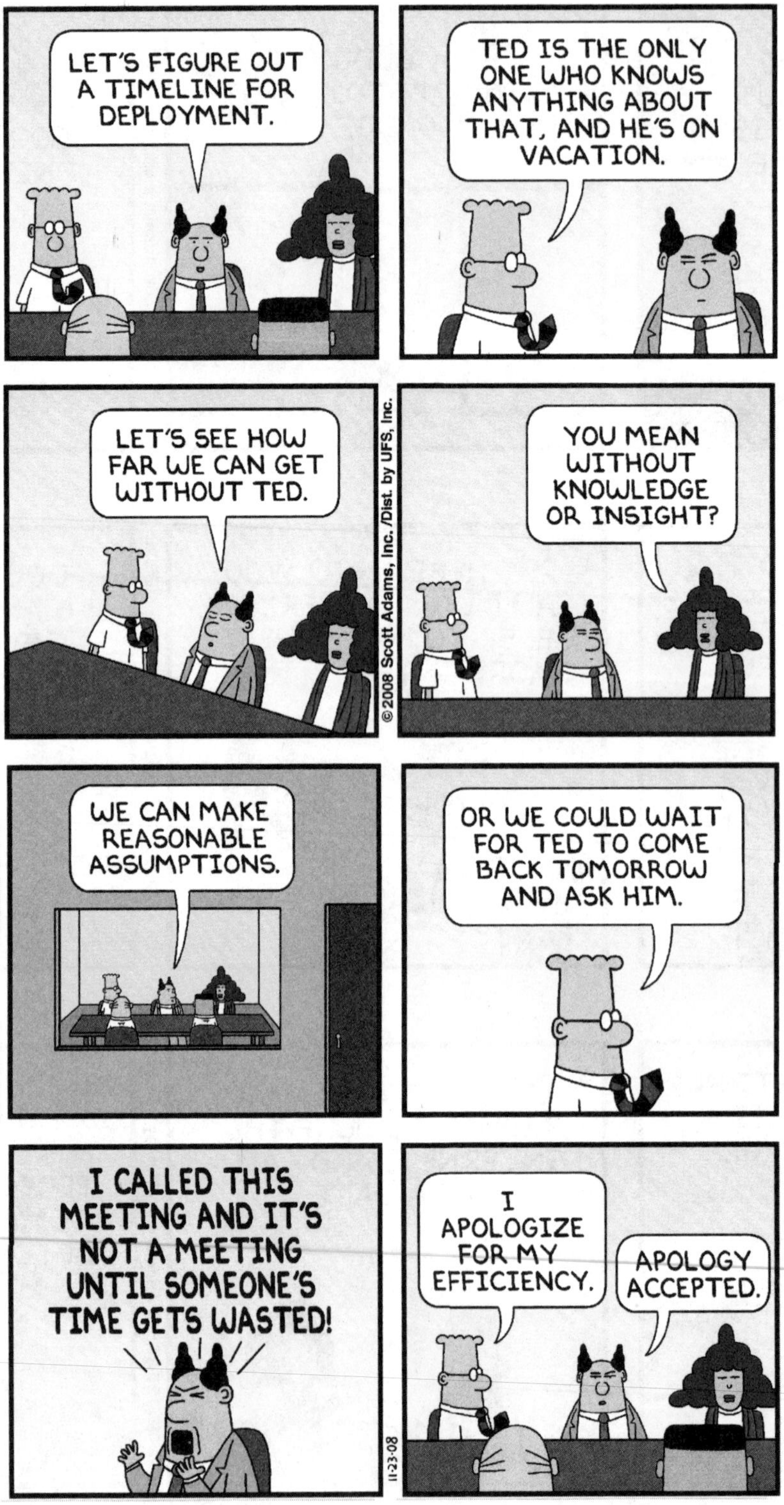
LET'S FIGURE OUT A TIMELINE FOR DEPLOYMENT.
TED IS THE ONLY ONE WHO KNOWS ANYTHING ABOUT THAT, AND HE'S ON VACATION.
LET'S SEE HOW FAR WE CAN GET WITHOUT TED.
YOU MEAN WITHOUT KNOWLEDGE OR INSIGHT?
WE CAN MAKE REASONABLE ASSUMPTIONS.
OR WE COULD WAIT FOR TED TO COME BACK TOMORROW AND ASK HIM.
I CALLED THIS MEETING AND IT'S NOT A MEETING UNTIL SOMEONE'S TIME GETS WASTED!
I APOLOGIZE FOR MY EFFICIENCY.
APOLOGY ACCEPTED.
11-23-08

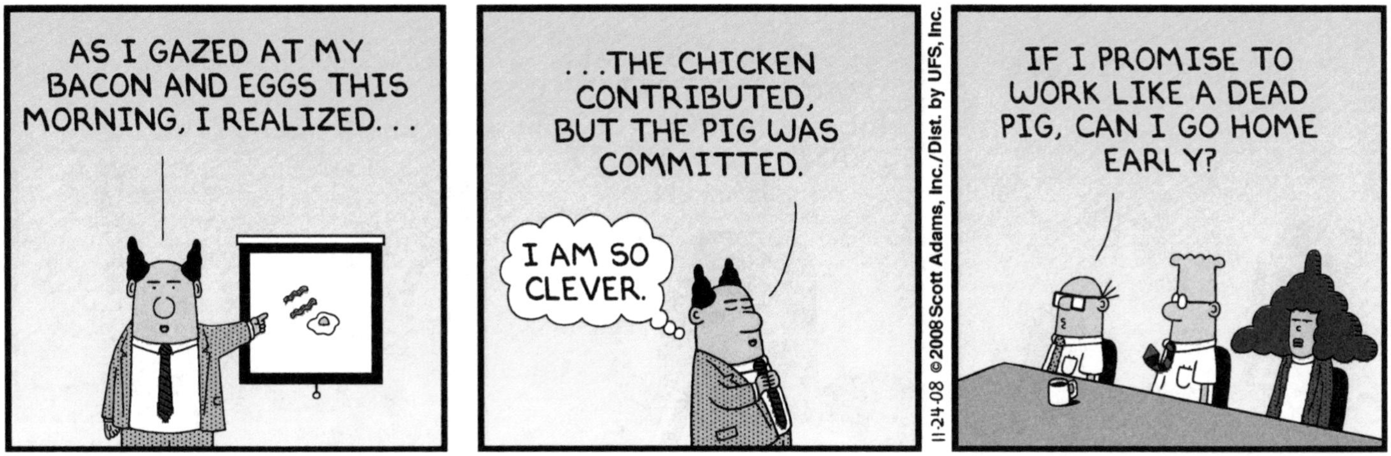
AS I GAZED AT MY BACON AND EGGS THIS MORNING, I REALIZED. . .
. . .THE CHICKEN CONTRIBUTED, BUT THE PIG WAS COMMITTED.
I AM SO CLEVER.
11-24-08 ©2008 Scott Adams, Inc./Dist. by UFS, Inc.
IF I PROMISE TO WORK LIKE A DEAD PIG, CAN I GO HOME EARLY?

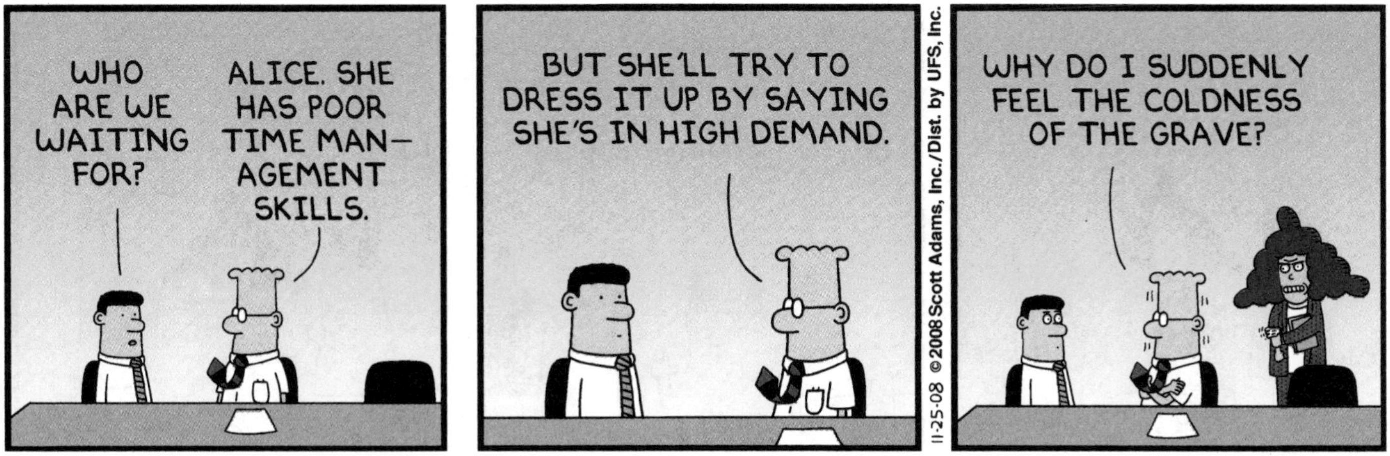
WHO ARE WE WAITING FOR?
ALICE. SHE HAS POOR TIME MAN-AGEMENT SKILLS.
BUT SHE'LL TRY TO DRESS IT UP BY SAYING SHE'S IN HIGH DEMAND.
11-25-08 ©2008 Scott Adams, Inc./Dist. by UFS, Inc.
WHY DO I SUDDENLY FEEL THE COLDNESS OF THE GRAVE?

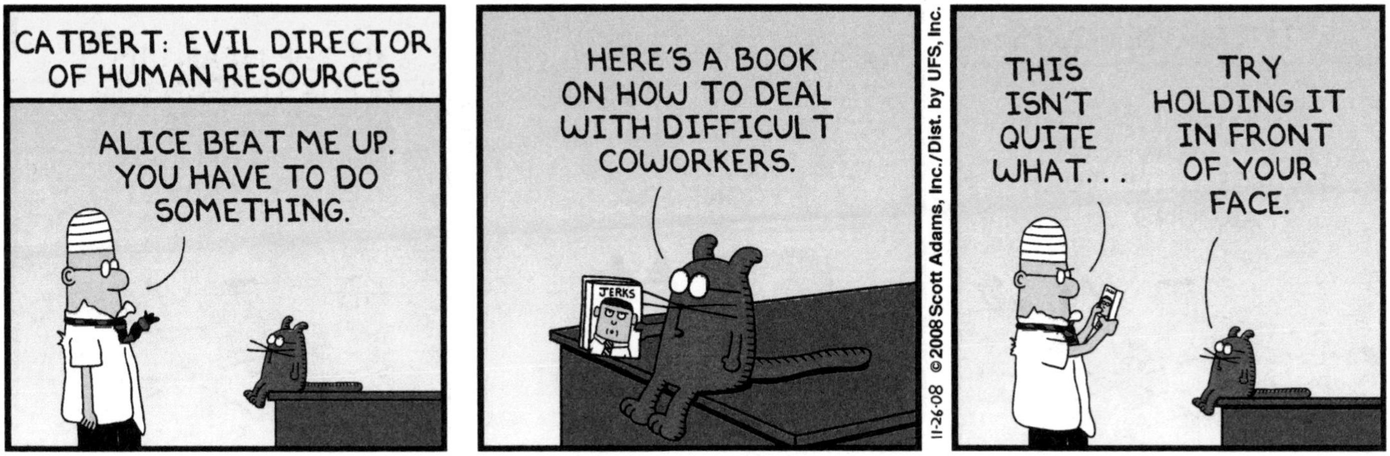
CATBERT: EVIL DIRECTOR OF HUMAN RESOURCES
ALICE BEAT ME UP. YOU HAVE TO DO SOMETHING.
HERE'S A BOOK ON HOW TO DEAL WITH DIFFICULT COWORKERS.
JERKS
11-26-08 ©2008 Scott Adams, Inc./Dist. by UFS, Inc.
THIS ISN'T QUITE WHAT. . .
TRY HOLDING IT IN FRONT OF YOUR FACE.

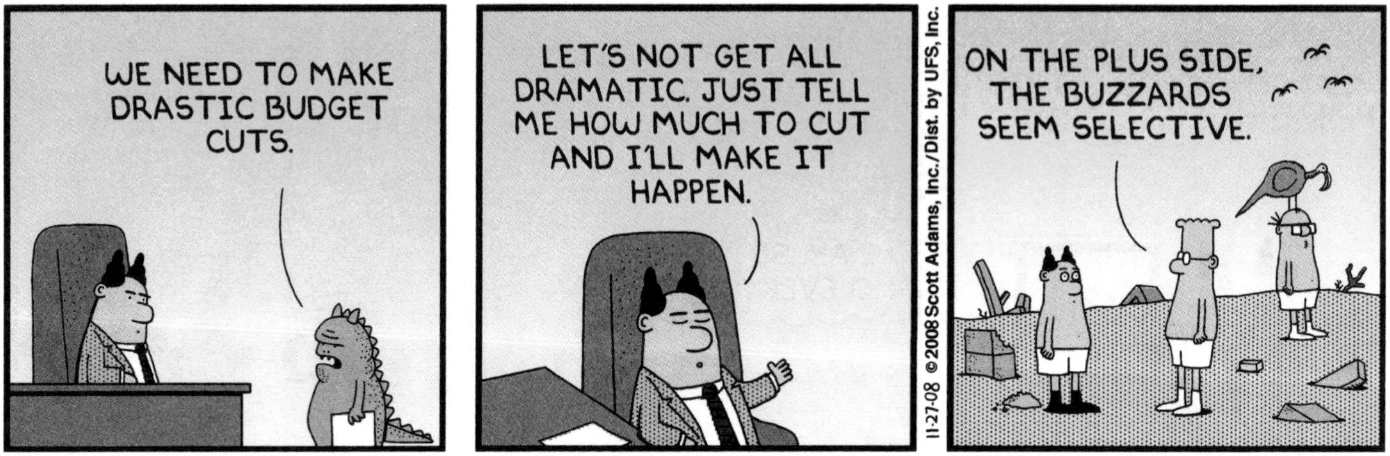
WE NEED TO MAKE DRASTIC BUDGET CUTS.
LET'S NOT GET ALL DRAMATIC. JUST TELL ME HOW MUCH TO CUT AND I'LL MAKE IT HAPPEN.
11-27-08 ©2008 Scott Adams, Inc./Dist. by UFS, Inc.
ON THE PLUS SIDE, THE BUZZARDS SEEM SELECTIVE.

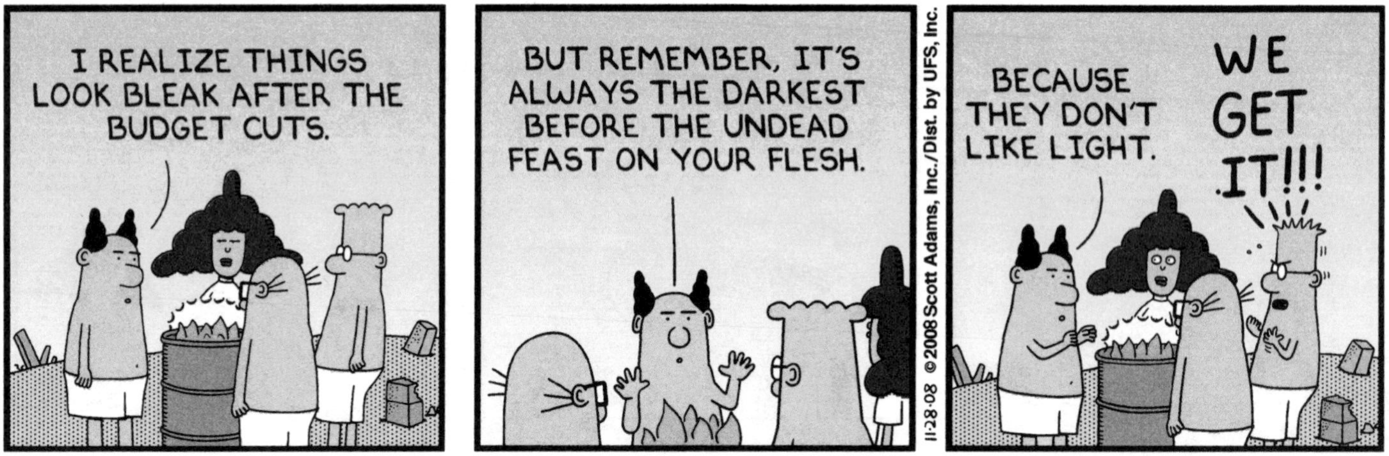
I REALIZE THINGS LOOK BLEAK AFTER THE BUDGET CUTS.
BUT REMEMBER, IT'S ALWAYS THE DARKEST BEFORE THE UNDEAD FEAST ON YOUR FLESH.
11-28-08 ©2008 Scott Adams, Inc./Dist. by UFS, Inc.
BECAUSE THEY DON'T LIKE LIGHT.
WE GET IT!!!

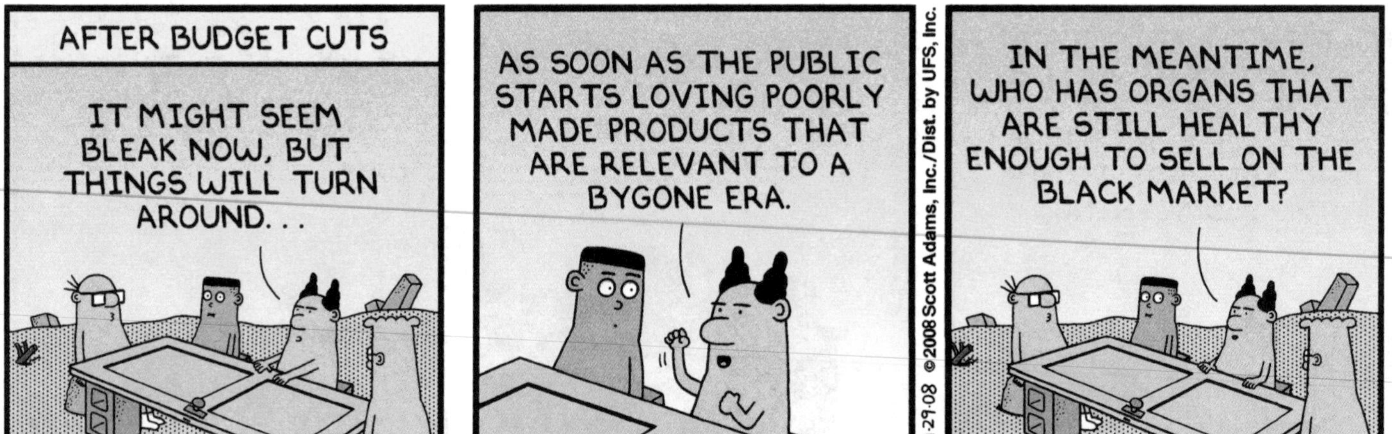
AFTER BUDGET CUTS
IT MIGHT SEEM BLEAK NOW, BUT THINGS WILL TURN AROUND. . .
AS SOON AS THE PUBLIC STARTS LOVING POORLY MADE PRODUCTS THAT ARE RELEVANT TO A BYGONE ERA.
11-29-08 ©2008 Scott Adams, Inc./Dist. by UFS, Inc.
IN THE MEANTIME, WHO HAS ORGANS THAT ARE STILL HEALTHY ENOUGH TO SELL ON THE BLACK MARKET?

UH—OH. I DON'T UNDERSTAND A WORD OF THIS.
WHAT DID OTHER PEOPLE SAY ABOUT IT?
A FEW PEOPLE QUIBBLED ABOUT THE METHODOLOGY.
RIGHT, WELL, YES, THE METHODOLOGY DOES HAVE A FEW ISSUES.
©2008 Scott Adams, Inc./Dist. by UFS, Inc.
CAN YOU BE MORE SPECIFIC?
I BROUGHT SOME CRICKETS TO KEEP ME COMPANY WHILE I WAIT FOR YOUR ANSWER.
CHIRP CHIRP CHIRP CHIRP CHIRP CHIRP CHIRP CHIRP
11-30-08
I'M UP NEXT. CAN I BORROW THE CRICKETS?
THEY'RE A LITTLE TIRED.

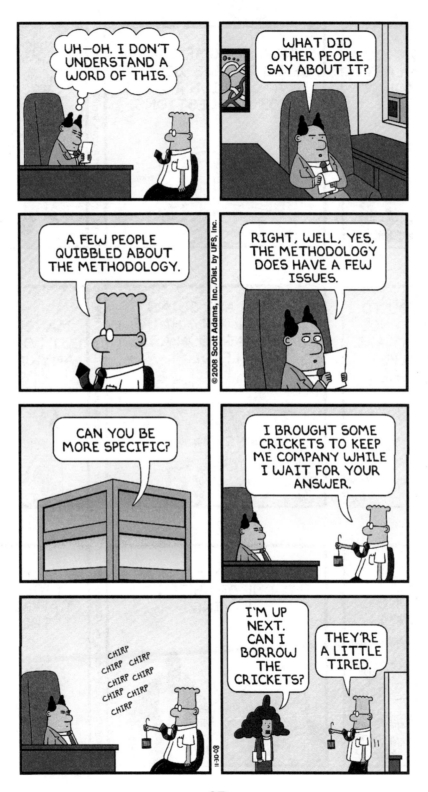

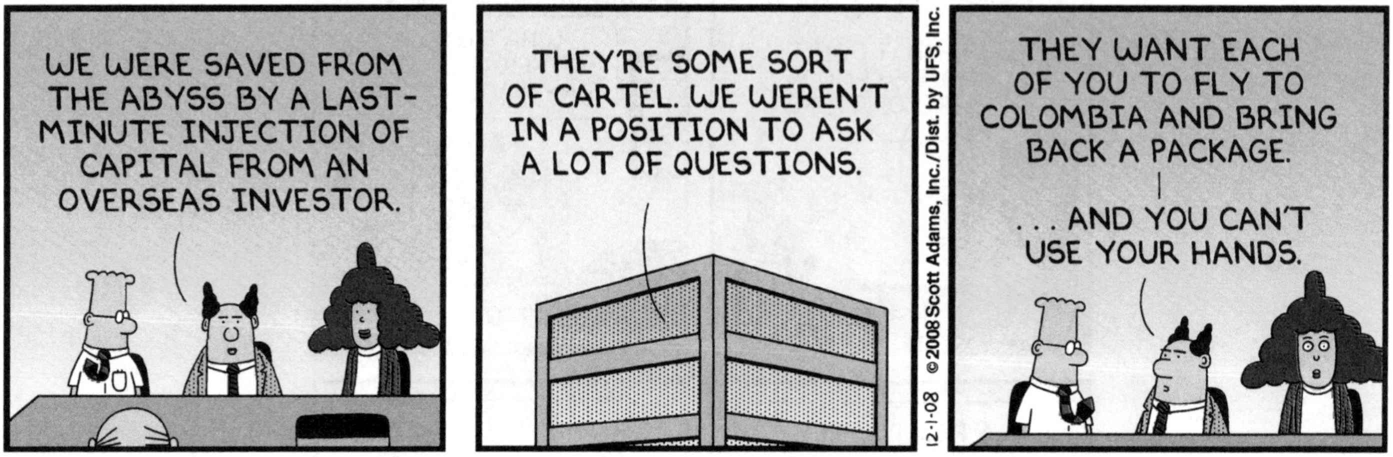
WE WERE SAVED FROM THE ABYSS BY A LAST-MINUTE INJECTION OF CAPITAL FROM AN OVERSEAS INVESTOR.
THEY'RE SOME SORT OF CARTEL. WE WEREN'T IN A POSITION TO ASK A LOT OF QUESTIONS.
12-1-08 ©2008 Scott Adams, Inc./Dist. by UFS, Inc.
THEY WANT EACH OF YOU TO FLY TO COLOMBIA AND BRING BACK A PACKAGE.
. . . AND YOU CAN'T USE YOUR HANDS.

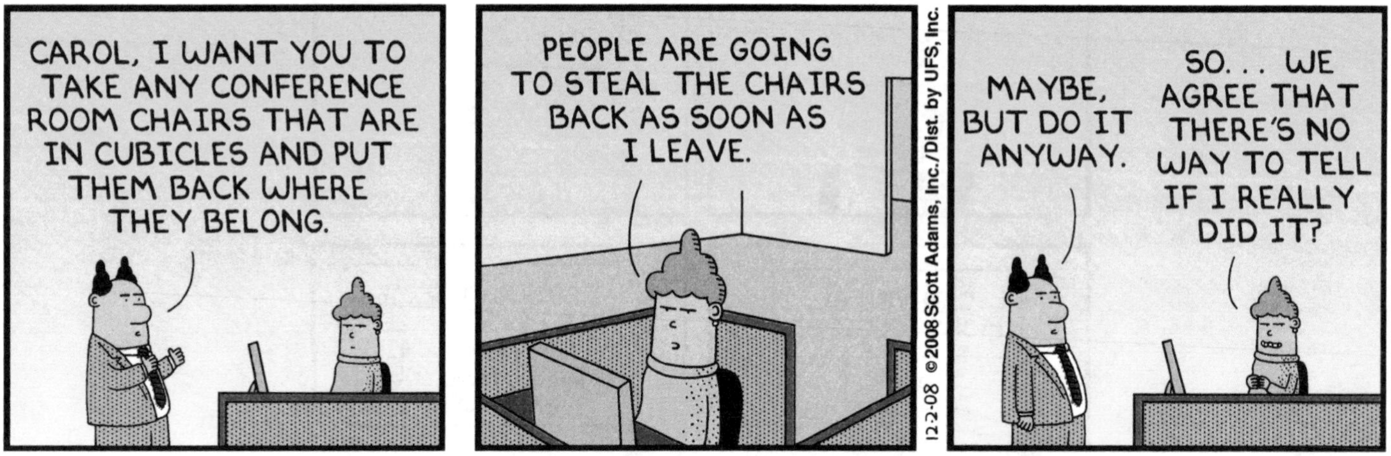
CAROL, I WANT YOU TO TAKE ANY CONFERENCE ROOM CHAIRS THAT ARE IN CUBICLES AND PUT THEM BACK WHERE THEY BELONG.
PEOPLE ARE GOING TO STEAL THE CHAIRS BACK AS SOON AS I LEAVE.
12-2-08 ©2008 Scott Adams, Inc./Dist. by UFS, Inc.
MAYBE, BUT DO IT ANYWAY.
SO. . . WE AGREE THAT THERE'S NO WAY TO TELL IF I REALLY DID IT?

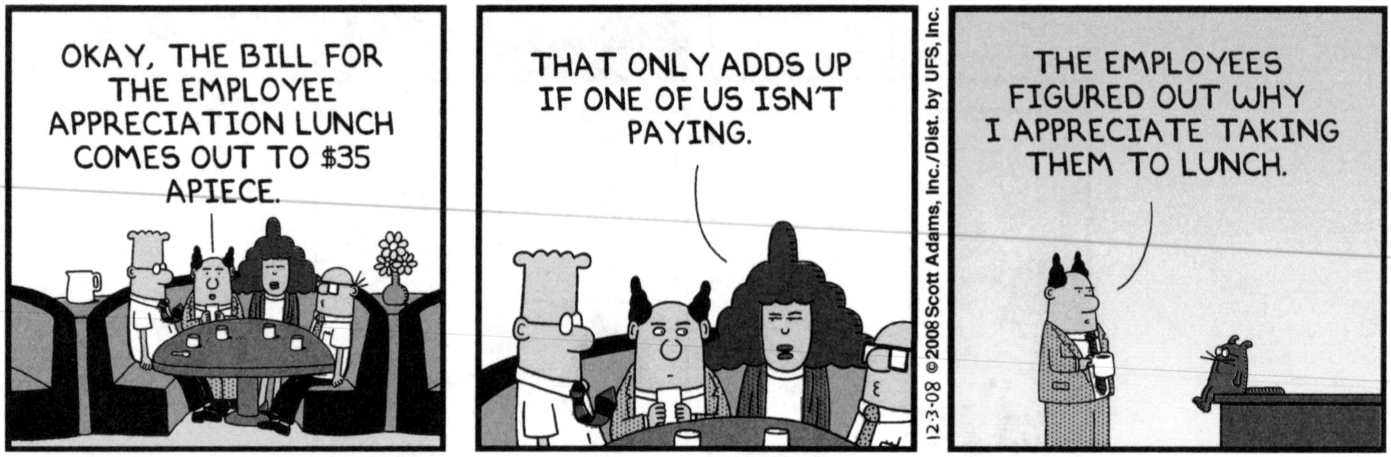
OKAY, THE BILL FOR THE EMPLOYEE APPRECIATION LUNCH COMES OUT TO $35 APIECE.
THAT ONLY ADDS UP IF ONE OF US ISN'T PAYING.
12-3-08 ©2008 Scott Adams, Inc./Dist. by UFS, Inc.
THE EMPLOYEES FIGURED OUT WHY I APPRECIATE TAKING THEM TO LUNCH.

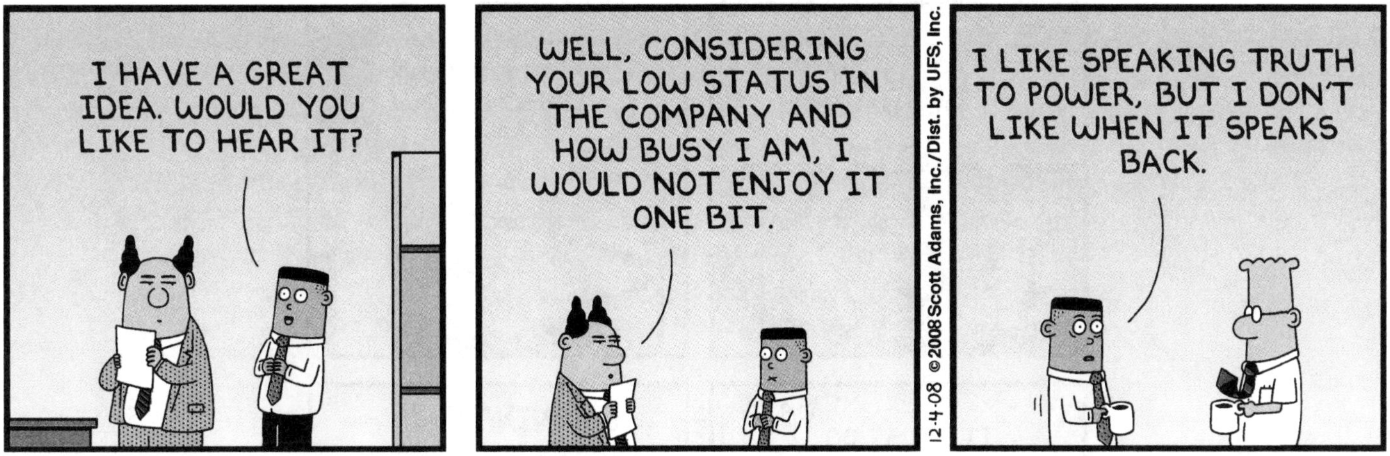
I HAVE A GREAT IDEA. WOULD YOU LIKE TO HEAR IT?
WELL, CONSIDERING YOUR LOW STATUS IN THE COMPANY AND HOW BUSY I AM, I WOULD NOT ENJOY IT ONE BIT.
12-4-08 © 2008 Scott Adams, Inc./Dist. by UFS, Inc.
I LIKE SPEAKING TRUTH TO POWER, BUT I DON'T LIKE WHEN IT SPEAKS BACK.

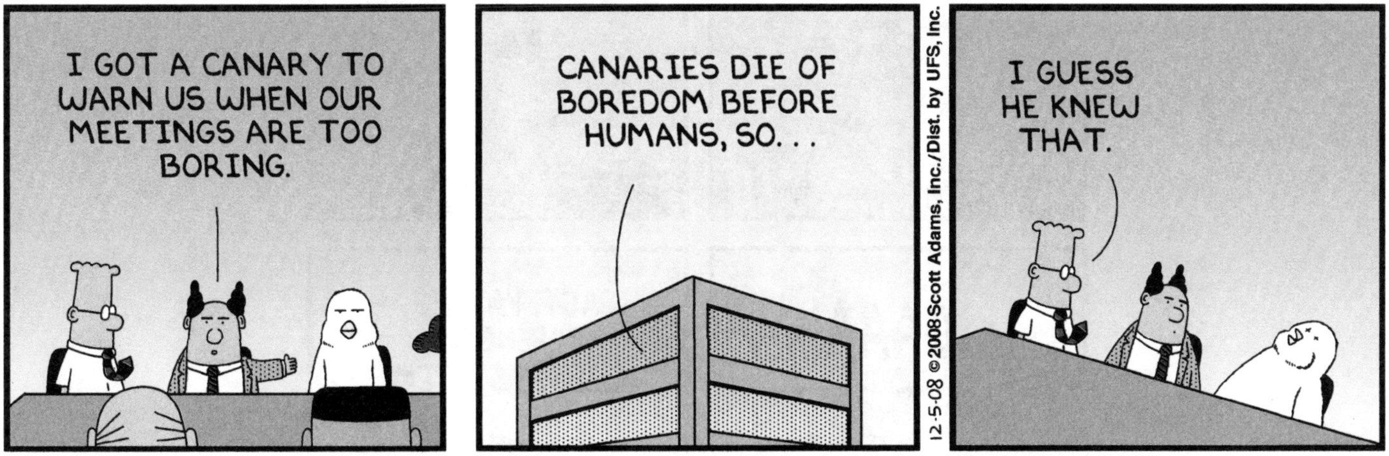
I GOT A CANARY TO WARN US WHEN OUR MEETINGS ARE TOO BORING.
CANARIES DIE OF BOREDOM BEFORE HUMANS, SO. . .
12-5-08 © 2008 Scott Adams, Inc./Dist. by UFS, Inc.
I GUESS HE KNEW THAT.

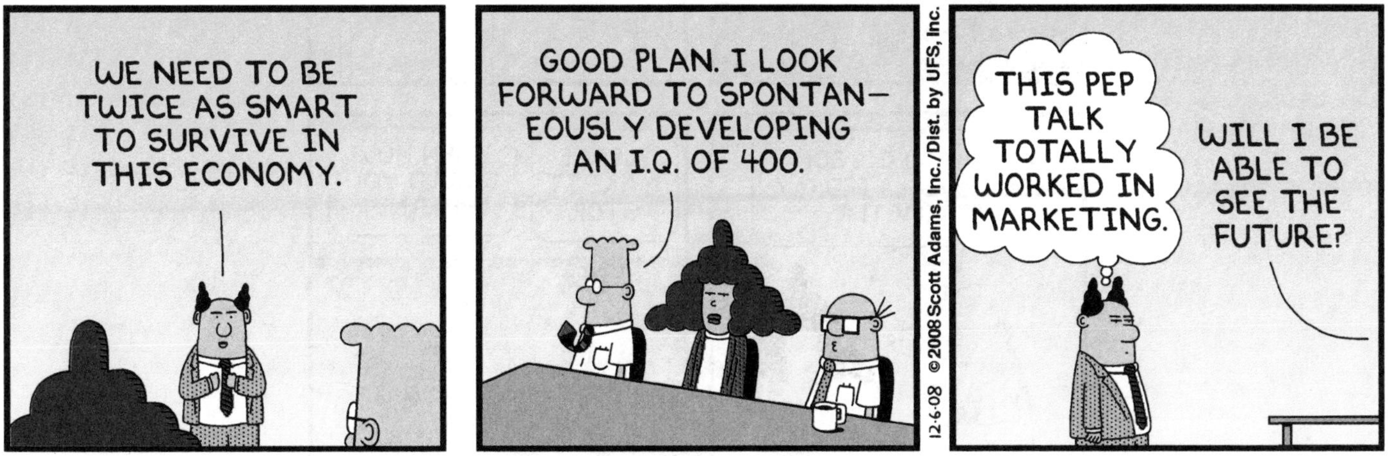
WE NEED TO BE TWICE AS SMART TO SURVIVE IN THIS ECONOMY.
GOOD PLAN. I LOOK FORWARD TO SPONTAN-EOUSLY DEVELOPING AN I.Q. OF 400.
12-6-08 © 2008 Scott Adams, Inc./Dist. by UFS, Inc.
THIS PEP TALK TOTALLY WORKED IN MARKETING.
WILL I BE ABLE TO SEE THE FUTURE?

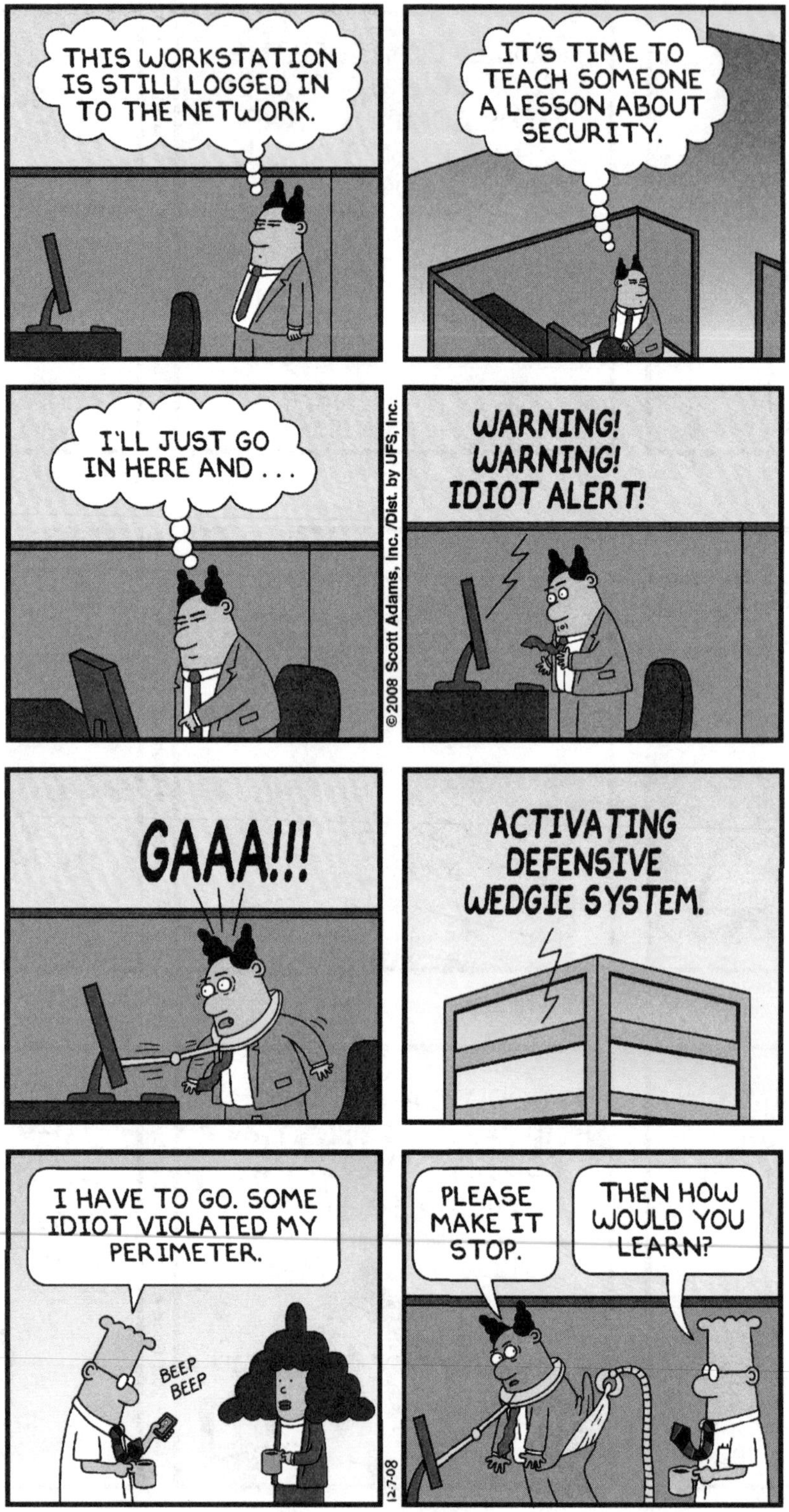
THIS WORKSTATION IS STILL LOGGED IN TO THE NETWORK.
IT'S TIME TO TEACH SOMEONE A LESSON ABOUT SECURITY.
I'LL JUST GO IN HERE AND . . .
©2008 Scott Adams, Inc./Dist. by UFS, Inc.
WARNING! WARNING! IDIOT ALERT!
GAAA!!!
ACTIVATING DEFENSIVE WEDGIE SYSTEM.
I HAVE TO GO. SOME IDIOT VIOLATED MY PERIMETER.
BEEP BEEP
12-7-08
PLEASE MAKE IT STOP.
THEN HOW WOULD YOU LEARN?

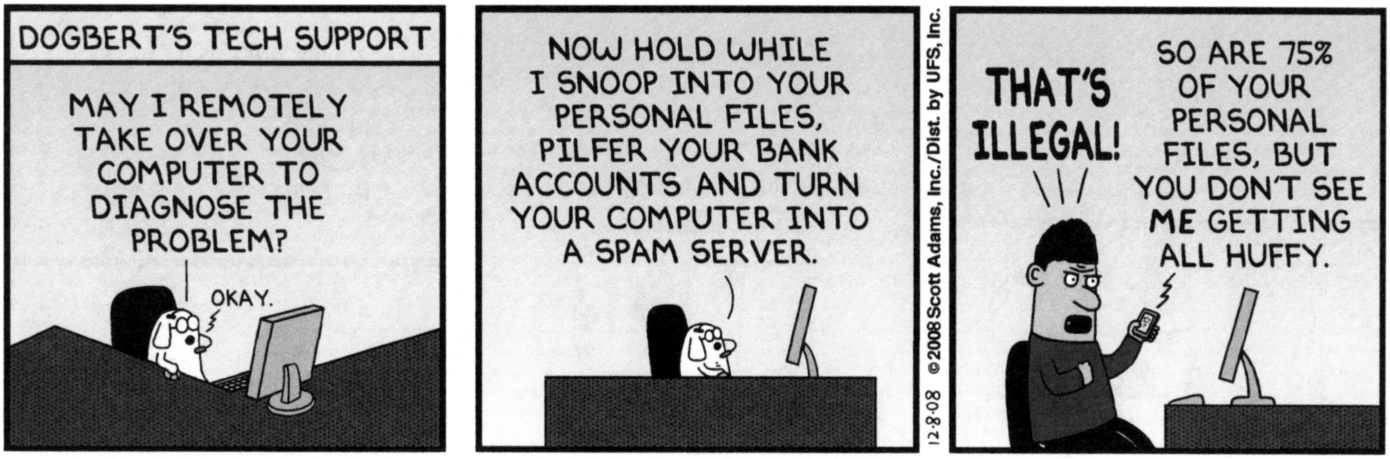
DOGBERT'S TECH SUPPORT
MAY I REMOTELY TAKE OVER YOUR COMPUTER TO DIAGNOSE THE PROBLEM?
OKAY.
NOW HOLD WHILE I SNOOP INTO YOUR PERSONAL FILES, PILFER YOUR BANK ACCOUNTS AND TURN YOUR COMPUTER INTO A SPAM SERVER.
12-8-08 © 2008 Scott Adams, Inc./Dist. by UFS, Inc.
THAT'S ILLEGAL!
SO ARE 75% OF YOUR PERSONAL FILES, BUT YOU DON'T SEE ME GETTING ALL HUFFY.

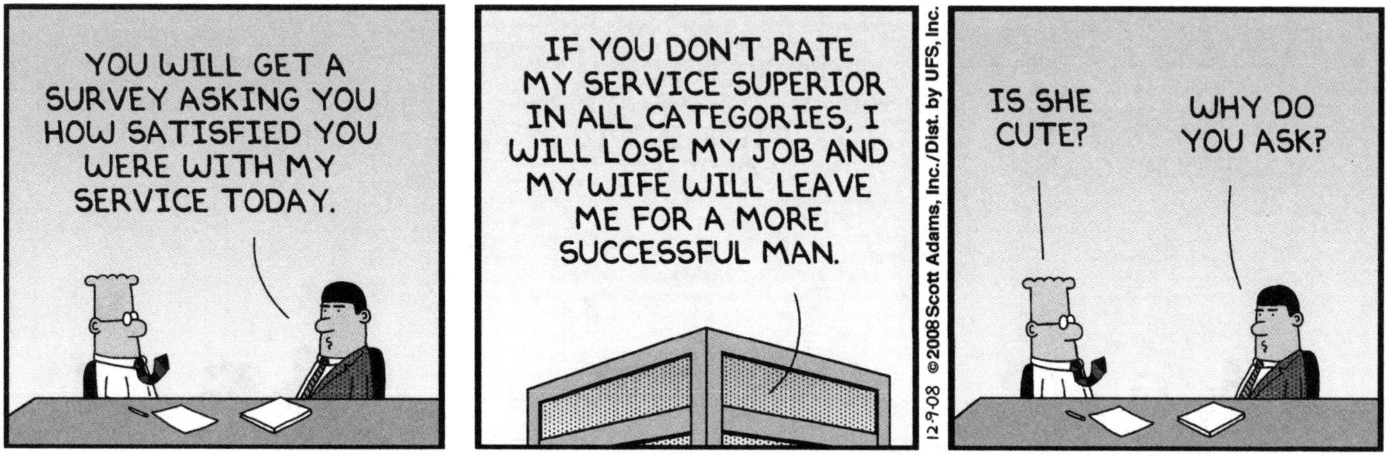
YOU WILL GET A SURVEY ASKING YOU HOW SATISFIED YOU WERE WITH MY SERVICE TODAY.
IF YOU DON'T RATE MY SERVICE SUPERIOR IN ALL CATEGORIES, I WILL LOSE MY JOB AND MY WIFE WILL LEAVE ME FOR A MORE SUCCESSFUL MAN.
12-9-08 © 2008 Scott Adams, Inc./Dist. by UFS, Inc.
IS SHE CUTE?
WHY DO YOU ASK?

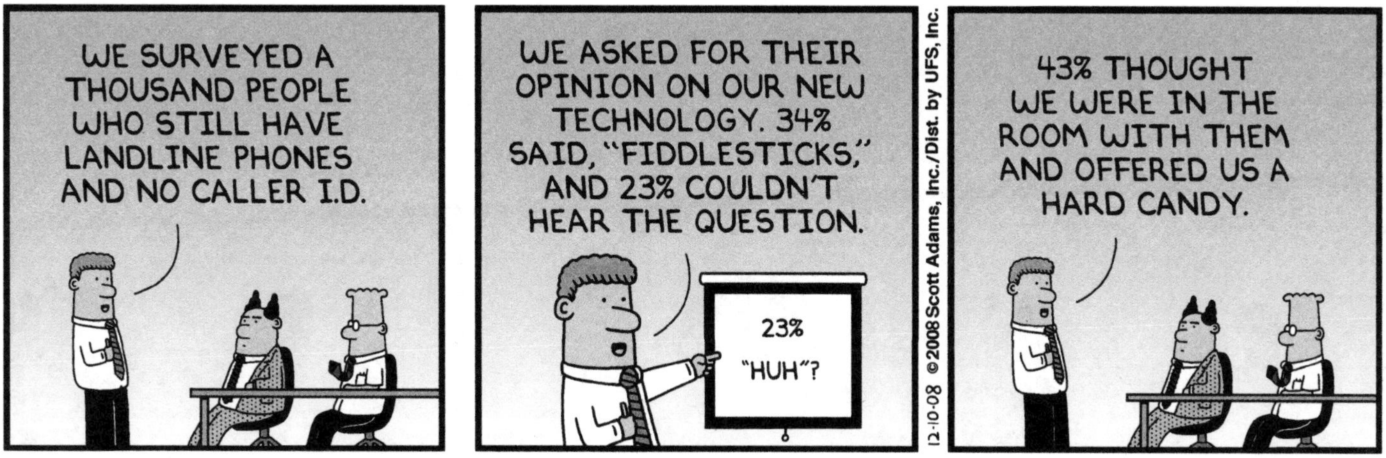
WE SURVEYED A THOUSAND PEOPLE WHO STILL HAVE LANDLINE PHONES AND NO CALLER I.D.
WE ASKED FOR THEIR OPINION ON OUR NEW TECHNOLOGY. 34% SAID, "FIDDLESTICKS," AND 23% COULDN'T HEAR THE QUESTION.
23% "HUH"?
12-10-08 © 2008 Scott Adams, Inc./Dist. by UFS, Inc.
43% THOUGHT WE WERE IN THE ROOM WITH THEM AND OFFERED US A HARD CANDY.

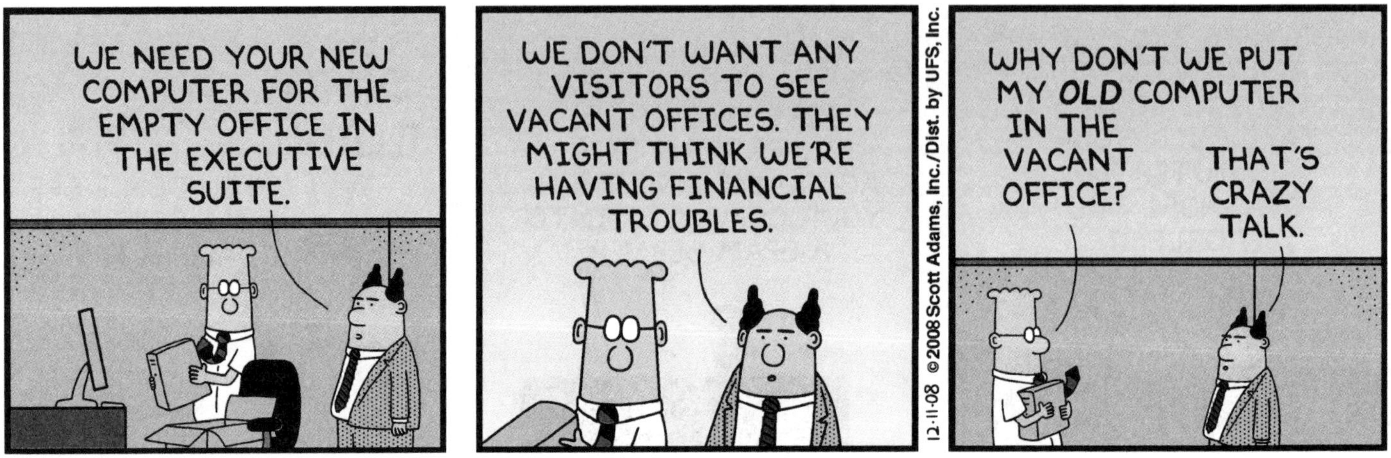
WE NEED YOUR NEW COMPUTER FOR THE EMPTY OFFICE IN THE EXECUTIVE SUITE.
WE DON'T WANT ANY VISITORS TO SEE VACANT OFFICES. THEY MIGHT THINK WE'RE HAVING FINANCIAL TROUBLES.
12-11-08 © 2008 Scott Adams, Inc./Dist. by UFS, Inc.
WHY DON'T WE PUT MY *OLD* COMPUTER IN THE VACANT OFFICE?
THAT'S CRAZY TALK.

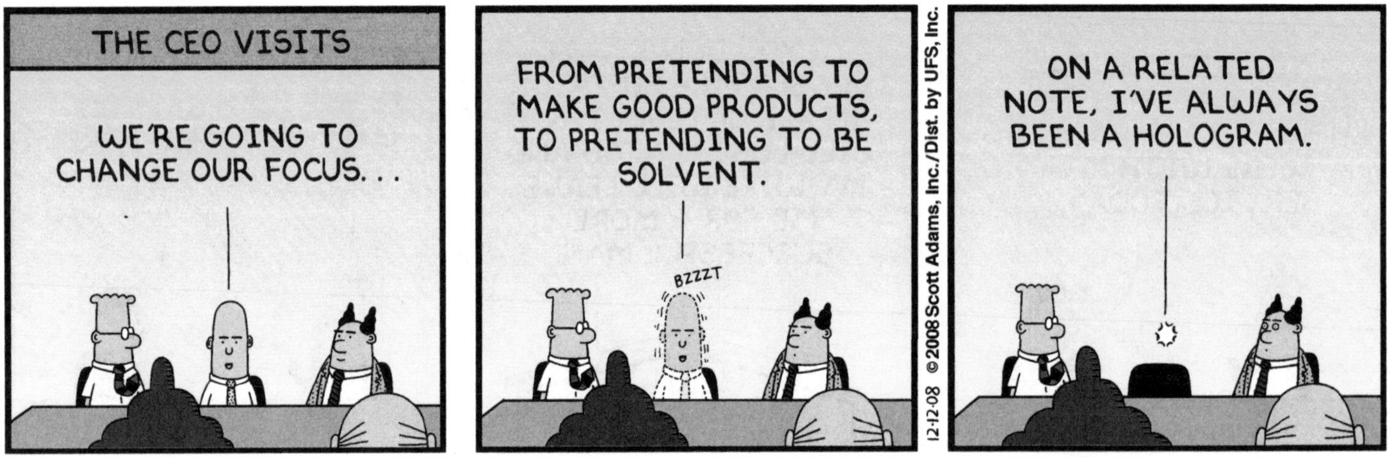
THE CEO VISITS
WE'RE GOING TO CHANGE OUR FOCUS...
FROM PRETENDING TO MAKE GOOD PRODUCTS, TO PRETENDING TO BE SOLVENT.
BZZZT
12-12-08 © 2008 Scott Adams, Inc./Dist. by UFS, Inc.
ON A RELATED NOTE, I'VE ALWAYS BEEN A HOLOGRAM.

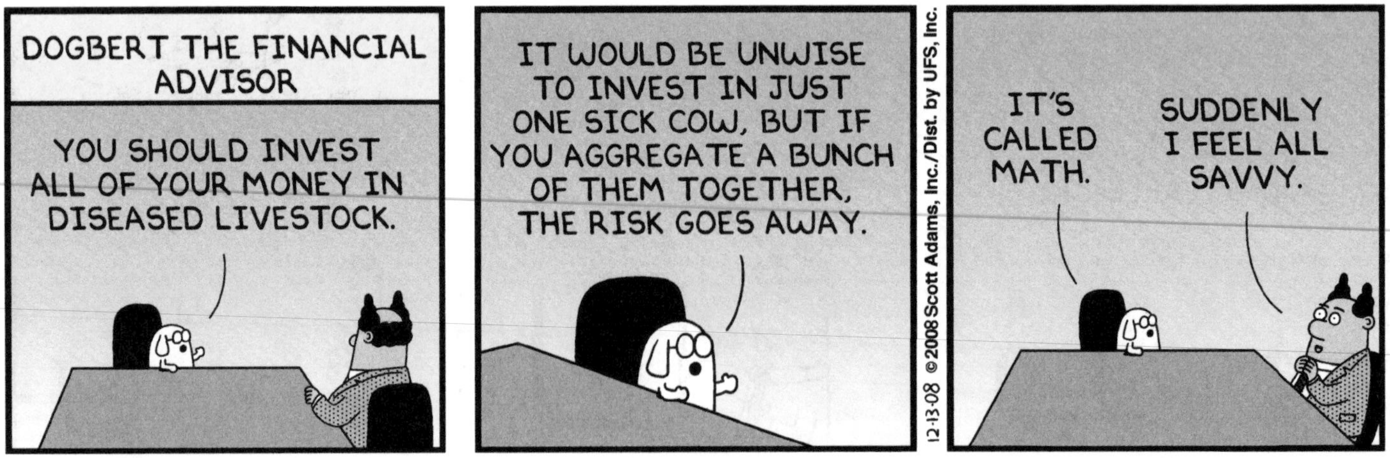
DOGBERT THE FINANCIAL ADVISOR
YOU SHOULD INVEST ALL OF YOUR MONEY IN DISEASED LIVESTOCK.
IT WOULD BE UNWISE TO INVEST IN JUST ONE SICK COW, BUT IF YOU AGGREGATE A BUNCH OF THEM TOGETHER, THE RISK GOES AWAY.
12-13-08 © 2008 Scott Adams, Inc./Dist. by UFS, Inc.
IT'S CALLED MATH.
SUDDENLY I FEEL ALL SAVVY.

DO YOU HAVE A MINUTE TO LOOK AT MY TERRIBLE IDEA?
IT'S THE WORST IDEA EVER. TOTALLY IMPRACTICAL, AND BORDERING ON IRRESPONSIBLE.
WHY ARE YOU SAYING THAT ABOUT YOUR OWN IDEA?
BECAUSE YOU'RE ONE OF THOSE JERKS WHO AUTOMATICALLY DISAGREES WITH EVERYONE.
© 2008 Scott Adams, Inc./Dist. by UFS, Inc.
I'M TELLING YOU MY IDEA IS AWFUL SO YOU WILL FEEL COMPELLED TO SAY IT IS GREAT.
NOW THAT I KNOW HOW YOU PLAN TO MANIPULATE ME, IT WON'T WORK.
I'M SO SURPRISED TO HEAR THAT YOU DISAGREE.
NOW LOOK AT MY TERRIBLE, TERRIBLE IDEA.
12-14-08
DANCE, PUPPET, DANCE.
THIS IS A GREAT IDEA!

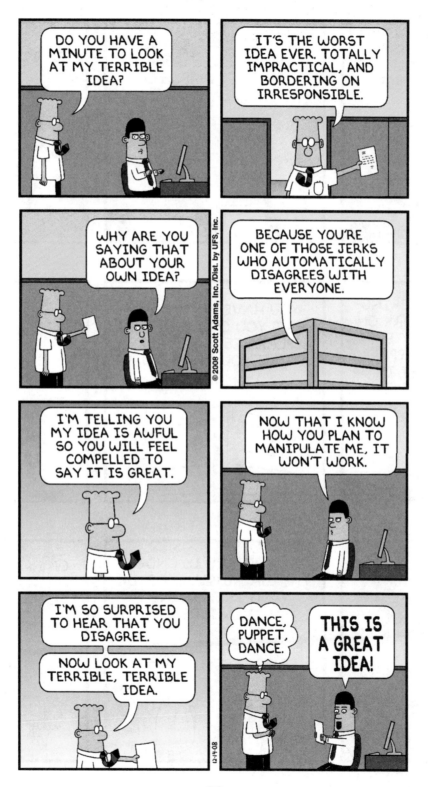

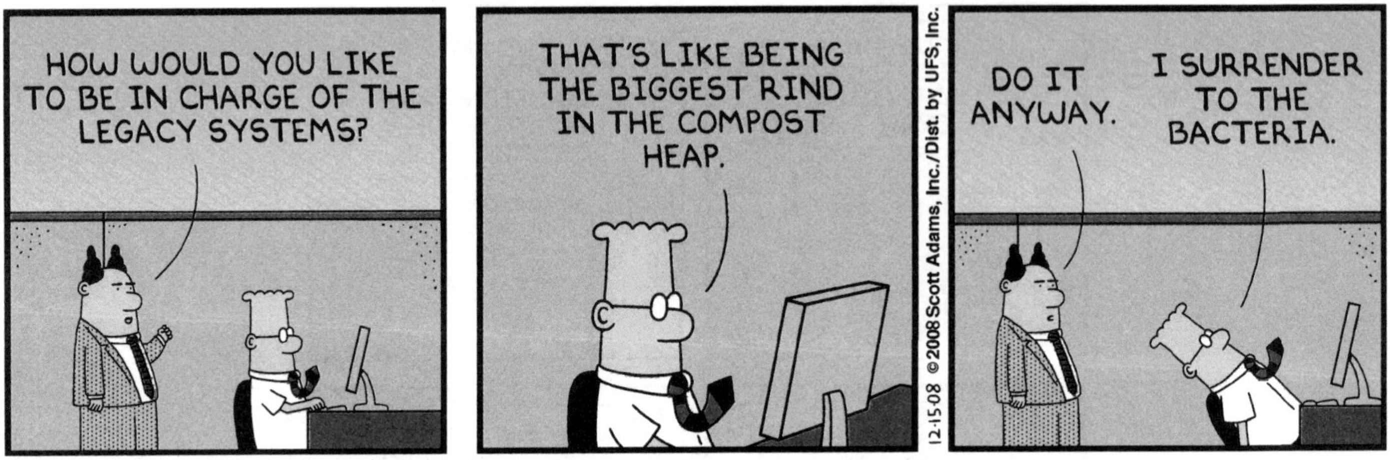
HOW WOULD YOU LIKE TO BE IN CHARGE OF THE LEGACY SYSTEMS?
THAT'S LIKE BEING THE BIGGEST RIND IN THE COMPOST HEAP.
12-15-08 ©2008 Scott Adams, Inc./Dist. by UFS, Inc.
DO IT ANYWAY.
I SURRENDER TO THE BACTERIA.

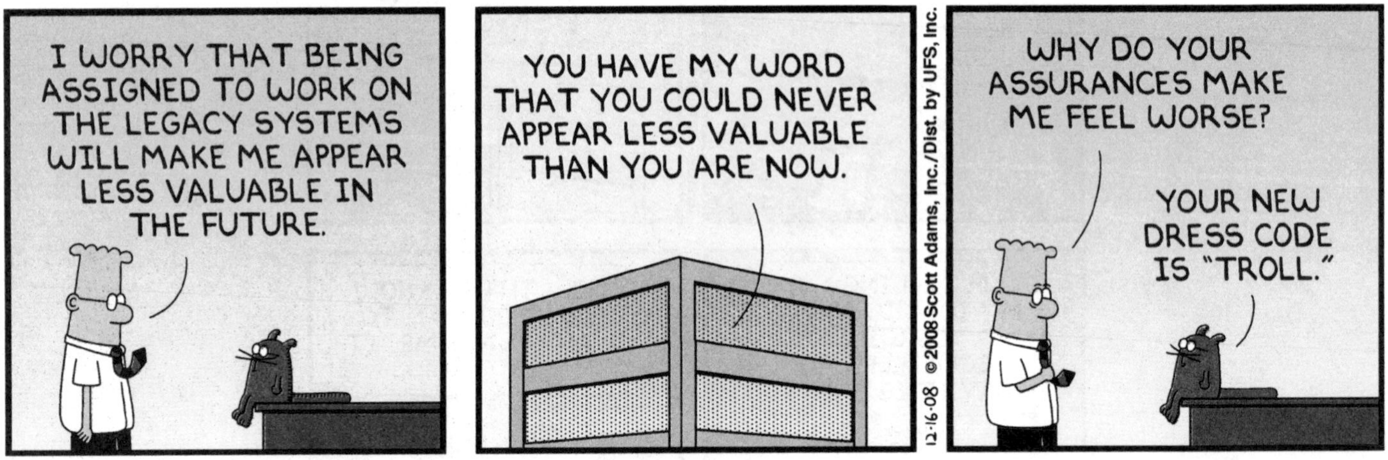
I WORRY THAT BEING ASSIGNED TO WORK ON THE LEGACY SYSTEMS WILL MAKE ME APPEAR LESS VALUABLE IN THE FUTURE.
YOU HAVE MY WORD THAT YOU COULD NEVER APPEAR LESS VALUABLE THAN YOU ARE NOW.
12-16-08 ©2008 Scott Adams, Inc./Dist. by UFS, Inc.
WHY DO YOUR ASSURANCES MAKE ME FEEL WORSE?
YOUR NEW DRESS CODE IS "TROLL."

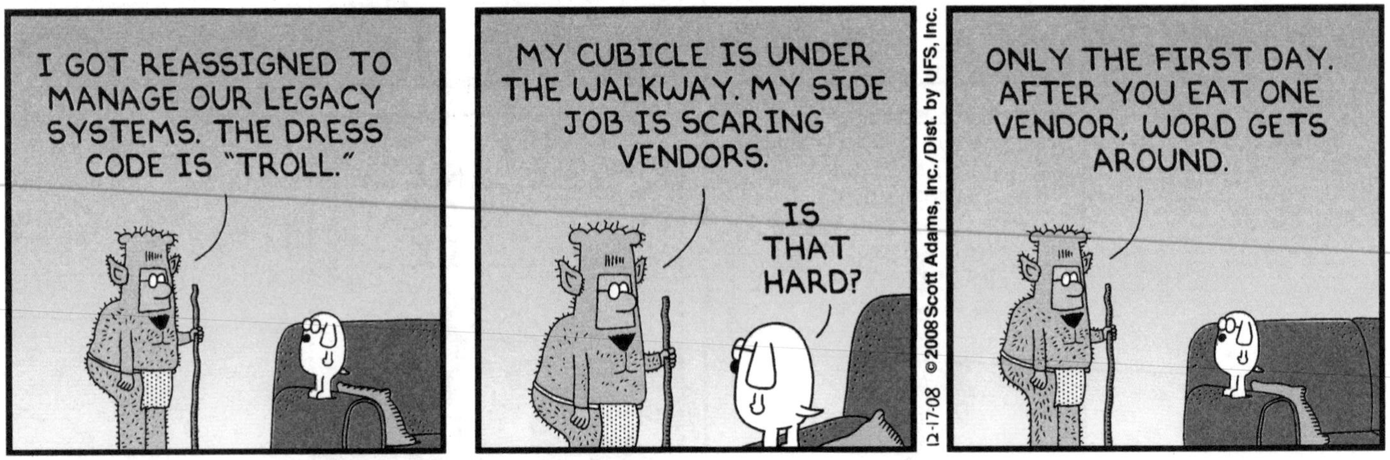
I GOT REASSIGNED TO MANAGE OUR LEGACY SYSTEMS. THE DRESS CODE IS "TROLL."
MY CUBICLE IS UNDER THE WALKWAY. MY SIDE JOB IS SCARING VENDORS.
IS THAT HARD?
12-17-08 ©2008 Scott Adams, Inc./Dist. by UFS, Inc.
ONLY THE FIRST DAY. AFTER YOU EAT ONE VENDOR, WORD GETS AROUND.

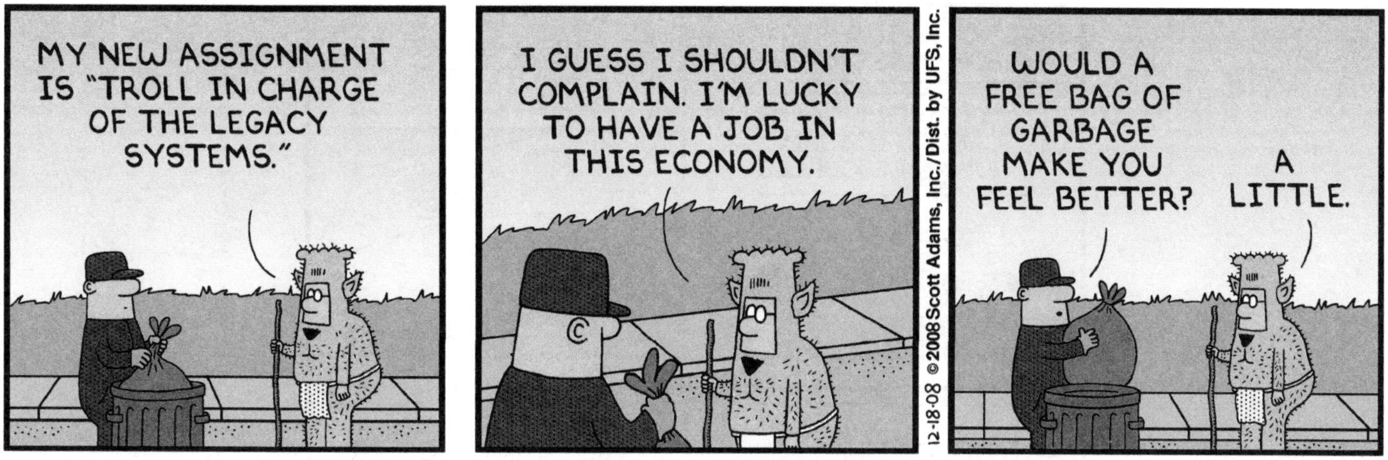
MY NEW ASSIGNMENT IS "TROLL IN CHARGE OF THE LEGACY SYSTEMS."
I GUESS I SHOULDN'T COMPLAIN. I'M LUCKY TO HAVE A JOB IN THIS ECONOMY.
12-18-08 ©2008 Scott Adams, Inc./Dist. by UFS, Inc.
WOULD A FREE BAG OF GARBAGE MAKE YOU FEEL BETTER?
A LITTLE.

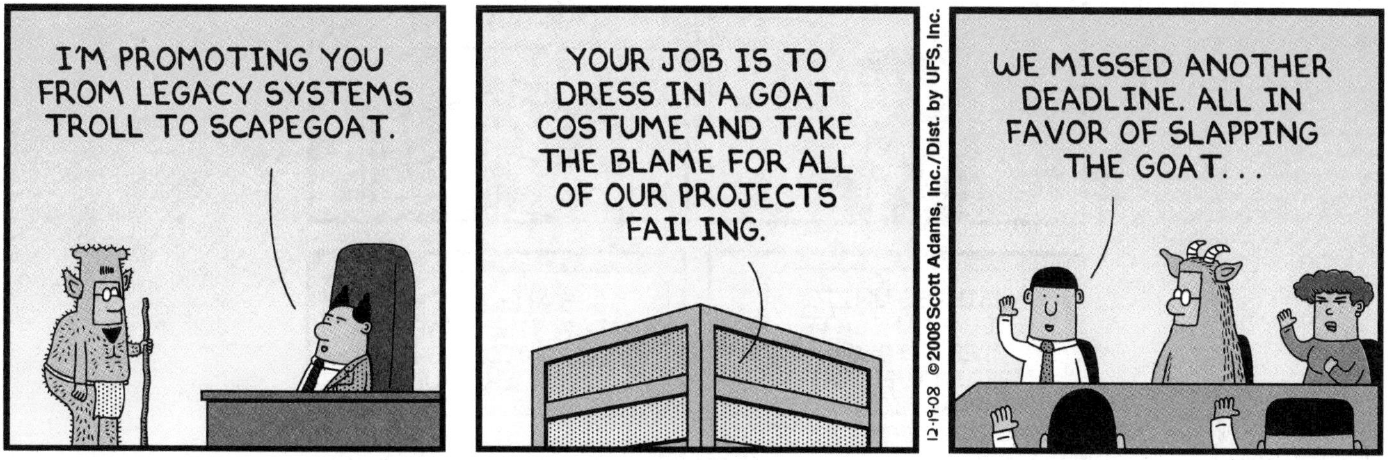
I'M PROMOTING YOU FROM LEGACY SYSTEMS TROLL TO SCAPEGOAT.
YOUR JOB IS TO DRESS IN A GOAT COSTUME AND TAKE THE BLAME FOR ALL OF OUR PROJECTS FAILING.
12-19-08 ©2008 Scott Adams, Inc./Dist. by UFS, Inc.
WE MISSED ANOTHER DEADLINE. ALL IN FAVOR OF SLAPPING THE GOAT...

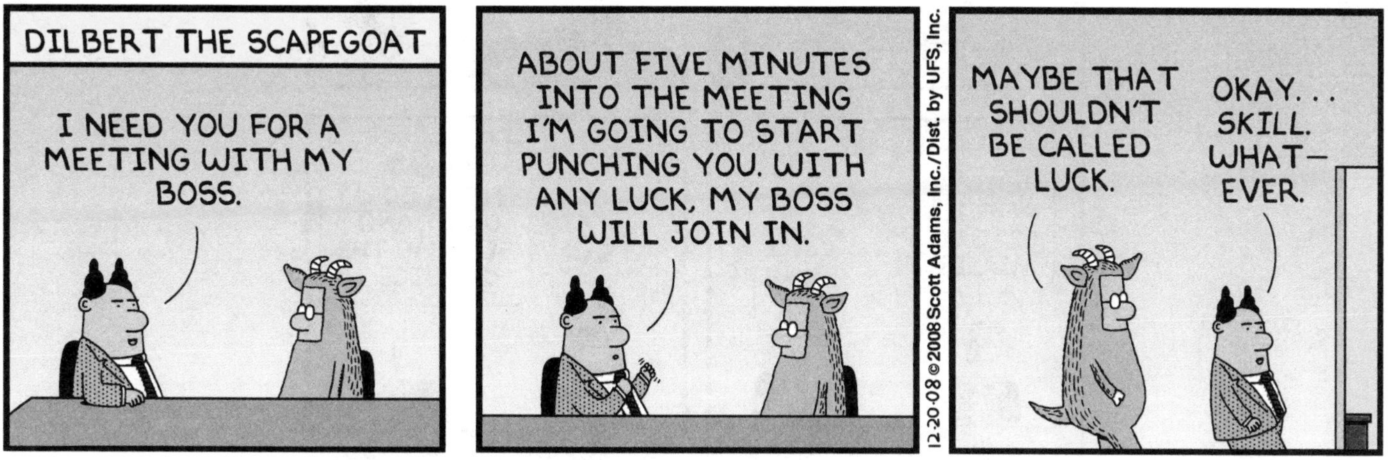
DILBERT THE SCAPEGOAT
I NEED YOU FOR A MEETING WITH MY BOSS.
ABOUT FIVE MINUTES INTO THE MEETING I'M GOING TO START PUNCHING YOU. WITH ANY LUCK, MY BOSS WILL JOIN IN.
12-20-08 ©2008 Scott Adams, Inc./Dist. by UFS, Inc.
MAYBE THAT SHOULDN'T BE CALLED LUCK.
OKAY... SKILL. WHAT—EVER.

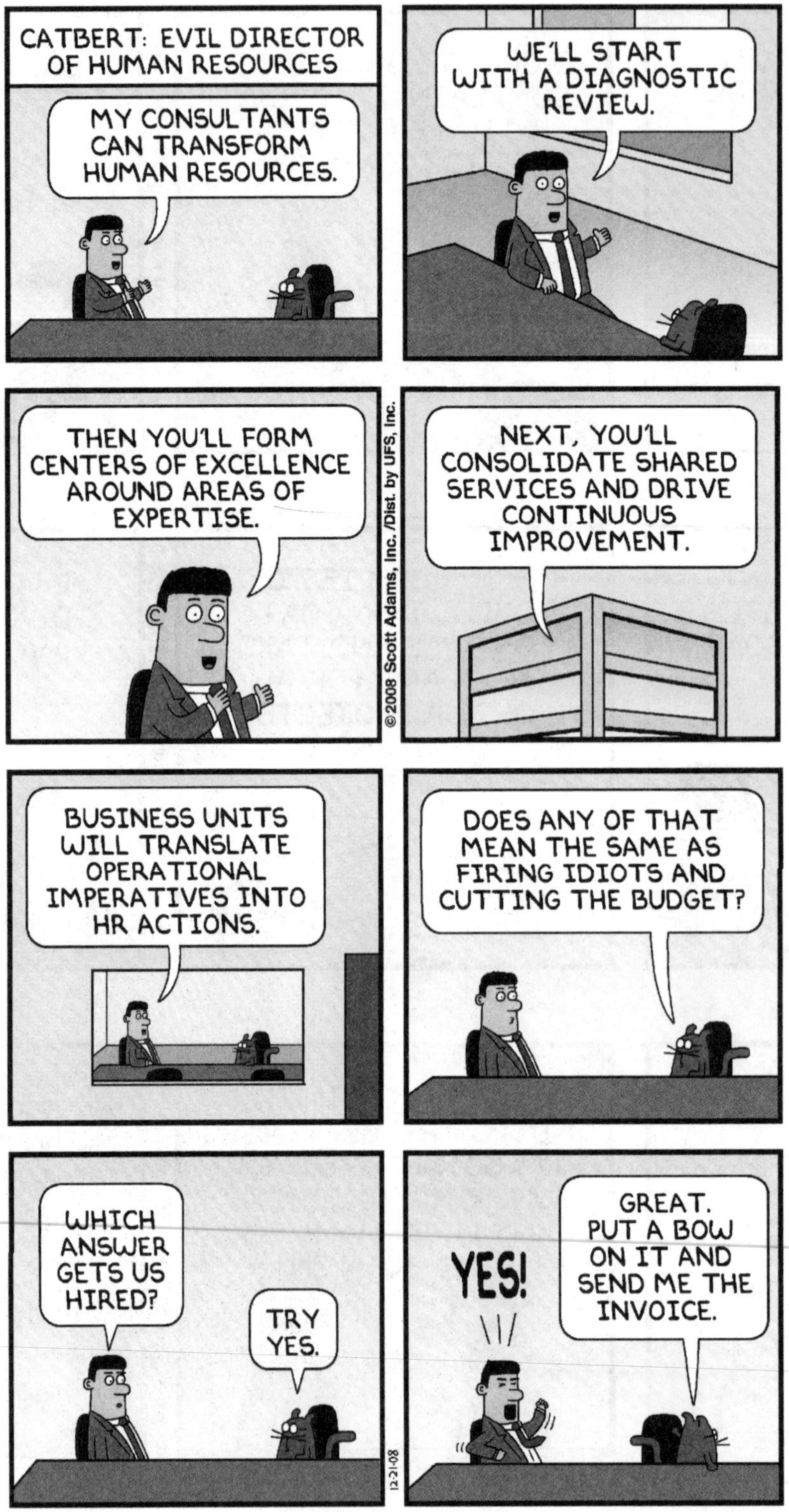
CATBERT: EVIL DIRECTOR OF HUMAN RESOURCES
MY CONSULTANTS CAN TRANSFORM HUMAN RESOURCES.
WE'LL START WITH A DIAGNOSTIC REVIEW.
THEN YOU'LL FORM CENTERS OF EXCELLENCE AROUND AREAS OF EXPERTISE.
NEXT, YOU'LL CONSOLIDATE SHARED SERVICES AND DRIVE CONTINUOUS IMPROVEMENT.
BUSINESS UNITS WILL TRANSLATE OPERATIONAL IMPERATIVES INTO HR ACTIONS.
DOES ANY OF THAT MEAN THE SAME AS FIRING IDIOTS AND CUTTING THE BUDGET?
WHICH ANSWER GETS US HIRED?
TRY YES.
YES!
GREAT. PUT A BOW ON IT AND SEND ME THE INVOICE.
©2008 Scott Adams, Inc./Dist. by UFS, Inc.
12-21-08

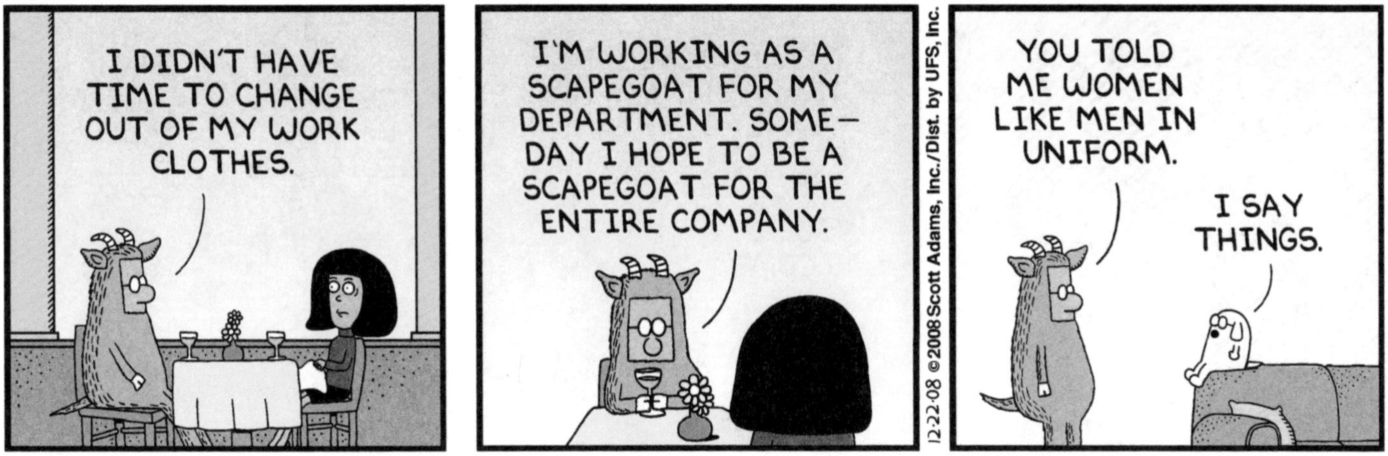
I DIDN'T HAVE TIME TO CHANGE OUT OF MY WORK CLOTHES.
I'M WORKING AS A SCAPEGOAT FOR MY DEPARTMENT. SOME-DAY I HOPE TO BE A SCAPEGOAT FOR THE ENTIRE COMPANY.
12-22-08 ©2008 Scott Adams, Inc./Dist. by UFS, Inc.
YOU TOLD ME WOMEN LIKE MEN IN UNIFORM.
I SAY THINGS.

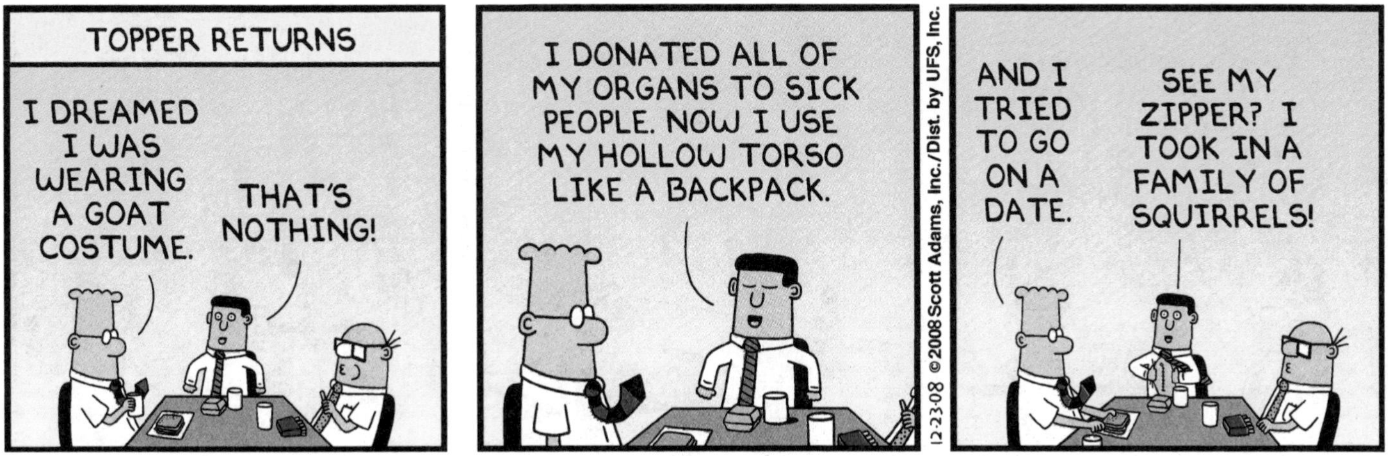
TOPPER RETURNS
I DREAMED I WAS WEARING A GOAT COSTUME.
THAT'S NOTHING!
I DONATED ALL OF MY ORGANS TO SICK PEOPLE. NOW I USE MY HOLLOW TORSO LIKE A BACKPACK.
12-23-08 ©2008 Scott Adams, Inc./Dist. by UFS, Inc.
AND I TRIED TO GO ON A DATE.
SEE MY ZIPPER? I TOOK IN A FAMILY OF SQUIRRELS!

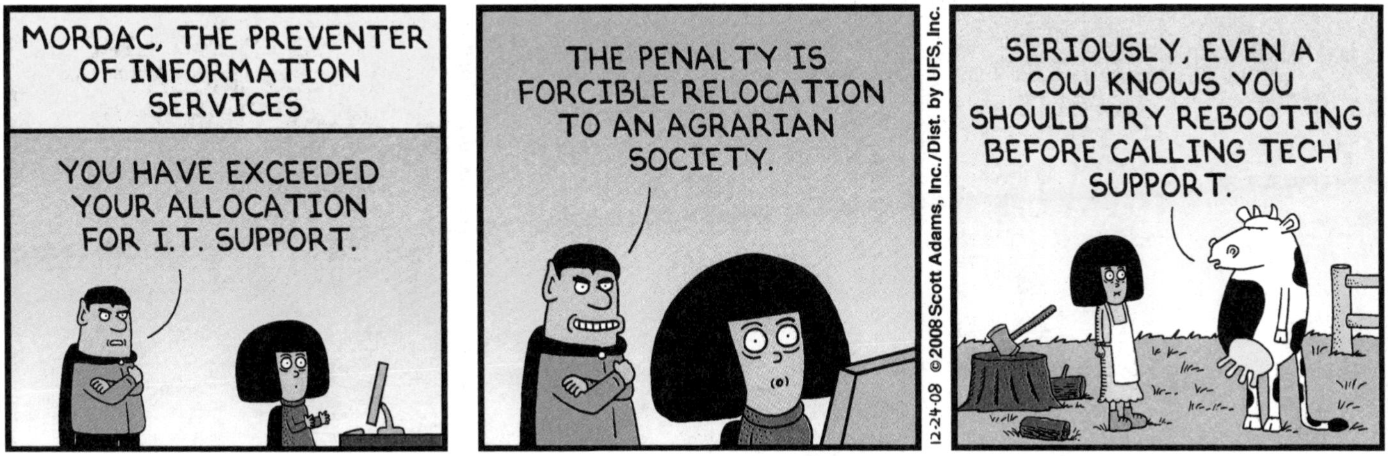
MORDAC, THE PREVENTER OF INFORMATION SERVICES
YOU HAVE EXCEEDED YOUR ALLOCATION FOR I.T. SUPPORT.
THE PENALTY IS FORCIBLE RELOCATION TO AN AGRARIAN SOCIETY.
12-24-08 ©2008 Scott Adams, Inc./Dist. by UFS, Inc.
SERIOUSLY, EVEN A COW KNOWS YOU SHOULD TRY REBOOTING BEFORE CALLING TECH SUPPORT.

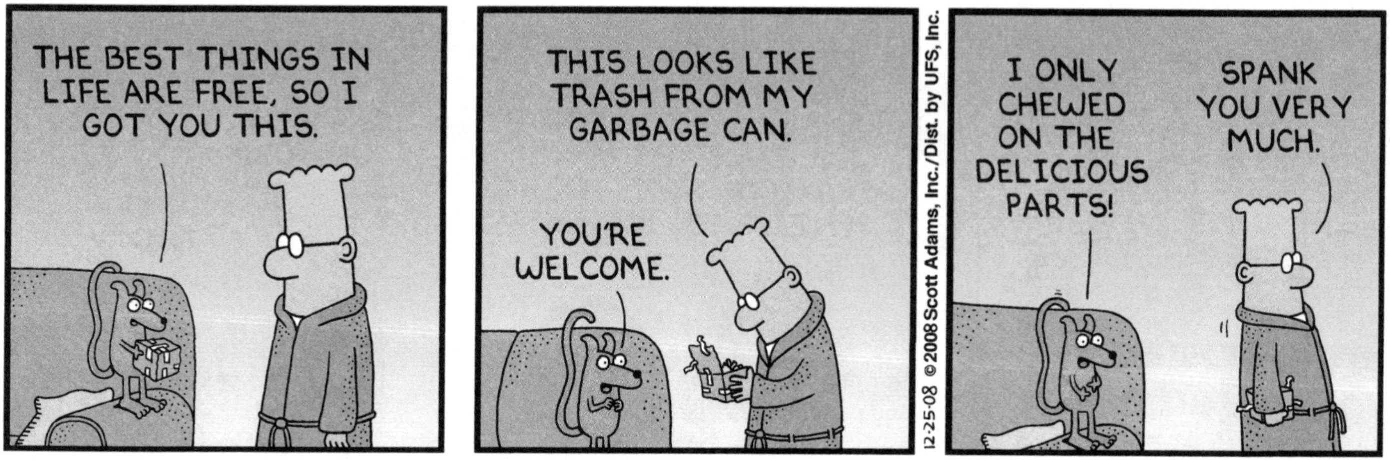
THE BEST THINGS IN LIFE ARE FREE, SO I GOT YOU THIS.
THIS LOOKS LIKE TRASH FROM MY GARBAGE CAN.
YOU'RE WELCOME.
I ONLY CHEWED ON THE DELICIOUS PARTS!
SPANK YOU VERY MUCH.
12-25-08 ©2008 Scott Adams, Inc./Dist. by UFS, Inc.

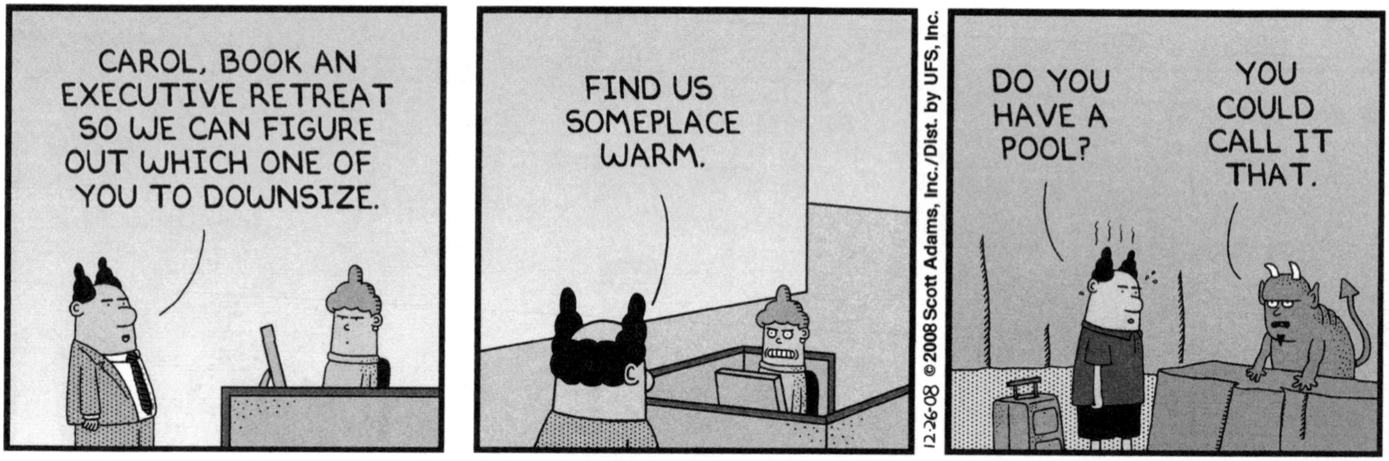
CAROL, BOOK AN EXECUTIVE RETREAT SO WE CAN FIGURE OUT WHICH ONE OF YOU TO DOWNSIZE.
FIND US SOMEPLACE WARM.
DO YOU HAVE A POOL?
YOU COULD CALL IT THAT.
12-26-08 ©2008 Scott Adams, Inc./Dist. by UFS, Inc.

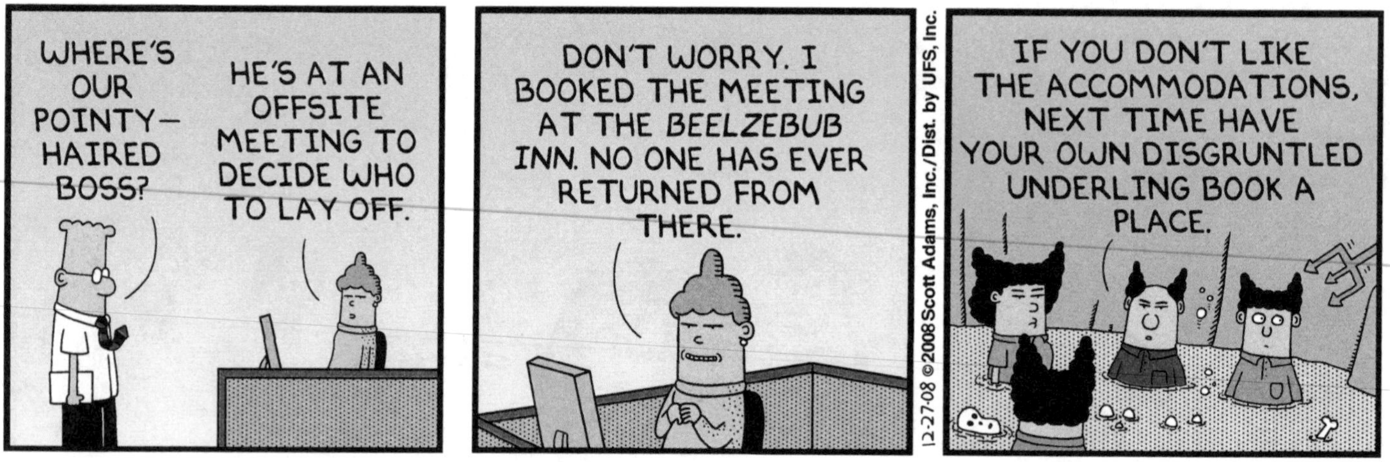
WHERE'S OUR POINTY-HAIRED BOSS?
HE'S AT AN OFFSITE MEETING TO DECIDE WHO TO LAY OFF.
DON'T WORRY. I BOOKED THE MEETING AT THE *BEELZEBUB INN*. NO ONE HAS EVER RETURNED FROM THERE.
IF YOU DON'T LIKE THE ACCOMMODATIONS, NEXT TIME HAVE YOUR OWN DISGRUNTLED UNDERLING BOOK A PLACE.
12-27-08 ©2008 Scott Adams, Inc./Dist. by UFS, Inc.

IT'S OUR VICE PRESIDENT OF ENGINEERING.
HELLO. I AM ASOK THE INTERN. MAY I TELL YOU ABOUT AN IDEA I HAVE?
©2008 Scott Adams, Inc./Dist. by UFS, Inc.
VICE PRESIDENTS CAN'T HEAR US, ASOK. TO THEM, OUR VOICES SOUND LIKE THE FAINT BUZZING OF FLIES.
IF YOU WANT TO GIVE HIM YOUR IDEA, YOU HAVE TO DO IT INDIRECTLY.
TELL SOMEONE WHO KNOWS SOMEONE, WHO KNOWS SOMEONE ELSE, WHO KNOWS THE VICE PRESIDENT.
OR DO WHAT I DO AND CHANNEL YOUR IRRATIONAL IMPULSE TO BE USEFUL INTO AN UNQUENCHABLE THIRST FOR COFFEE.
12-28-08
SO... WHY ARE YOU HELPING ME?
THE COFFEE MACHINE IS BROKEN.

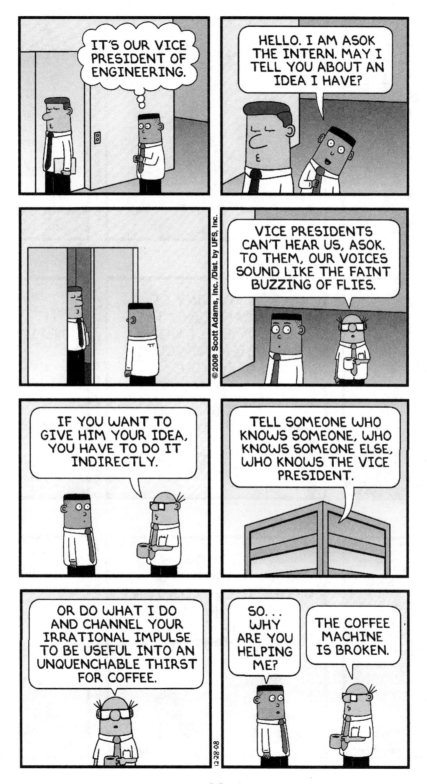

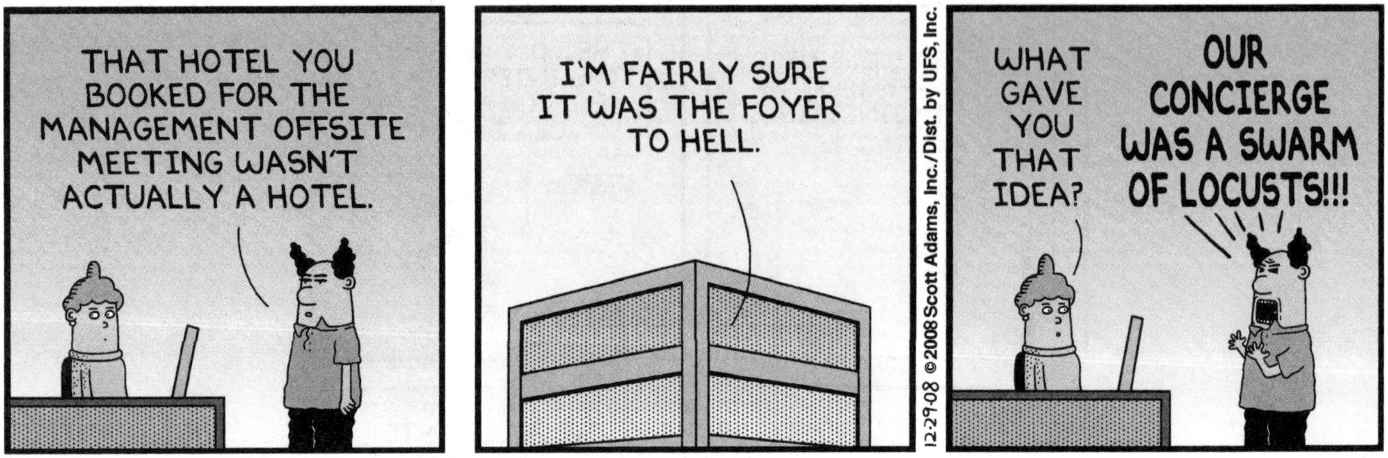
THAT HOTEL YOU BOOKED FOR THE MANAGEMENT OFFSITE MEETING WASN'T ACTUALLY A HOTEL.
I'M FAIRLY SURE IT WAS THE FOYER TO HELL.
WHAT GAVE YOU THAT IDEA?
OUR CONCIERGE WAS A SWARM OF LOCUSTS!!!

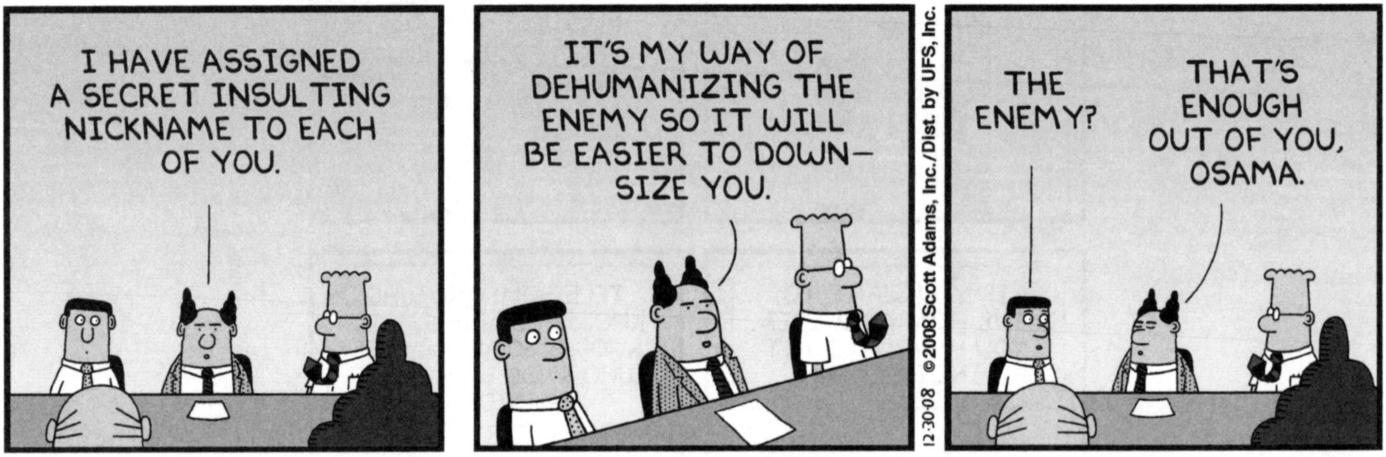
I HAVE ASSIGNED A SECRET INSULTING NICKNAME TO EACH OF YOU.
IT'S MY WAY OF DEHUMANIZING THE ENEMY SO IT WILL BE EASIER TO DOWN-SIZE YOU.
THE ENEMY?
THAT'S ENOUGH OUT OF YOU, OSAMA.

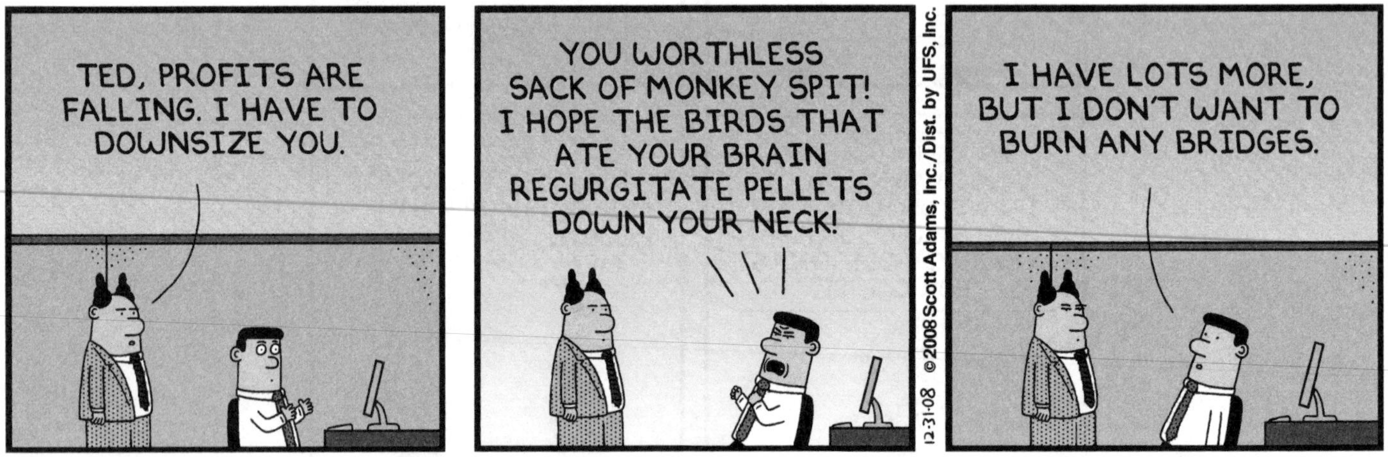
TED, PROFITS ARE FALLING. I HAVE TO DOWNSIZE YOU.
YOU WORTHLESS SACK OF MONKEY SPIT! I HOPE THE BIRDS THAT ATE YOUR BRAIN REGURGITATE PELLETS DOWN YOUR NECK!
I HAVE LOTS MORE, BUT I DON'T WANT TO BURN ANY BRIDGES.

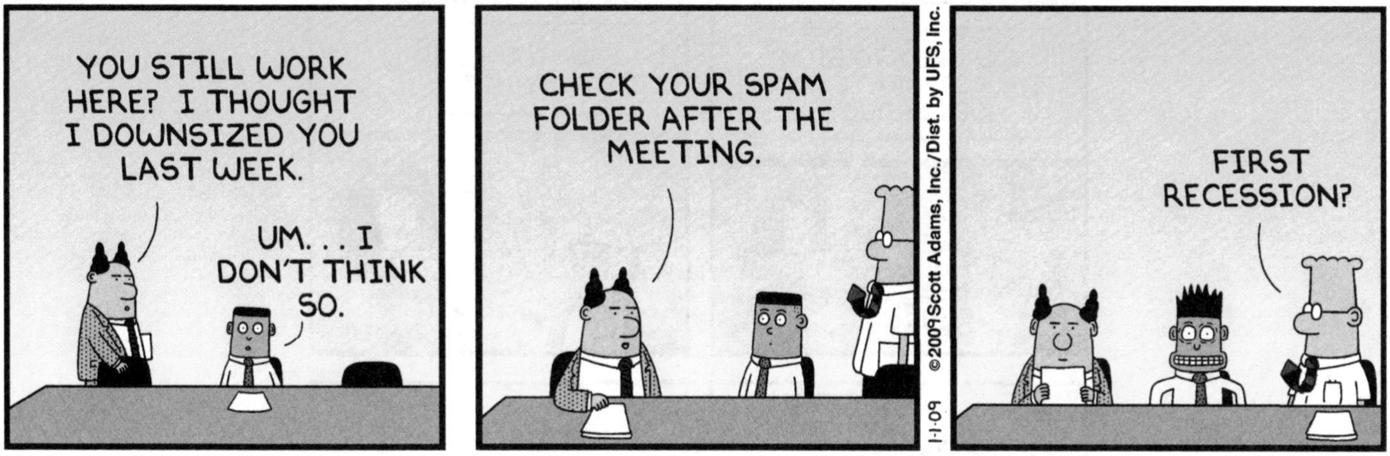
YOU STILL WORK HERE? I THOUGHT I DOWNSIZED YOU LAST WEEK.
UM. . . I DON'T THINK SO.
CHECK YOUR SPAM FOLDER AFTER THE MEETING.
©2009 Scott Adams, Inc./Dist. by UFS, Inc.
1-1-09
FIRST RECESSION?

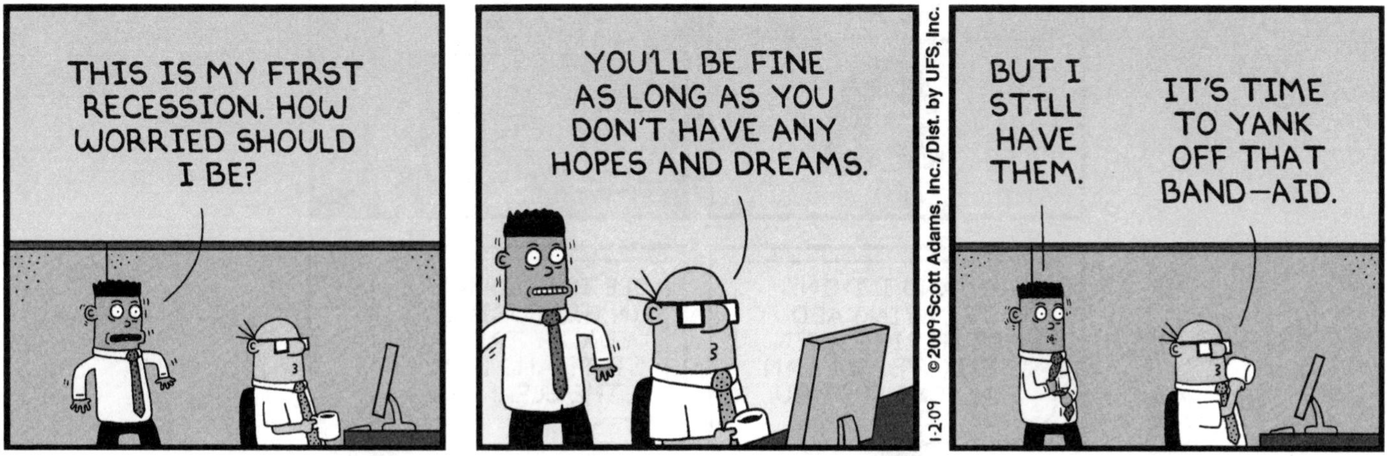
THIS IS MY FIRST RECESSION. HOW WORRIED SHOULD I BE?
YOU'LL BE FINE AS LONG AS YOU DON'T HAVE ANY HOPES AND DREAMS.
©2009 Scott Adams, Inc./Dist. by UFS, Inc.
1-2-09
BUT I STILL HAVE THEM.
IT'S TIME TO YANK OFF THAT BAND-AID.

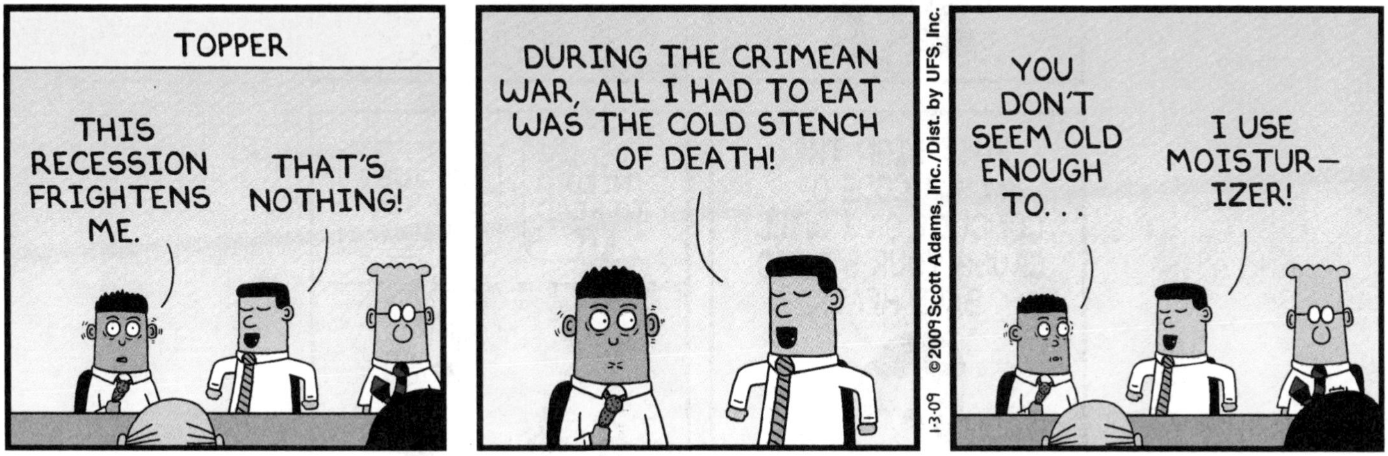
TOPPER
THIS RECESSION FRIGHTENS ME.
THAT'S NOTHING!
DURING THE CRIMEAN WAR, ALL I HAD TO EAT WAS THE COLD STENCH OF DEATH!
©2009 Scott Adams, Inc./Dist. by UFS, Inc.
1-3-09
YOU DON'T SEEM OLD ENOUGH TO. . .
I USE MOISTUR-IZER!

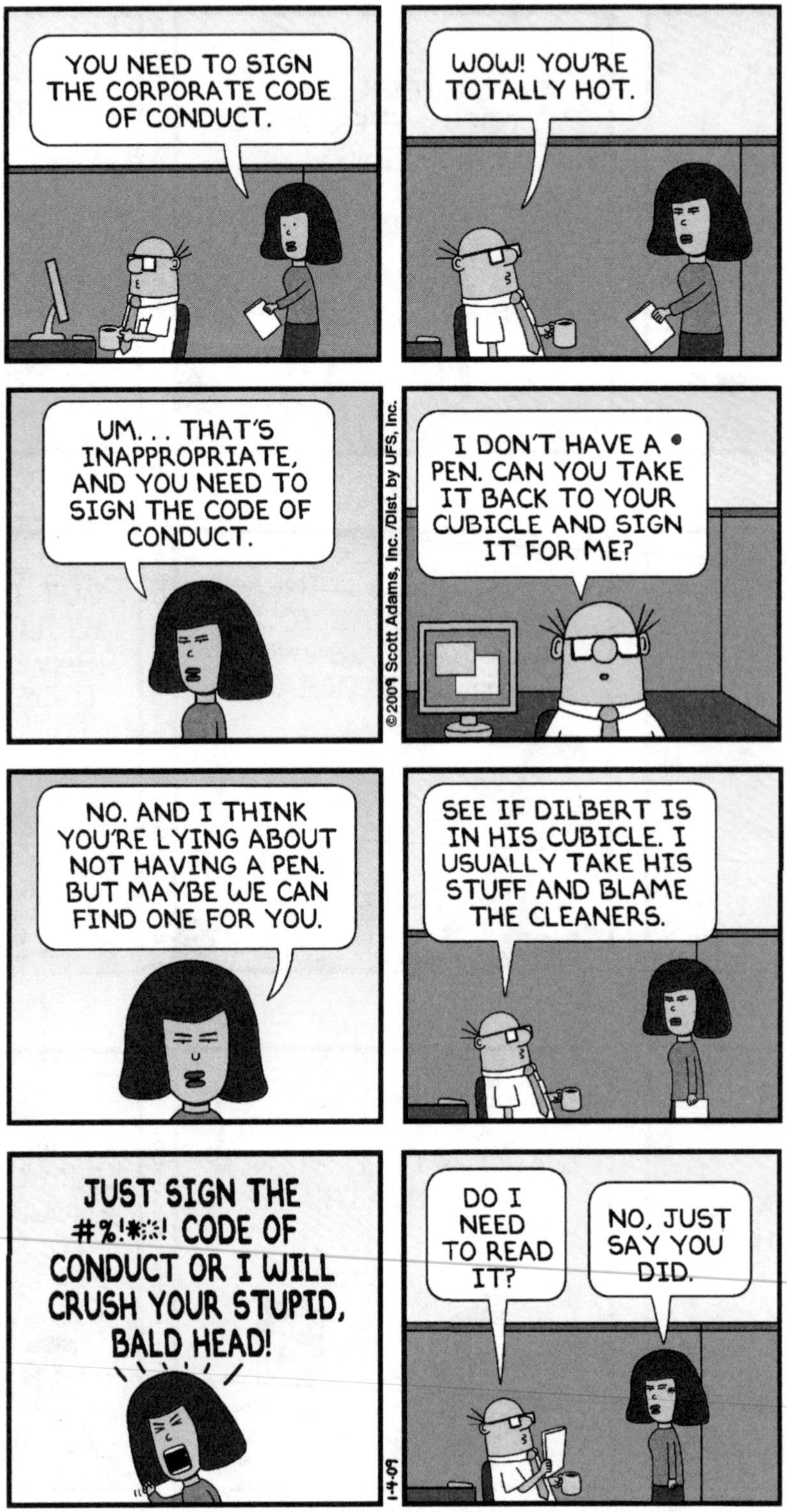
YOU NEED TO SIGN THE CORPORATE CODE OF CONDUCT.
WOW! YOU'RE TOTALLY HOT.
UM. . . THAT'S INAPPROPRIATE, AND YOU NEED TO SIGN THE CODE OF CONDUCT.
I DON'T HAVE A PEN. CAN YOU TAKE IT BACK TO YOUR CUBICLE AND SIGN IT FOR ME?
NO. AND I THINK YOU'RE LYING ABOUT NOT HAVING A PEN. BUT MAYBE WE CAN FIND ONE FOR YOU.
SEE IF DILBERT IS IN HIS CUBICLE. I USUALLY TAKE HIS STUFF AND BLAME THE CLEANERS.
JUST SIGN THE #%!*☼! CODE OF CONDUCT OR I WILL CRUSH YOUR STUPID, BALD HEAD!
DO I NEED TO READ IT?
NO, JUST SAY YOU DID.
©2009 Scott Adams, Inc./Dist. by UFS, Inc.
1-4-09

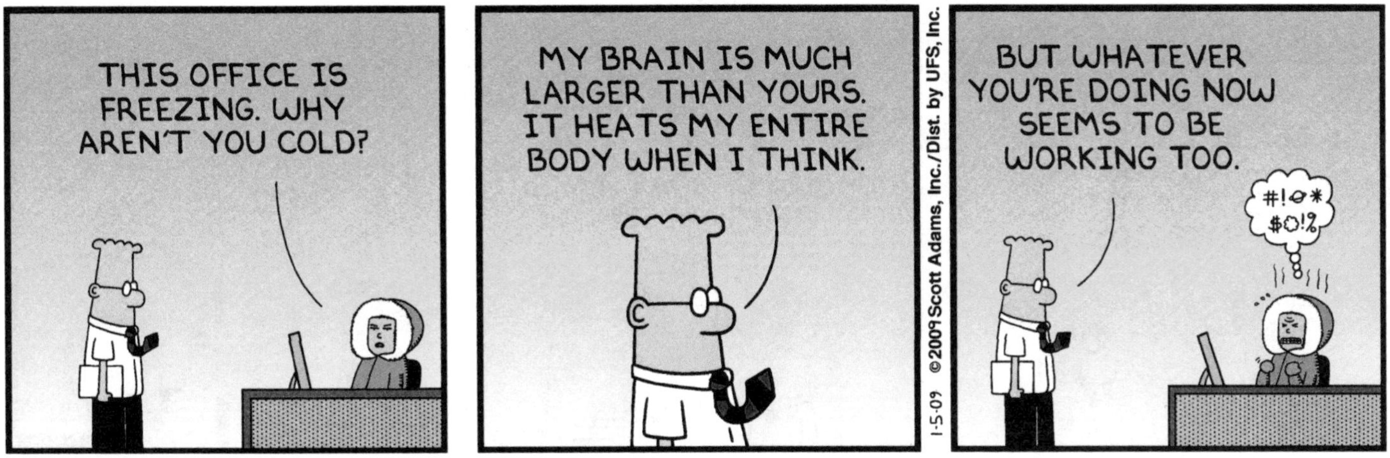
THIS OFFICE IS FREEZING. WHY AREN'T YOU COLD?
MY BRAIN IS MUCH LARGER THAN YOURS. IT HEATS MY ENTIRE BODY WHEN I THINK.
BUT WHATEVER YOU'RE DOING NOW SEEMS TO BE WORKING TOO.
1-5-09 ©2009 Scott Adams, Inc./Dist. by UFS, Inc.

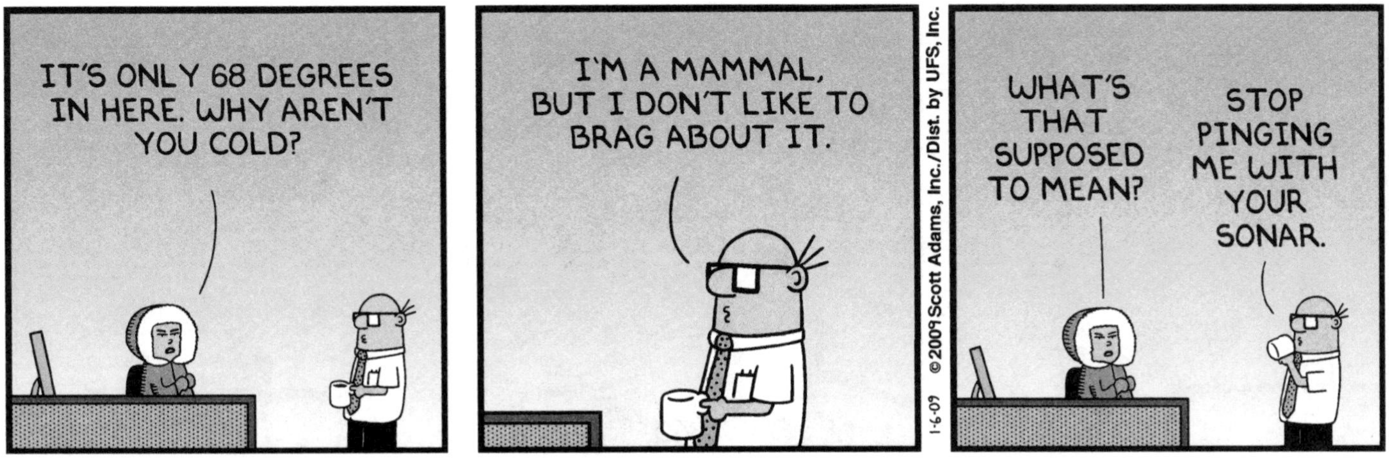
IT'S ONLY 68 DEGREES IN HERE. WHY AREN'T YOU COLD?
I'M A MAMMAL, BUT I DON'T LIKE TO BRAG ABOUT IT.
WHAT'S THAT SUPPOSED TO MEAN?
STOP PINGING ME WITH YOUR SONAR.
1-6-09 ©2009 Scott Adams, Inc./Dist. by UFS, Inc.

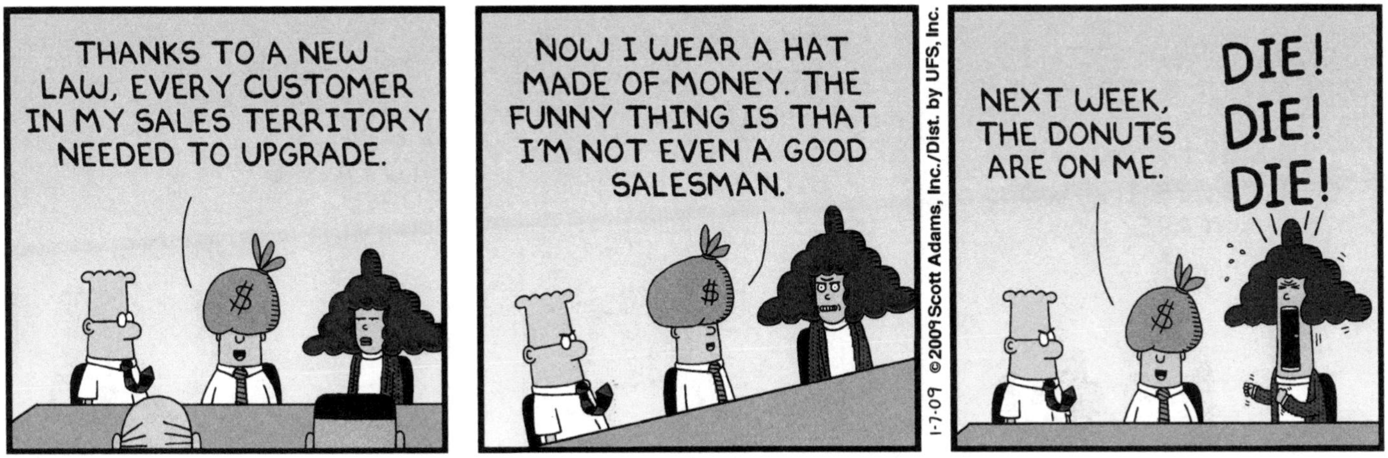
THANKS TO A NEW LAW, EVERY CUSTOMER IN MY SALES TERRITORY NEEDED TO UPGRADE.
NOW I WEAR A HAT MADE OF MONEY. THE FUNNY THING IS THAT I'M NOT EVEN A GOOD SALESMAN.
NEXT WEEK, THE DONUTS ARE ON ME.
DIE! DIE! DIE!
1-7-09 ©2009 Scott Adams, Inc./Dist. by UFS, Inc.

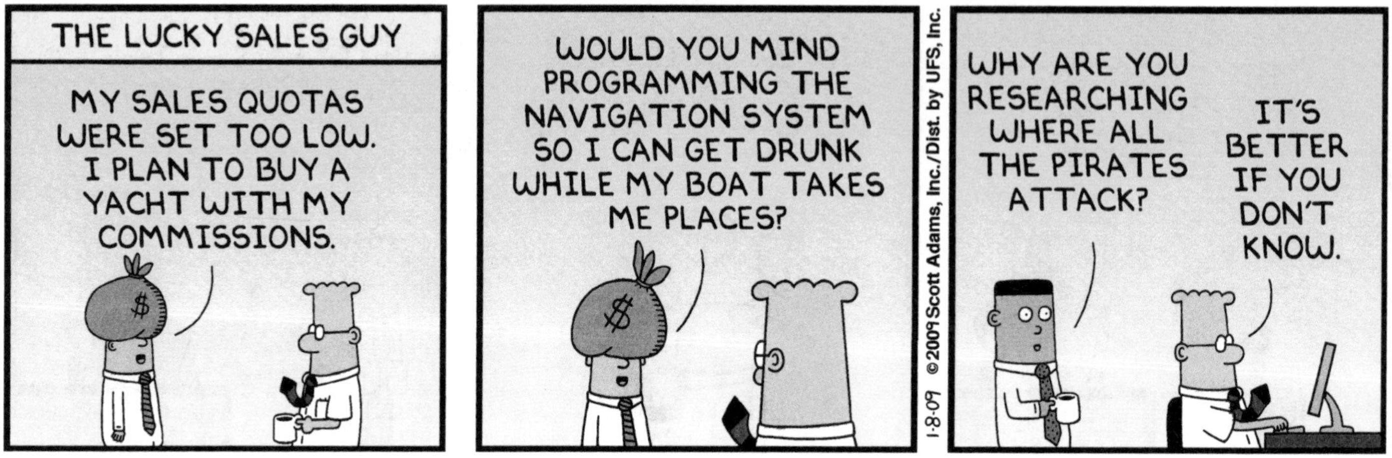
THE LUCKY SALES GUY
MY SALES QUOTAS WERE SET TOO LOW. I PLAN TO BUY A YACHT WITH MY COMMISSIONS.
WOULD YOU MIND PROGRAMMING THE NAVIGATION SYSTEM SO I CAN GET DRUNK WHILE MY BOAT TAKES ME PLACES?
1-8-09 ©2009 Scott Adams, Inc./Dist. by UFS, Inc.
WHY ARE YOU RESEARCHING WHERE ALL THE PIRATES ATTACK?
IT'S BETTER IF YOU DON'T KNOW.

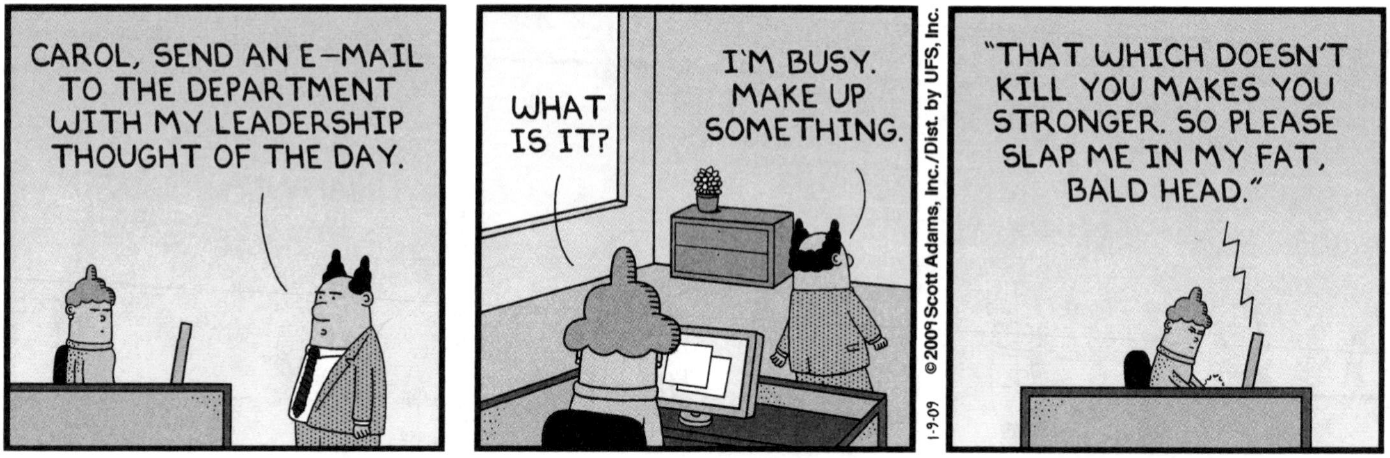
CAROL, SEND AN E-MAIL TO THE DEPARTMENT WITH MY LEADERSHIP THOUGHT OF THE DAY.
WHAT IS IT?
I'M BUSY. MAKE UP SOMETHING.
1-9-09 ©2009 Scott Adams, Inc./Dist. by UFS, Inc.
"THAT WHICH DOESN'T KILL YOU MAKES YOU STRONGER. SO PLEASE SLAP ME IN MY FAT, BALD HEAD."

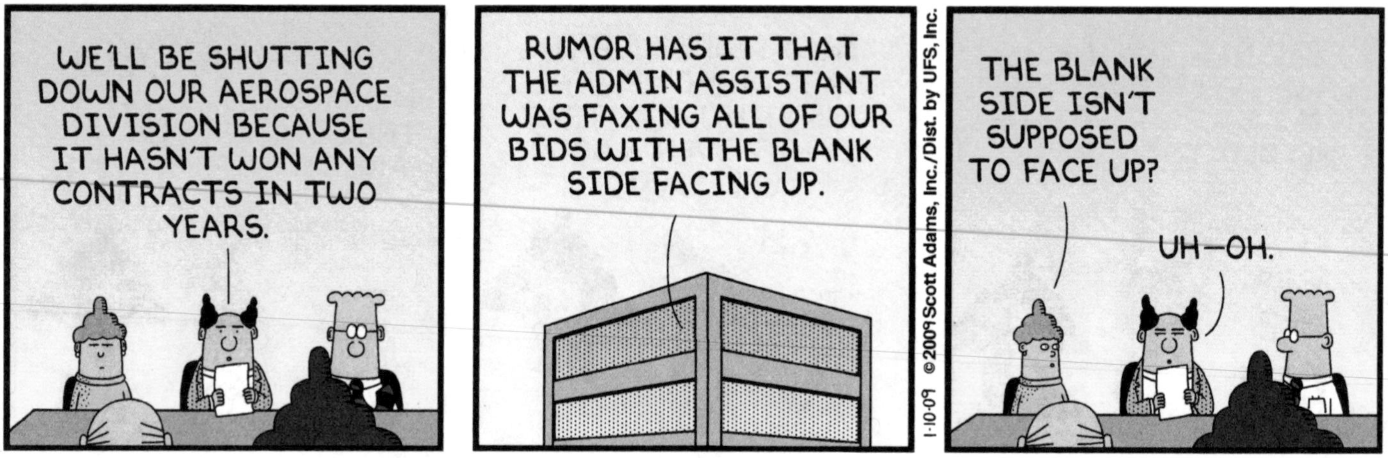
WE'LL BE SHUTTING DOWN OUR AEROSPACE DIVISION BECAUSE IT HASN'T WON ANY CONTRACTS IN TWO YEARS.
RUMOR HAS IT THAT THE ADMIN ASSISTANT WAS FAXING ALL OF OUR BIDS WITH THE BLANK SIDE FACING UP.
1-10-09 ©2009 Scott Adams, Inc./Dist. by UFS, Inc.
THE BLANK SIDE ISN'T SUPPOSED TO FACE UP?
UH-OH.

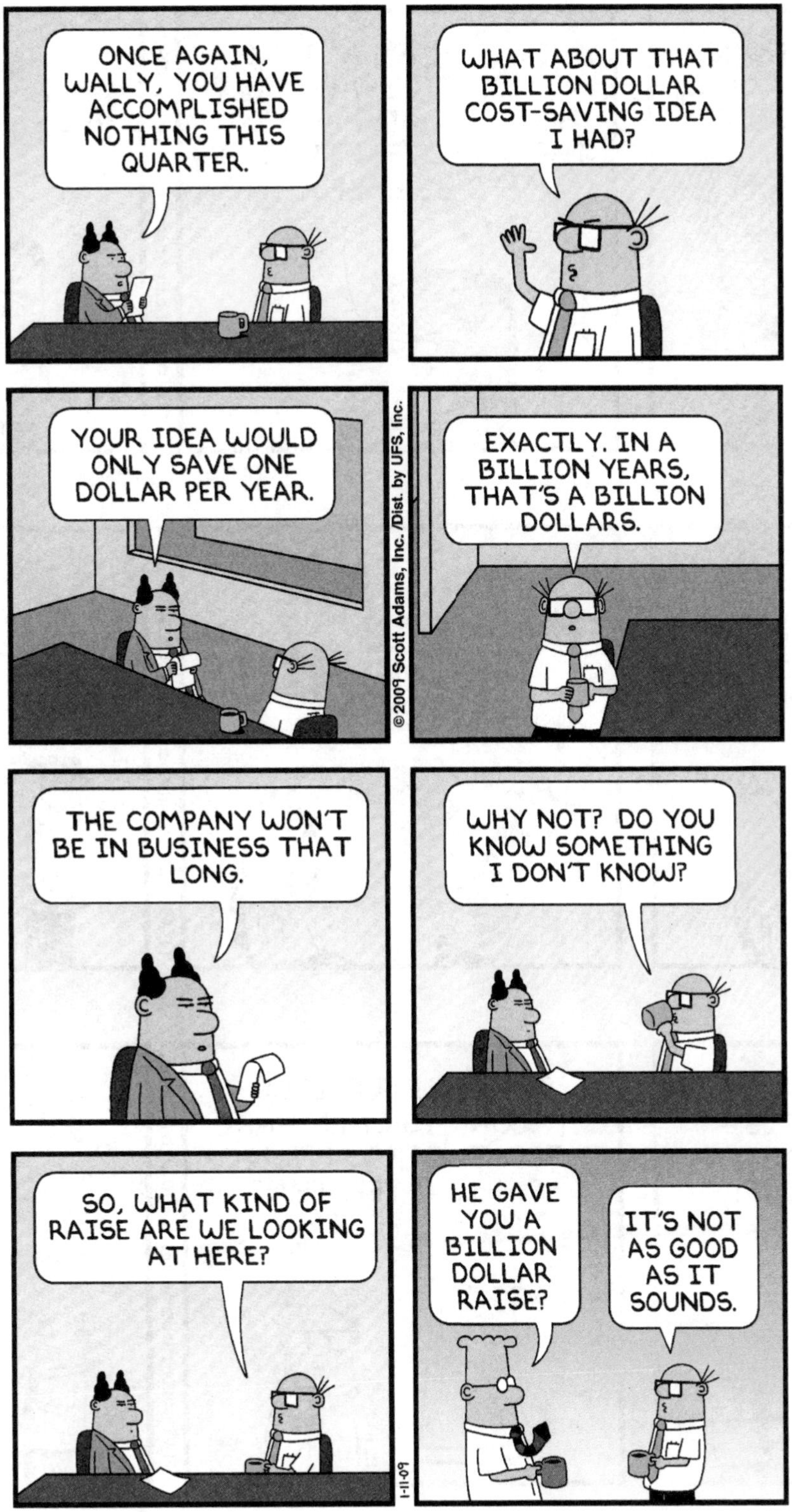
ONCE AGAIN, WALLY, YOU HAVE ACCOMPLISHED NOTHING THIS QUARTER.
WHAT ABOUT THAT BILLION DOLLAR COST-SAVING IDEA I HAD?
YOUR IDEA WOULD ONLY SAVE ONE DOLLAR PER YEAR.
EXACTLY. IN A BILLION YEARS, THAT'S A BILLION DOLLARS.
THE COMPANY WON'T BE IN BUSINESS THAT LONG.
WHY NOT? DO YOU KNOW SOMETHING I DON'T KNOW?
SO, WHAT KIND OF RAISE ARE WE LOOKING AT HERE?
HE GAVE YOU A BILLION DOLLAR RAISE?
IT'S NOT AS GOOD AS IT SOUNDS.
1-11-09

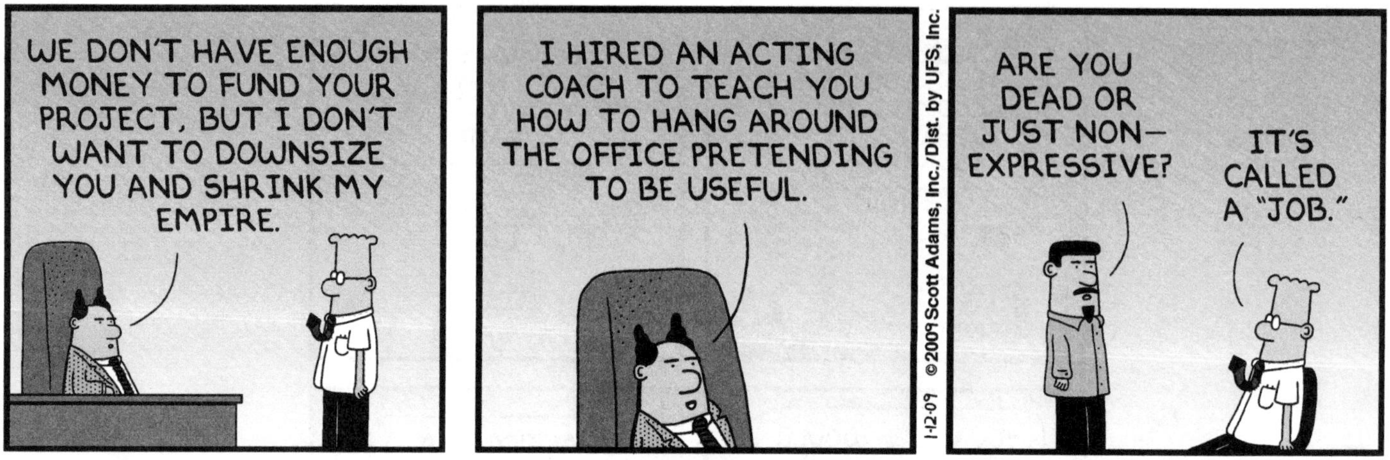
WE DON'T HAVE ENOUGH MONEY TO FUND YOUR PROJECT, BUT I DON'T WANT TO DOWNSIZE YOU AND SHRINK MY EMPIRE.
I HIRED AN ACTING COACH TO TEACH YOU HOW TO HANG AROUND THE OFFICE PRETENDING TO BE USEFUL.
1-12-09 ©2009 Scott Adams, Inc./Dist. by UFS, Inc.
ARE YOU DEAD OR JUST NON-EXPRESSIVE?
IT'S CALLED A "JOB."

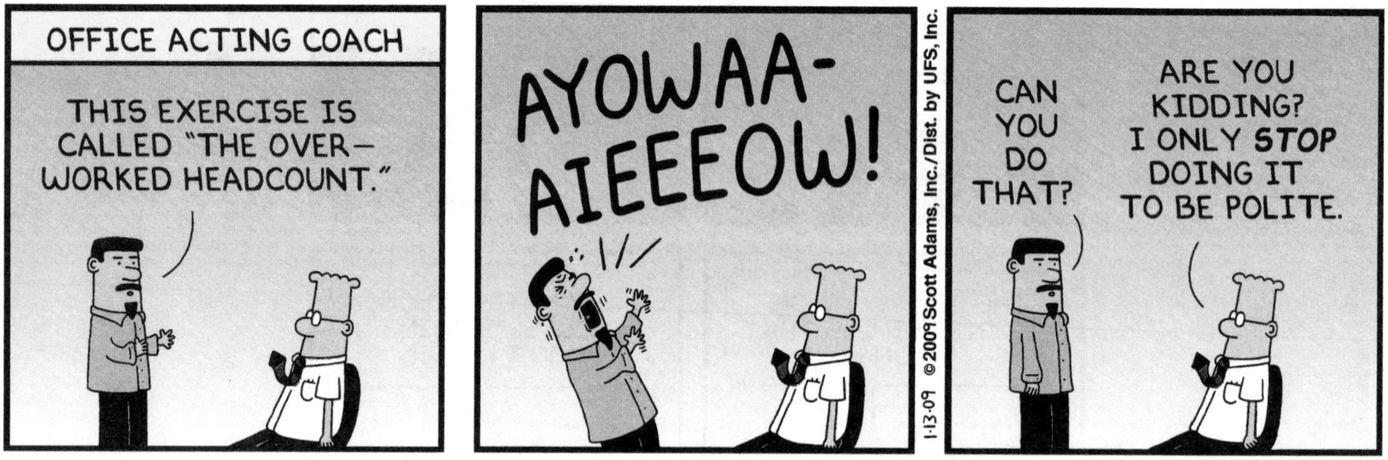
OFFICE ACTING COACH
THIS EXERCISE IS CALLED "THE OVER-WORKED HEADCOUNT."
AYOWAA-AIEEEOW!
1-13-09 ©2009 Scott Adams, Inc./Dist. by UFS, Inc.
CAN YOU DO THAT?
ARE YOU KIDDING? I ONLY STOP DOING IT TO BE POLITE.

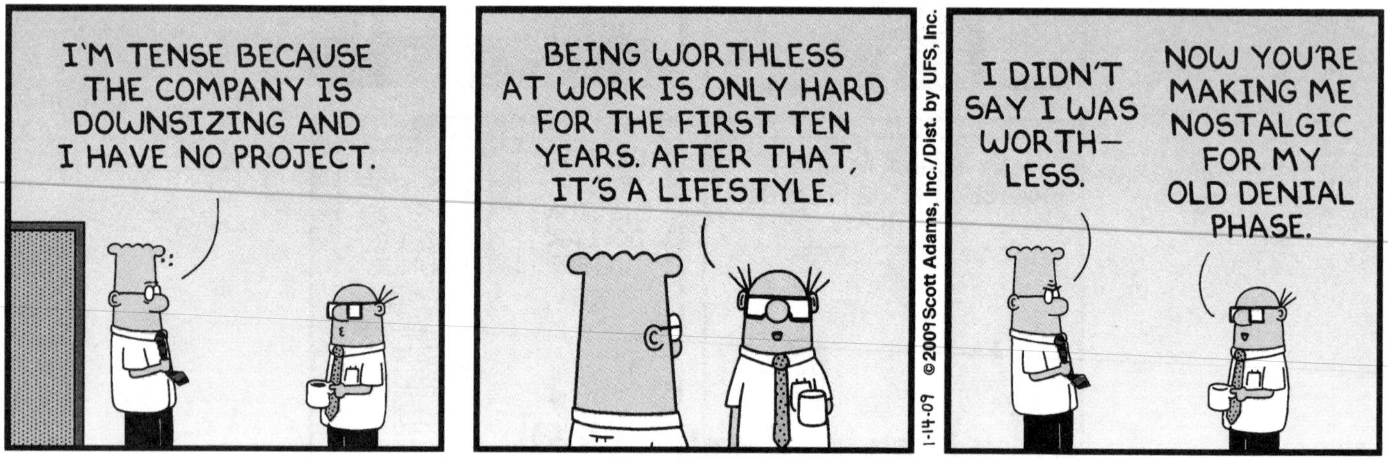
I'M TENSE BECAUSE THE COMPANY IS DOWNSIZING AND I HAVE NO PROJECT.
BEING WORTHLESS AT WORK IS ONLY HARD FOR THE FIRST TEN YEARS. AFTER THAT, IT'S A LIFESTYLE.
1-14-09 ©2009 Scott Adams, Inc./Dist. by UFS, Inc.
I DIDN'T SAY I WAS WORTH-LESS.
NOW YOU'RE MAKING ME NOSTALGIC FOR MY OLD DENIAL PHASE.

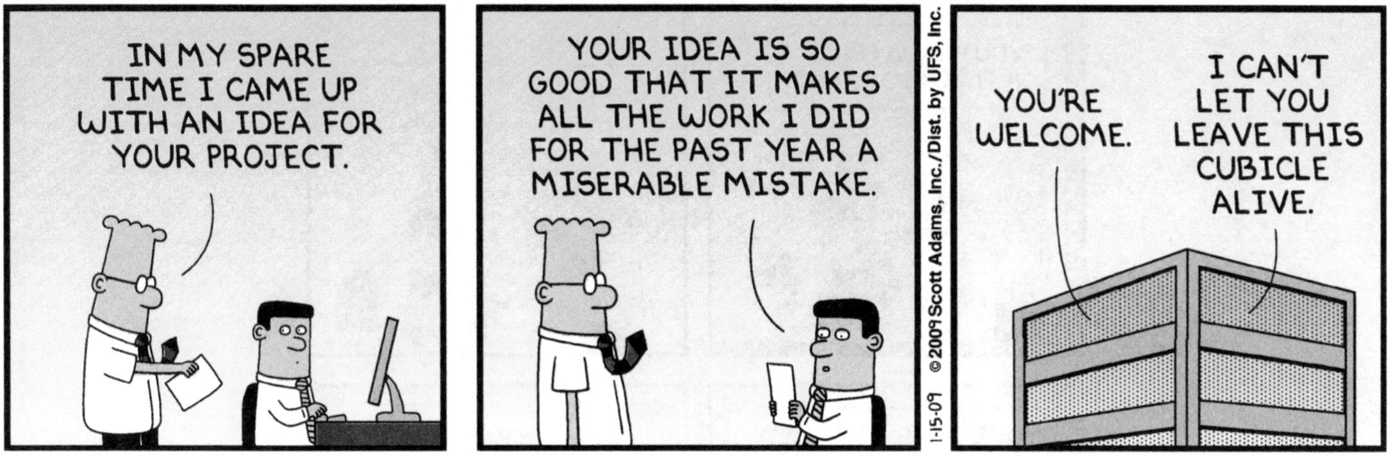
IN MY SPARE TIME I CAME UP WITH AN IDEA FOR YOUR PROJECT.
YOUR IDEA IS SO GOOD THAT IT MAKES ALL THE WORK I DID FOR THE PAST YEAR A MISERABLE MISTAKE.
YOU'RE WELCOME.
I CAN'T LET YOU LEAVE THIS CUBICLE ALIVE.
1-15-09 ©2009 Scott Adams, Inc./Dist. by UFS, Inc.

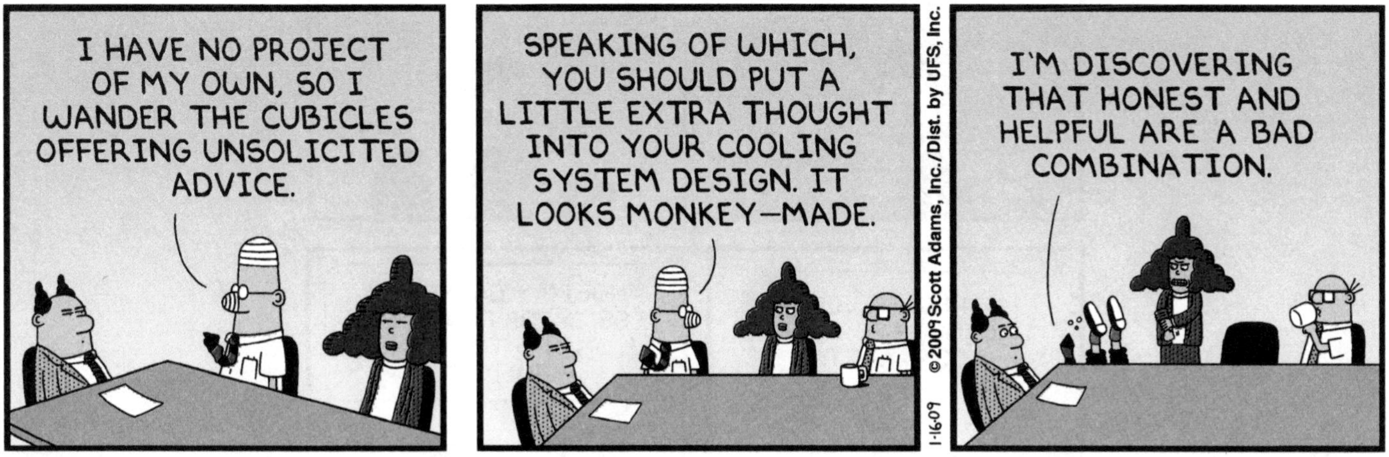
I HAVE NO PROJECT OF MY OWN, SO I WANDER THE CUBICLES OFFERING UNSOLICITED ADVICE.
SPEAKING OF WHICH, YOU SHOULD PUT A LITTLE EXTRA THOUGHT INTO YOUR COOLING SYSTEM DESIGN. IT LOOKS MONKEY—MADE.
I'M DISCOVERING THAT HONEST AND HELPFUL ARE A BAD COMBINATION.
1-16-09 ©2009 Scott Adams, Inc./Dist. by UFS, Inc.

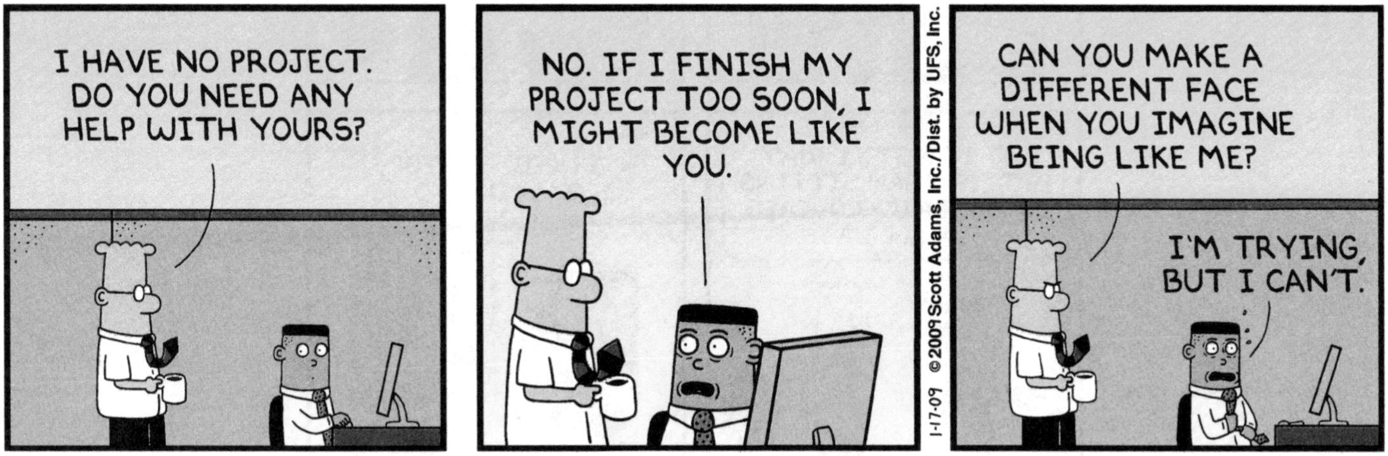
I HAVE NO PROJECT. DO YOU NEED ANY HELP WITH YOURS?
NO. IF I FINISH MY PROJECT TOO SOON, I MIGHT BECOME LIKE YOU.
CAN YOU MAKE A DIFFERENT FACE WHEN YOU IMAGINE BEING LIKE ME?
I'M TRYING, BUT I CAN'T.
1-17-09 ©2009 Scott Adams, Inc./Dist. by UFS, Inc.

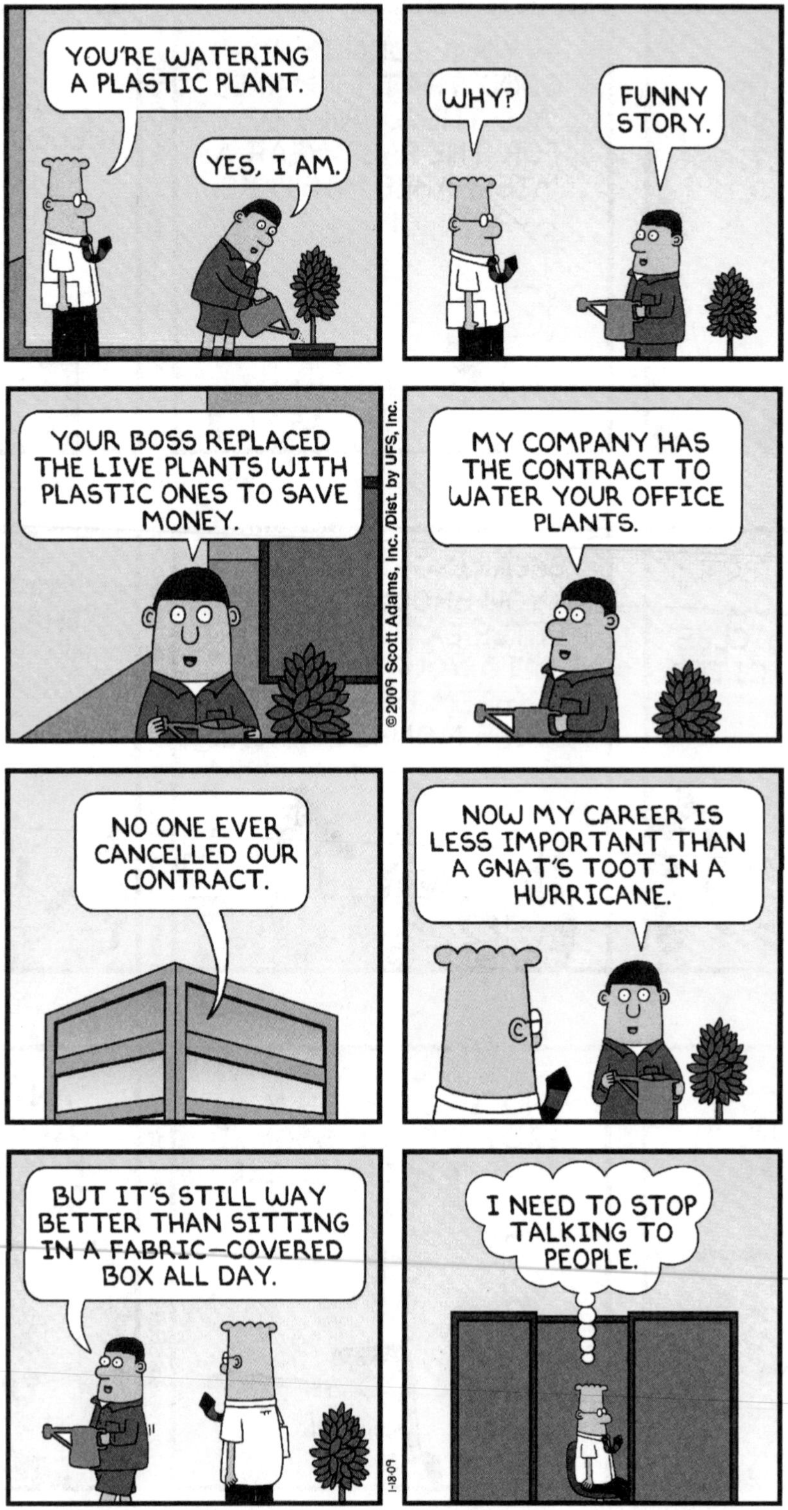
YOU'RE WATERING A PLASTIC PLANT.
YES, I AM.
WHY?
FUNNY STORY.
YOUR BOSS REPLACED THE LIVE PLANTS WITH PLASTIC ONES TO SAVE MONEY.
MY COMPANY HAS THE CONTRACT TO WATER YOUR OFFICE PLANTS.
NO ONE EVER CANCELLED OUR CONTRACT.
NOW MY CAREER IS LESS IMPORTANT THAN A GNAT'S TOOT IN A HURRICANE.
BUT IT'S STILL WAY BETTER THAN SITTING IN A FABRIC-COVERED BOX ALL DAY.
I NEED TO STOP TALKING TO PEOPLE.
© 2009 Scott Adams, Inc./Dist. by UFS, Inc.
1-18-09

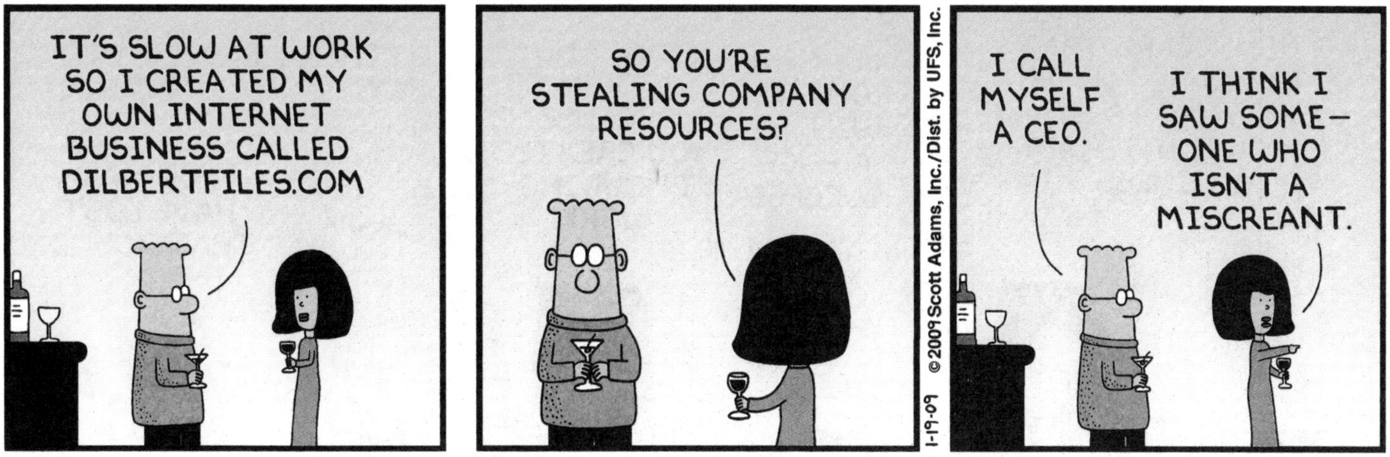
IT'S SLOW AT WORK SO I CREATED MY OWN INTERNET BUSINESS CALLED DILBERTFILES.COM
SO YOU'RE STEALING COMPANY RESOURCES?
1-19-09 © 2009 Scott Adams, Inc./Dist. by UFS, Inc.
I CALL MYSELF A CEO.
I THINK I SAW SOME-ONE WHO ISN'T A MISCREANT.

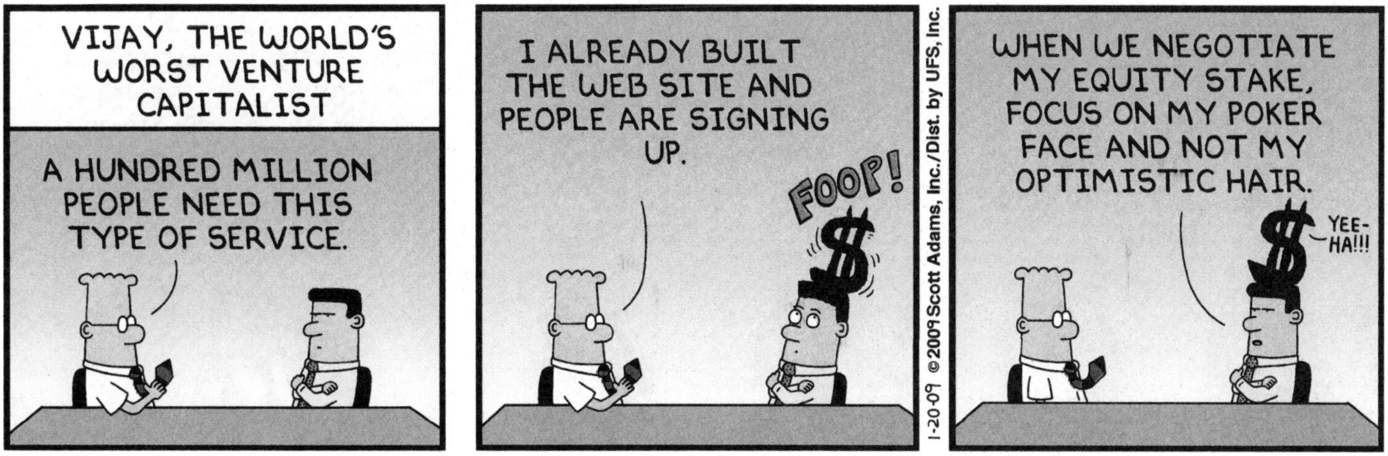
VIJAY, THE WORLD'S WORST VENTURE CAPITALIST
A HUNDRED MILLION PEOPLE NEED THIS TYPE OF SERVICE.
I ALREADY BUILT THE WEB SITE AND PEOPLE ARE SIGNING UP.
FOOP!
1-20-09 © 2009 Scott Adams, Inc./Dist. by UFS, Inc.
WHEN WE NEGOTIATE MY EQUITY STAKE, FOCUS ON MY POKER FACE AND NOT MY OPTIMISTIC HAIR.
YEE-HA!!!

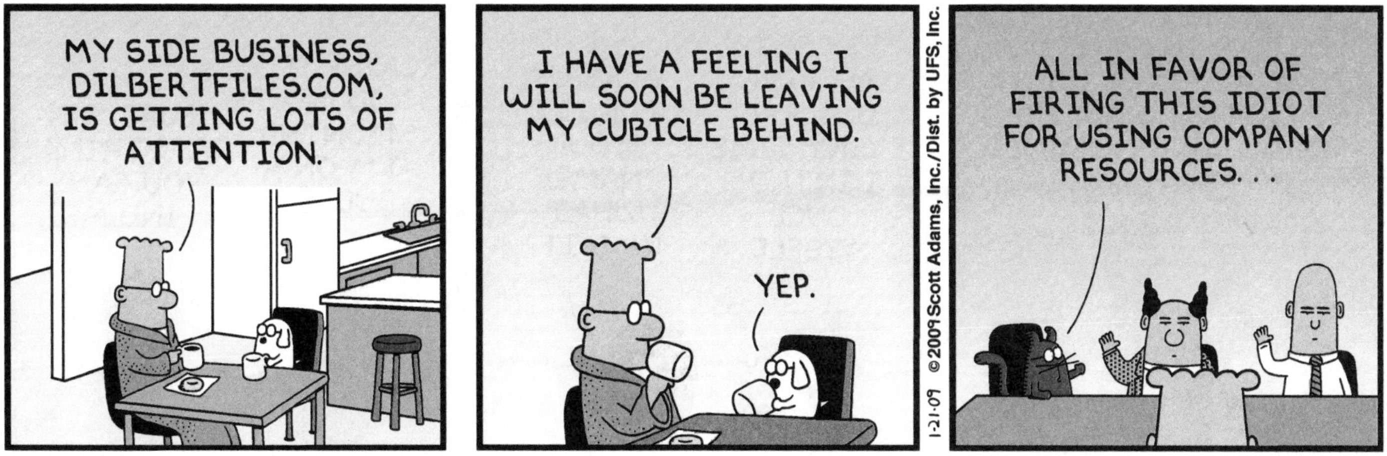
MY SIDE BUSINESS, DILBERTFILES.COM, IS GETTING LOTS OF ATTENTION.
I HAVE A FEELING I WILL SOON BE LEAVING MY CUBICLE BEHIND.
YEP.
1-21-09 © 2009 Scott Adams, Inc./Dist. by UFS, Inc.
ALL IN FAVOR OF FIRING THIS IDIOT FOR USING COMPANY RESOURCES. . .

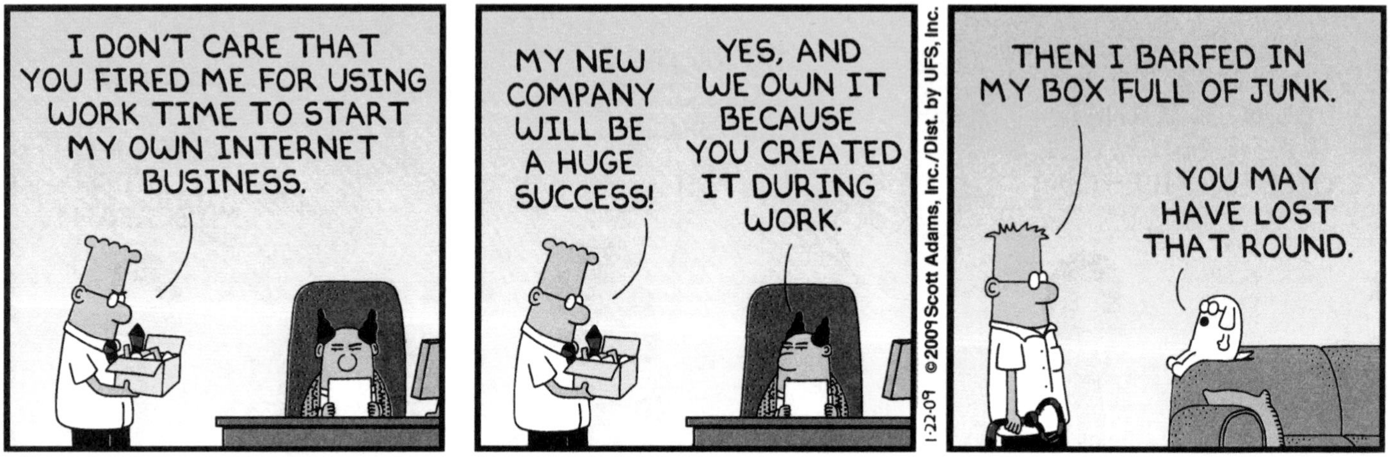
I DON'T CARE THAT YOU FIRED ME FOR USING WORK TIME TO START MY OWN INTERNET BUSINESS.
MY NEW COMPANY WILL BE A HUGE SUCCESS!
YES, AND WE OWN IT BECAUSE YOU CREATED IT DURING WORK.
1-22-09 ©2009 Scott Adams, Inc./Dist. by UFS, Inc.
THEN I BARFED IN MY BOX FULL OF JUNK.
YOU MAY HAVE LOST THAT ROUND.

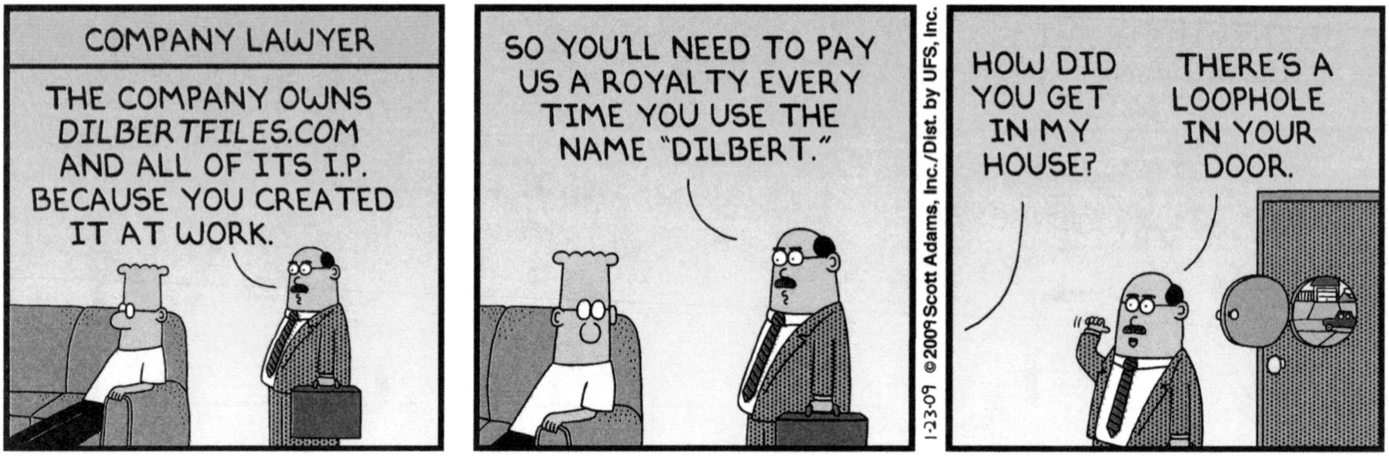
COMPANY LAWYER
THE COMPANY OWNS DILBERTFILES.COM AND ALL OF ITS I.P. BECAUSE YOU CREATED IT AT WORK.
SO YOU'LL NEED TO PAY US A ROYALTY EVERY TIME YOU USE THE NAME "DILBERT."
1-23-09 ©2009 Scott Adams, Inc./Dist. by UFS, Inc.
HOW DID YOU GET IN MY HOUSE?
THERE'S A LOOPHOLE IN YOUR DOOR.

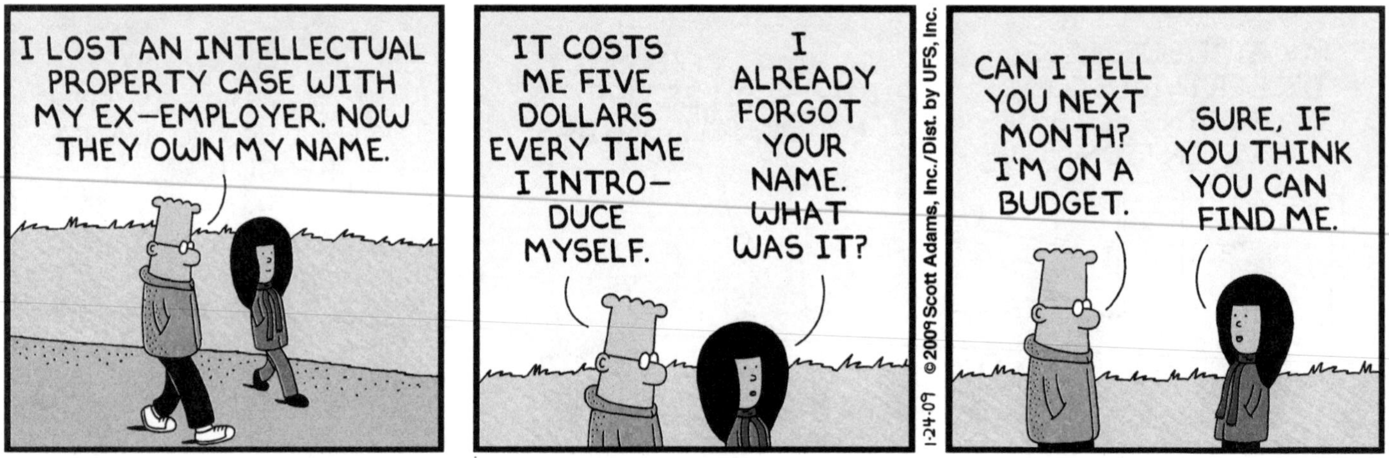
I LOST AN INTELLECTUAL PROPERTY CASE WITH MY EX-EMPLOYER. NOW THEY OWN MY NAME.
IT COSTS ME FIVE DOLLARS EVERY TIME I INTRO-DUCE MYSELF.
I ALREADY FORGOT YOUR NAME. WHAT WAS IT?
1-24-09 ©2009 Scott Adams, Inc./Dist. by UFS, Inc.
CAN I TELL YOU NEXT MONTH? I'M ON A BUDGET.
SURE, IF YOU THINK YOU CAN FIND ME.

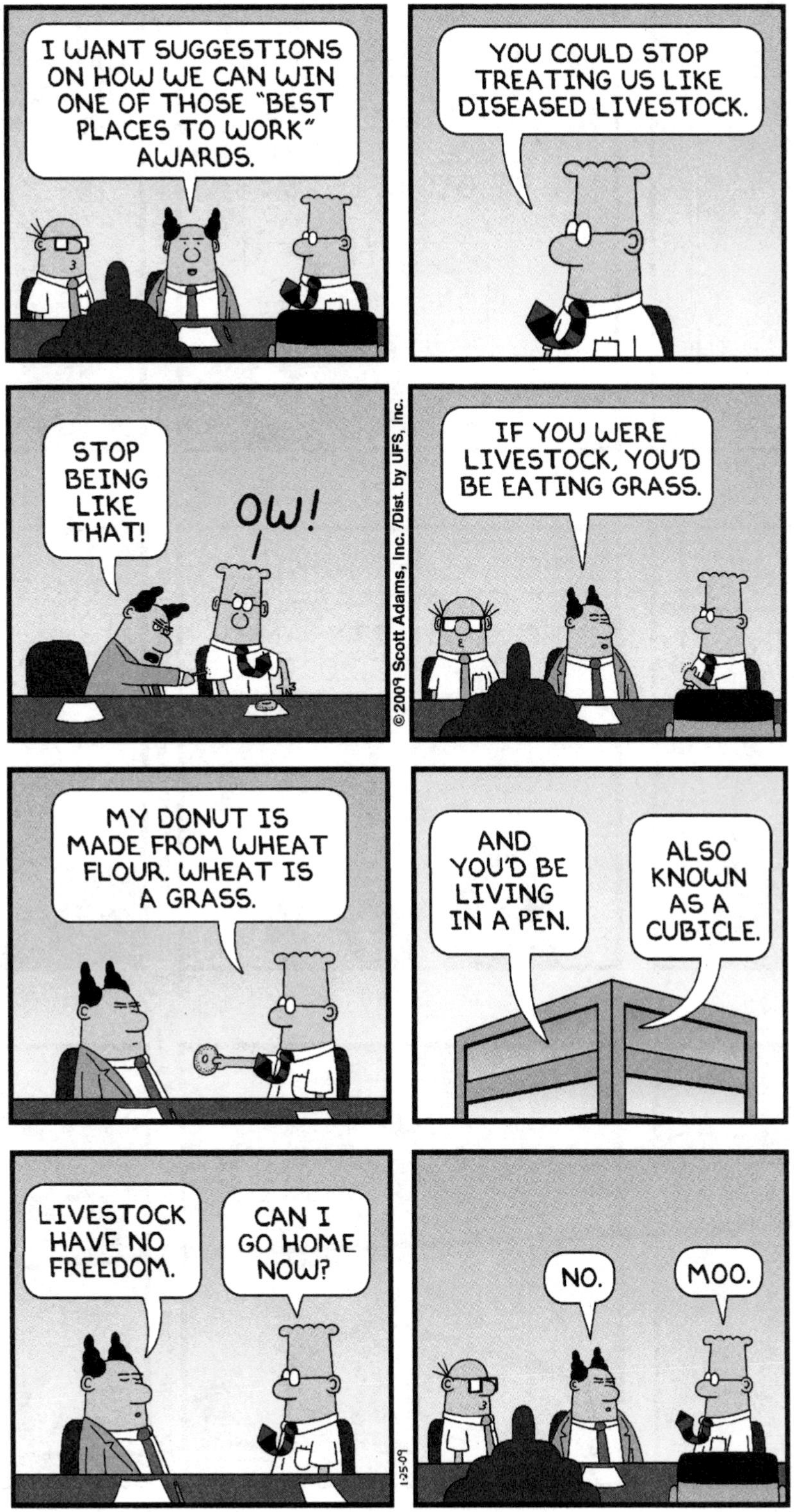
I WANT SUGGESTIONS ON HOW WE CAN WIN ONE OF THOSE "BEST PLACES TO WORK" AWARDS.
YOU COULD STOP TREATING US LIKE DISEASED LIVESTOCK.
STOP BEING LIKE THAT!
OW!
©2009 Scott Adams, Inc./Dist. by UFS, Inc.
IF YOU WERE LIVESTOCK, YOU'D BE EATING GRASS.
MY DONUT IS MADE FROM WHEAT FLOUR. WHEAT IS A GRASS.
AND YOU'D BE LIVING IN A PEN.
ALSO KNOWN AS A CUBICLE.
LIVESTOCK HAVE NO FREEDOM.
CAN I GO HOME NOW?
1-25-09
NO.
MOO.

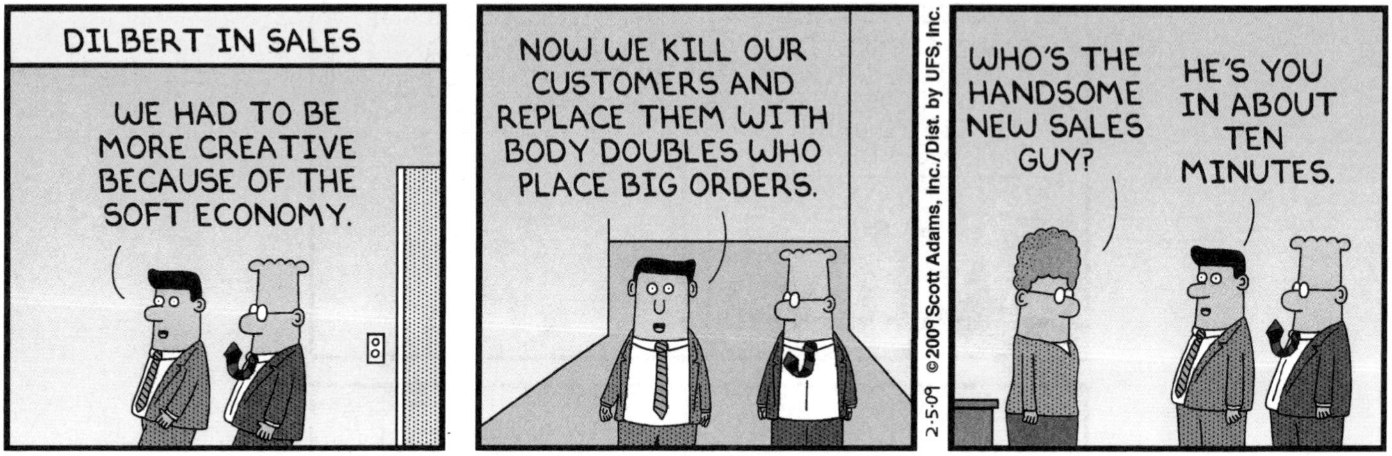
DILBERT IN SALES
WE HAD TO BE MORE CREATIVE BECAUSE OF THE SOFT ECONOMY.
NOW WE KILL OUR CUSTOMERS AND REPLACE THEM WITH BODY DOUBLES WHO PLACE BIG ORDERS.
2-5-09 © 2009 Scott Adams, Inc./Dist. by UFS, Inc.
WHO'S THE HANDSOME NEW SALES GUY?
HE'S YOU IN ABOUT TEN MINUTES.

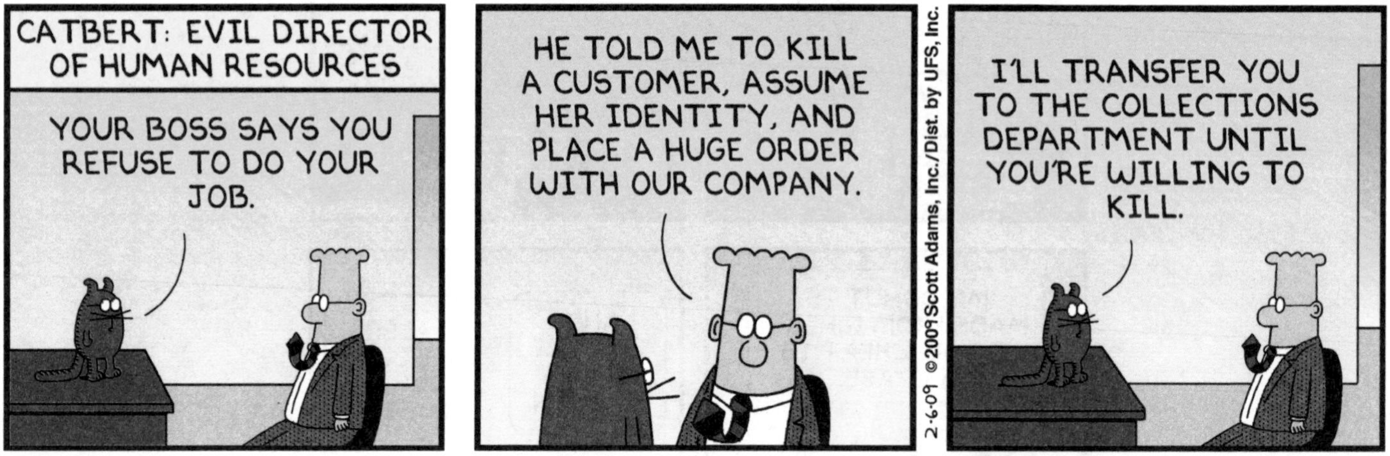
CATBERT: EVIL DIRECTOR OF HUMAN RESOURCES
YOUR BOSS SAYS YOU REFUSE TO DO YOUR JOB.
HE TOLD ME TO KILL A CUSTOMER, ASSUME HER IDENTITY, AND PLACE A HUGE ORDER WITH OUR COMPANY.
2-6-09 © 2009 Scott Adams, Inc./Dist. by UFS, Inc.
I'LL TRANSFER YOU TO THE COLLECTIONS DEPARTMENT UNTIL YOU'RE WILLING TO KILL.

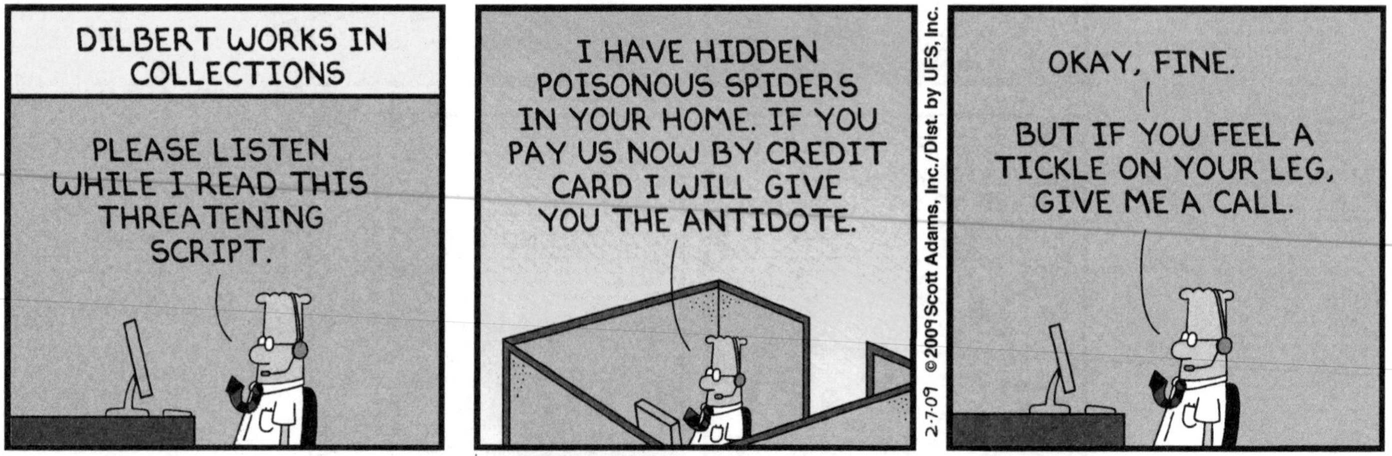
DILBERT WORKS IN COLLECTIONS
PLEASE LISTEN WHILE I READ THIS THREATENING SCRIPT.
I HAVE HIDDEN POISONOUS SPIDERS IN YOUR HOME. IF YOU PAY US NOW BY CREDIT CARD I WILL GIVE YOU THE ANTIDOTE.
2-7-09 © 2009 Scott Adams, Inc./Dist. by UFS, Inc.
OKAY, FINE.
BUT IF YOU FEEL A TICKLE ON YOUR LEG, GIVE ME A CALL.

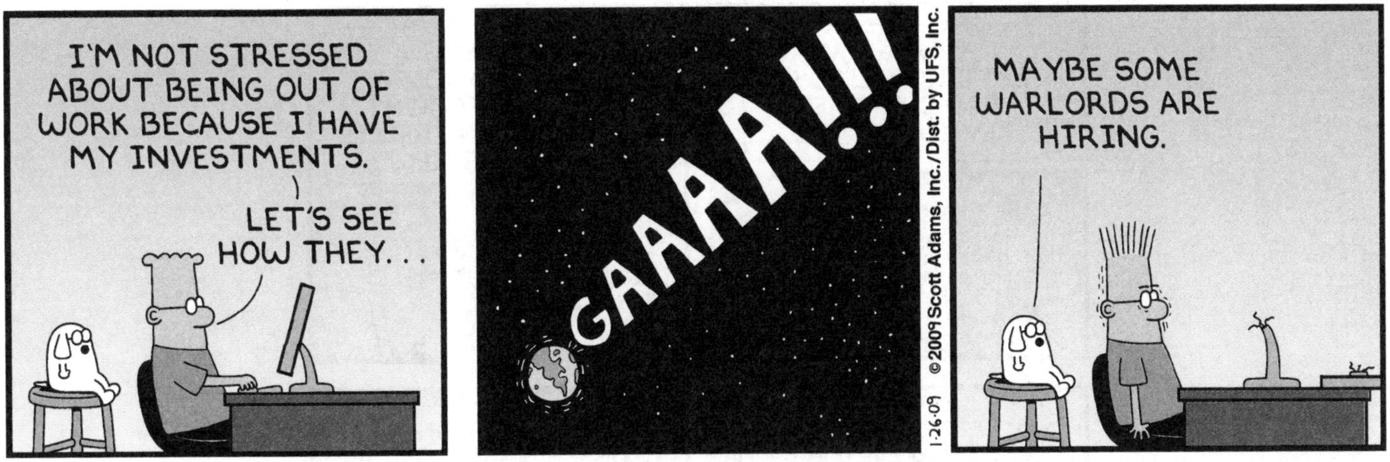
I'M NOT STRESSED ABOUT BEING OUT OF WORK BECAUSE I HAVE MY INVESTMENTS.
LET'S SEE HOW THEY. . .
GAAAA!!!
1-26-09 ©2009 Scott Adams, Inc./Dist. by UFS, Inc.
MAYBE SOME WARLORDS ARE HIRING.

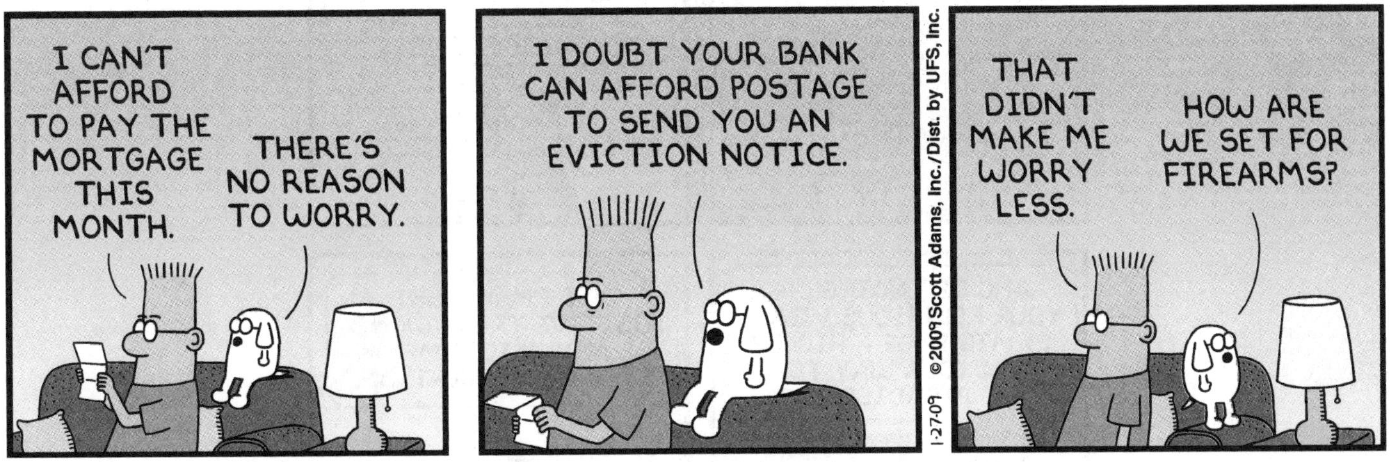
I CAN'T AFFORD TO PAY THE MORTGAGE THIS MONTH.
THERE'S NO REASON TO WORRY.
I DOUBT YOUR BANK CAN AFFORD POSTAGE TO SEND YOU AN EVICTION NOTICE.
1-27-09 ©2009 Scott Adams, Inc./Dist. by UFS, Inc.
THAT DIDN'T MAKE ME WORRY LESS.
HOW ARE WE SET FOR FIREARMS?

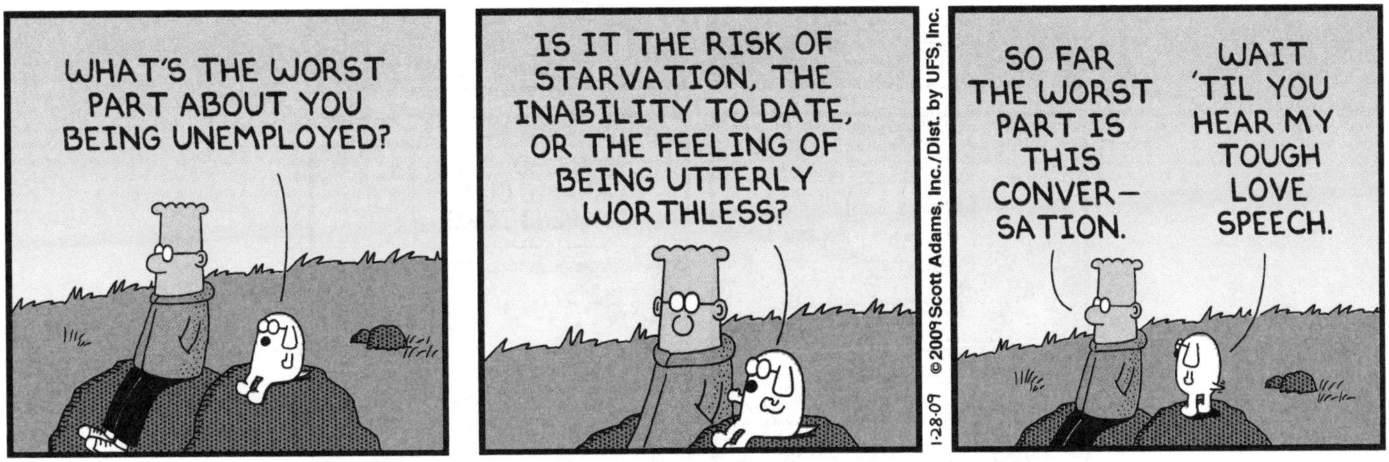
WHAT'S THE WORST PART ABOUT YOU BEING UNEMPLOYED?
IS IT THE RISK OF STARVATION, THE INABILITY TO DATE, OR THE FEELING OF BEING UTTERLY WORTHLESS?
1-28-09 ©2009 Scott Adams, Inc./Dist. by UFS, Inc.
SO FAR THE WORST PART IS THIS CONVER-SATION.
WAIT 'TIL YOU HEAR MY TOUGH LOVE SPEECH.

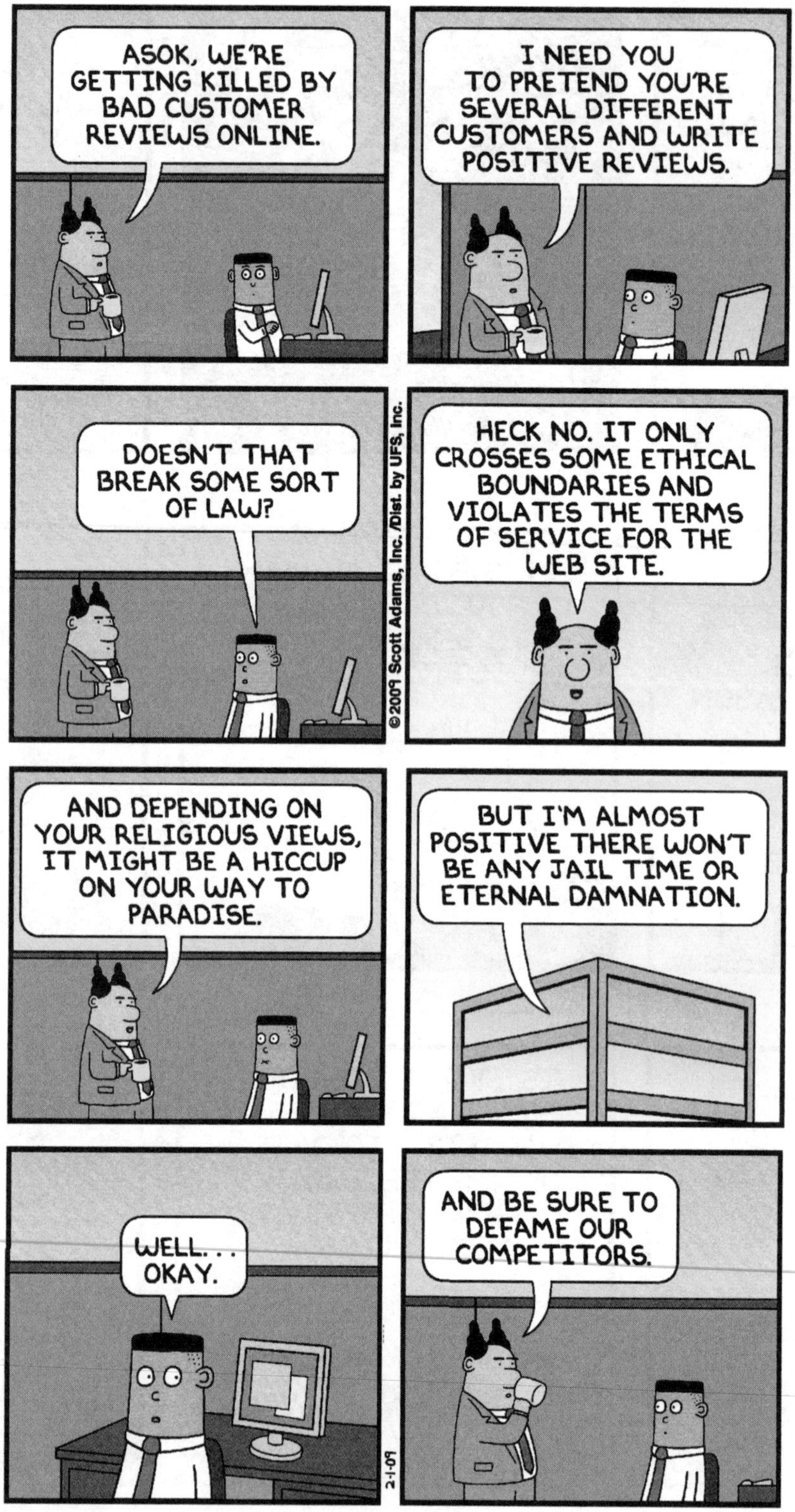
ASOK, WE'RE GETTING KILLED BY BAD CUSTOMER REVIEWS ONLINE.
I NEED YOU TO PRETEND YOU'RE SEVERAL DIFFERENT CUSTOMERS AND WRITE POSITIVE REVIEWS.
DOESN'T THAT BREAK SOME SORT OF LAW?
HECK NO. IT ONLY CROSSES SOME ETHICAL BOUNDARIES AND VIOLATES THE TERMS OF SERVICE FOR THE WEB SITE.
AND DEPENDING ON YOUR RELIGIOUS VIEWS, IT MIGHT BE A HICCUP ON YOUR WAY TO PARADISE.
BUT I'M ALMOST POSITIVE THERE WON'T BE ANY JAIL TIME OR ETERNAL DAMNATION.
WELL. . . OKAY.
AND BE SURE TO DEFAME OUR COMPETITORS.
©2009 Scott Adams, Inc./Dist. by UFS, Inc.
2-1-09

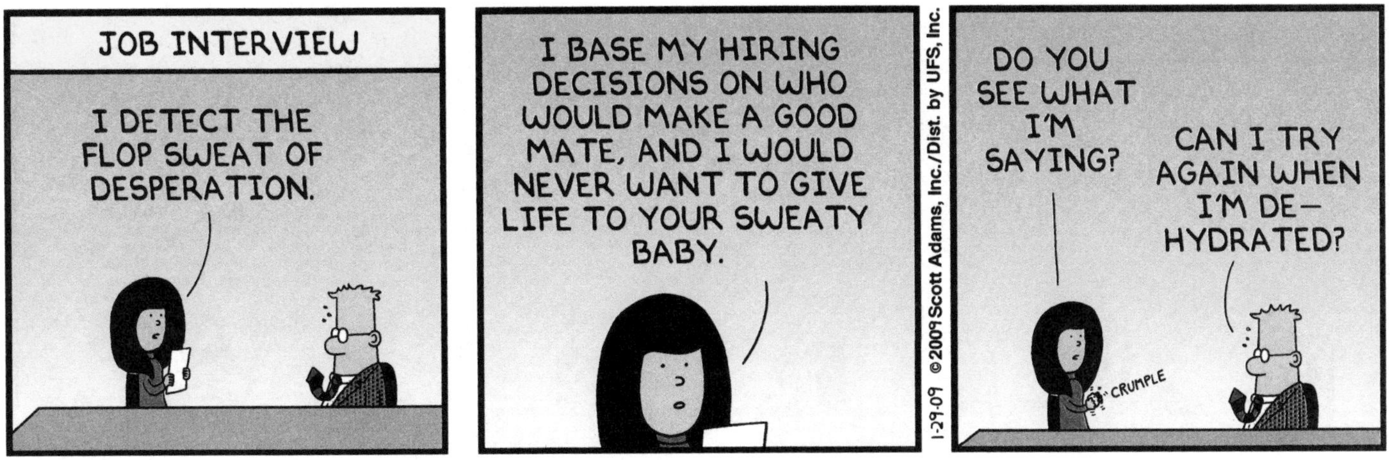
JOB INTERVIEW
I DETECT THE FLOP SWEAT OF DESPERATION.
I BASE MY HIRING DECISIONS ON WHO WOULD MAKE A GOOD MATE, AND I WOULD NEVER WANT TO GIVE LIFE TO YOUR SWEATY BABY.
1-29-09 ©2009 Scott Adams, Inc./Dist. by UFS, Inc.
DO YOU SEE WHAT I'M SAYING?
CRUMPLE
CAN I TRY AGAIN WHEN I'M DE-HYDRATED?

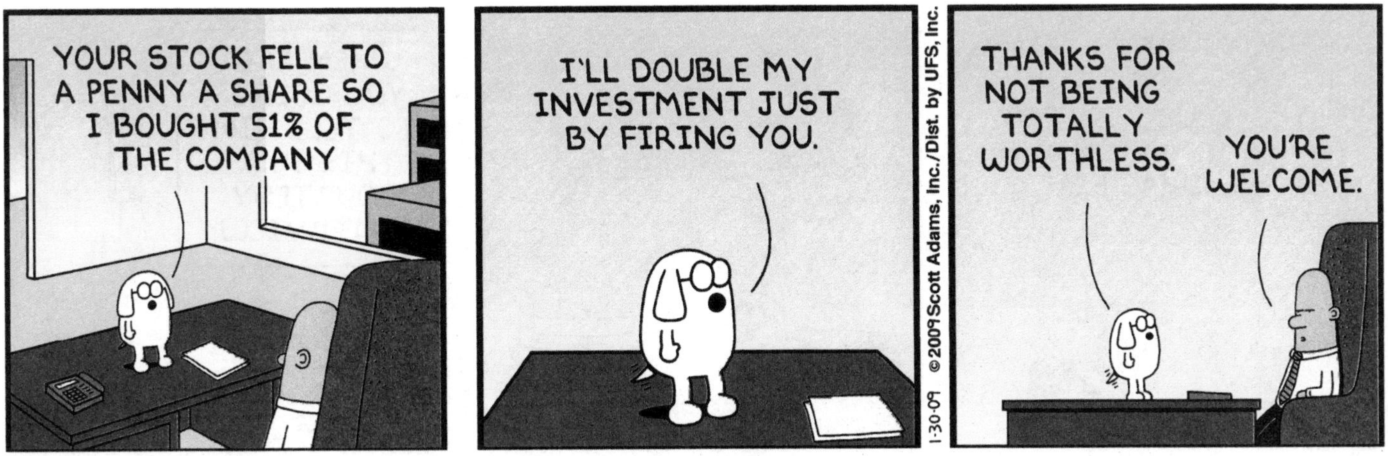
YOUR STOCK FELL TO A PENNY A SHARE SO I BOUGHT 51% OF THE COMPANY
I'LL DOUBLE MY INVESTMENT JUST BY FIRING YOU.
1-30-09 ©2009 Scott Adams, Inc./Dist. by UFS, Inc.
THANKS FOR NOT BEING TOTALLY WORTHLESS.
YOU'RE WELCOME.

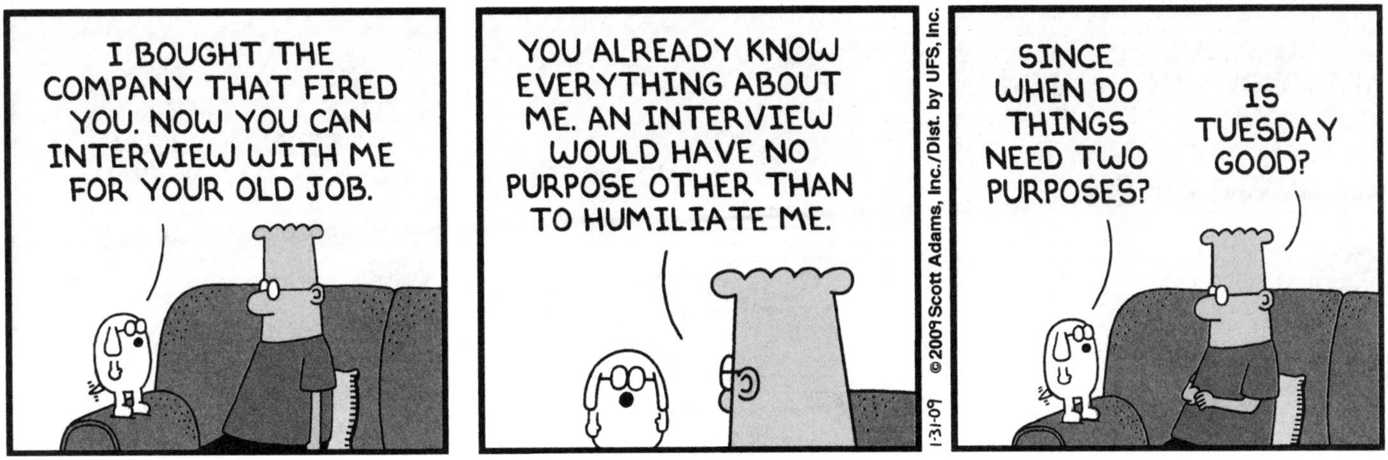
I BOUGHT THE COMPANY THAT FIRED YOU. NOW YOU CAN INTERVIEW WITH ME FOR YOUR OLD JOB.
YOU ALREADY KNOW EVERYTHING ABOUT ME. AN INTERVIEW WOULD HAVE NO PURPOSE OTHER THAN TO HUMILIATE ME.
1-31-09 ©2009 Scott Adams, Inc./Dist. by UFS, Inc.
SINCE WHEN DO THINGS NEED TWO PURPOSES?
IS TUESDAY GOOD?

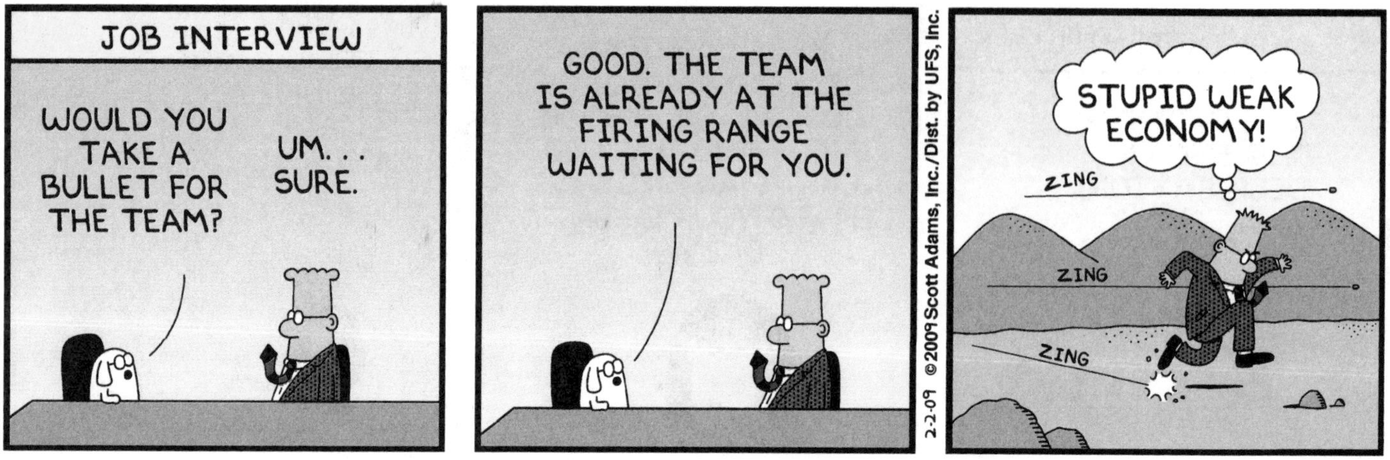
JOB INTERVIEW
WOULD YOU TAKE A BULLET FOR THE TEAM?
UM... SURE.
GOOD. THE TEAM IS ALREADY AT THE FIRING RANGE WAITING FOR YOU.
2-2-09 ©2009 Scott Adams, Inc./Dist. by UFS, Inc.
STUPID WEAK ECONOMY!
ZING
ZING
ZING

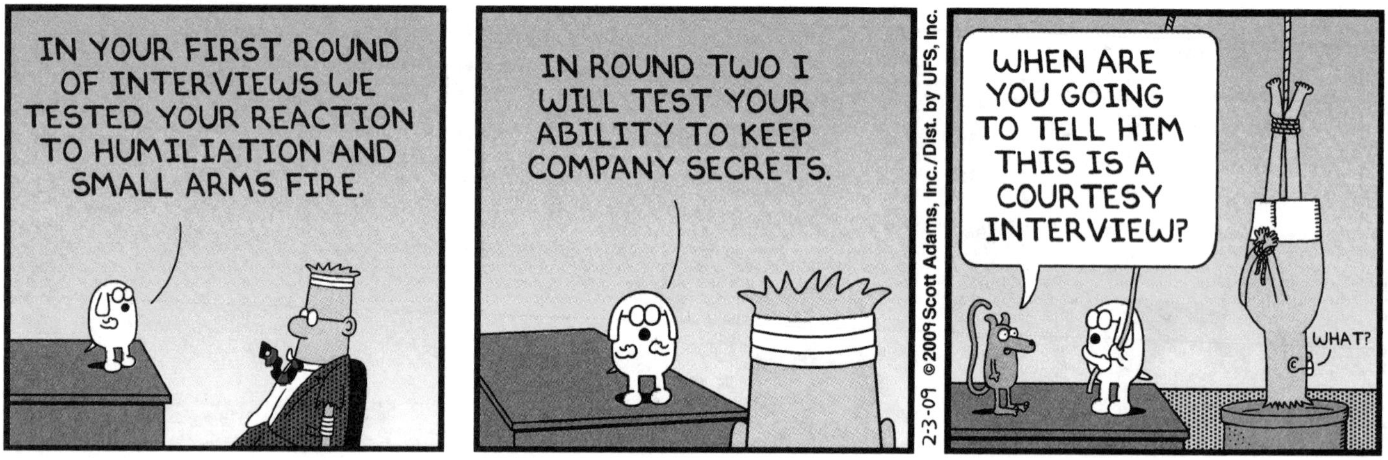
IN YOUR FIRST ROUND OF INTERVIEWS WE TESTED YOUR REACTION TO HUMILIATION AND SMALL ARMS FIRE.
IN ROUND TWO I WILL TEST YOUR ABILITY TO KEEP COMPANY SECRETS.
2-3-09 ©2009 Scott Adams, Inc./Dist. by UFS, Inc.
WHEN ARE YOU GOING TO TELL HIM THIS IS A COURTESY INTERVIEW?
WHAT?

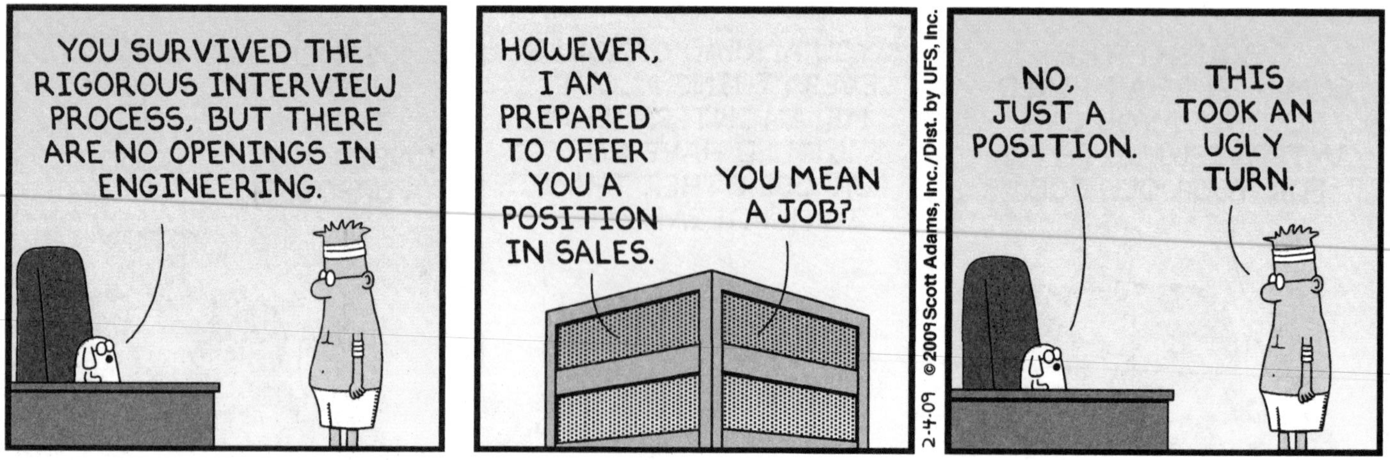
YOU SURVIVED THE RIGOROUS INTERVIEW PROCESS, BUT THERE ARE NO OPENINGS IN ENGINEERING.
HOWEVER, I AM PREPARED TO OFFER YOU A POSITION IN SALES.
YOU MEAN A JOB?
2-4-09 ©2009 Scott Adams, Inc./Dist. by UFS, Inc.
NO, JUST A POSITION.
THIS TOOK AN UGLY TURN.

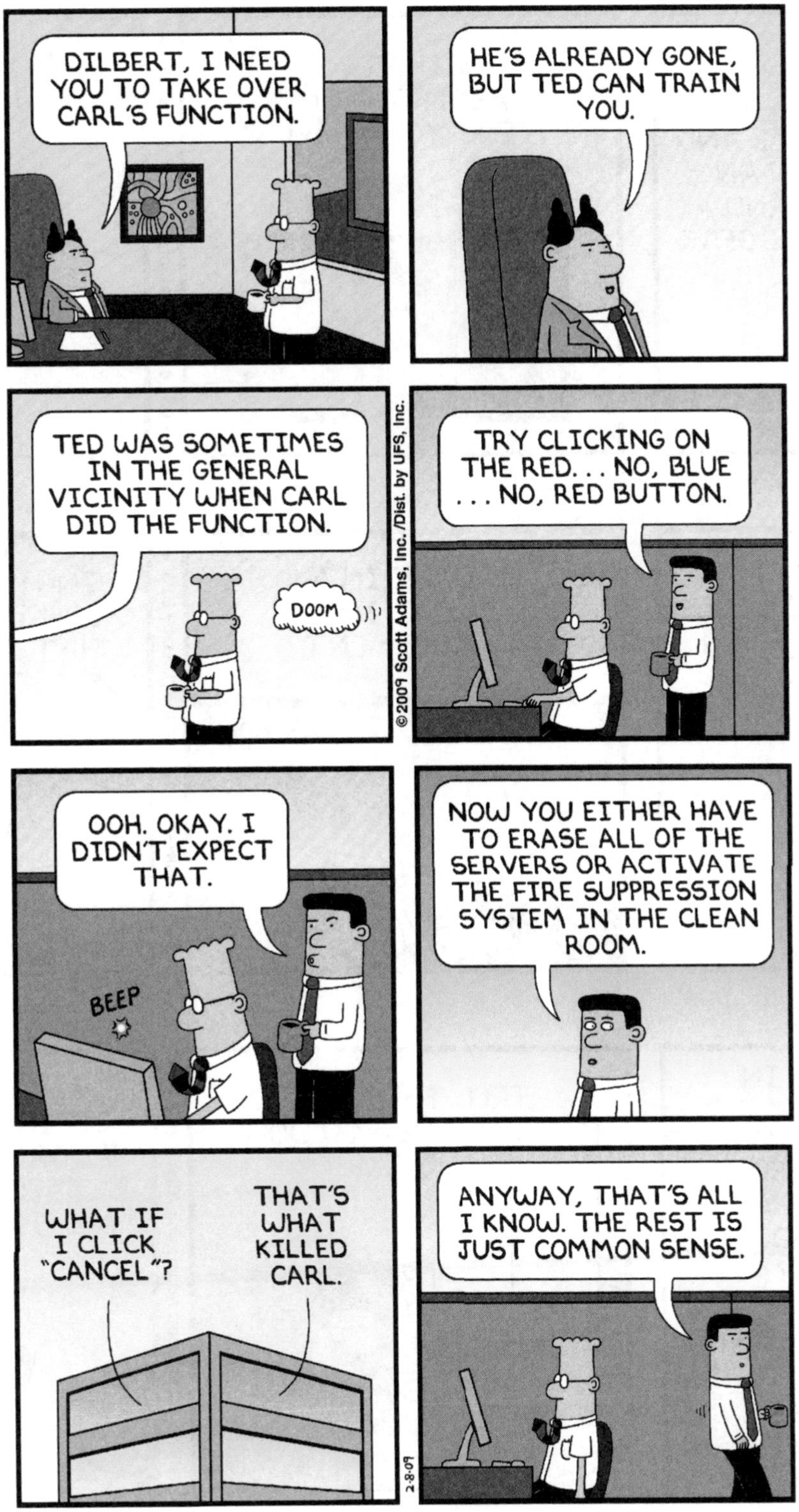
DILBERT, I NEED YOU TO TAKE OVER CARL'S FUNCTION.
HE'S ALREADY GONE, BUT TED CAN TRAIN YOU.
TED WAS SOMETIMES IN THE GENERAL VICINITY WHEN CARL DID THE FUNCTION.
DOOM
©2009 Scott Adams, Inc./Dist. by UFS, Inc.
TRY CLICKING ON THE RED. . . NO, BLUE . . . NO, RED BUTTON.
OOH. OKAY. I DIDN'T EXPECT THAT.
BEEP
NOW YOU EITHER HAVE TO ERASE ALL OF THE SERVERS OR ACTIVATE THE FIRE SUPPRESSION SYSTEM IN THE CLEAN ROOM.
WHAT IF I CLICK "CANCEL"?
THAT'S WHAT KILLED CARL.
2-8-09
ANYWAY, THAT'S ALL I KNOW. THE REST IS JUST COMMON SENSE.

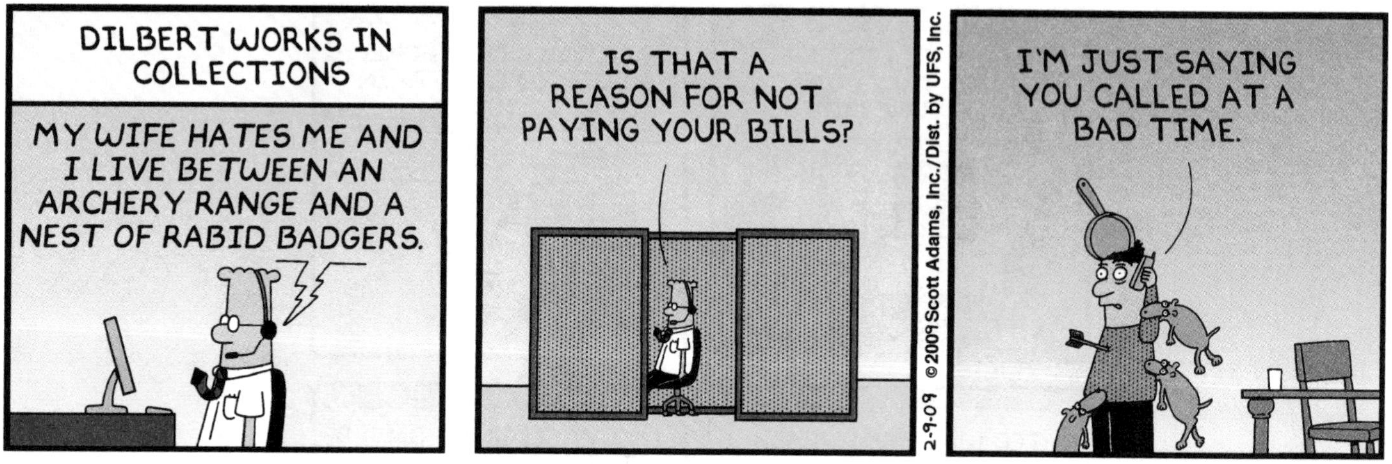
DILBERT WORKS IN COLLECTIONS
MY WIFE HATES ME AND I LIVE BETWEEN AN ARCHERY RANGE AND A NEST OF RABID BADGERS.
IS THAT A REASON FOR NOT PAYING YOUR BILLS?
2-9-09 ©2009 Scott Adams, Inc./Dist. by UFS, Inc.
I'M JUST SAYING YOU CALLED AT A BAD TIME.

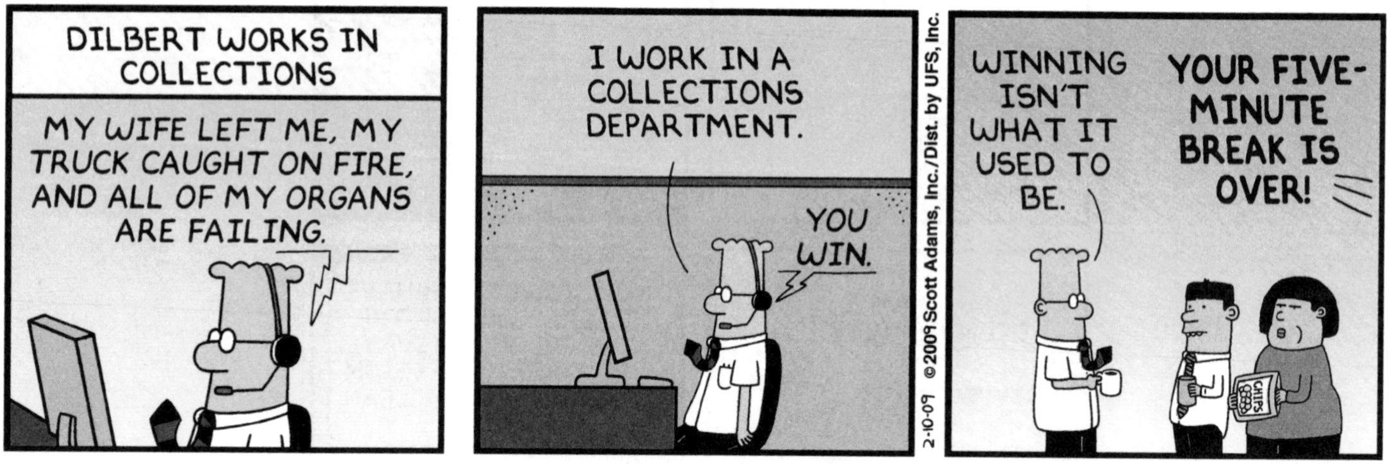
DILBERT WORKS IN COLLECTIONS
MY WIFE LEFT ME, MY TRUCK CAUGHT ON FIRE, AND ALL OF MY ORGANS ARE FAILING.
I WORK IN A COLLECTIONS DEPARTMENT.
YOU WIN.
2-10-09 ©2009 Scott Adams, Inc./Dist. by UFS, Inc.
WINNING ISN'T WHAT IT USED TO BE.
YOUR FIVE-MINUTE BREAK IS OVER!
CHIPS

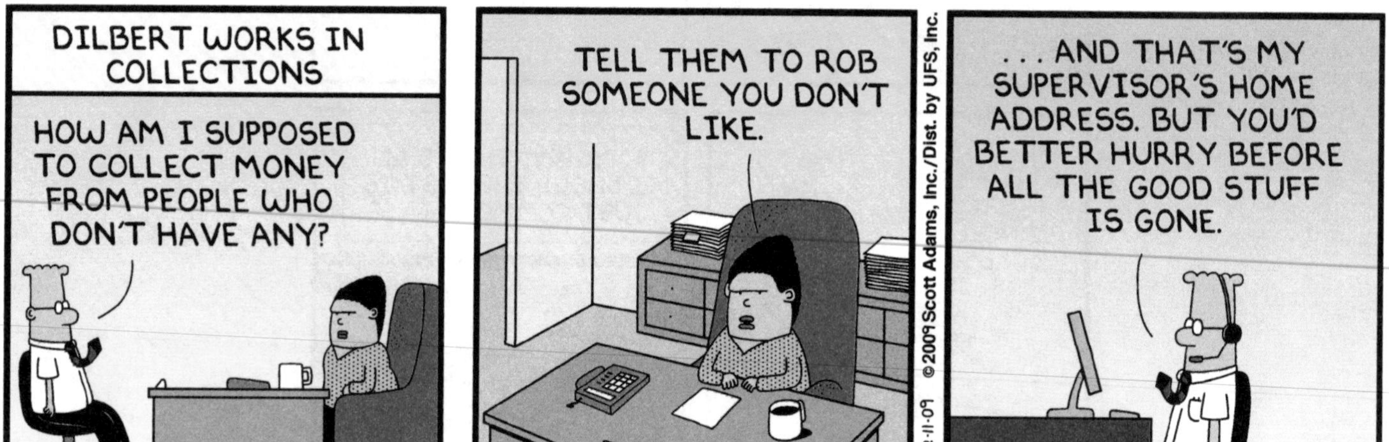
DILBERT WORKS IN COLLECTIONS
HOW AM I SUPPOSED TO COLLECT MONEY FROM PEOPLE WHO DON'T HAVE ANY?
TELL THEM TO ROB SOMEONE YOU DON'T LIKE.
2-11-09 ©2009 Scott Adams, Inc./Dist. by UFS, Inc.
. . . AND THAT'S MY SUPERVISOR'S HOME ADDRESS. BUT YOU'D BETTER HURRY BEFORE ALL THE GOOD STUFF IS GONE.

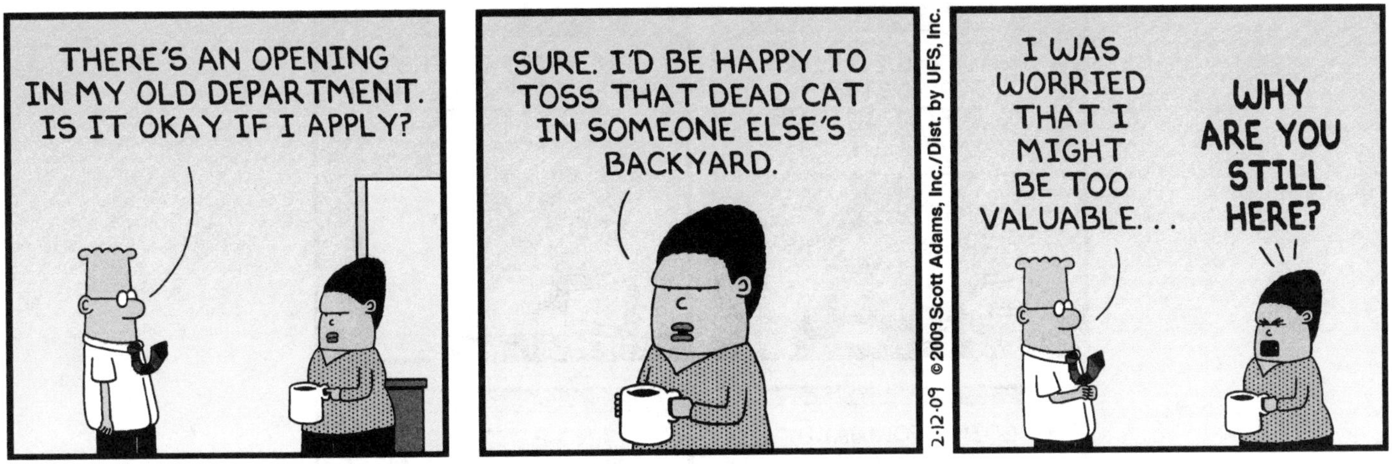
THERE'S AN OPENING IN MY OLD DEPARTMENT. IS IT OKAY IF I APPLY?
SURE. I'D BE HAPPY TO TOSS THAT DEAD CAT IN SOMEONE ELSE'S BACKYARD.
2·12·09 ©2009 Scott Adams, Inc./Dist. by UFS, Inc.
I WAS WORRIED THAT I MIGHT BE TOO VALUABLE...
WHY ARE YOU STILL HERE?

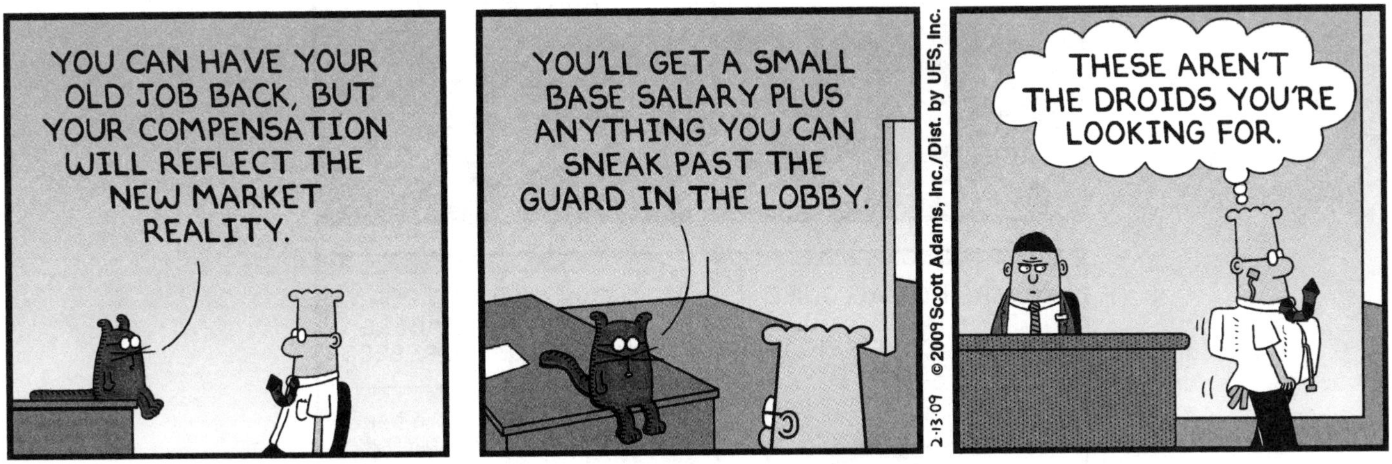
YOU CAN HAVE YOUR OLD JOB BACK, BUT YOUR COMPENSATION WILL REFLECT THE NEW MARKET REALITY.
YOU'LL GET A SMALL BASE SALARY PLUS ANYTHING YOU CAN SNEAK PAST THE GUARD IN THE LOBBY.
2·13·09 ©2009 Scott Adams, Inc./Dist. by UFS, Inc.
THESE AREN'T THE DROIDS YOU'RE LOOKING FOR.

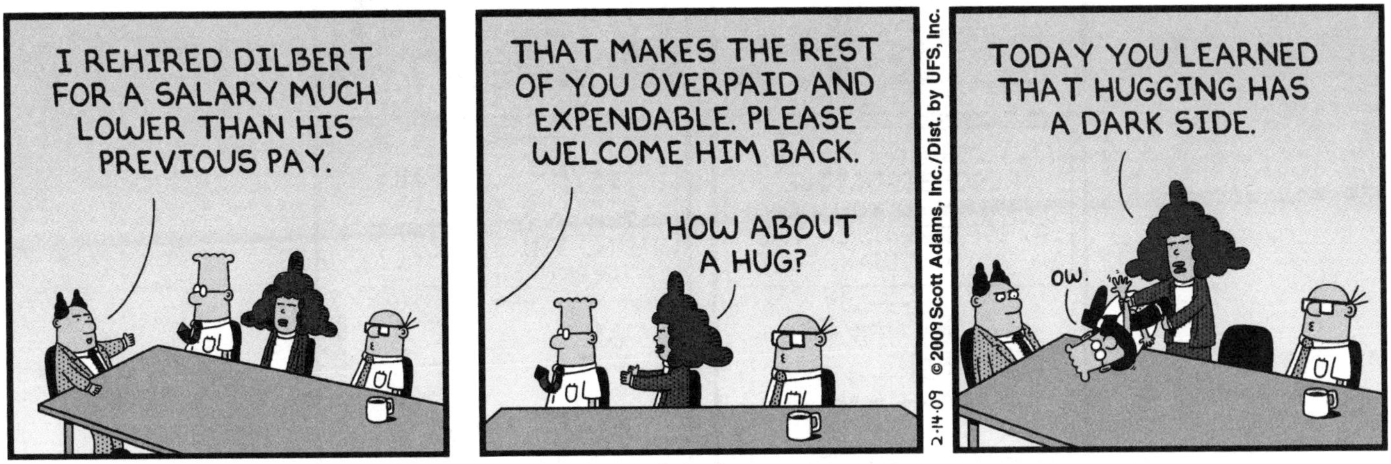
I REHIRED DILBERT FOR A SALARY MUCH LOWER THAN HIS PREVIOUS PAY.
THAT MAKES THE REST OF YOU OVERPAID AND EXPENDABLE. PLEASE WELCOME HIM BACK.
HOW ABOUT A HUG?
2·14·09 ©2009 Scott Adams, Inc./Dist. by UFS, Inc.
TODAY YOU LEARNED THAT HUGGING HAS A DARK SIDE.
OW.

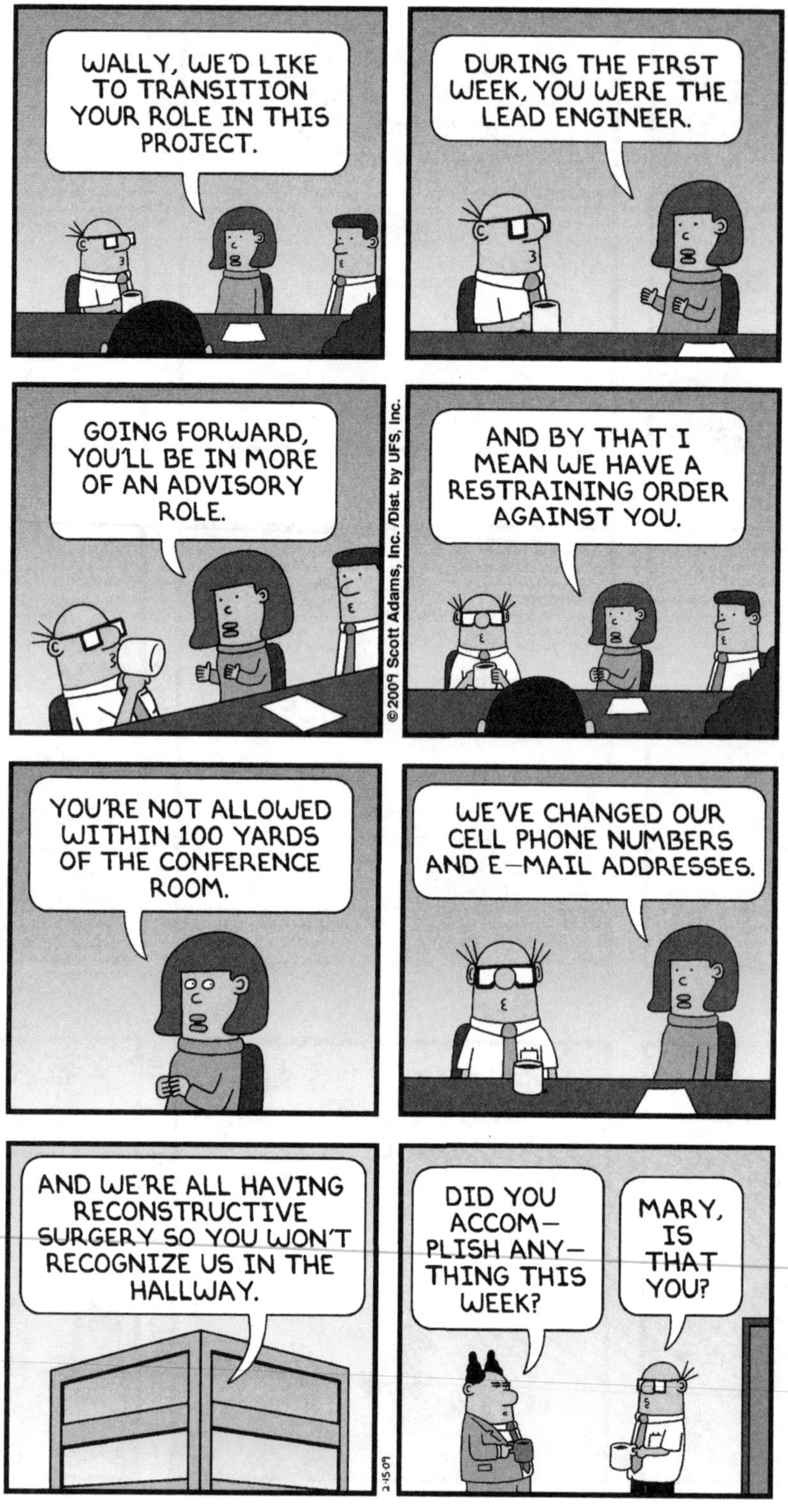
WALLY, WE'D LIKE TO TRANSITION YOUR ROLE IN THIS PROJECT.
DURING THE FIRST WEEK, YOU WERE THE LEAD ENGINEER.
GOING FORWARD, YOU'LL BE IN MORE OF AN ADVISORY ROLE.
AND BY THAT I MEAN WE HAVE A RESTRAINING ORDER AGAINST YOU.
©2009 Scott Adams, Inc./Dist. by UFS, Inc.
YOU'RE NOT ALLOWED WITHIN 100 YARDS OF THE CONFERENCE ROOM.
WE'VE CHANGED OUR CELL PHONE NUMBERS AND E-MAIL ADDRESSES.
AND WE'RE ALL HAVING RECONSTRUCTIVE SURGERY SO YOU WON'T RECOGNIZE US IN THE HALLWAY.
2-15-09
DID YOU ACCOM-PLISH ANY-THING THIS WEEK?
MARY, IS THAT YOU?

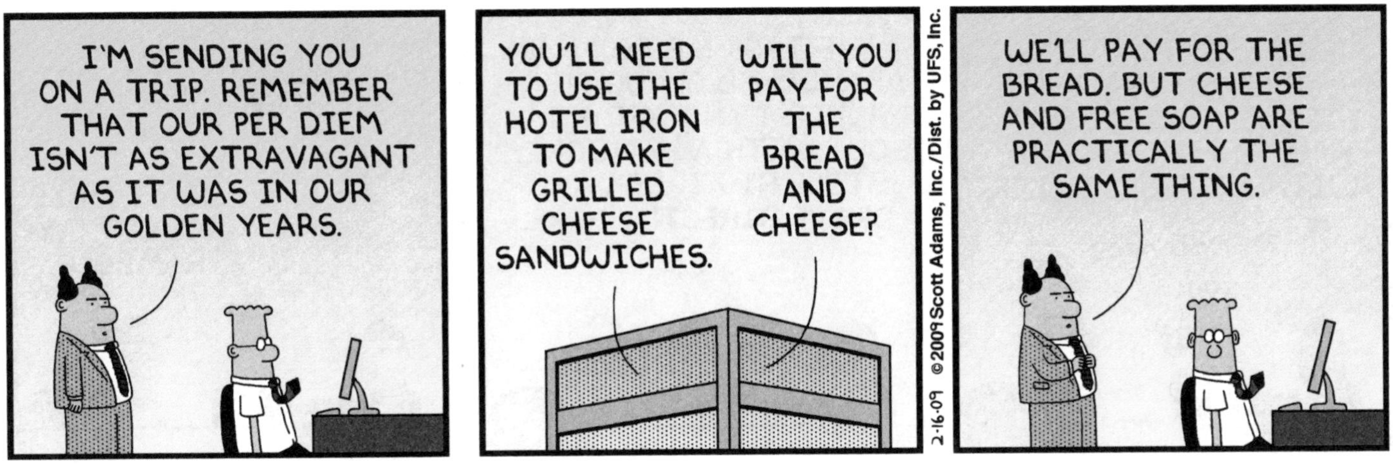
I'M SENDING YOU ON A TRIP. REMEMBER THAT OUR PER DIEM ISN'T AS EXTRAVAGANT AS IT WAS IN OUR GOLDEN YEARS.
YOU'LL NEED TO USE THE HOTEL IRON TO MAKE GRILLED CHEESE SANDWICHES.
WILL YOU PAY FOR THE BREAD AND CHEESE?
2-16-09 ©2009 Scott Adams, Inc./Dist. by UFS, Inc.
WE'LL PAY FOR THE BREAD. BUT CHEESE AND FREE SOAP ARE PRACTICALLY THE SAME THING.

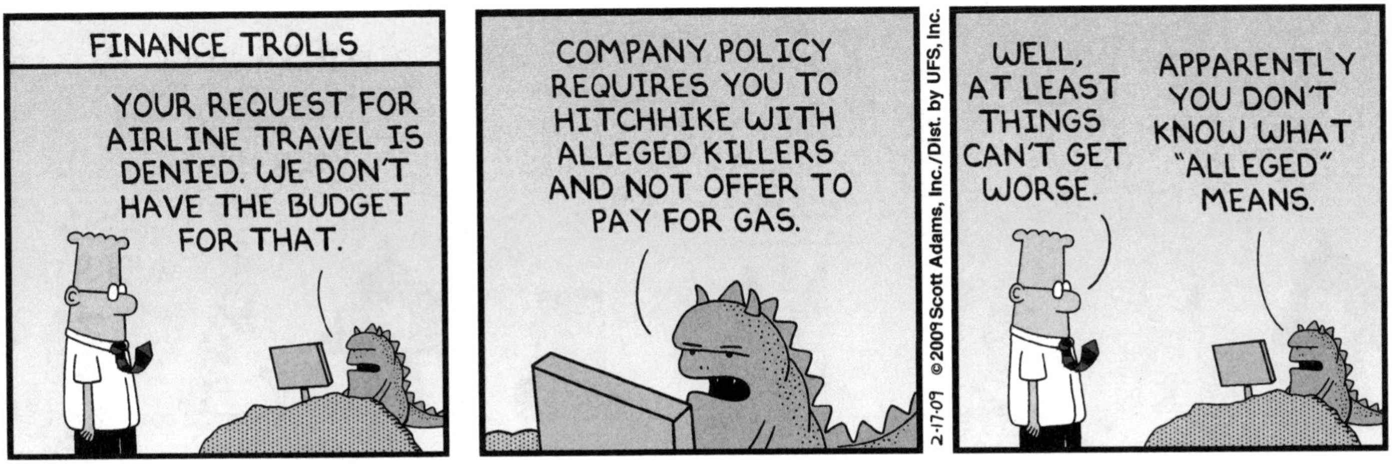
FINANCE TROLLS
YOUR REQUEST FOR AIRLINE TRAVEL IS DENIED. WE DON'T HAVE THE BUDGET FOR THAT.
COMPANY POLICY REQUIRES YOU TO HITCHHIKE WITH ALLEGED KILLERS AND NOT OFFER TO PAY FOR GAS.
2-17-09 ©2009 Scott Adams, Inc./Dist. by UFS, Inc.
WELL, AT LEAST THINGS CAN'T GET WORSE.
APPARENTLY YOU DON'T KNOW WHAT "ALLEGED" MEANS.

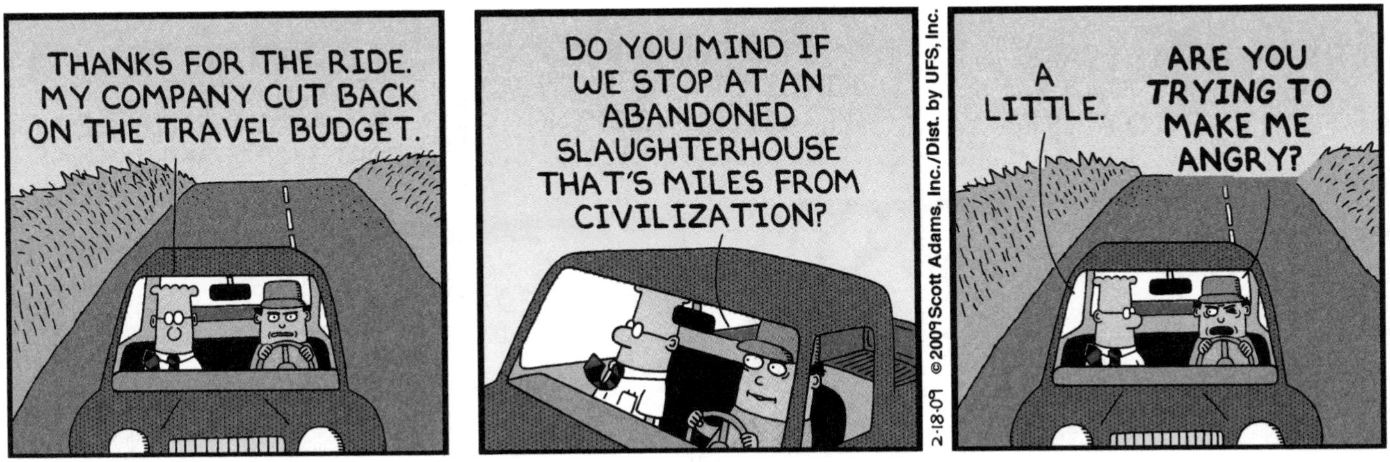
THANKS FOR THE RIDE. MY COMPANY CUT BACK ON THE TRAVEL BUDGET.
DO YOU MIND IF WE STOP AT AN ABANDONED SLAUGHTERHOUSE THAT'S MILES FROM CIVILIZATION?
2-18-09 ©2009 Scott Adams, Inc./Dist. by UFS, Inc.
A LITTLE.
ARE YOU *TRYING* TO MAKE ME ANGRY?

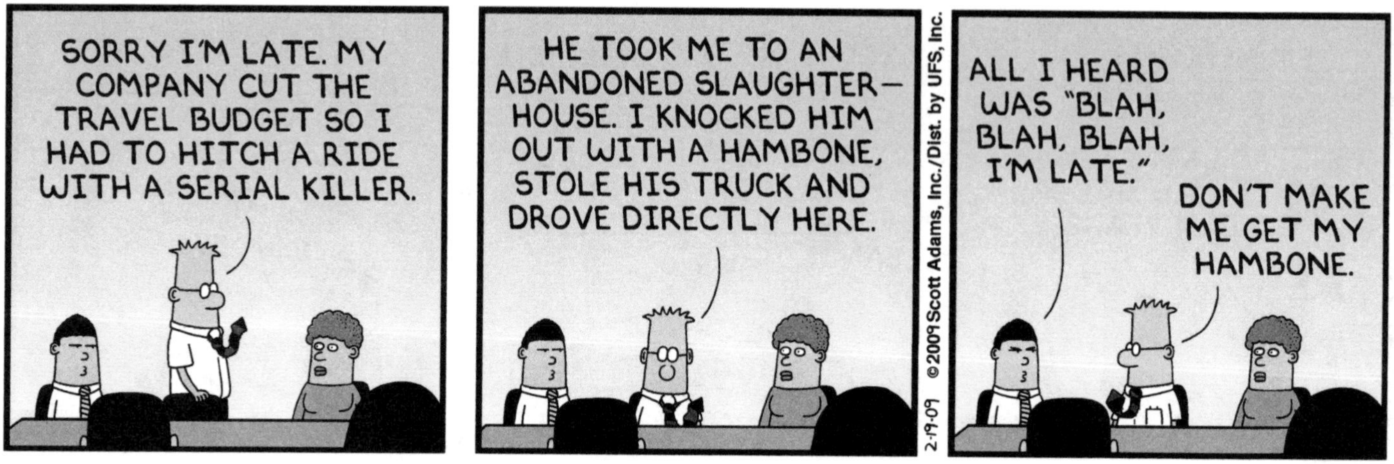
SORRY I'M LATE. MY COMPANY CUT THE TRAVEL BUDGET SO I HAD TO HITCH A RIDE WITH A SERIAL KILLER.
HE TOOK ME TO AN ABANDONED SLAUGHTER-HOUSE. I KNOCKED HIM OUT WITH A HAMBONE, STOLE HIS TRUCK AND DROVE DIRECTLY HERE.
ALL I HEARD WAS "BLAH, BLAH, BLAH, I'M LATE."
DON'T MAKE ME GET MY HAMBONE.
2-19-09 ©2009 Scott Adams, Inc./Dist. by UFS, Inc.

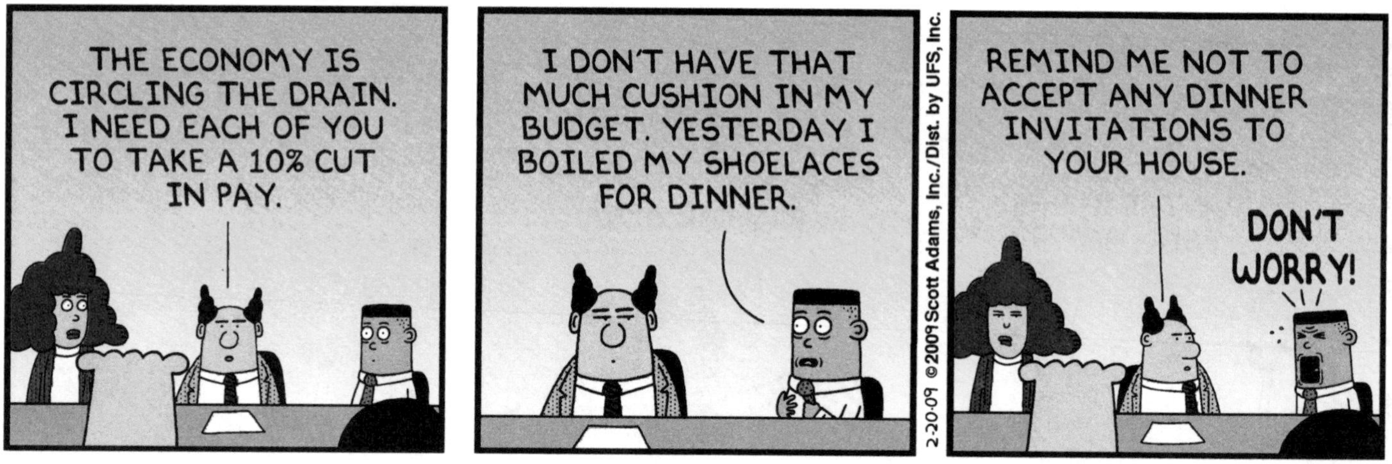
THE ECONOMY IS CIRCLING THE DRAIN. I NEED EACH OF YOU TO TAKE A 10% CUT IN PAY.
I DON'T HAVE THAT MUCH CUSHION IN MY BUDGET. YESTERDAY I BOILED MY SHOELACES FOR DINNER.
REMIND ME NOT TO ACCEPT ANY DINNER INVITATIONS TO YOUR HOUSE.
DON'T WORRY!
2-20-09 ©2009 Scott Adams, Inc./Dist. by UFS, Inc.

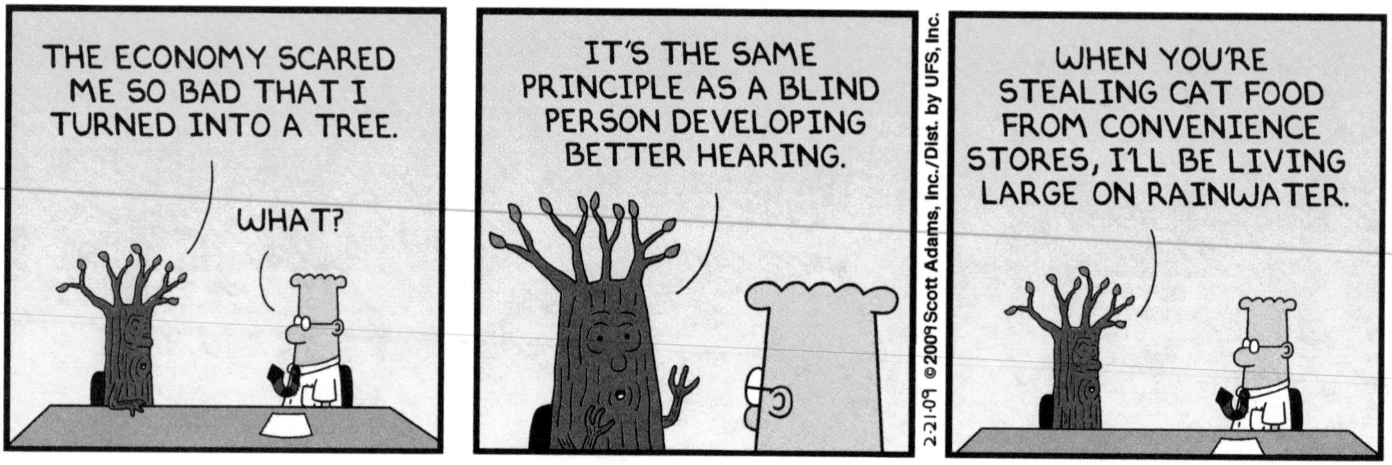
THE ECONOMY SCARED ME SO BAD THAT I TURNED INTO A TREE.
WHAT?
IT'S THE SAME PRINCIPLE AS A BLIND PERSON DEVELOPING BETTER HEARING.
WHEN YOU'RE STEALING CAT FOOD FROM CONVENIENCE STORES, I'LL BE LIVING LARGE ON RAINWATER.
2-21-09 ©2009 Scott Adams, Inc./Dist. by UFS, Inc.

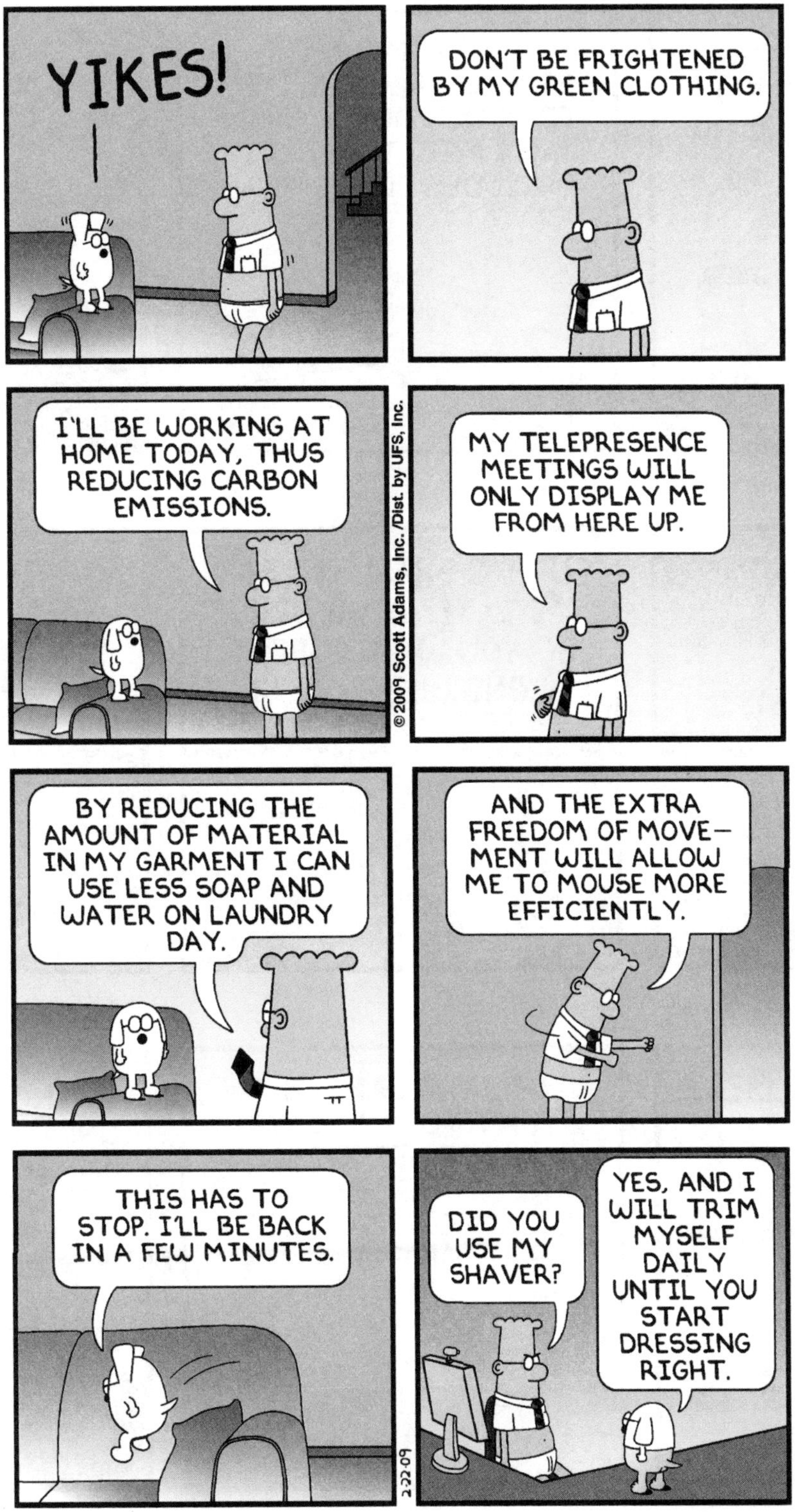
YIKES!
DON'T BE FRIGHTENED BY MY GREEN CLOTHING.
I'LL BE WORKING AT HOME TODAY, THUS REDUCING CARBON EMISSIONS.
MY TELEPRESENCE MEETINGS WILL ONLY DISPLAY ME FROM HERE UP.
BY REDUCING THE AMOUNT OF MATERIAL IN MY GARMENT I CAN USE LESS SOAP AND WATER ON LAUNDRY DAY.
AND THE EXTRA FREEDOM OF MOVE—MENT WILL ALLOW ME TO MOUSE MORE EFFICIENTLY.
THIS HAS TO STOP. I'LL BE BACK IN A FEW MINUTES.
DID YOU USE MY SHAVER?
YES, AND I WILL TRIM MYSELF DAILY UNTIL YOU START DRESSING RIGHT.
©2009 Scott Adams, Inc./Dist. by UFS, Inc.
2-22-09

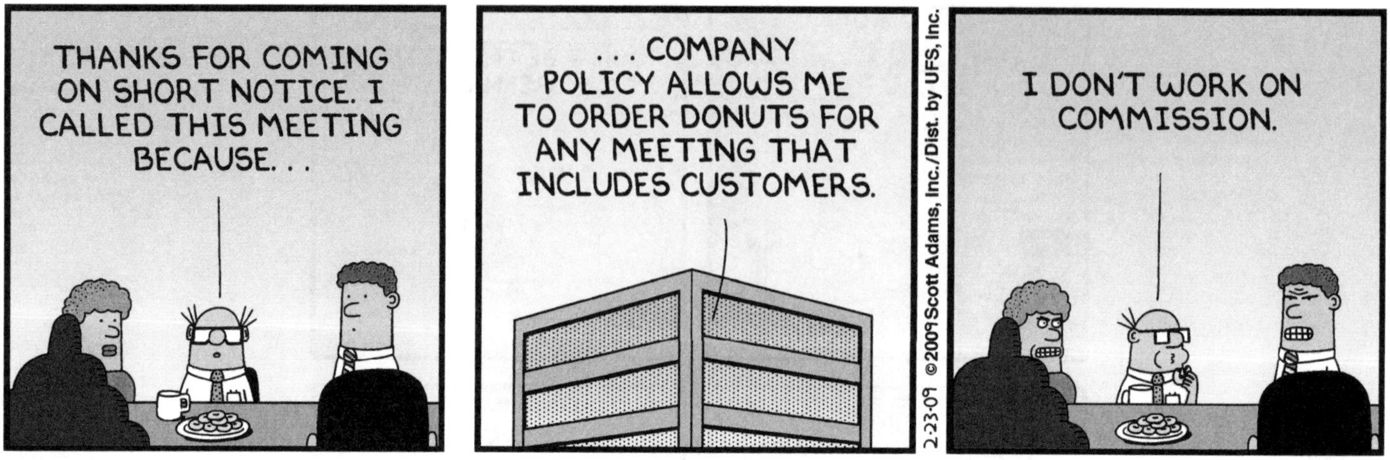
THANKS FOR COMING ON SHORT NOTICE. I CALLED THIS MEETING BECAUSE. . .
. . . COMPANY POLICY ALLOWS ME TO ORDER DONUTS FOR ANY MEETING THAT INCLUDES CUSTOMERS.
2-23-09 ©2009 Scott Adams, Inc./Dist. by UFS, Inc.
I DON'T WORK ON COMMISSION.

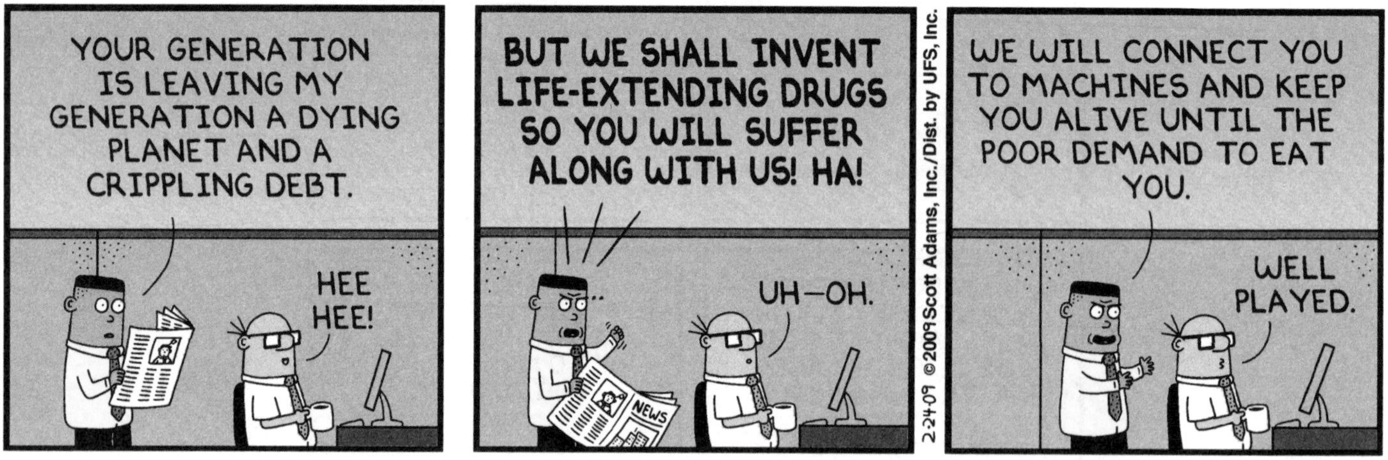
YOUR GENERATION IS LEAVING MY GENERATION A DYING PLANET AND A CRIPPLING DEBT.
HEE HEE!
BUT WE SHALL INVENT LIFE-EXTENDING DRUGS SO YOU WILL SUFFER ALONG WITH US! HA!
UH—OH.
NEWS
2-24-09 ©2009 Scott Adams, Inc./Dist. by UFS, Inc.
WE WILL CONNECT YOU TO MACHINES AND KEEP YOU ALIVE UNTIL THE POOR DEMAND TO EAT YOU.
WELL PLAYED.

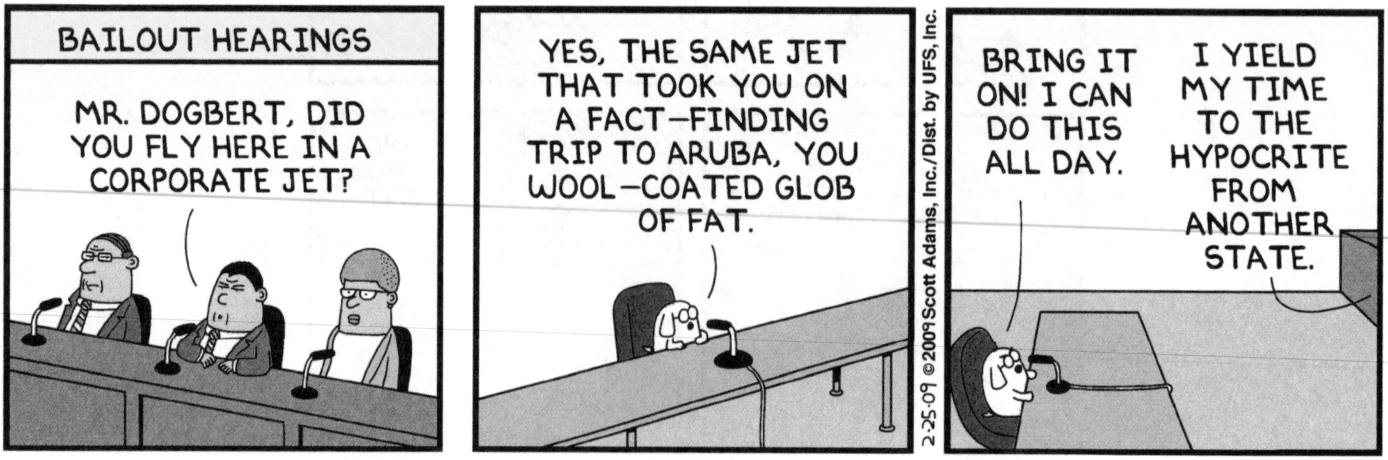
BAILOUT HEARINGS
MR. DOGBERT, DID YOU FLY HERE IN A CORPORATE JET?
YES, THE SAME JET THAT TOOK YOU ON A FACT—FINDING TRIP TO ARUBA, YOU WOOL—COATED GLOB OF FAT.
2-25-09 ©2009 Scott Adams, Inc./Dist. by UFS, Inc.
BRING IT ON! I CAN DO THIS ALL DAY.
I YIELD MY TIME TO THE HYPOCRITE FROM ANOTHER STATE.

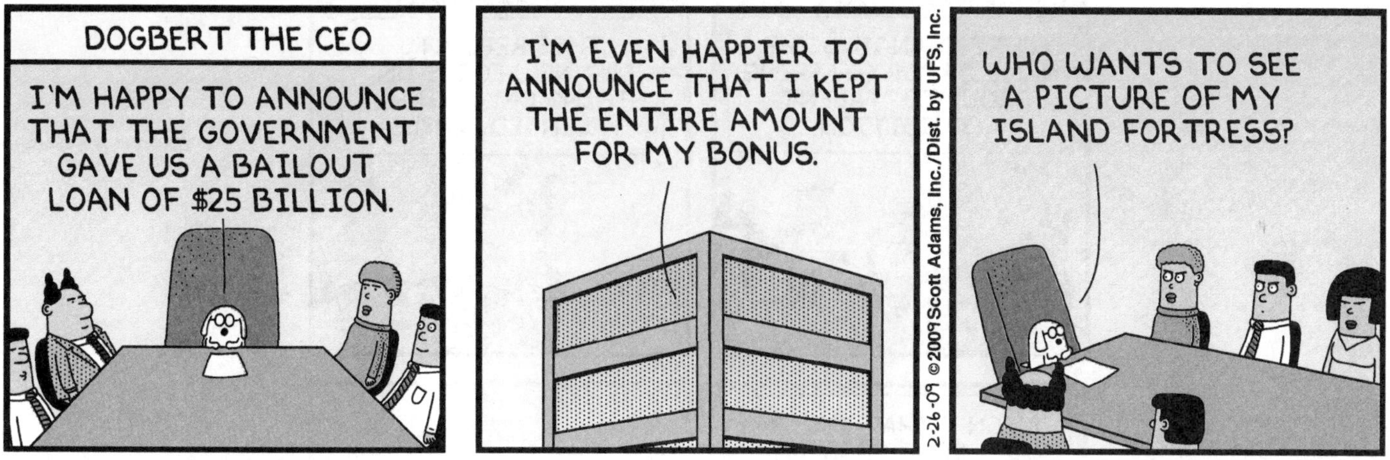
DOGBERT THE CEO
I'M HAPPY TO ANNOUNCE THAT THE GOVERNMENT GAVE US A BAILOUT LOAN OF $25 BILLION.
I'M EVEN HAPPIER TO ANNOUNCE THAT I KEPT THE ENTIRE AMOUNT FOR MY BONUS.
2-26-09 ©2009Scott Adams, Inc./Dist. by UFS, Inc.
WHO WANTS TO SEE A PICTURE OF MY ISLAND FORTRESS?

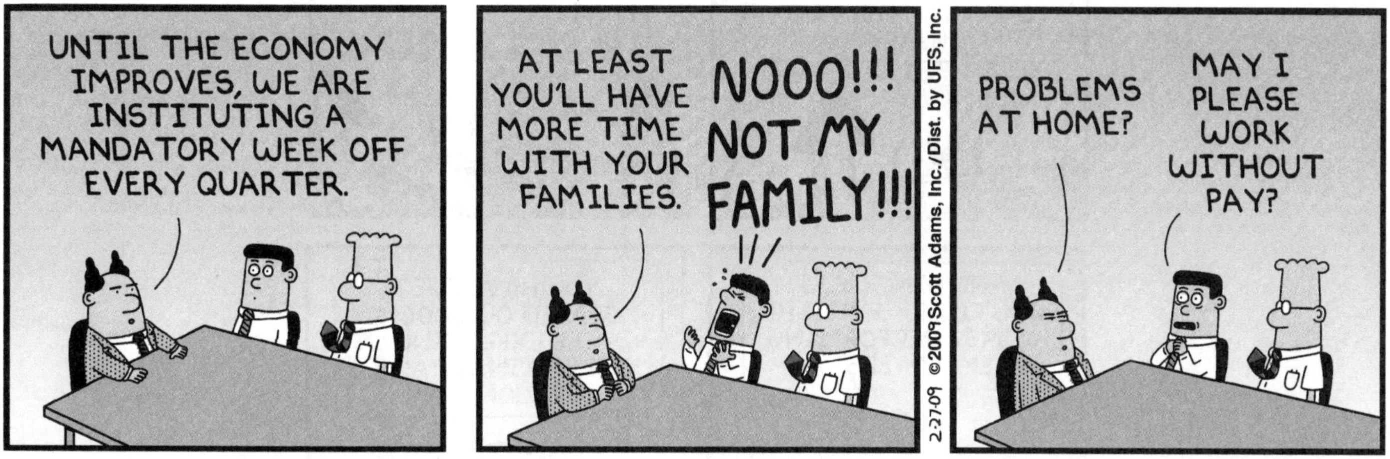
UNTIL THE ECONOMY IMPROVES, WE ARE INSTITUTING A MANDATORY WEEK OFF EVERY QUARTER.
AT LEAST YOU'LL HAVE MORE TIME WITH YOUR FAMILIES.
NOOO!!! NOT MY FAMILY!!!
2-27-09 ©2009Scott Adams, Inc./Dist. by UFS, Inc.
PROBLEMS AT HOME?
MAY I PLEASE WORK WITHOUT PAY?

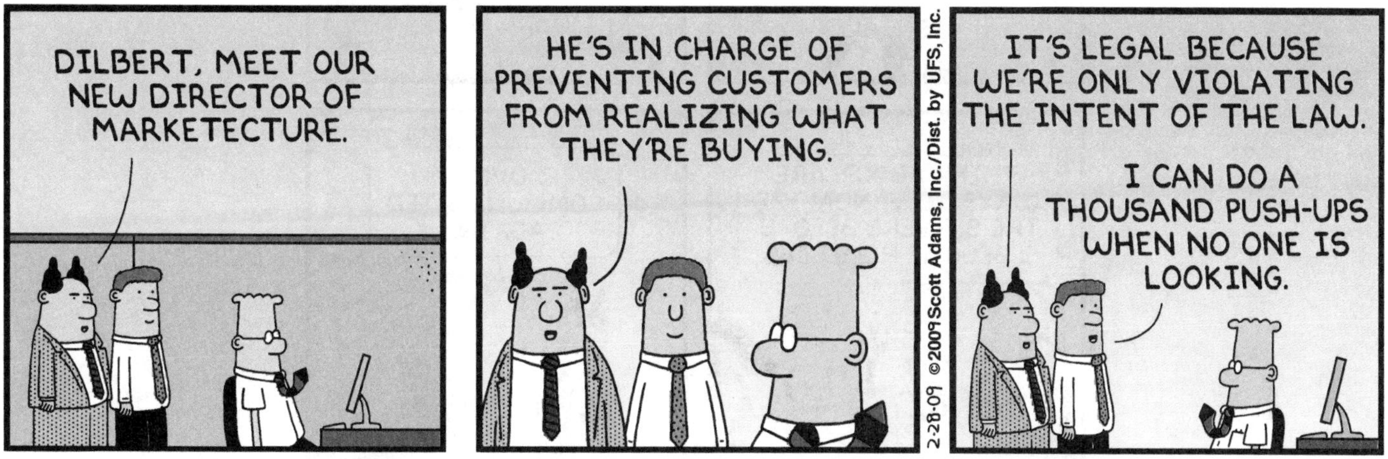
DILBERT, MEET OUR NEW DIRECTOR OF MARKETECTURE.
HE'S IN CHARGE OF PREVENTING CUSTOMERS FROM REALIZING WHAT THEY'RE BUYING.
2-28-09 ©2009Scott Adams, Inc./Dist. by UFS, Inc.
IT'S LEGAL BECAUSE WE'RE ONLY VIOLATING THE INTENT OF THE LAW.
I CAN DO A THOUSAND PUSH-UPS WHEN NO ONE IS LOOKING.

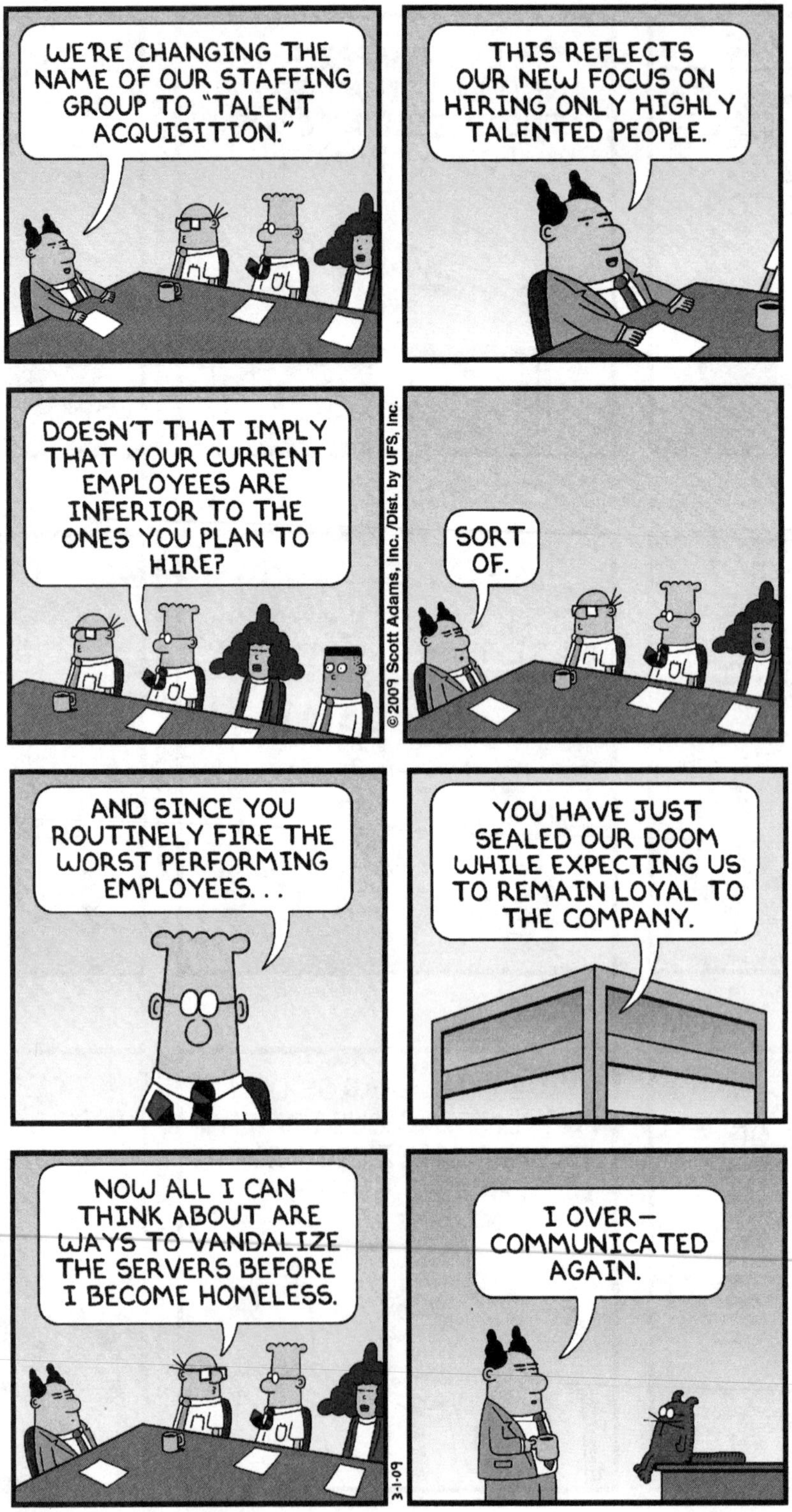
WE'RE CHANGING THE NAME OF OUR STAFFING GROUP TO "TALENT ACQUISITION."
THIS REFLECTS OUR NEW FOCUS ON HIRING ONLY HIGHLY TALENTED PEOPLE.
DOESN'T THAT IMPLY THAT YOUR CURRENT EMPLOYEES ARE INFERIOR TO THE ONES YOU PLAN TO HIRE?
SORT OF.
AND SINCE YOU ROUTINELY FIRE THE WORST PERFORMING EMPLOYEES. . .
YOU HAVE JUST SEALED OUR DOOM WHILE EXPECTING US TO REMAIN LOYAL TO THE COMPANY.
NOW ALL I CAN THINK ABOUT ARE WAYS TO VANDALIZE THE SERVERS BEFORE I BECOME HOMELESS.
I OVER-COMMUNICATED AGAIN.
© 2009 Scott Adams, Inc./Dist. by UFS, Inc.
3-1-09

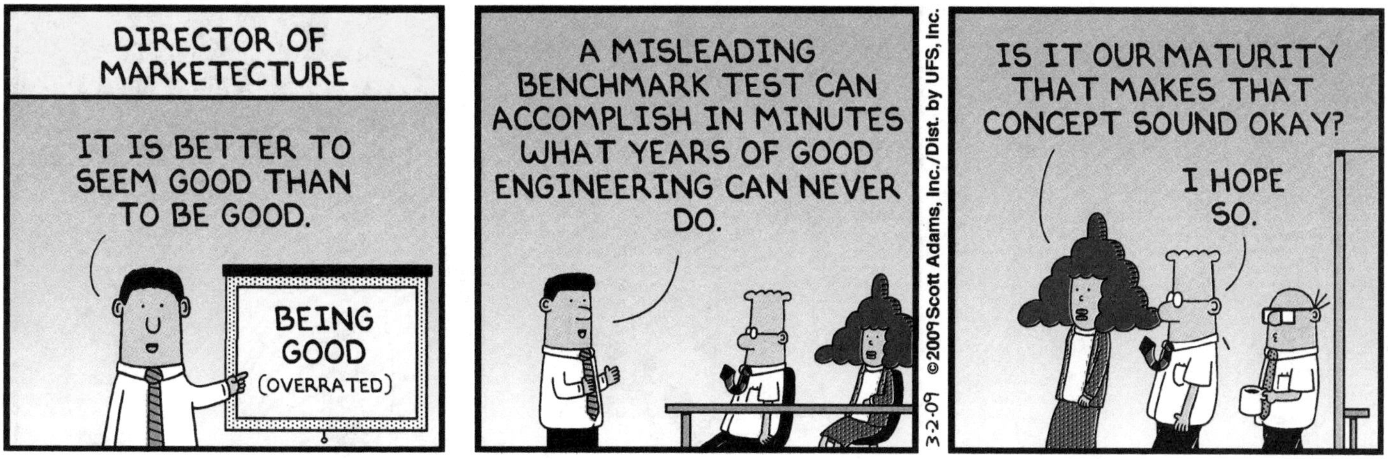
DIRECTOR OF MARKETECTURE
IT IS BETTER TO SEEM GOOD THAN TO BE GOOD.
BEING GOOD (OVERRATED)
A MISLEADING BENCHMARK TEST CAN ACCOMPLISH IN MINUTES WHAT YEARS OF GOOD ENGINEERING CAN NEVER DO.
IS IT OUR MATURITY THAT MAKES THAT CONCEPT SOUND OKAY?
I HOPE SO.
3-2-09 ©2009 Scott Adams, Inc./Dist. by UFS, Inc.

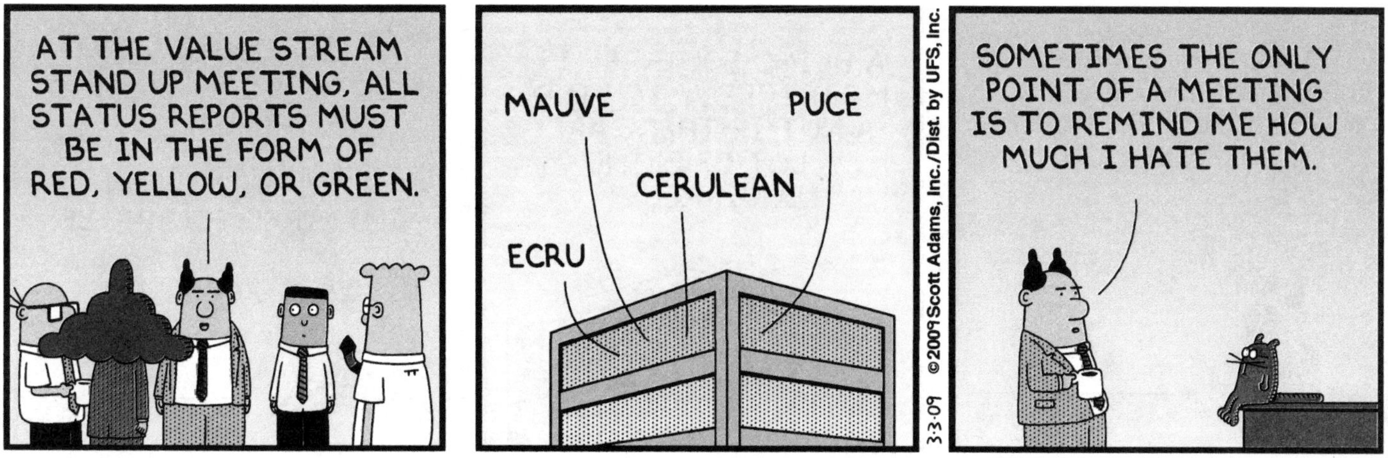
AT THE VALUE STREAM STAND UP MEETING, ALL STATUS REPORTS MUST BE IN THE FORM OF RED, YELLOW, OR GREEN.
MAUVE
PUCE
CERULEAN
ECRU
SOMETIMES THE ONLY POINT OF A MEETING IS TO REMIND ME HOW MUCH I HATE THEM.
3-3-09 ©2009 Scott Adams, Inc./Dist. by UFS, Inc.

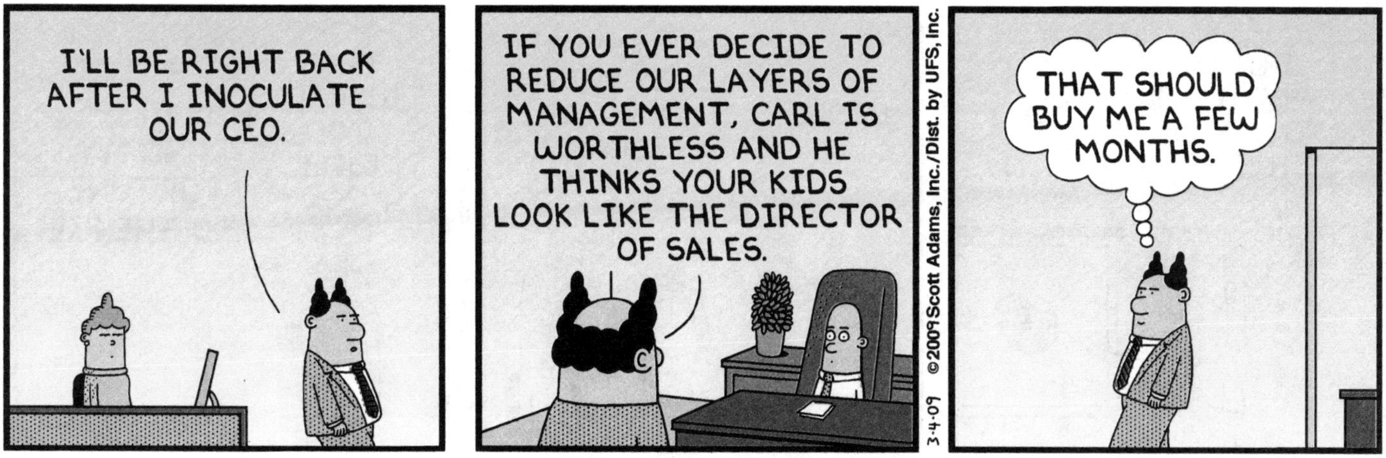
I'LL BE RIGHT BACK AFTER I INOCULATE OUR CEO.
IF YOU EVER DECIDE TO REDUCE OUR LAYERS OF MANAGEMENT, CARL IS WORTHLESS AND HE THINKS YOUR KIDS LOOK LIKE THE DIRECTOR OF SALES.
THAT SHOULD BUY ME A FEW MONTHS.
3-4-09 ©2009 Scott Adams, Inc./Dist. by UFS, Inc.

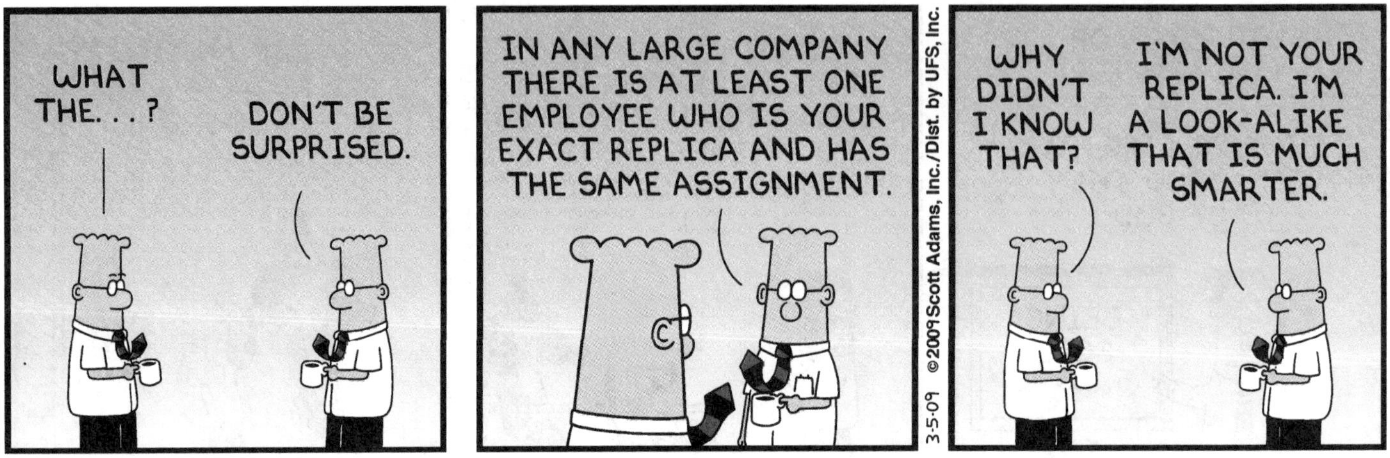
WHAT THE. . . ?
DON'T BE SURPRISED.
IN ANY LARGE COMPANY THERE IS AT LEAST ONE EMPLOYEE WHO IS YOUR EXACT REPLICA AND HAS THE SAME ASSIGNMENT.
3-5-09 ©2009 Scott Adams, Inc./Dist. by UFS, Inc.
WHY DIDN'T I KNOW THAT?
I'M NOT YOUR REPLICA. I'M A LOOK-ALIKE THAT IS MUCH SMARTER.

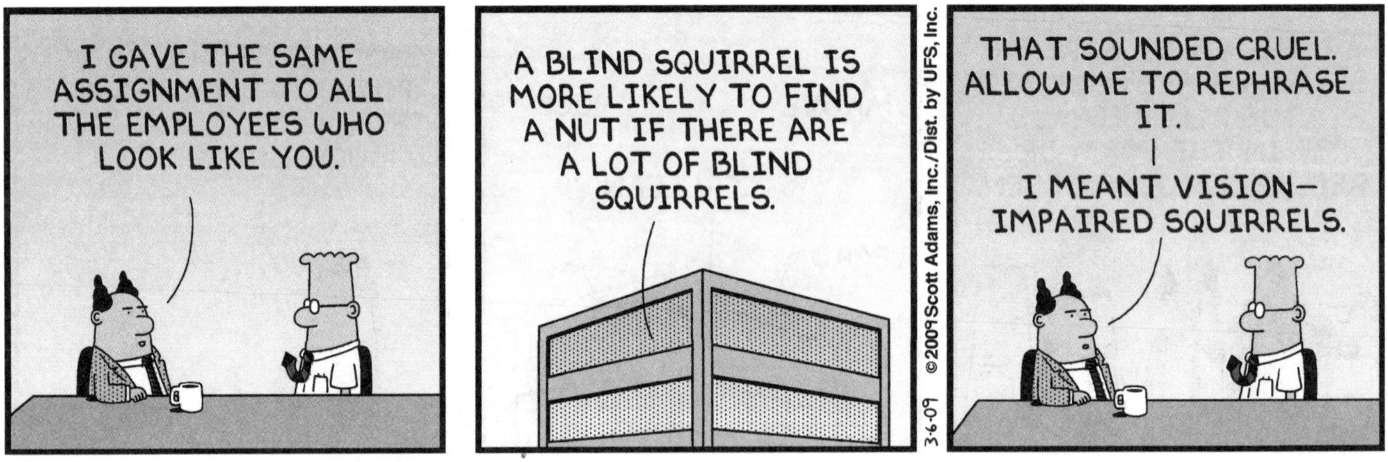
I GAVE THE SAME ASSIGNMENT TO ALL THE EMPLOYEES WHO LOOK LIKE YOU.
A BLIND SQUIRREL IS MORE LIKELY TO FIND A NUT IF THERE ARE A LOT OF BLIND SQUIRRELS.
3-6-09 ©2009 Scott Adams, Inc./Dist. by UFS, Inc.
THAT SOUNDED CRUEL. ALLOW ME TO REPHRASE IT.
I MEANT VISION-IMPAIRED SQUIRRELS.

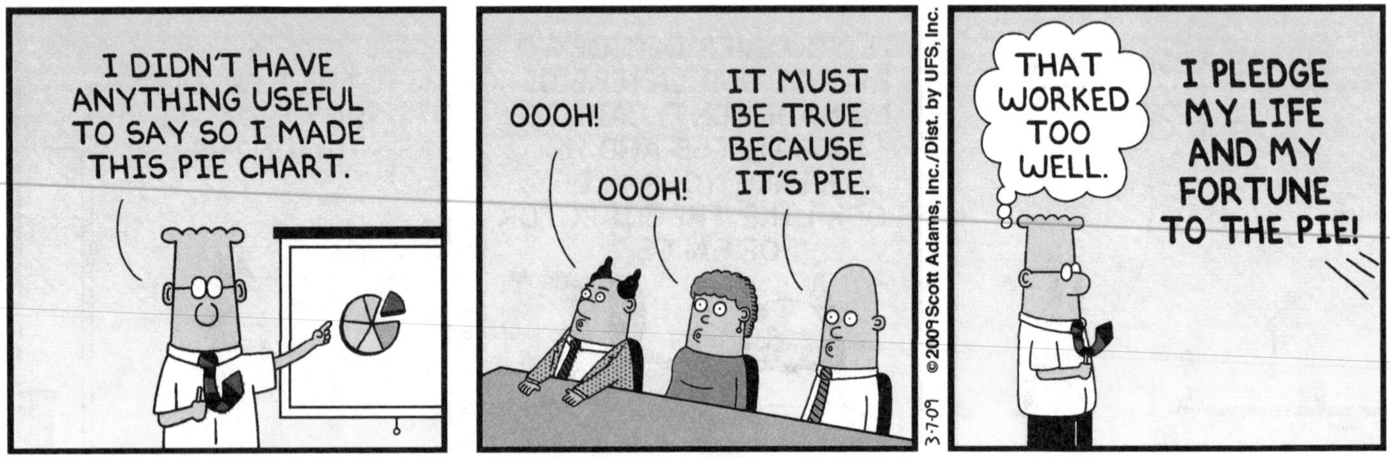
I DIDN'T HAVE ANYTHING USEFUL TO SAY SO I MADE THIS PIE CHART.
OOOH!
OOOH!
IT MUST BE TRUE BECAUSE IT'S PIE.
3-7-09 ©2009 Scott Adams, Inc./Dist. by UFS, Inc.
THAT WORKED TOO WELL.
I PLEDGE MY LIFE AND MY FORTUNE TO THE PIE!

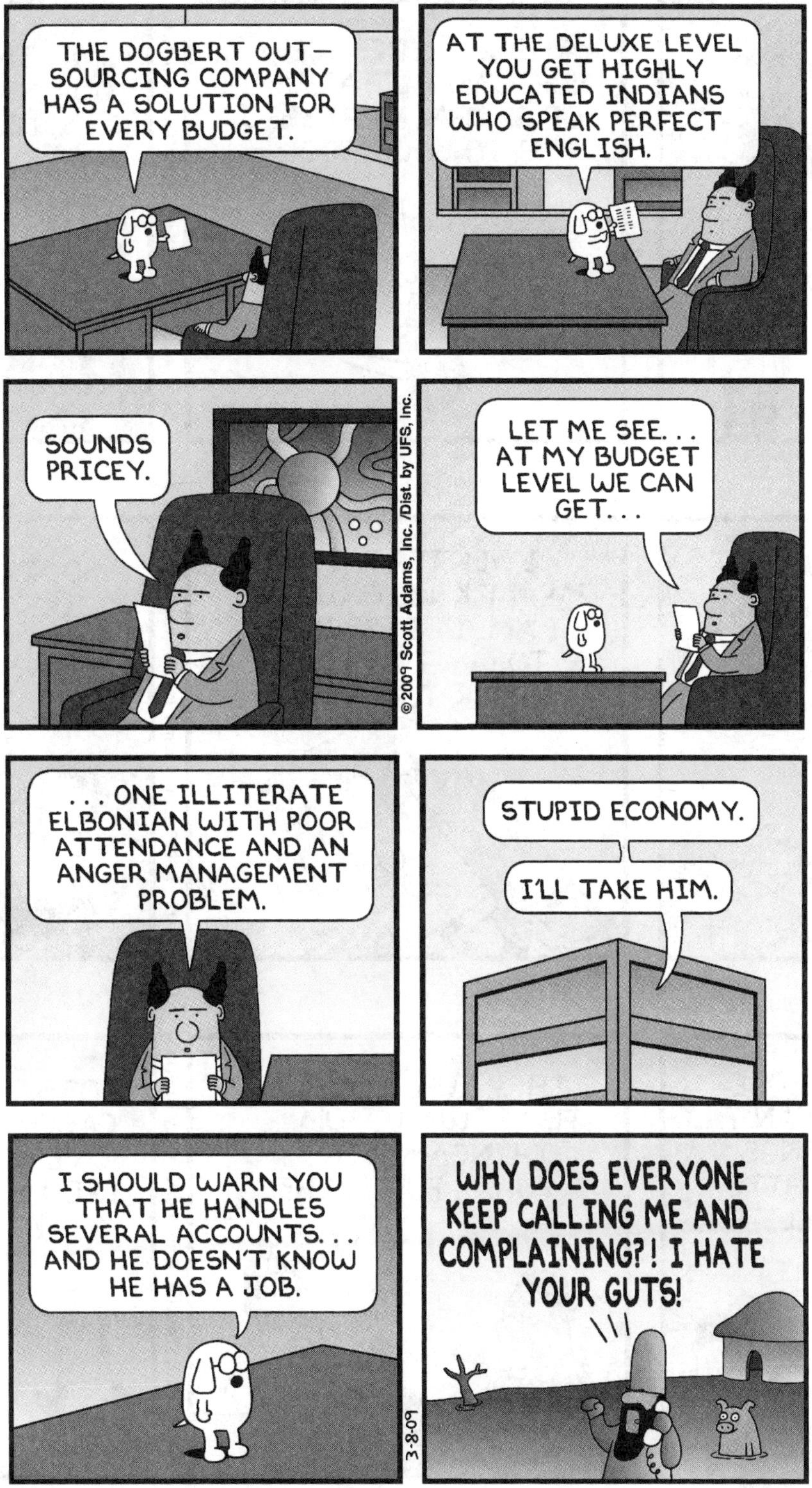
THE DOGBERT OUT-SOURCING COMPANY HAS A SOLUTION FOR EVERY BUDGET.
AT THE DELUXE LEVEL YOU GET HIGHLY EDUCATED INDIANS WHO SPEAK PERFECT ENGLISH.
SOUNDS PRICEY.
©2009 Scott Adams, Inc./Dist. by UFS, Inc.
LET ME SEE... AT MY BUDGET LEVEL WE CAN GET...
...ONE ILLITERATE ELBONIAN WITH POOR ATTENDANCE AND AN ANGER MANAGEMENT PROBLEM.
STUPID ECONOMY.
I'LL TAKE HIM.
I SHOULD WARN YOU THAT HE HANDLES SEVERAL ACCOUNTS... AND HE DOESN'T KNOW HE HAS A JOB.
3-8-09
WHY DOES EVERYONE KEEP CALLING ME AND COMPLAINING?! I HATE YOUR GUTS!

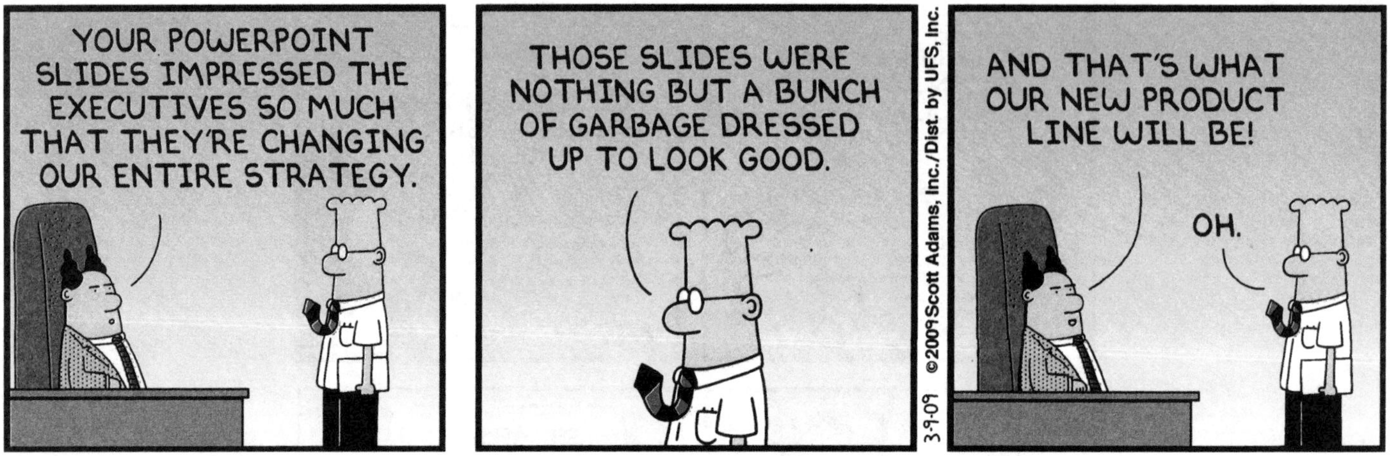
YOUR POWERPOINT SLIDES IMPRESSED THE EXECUTIVES SO MUCH THAT THEY'RE CHANGING OUR ENTIRE STRATEGY.
THOSE SLIDES WERE NOTHING BUT A BUNCH OF GARBAGE DRESSED UP TO LOOK GOOD.
3-9-09 ©2009 Scott Adams, Inc./Dist. by UFS, Inc.
AND THAT'S WHAT OUR NEW PRODUCT LINE WILL BE!
OH.

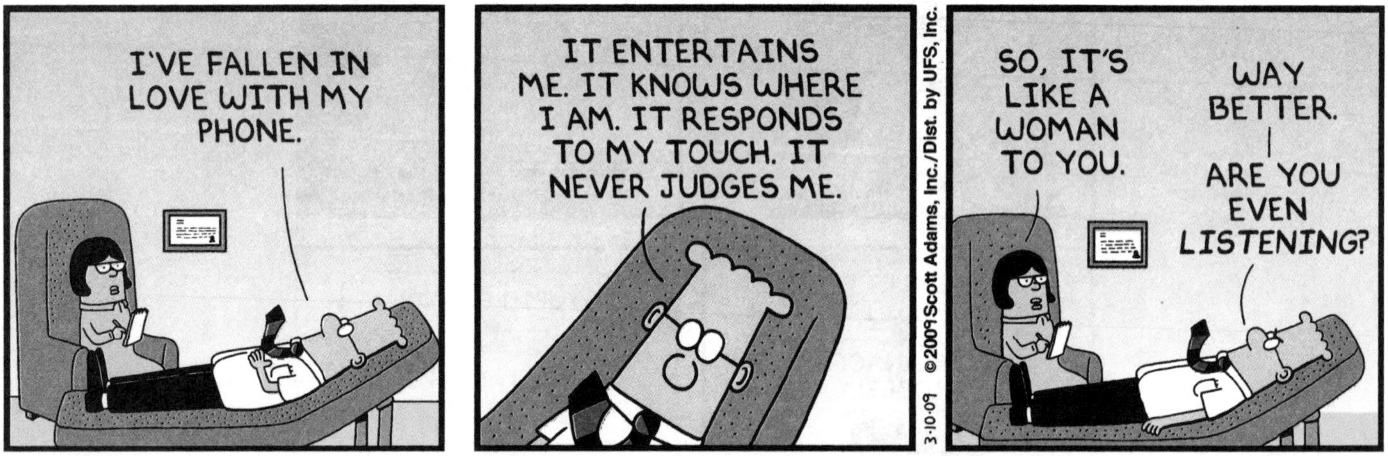
I'VE FALLEN IN LOVE WITH MY PHONE.
IT ENTERTAINS ME. IT KNOWS WHERE I AM. IT RESPONDS TO MY TOUCH. IT NEVER JUDGES ME.
3-10-09 ©2009 Scott Adams, Inc./Dist. by UFS, Inc.
SO, IT'S LIKE A WOMAN TO YOU.
WAY BETTER.
ARE YOU EVEN *LISTENING*?

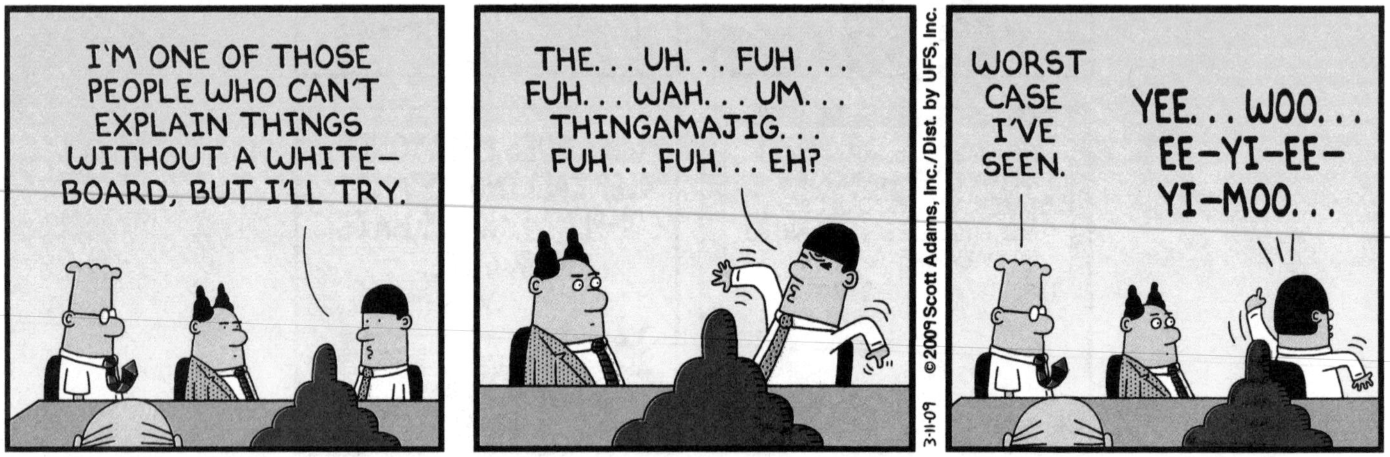
I'M ONE OF THOSE PEOPLE WHO CAN'T EXPLAIN THINGS WITHOUT A WHITE-BOARD, BUT I'LL TRY.
THE... UH... FUH... FUH... WAH... UM... THINGAMAJIG... FUH... FUH... EH?
3-11-09 ©2009 Scott Adams, Inc./Dist. by UFS, Inc.
WORST CASE I'VE SEEN.
YEE... WOO... EE-YI-EE-YI-MOO...

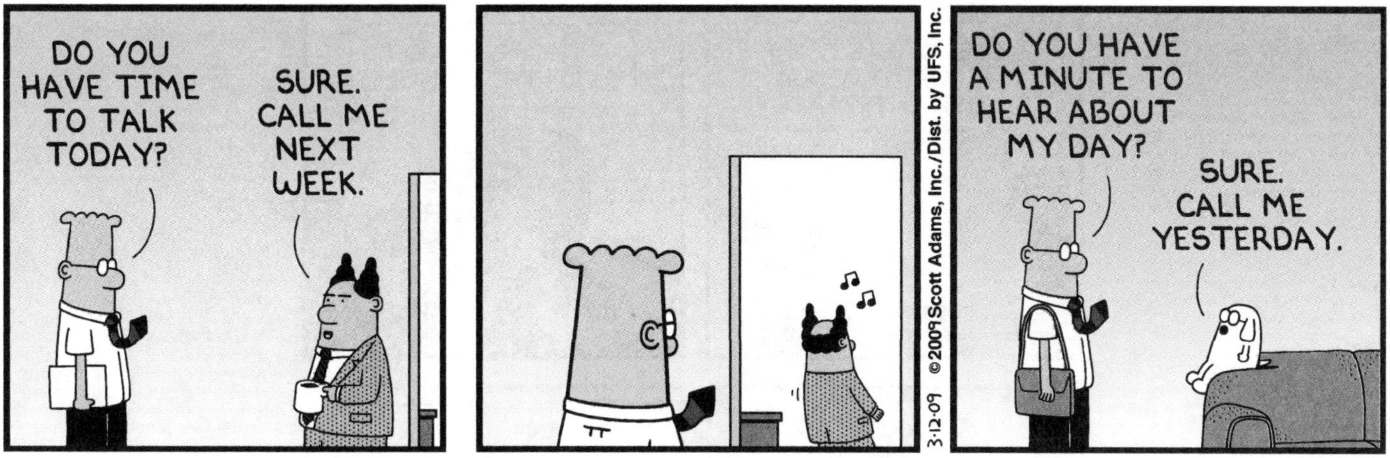
DO YOU HAVE TIME TO TALK TODAY?
SURE. CALL ME NEXT WEEK.
DO YOU HAVE A MINUTE TO HEAR ABOUT MY DAY?
SURE. CALL ME YESTERDAY.
3-12-09 ©2009 Scott Adams, Inc./Dist. by UFS, Inc.

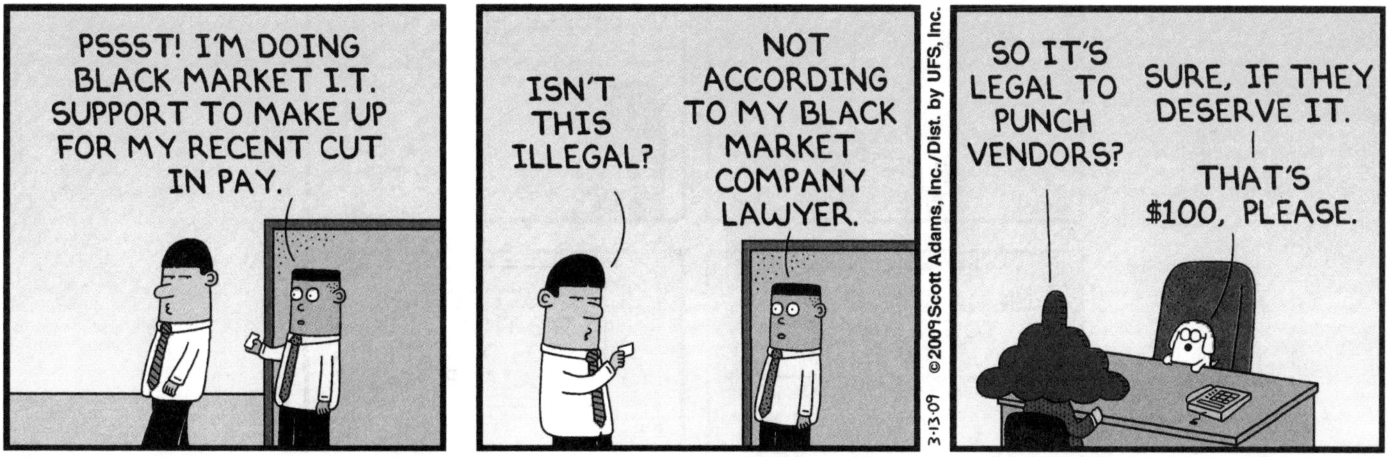
PSSST! I'M DOING BLACK MARKET I.T. SUPPORT TO MAKE UP FOR MY RECENT CUT IN PAY.
ISN'T THIS ILLEGAL?
NOT ACCORDING TO MY BLACK MARKET COMPANY LAWYER.
SO IT'S LEGAL TO PUNCH VENDORS?
SURE, IF THEY DESERVE IT.
THAT'S $100, PLEASE.
3-13-09 ©2009 Scott Adams, Inc./Dist. by UFS, Inc.

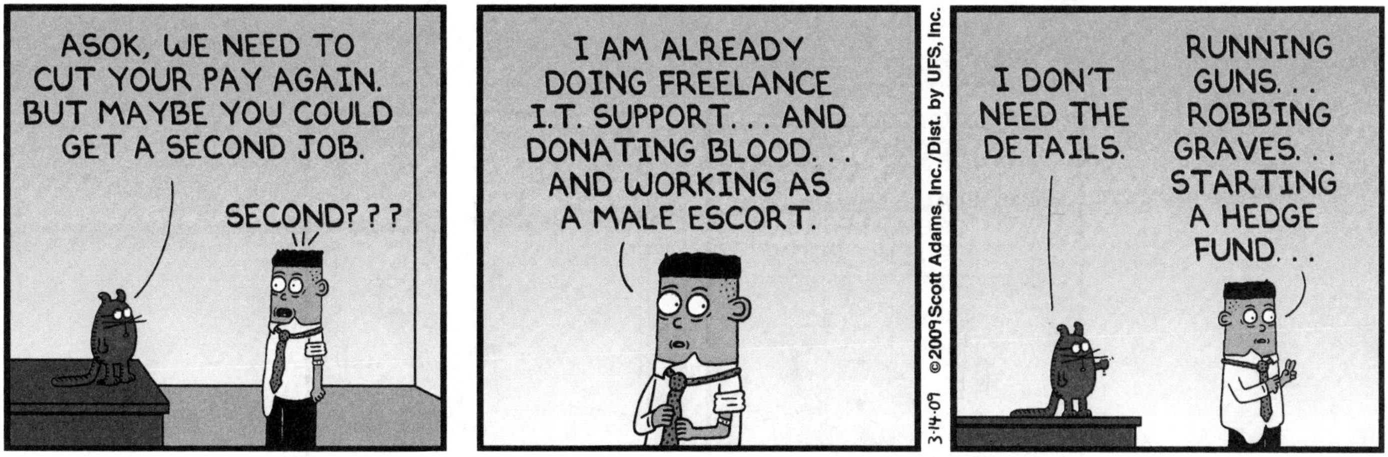
ASOK, WE NEED TO CUT YOUR PAY AGAIN. BUT MAYBE YOU COULD GET A SECOND JOB.
SECOND???
I AM ALREADY DOING FREELANCE I.T. SUPPORT... AND DONATING BLOOD... AND WORKING AS A MALE ESCORT.
I DON'T NEED THE DETAILS.
RUNNING GUNS... ROBBING GRAVES... STARTING A HEDGE FUND...
3-14-09 ©2009 Scott Adams, Inc./Dist. by UFS, Inc.

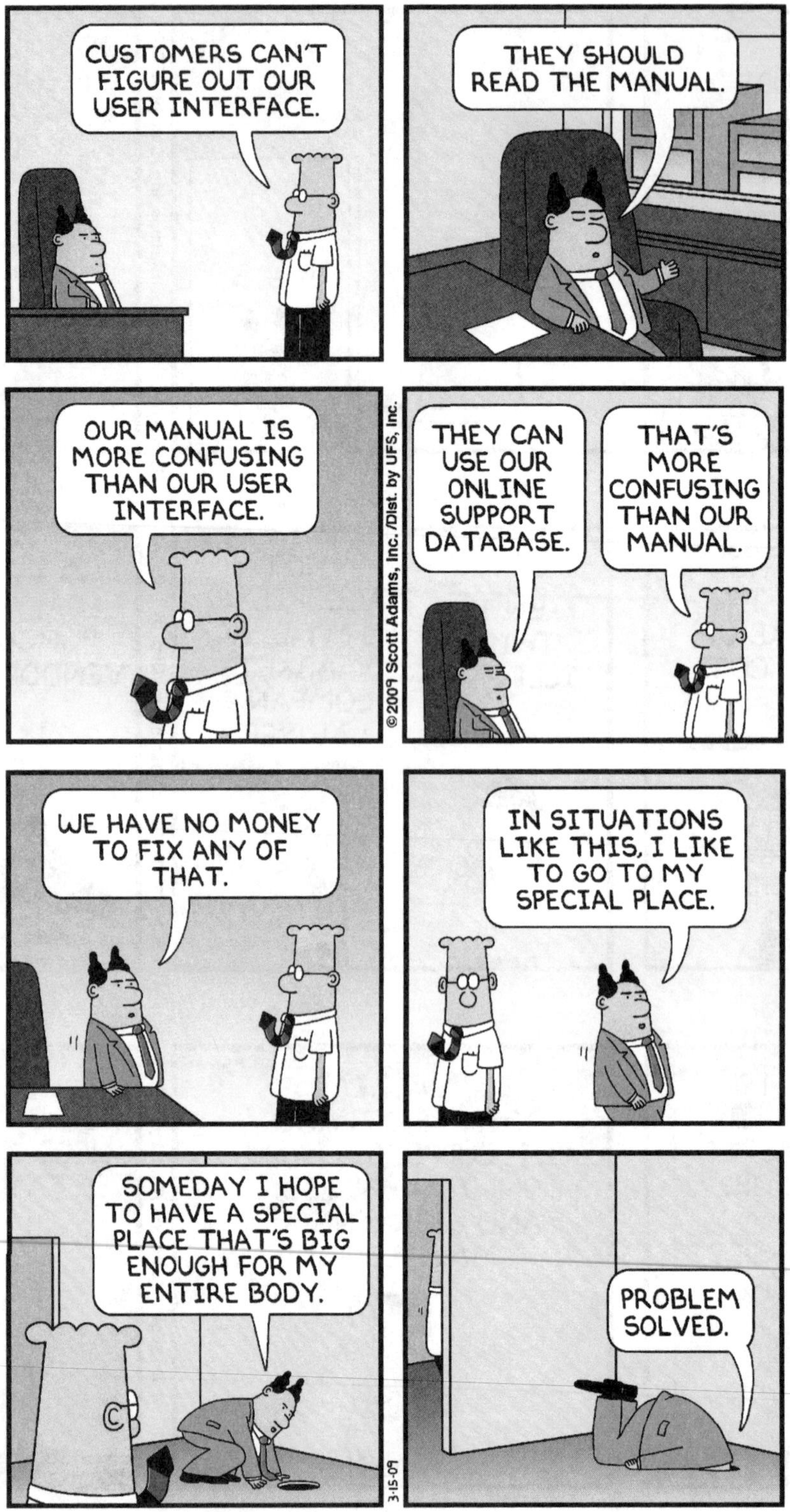
CUSTOMERS CAN'T FIGURE OUT OUR USER INTERFACE.
THEY SHOULD READ THE MANUAL.
OUR MANUAL IS MORE CONFUSING THAN OUR USER INTERFACE.
THEY CAN USE OUR ONLINE SUPPORT DATABASE.
THAT'S MORE CONFUSING THAN OUR MANUAL.
WE HAVE NO MONEY TO FIX ANY OF THAT.
IN SITUATIONS LIKE THIS, I LIKE TO GO TO MY SPECIAL PLACE.
SOMEDAY I HOPE TO HAVE A SPECIAL PLACE THAT'S BIG ENOUGH FOR MY ENTIRE BODY.
PROBLEM SOLVED.
©2009 Scott Adams, Inc./Dist. by UFS, Inc.
3-15-09

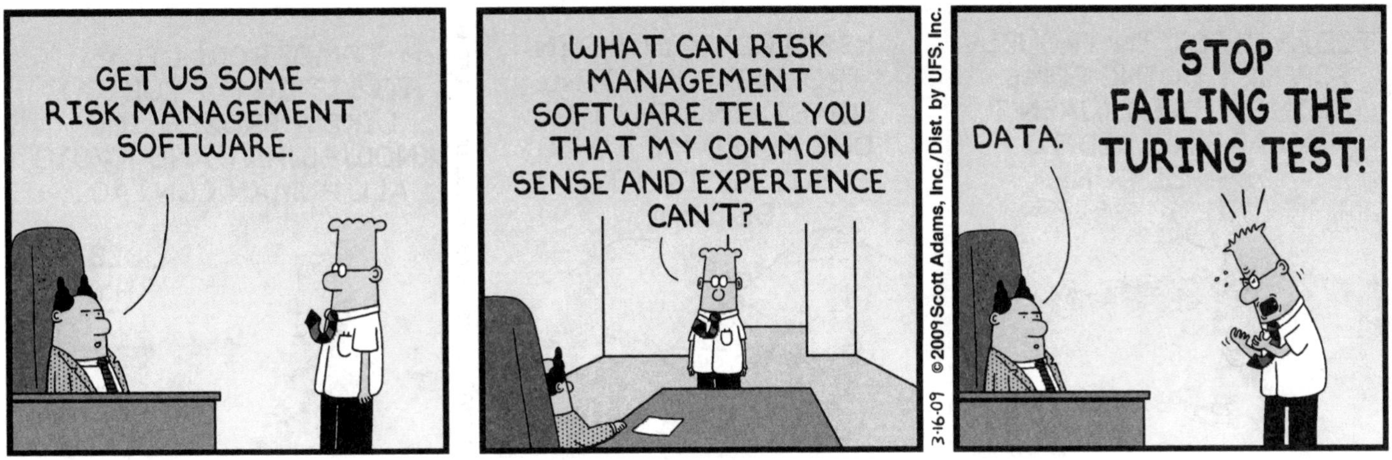
GET US SOME RISK MANAGEMENT SOFTWARE.
WHAT CAN RISK MANAGEMENT SOFTWARE TELL YOU THAT MY COMMON SENSE AND EXPERIENCE CAN'T?
DATA.
STOP FAILING THE TURING TEST!
3-16-09 ©2009 Scott Adams, Inc./Dist. by UFS, Inc.

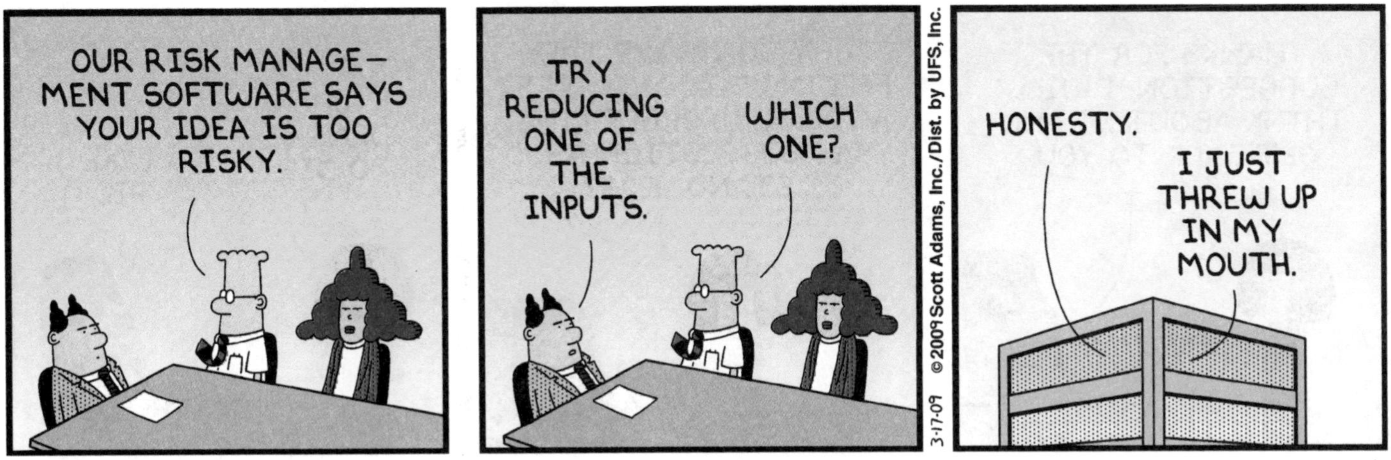
OUR RISK MANAGE— MENT SOFTWARE SAYS YOUR IDEA IS TOO RISKY.
TRY REDUCING ONE OF THE INPUTS.
WHICH ONE?
HONESTY.
I JUST THREW UP IN MY MOUTH.
3-17-09 ©2009 Scott Adams, Inc./Dist. by UFS, Inc.

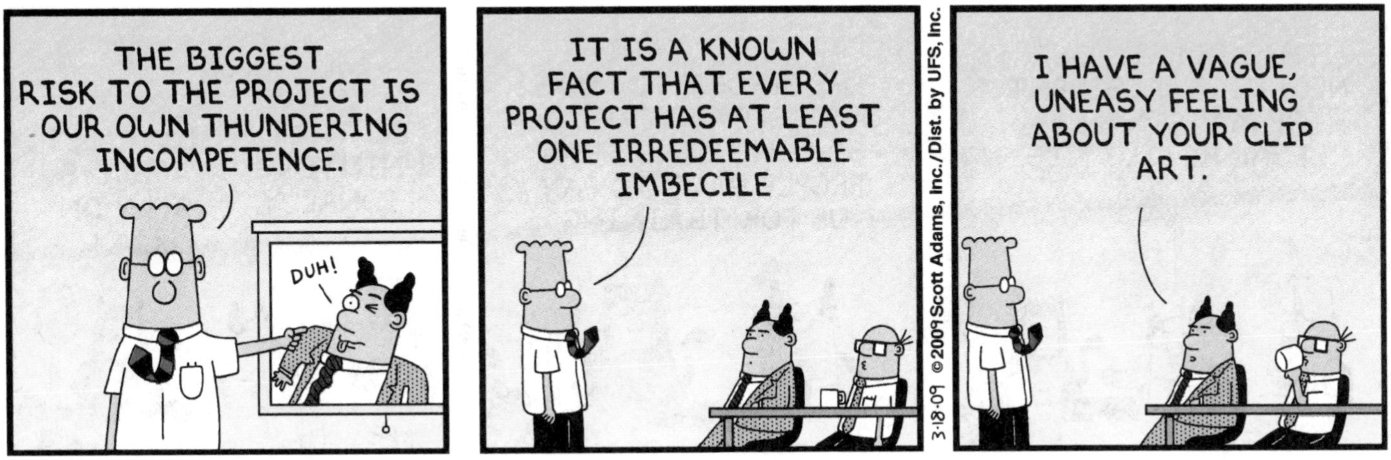
THE BIGGEST RISK TO THE PROJECT IS OUR OWN THUNDERING INCOMPETENCE.
DUH!
IT IS A KNOWN FACT THAT EVERY PROJECT HAS AT LEAST ONE IRREDEEMABLE IMBECILE
I HAVE A VAGUE, UNEASY FEELING ABOUT YOUR CLIP ART.
3-18-09 ©2009 Scott Adams, Inc./Dist. by UFS, Inc.

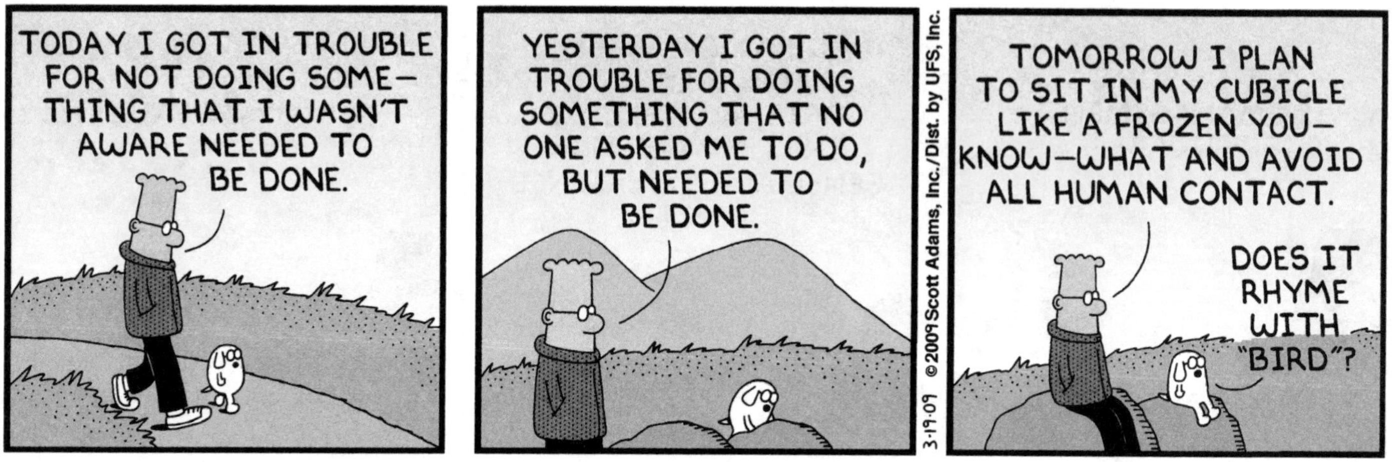
TODAY I GOT IN TROUBLE FOR NOT DOING SOME-THING THAT I WASN'T AWARE NEEDED TO BE DONE.
YESTERDAY I GOT IN TROUBLE FOR DOING SOMETHING THAT NO ONE ASKED ME TO DO, BUT NEEDED TO BE DONE.
TOMORROW I PLAN TO SIT IN MY CUBICLE LIKE A FROZEN YOU-KNOW-WHAT AND AVOID ALL HUMAN CONTACT.
DOES IT RHYME WITH "BIRD"?
3-19-09

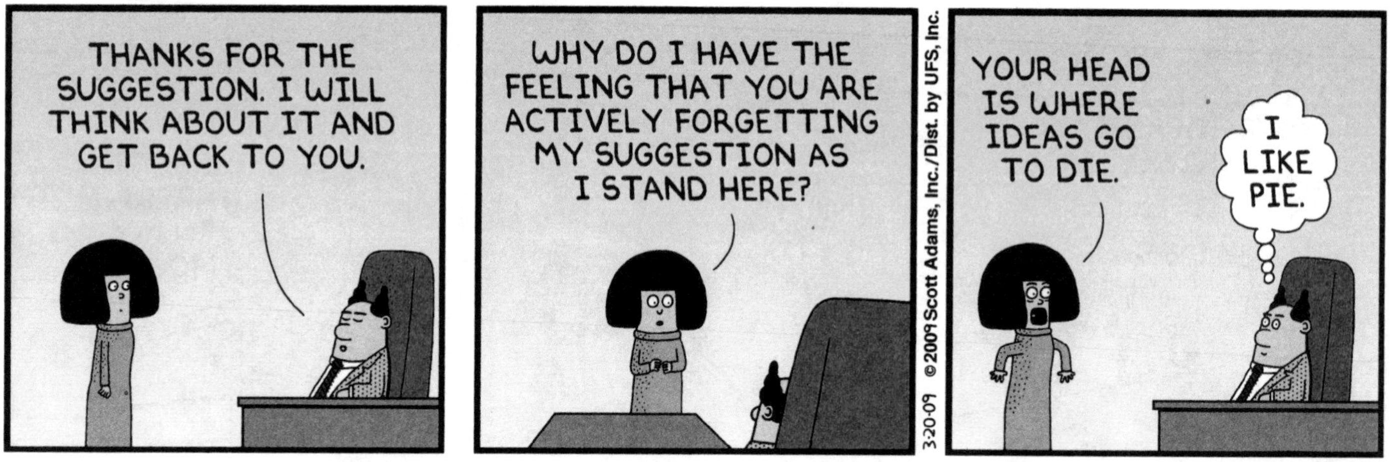
THANKS FOR THE SUGGESTION. I WILL THINK ABOUT IT AND GET BACK TO YOU.
WHY DO I HAVE THE FEELING THAT YOU ARE ACTIVELY FORGETTING MY SUGGESTION AS I STAND HERE?
YOUR HEAD IS WHERE IDEAS GO TO DIE.
I LIKE PIE.
3-20-09

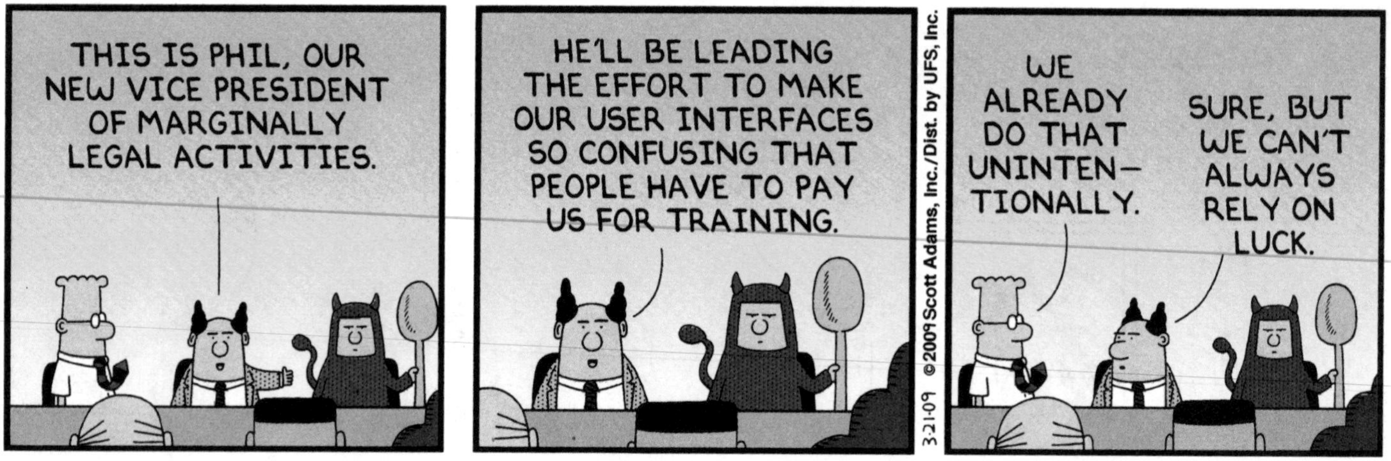
THIS IS PHIL, OUR NEW VICE PRESIDENT OF MARGINALLY LEGAL ACTIVITIES.
HE'LL BE LEADING THE EFFORT TO MAKE OUR USER INTERFACES SO CONFUSING THAT PEOPLE HAVE TO PAY US FOR TRAINING.
WE ALREADY DO THAT UNINTEN-TIONALLY.
SURE, BUT WE CAN'T ALWAYS RELY ON LUCK.
3-21-09

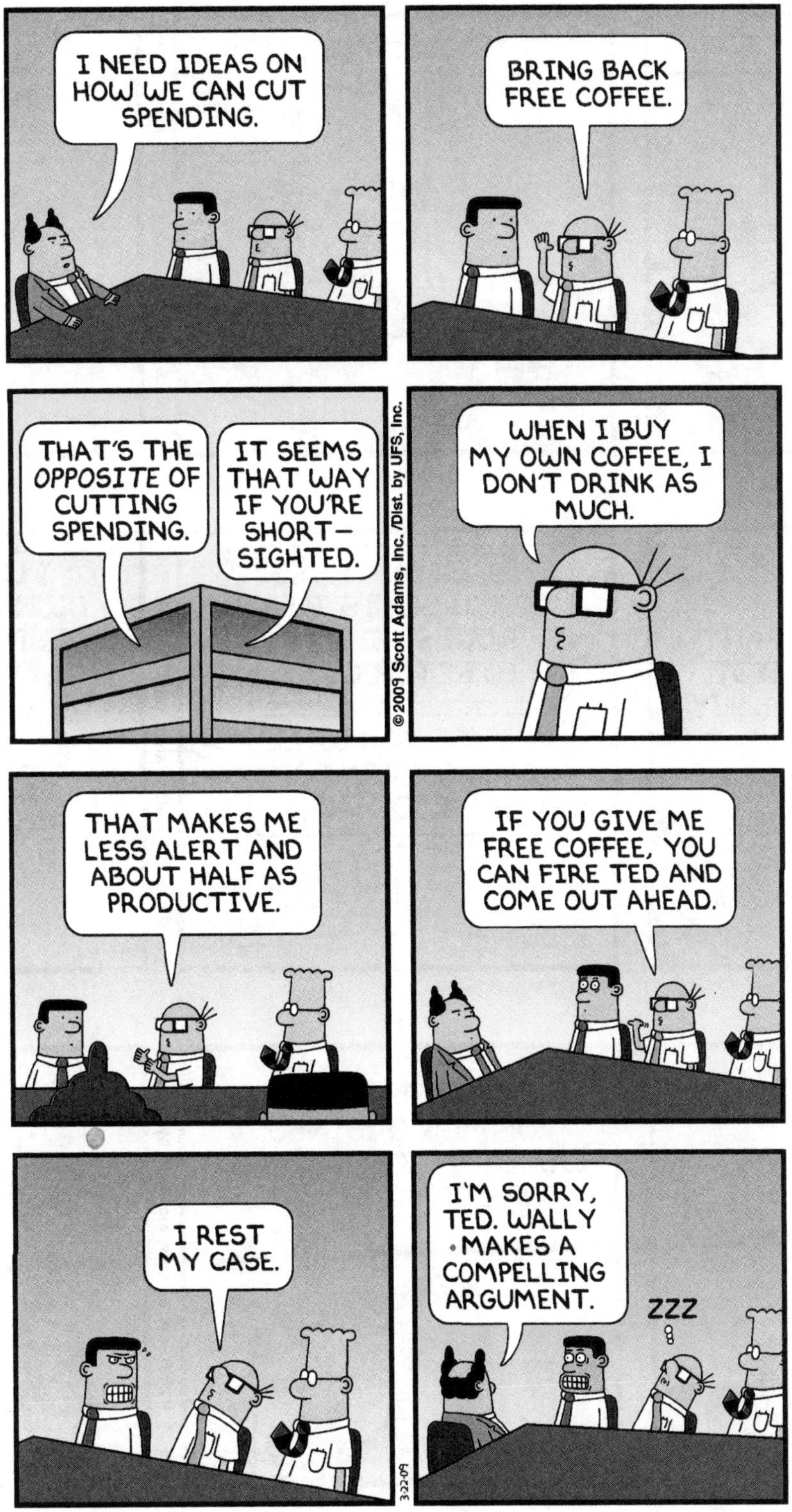
I NEED IDEAS ON HOW WE CAN CUT SPENDING.
BRING BACK FREE COFFEE.
THAT'S THE *OPPOSITE* OF CUTTING SPENDING.
IT SEEMS THAT WAY IF YOU'RE SHORT-SIGHTED.
©2009 Scott Adams, Inc./Dist. by UFS, Inc.
WHEN I BUY MY OWN COFFEE, I DON'T DRINK AS MUCH.
THAT MAKES ME LESS ALERT AND ABOUT HALF AS PRODUCTIVE.
IF YOU GIVE ME FREE COFFEE, YOU CAN FIRE TED AND COME OUT AHEAD.
I REST MY CASE.
I'M SORRY, TED. WALLY MAKES A COMPELLING ARGUMENT.
ZZZ
3-22-09

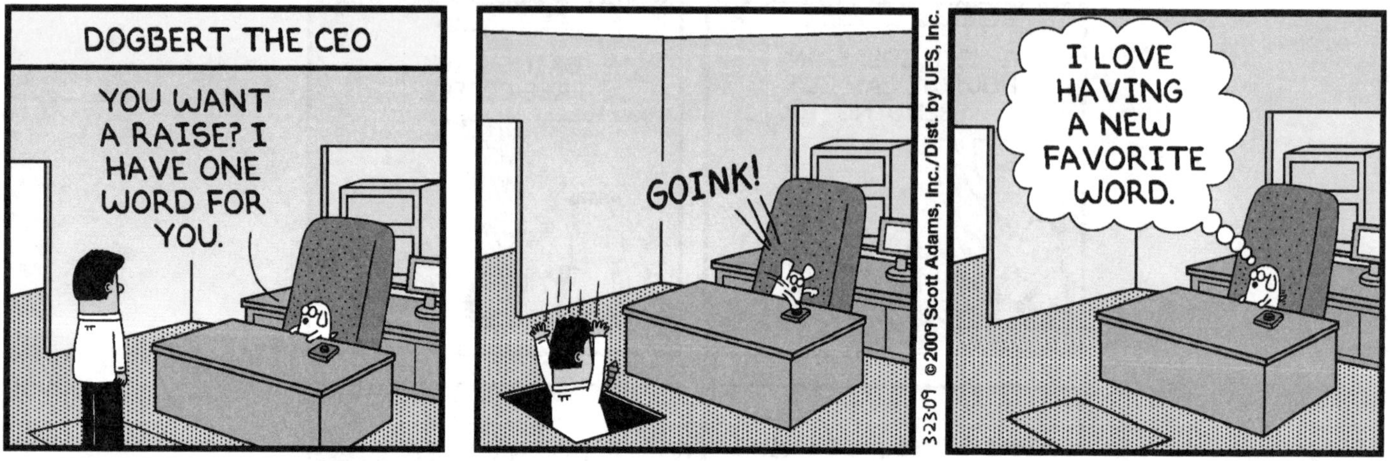
DOGBERT THE CEO
YOU WANT A RAISE? I HAVE ONE WORD FOR YOU.
GOINK!
3-23-09 ©2009 Scott Adams, Inc./Dist. by UFS, Inc.
I LOVE HAVING A NEW FAVORITE WORD.

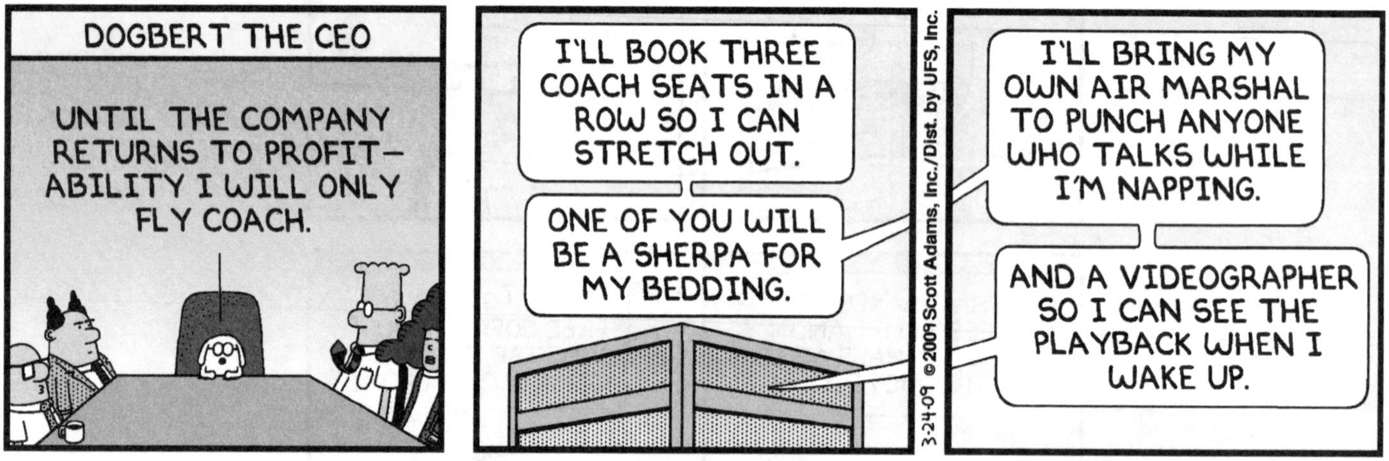
DOGBERT THE CEO
UNTIL THE COMPANY RETURNS TO PROFIT-ABILITY I WILL ONLY FLY COACH.
I'LL BOOK THREE COACH SEATS IN A ROW SO I CAN STRETCH OUT.
ONE OF YOU WILL BE A SHERPA FOR MY BEDDING.
3-24-09 ©2009 Scott Adams, Inc./Dist. by UFS, Inc.
I'LL BRING MY OWN AIR MARSHAL TO PUNCH ANYONE WHO TALKS WHILE I'M NAPPING.
AND A VIDEOGRAPHER SO I CAN SEE THE PLAYBACK WHEN I WAKE UP.

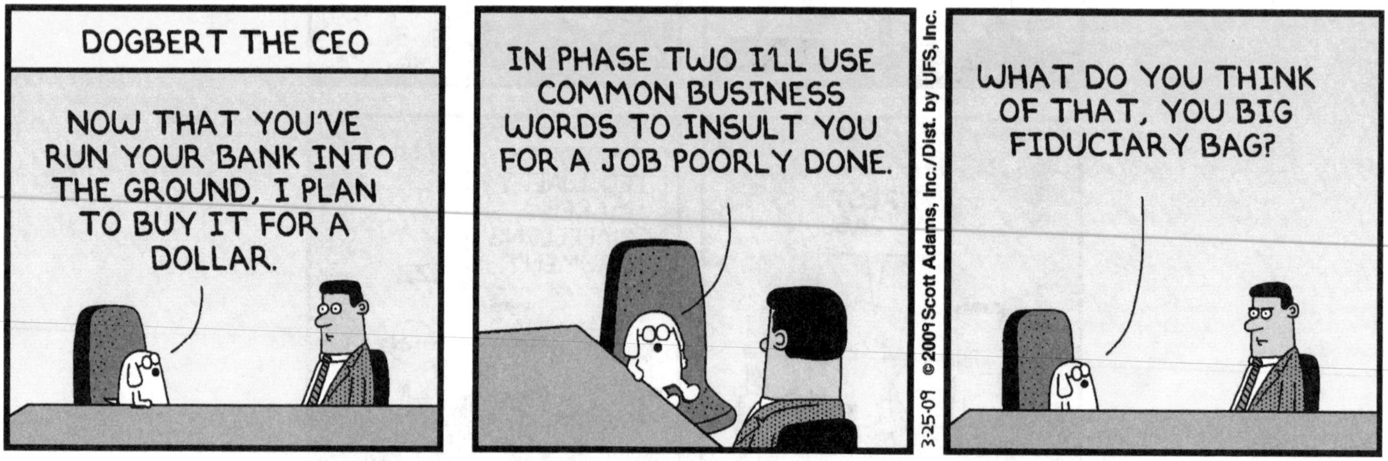
DOGBERT THE CEO
NOW THAT YOU'VE RUN YOUR BANK INTO THE GROUND, I PLAN TO BUY IT FOR A DOLLAR.
IN PHASE TWO I'LL USE COMMON BUSINESS WORDS TO INSULT YOU FOR A JOB POORLY DONE.
3-25-09 ©2009 Scott Adams, Inc./Dist. by UFS, Inc.
WHAT DO YOU THINK OF THAT, YOU BIG FIDUCIARY BAG?

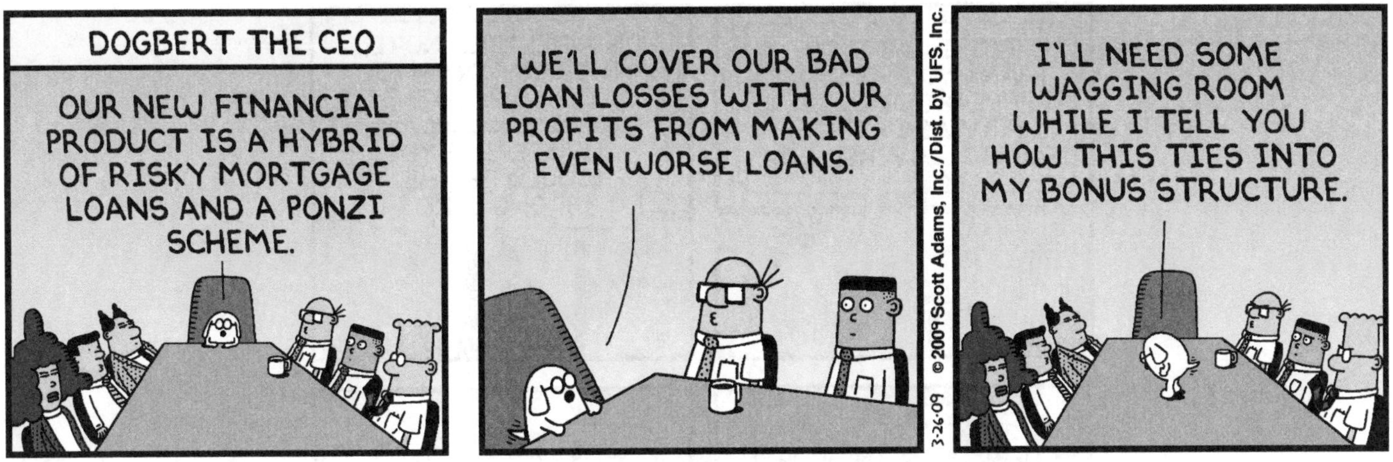
DOGBERT THE CEO
OUR NEW FINANCIAL PRODUCT IS A HYBRID OF RISKY MORTGAGE LOANS AND A PONZI SCHEME.
WE'LL COVER OUR BAD LOAN LOSSES WITH OUR PROFITS FROM MAKING EVEN WORSE LOANS.
I'LL NEED SOME WAGGING ROOM WHILE I TELL YOU HOW THIS TIES INTO MY BONUS STRUCTURE.
3-26-09 © 2009 Scott Adams, Inc./Dist. by UFS, Inc.

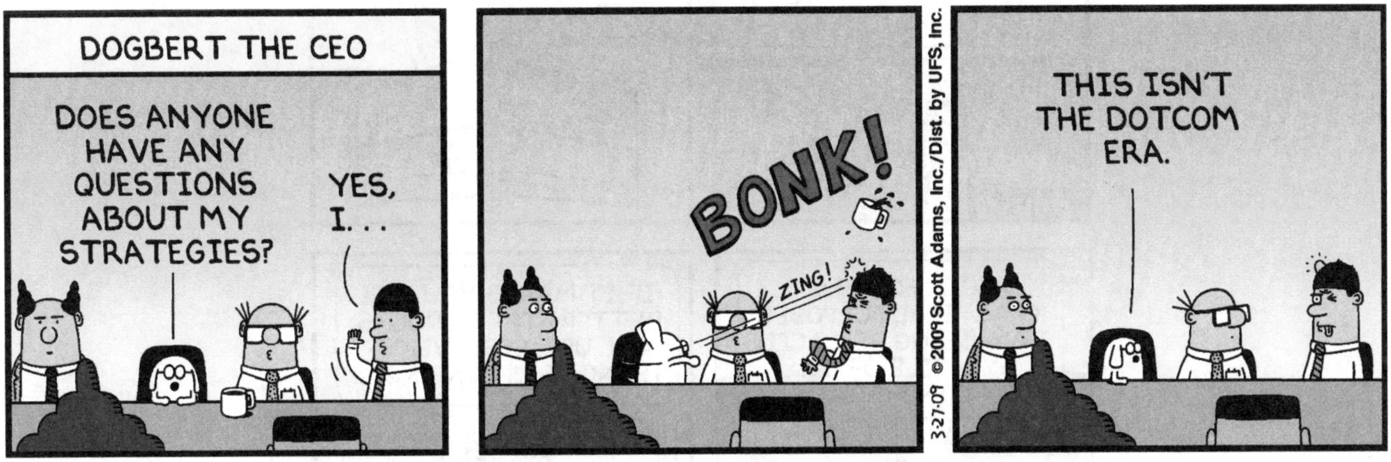
DOGBERT THE CEO
DOES ANYONE HAVE ANY QUESTIONS ABOUT MY STRATEGIES?
YES, I. . .
BONK!
ZING!
THIS ISN'T THE DOTCOM ERA.
3-27-09 © 2009 Scott Adams, Inc./Dist. by UFS, Inc.

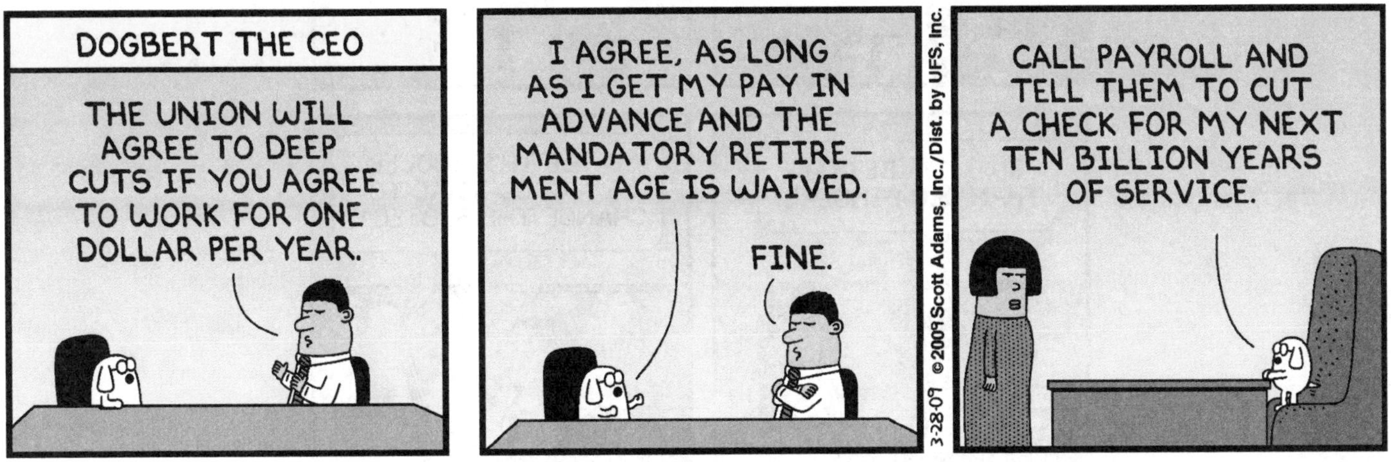
DOGBERT THE CEO
THE UNION WILL AGREE TO DEEP CUTS IF YOU AGREE TO WORK FOR ONE DOLLAR PER YEAR.
I AGREE, AS LONG AS I GET MY PAY IN ADVANCE AND THE MANDATORY RETIRE-MENT AGE IS WAIVED.
FINE.
CALL PAYROLL AND TELL THEM TO CUT A CHECK FOR MY NEXT TEN BILLION YEARS OF SERVICE.
3-28-09 © 2009 Scott Adams, Inc./Dist. by UFS, Inc.

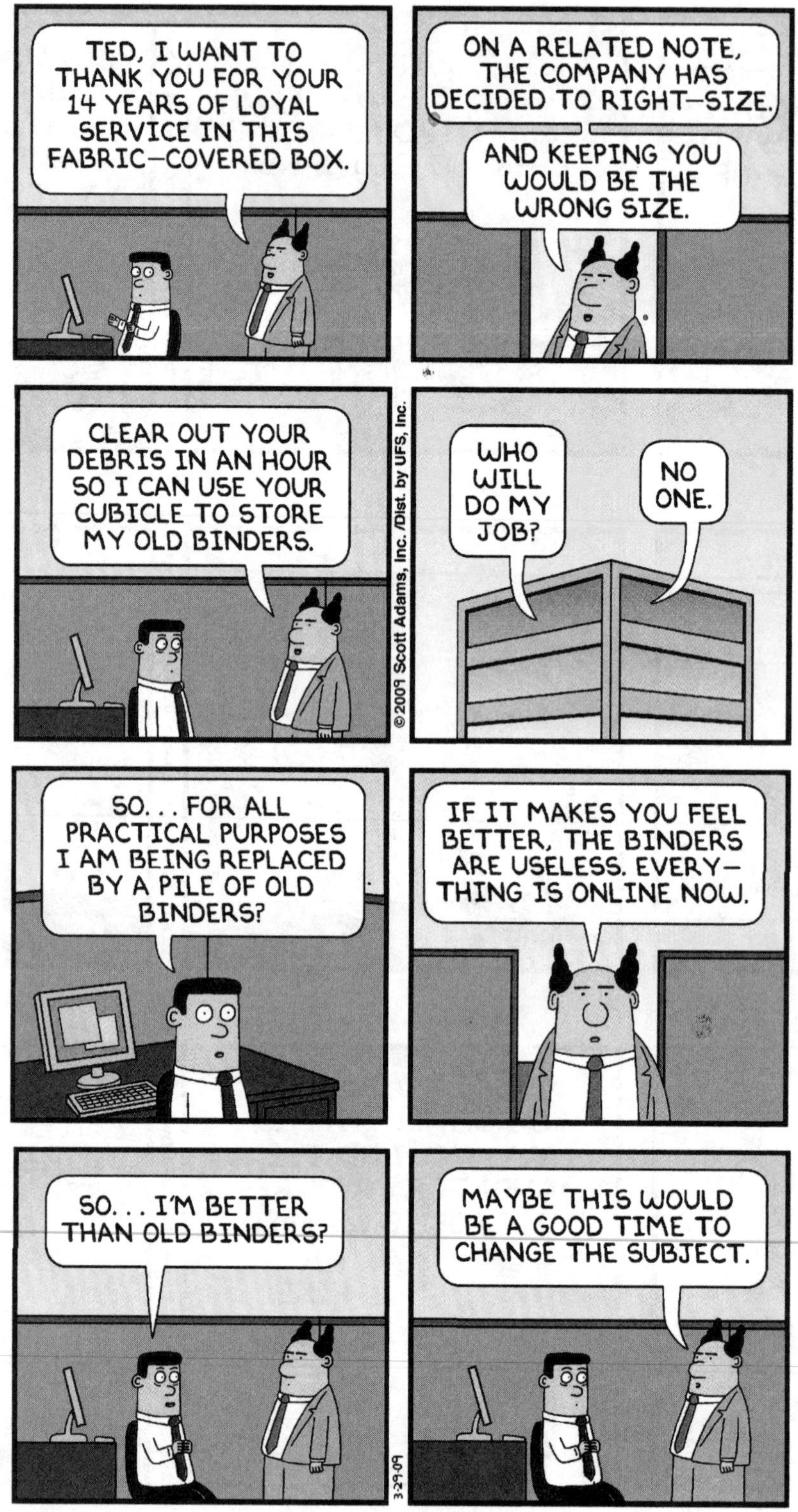
TED, I WANT TO THANK YOU FOR YOUR 14 YEARS OF LOYAL SERVICE IN THIS FABRIC-COVERED BOX.
ON A RELATED NOTE, THE COMPANY HAS DECIDED TO RIGHT-SIZE.
AND KEEPING YOU WOULD BE THE WRONG SIZE.
CLEAR OUT YOUR DEBRIS IN AN HOUR SO I CAN USE YOUR CUBICLE TO STORE MY OLD BINDERS.
WHO WILL DO MY JOB?
NO ONE.
SO. . . FOR ALL PRACTICAL PURPOSES I AM BEING REPLACED BY A PILE OF OLD BINDERS?
IF IT MAKES YOU FEEL BETTER, THE BINDERS ARE USELESS. EVERY-THING IS ONLINE NOW.
SO. . . I'M BETTER THAN OLD BINDERS?
MAYBE THIS WOULD BE A GOOD TIME TO CHANGE THE SUBJECT.
© 2009 Scott Adams, Inc. /Dist. by UFS, Inc.
3-29-09

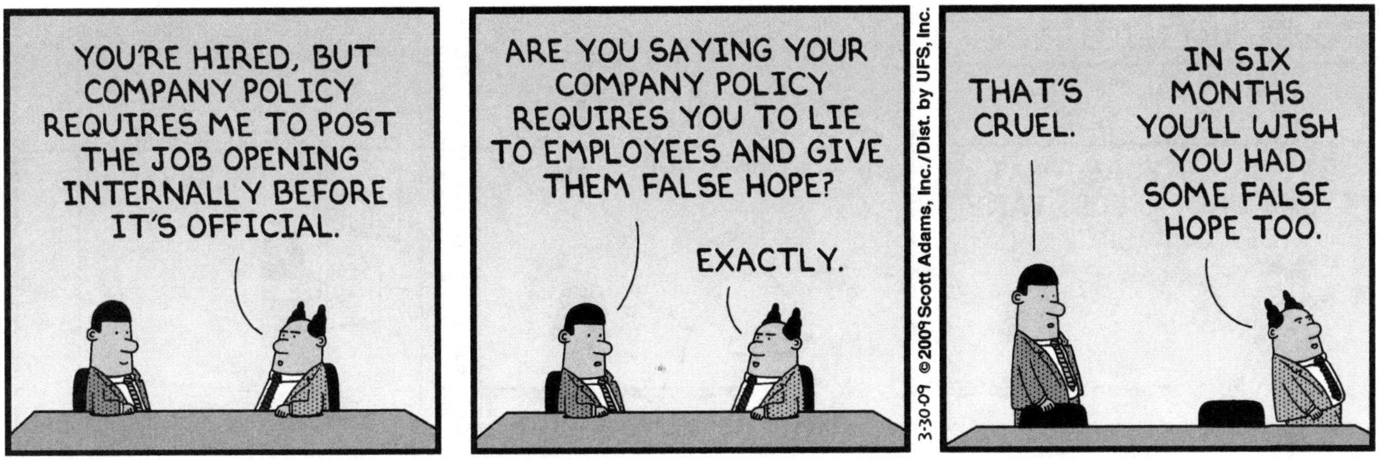
YOU'RE HIRED, BUT COMPANY POLICY REQUIRES ME TO POST THE JOB OPENING INTERNALLY BEFORE IT'S OFFICIAL.
ARE YOU SAYING YOUR COMPANY POLICY REQUIRES YOU TO LIE TO EMPLOYEES AND GIVE THEM FALSE HOPE?
EXACTLY.
3-30-09 © 2009 Scott Adams, Inc./Dist. by UFS, Inc.
THAT'S CRUEL.
IN SIX MONTHS YOU'LL WISH YOU HAD SOME FALSE HOPE TOO.

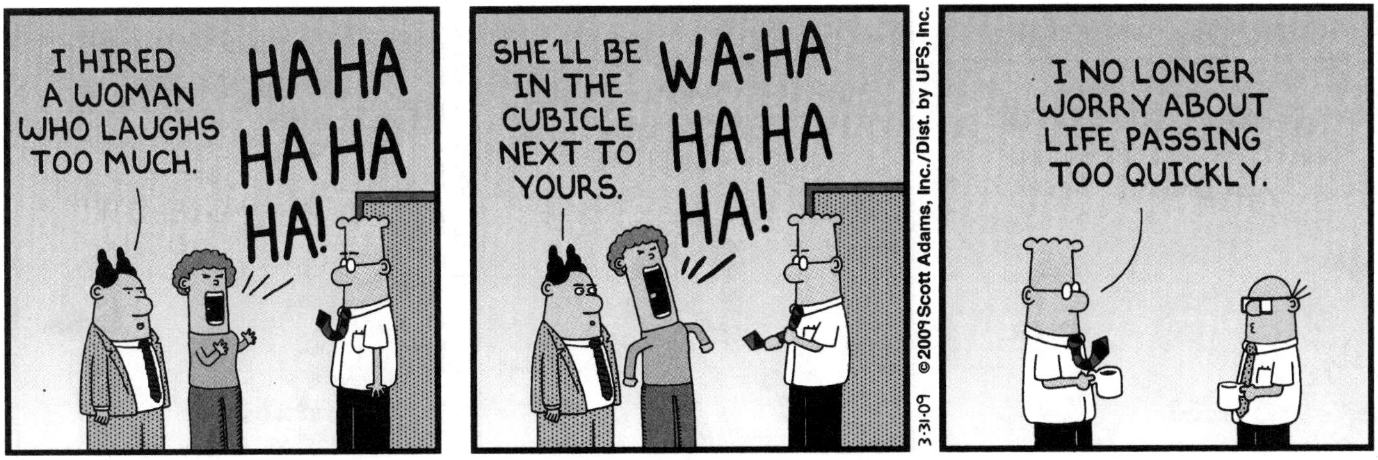
I HIRED A WOMAN WHO LAUGHS TOO MUCH.
HA HA HA HA HA!
SHE'LL BE IN THE CUBICLE NEXT TO YOURS.
WA-HA HA HA HA!
3-31-09 © 2009 Scott Adams, Inc./Dist. by UFS, Inc.
I NO LONGER WORRY ABOUT LIFE PASSING TOO QUICKLY.

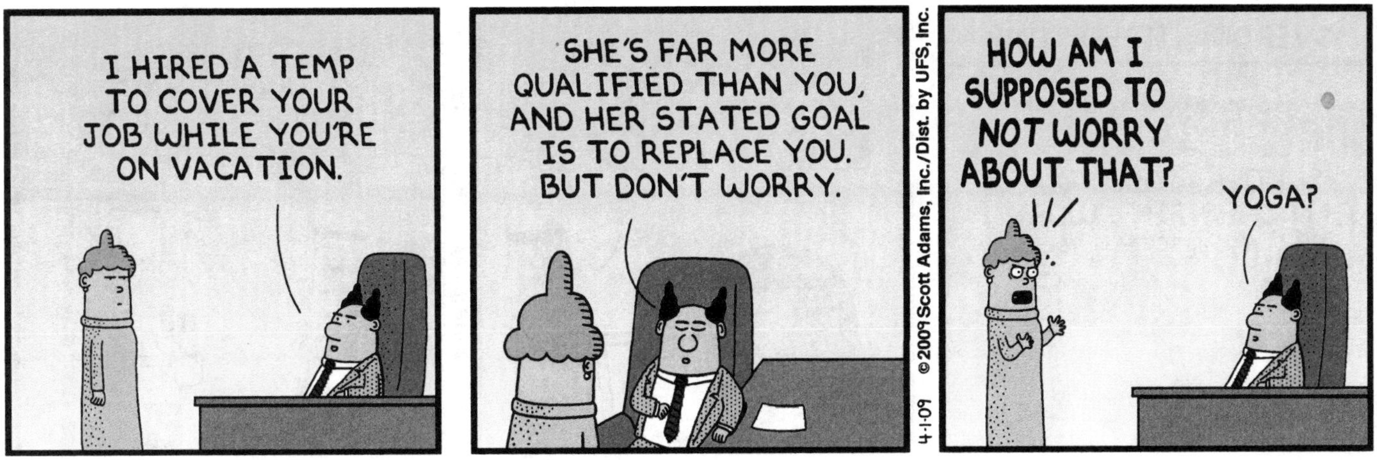
I HIRED A TEMP TO COVER YOUR JOB WHILE YOU'RE ON VACATION.
SHE'S FAR MORE QUALIFIED THAN YOU, AND HER STATED GOAL IS TO REPLACE YOU. BUT DON'T WORRY.
4-1-09 © 2009 Scott Adams, Inc./Dist. by UFS, Inc.
HOW AM I SUPPOSED TO NOT WORRY ABOUT THAT?
YOGA?

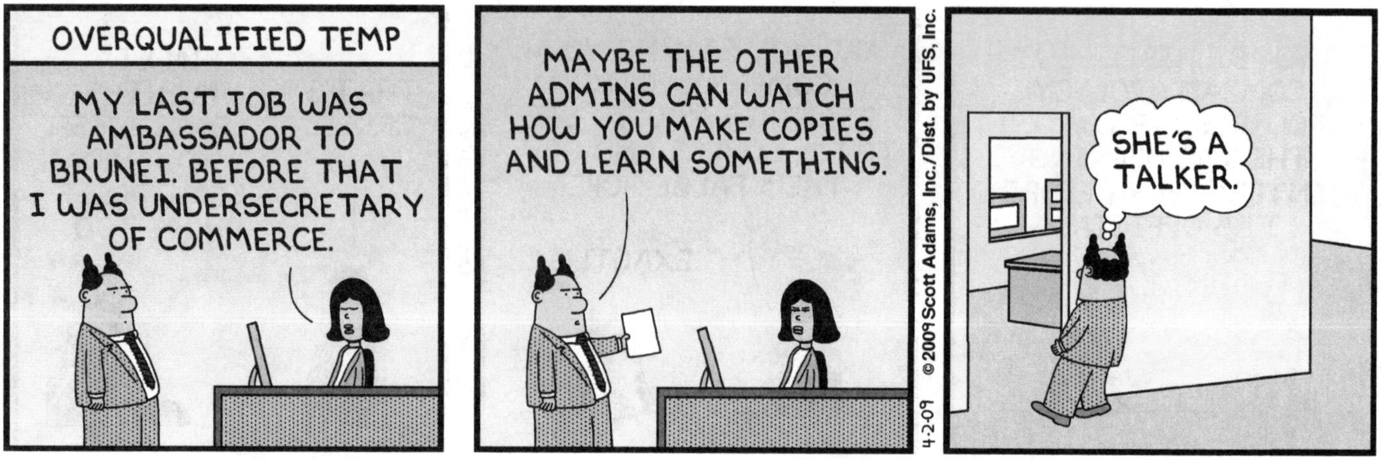
OVERQUALIFIED TEMP
MY LAST JOB WAS AMBASSADOR TO BRUNEI. BEFORE THAT I WAS UNDERSECRETARY OF COMMERCE.
MAYBE THE OTHER ADMINS CAN WATCH HOW YOU MAKE COPIES AND LEARN SOMETHING.
4-2-09 © 2009 Scott Adams, Inc./Dist. by UFS, Inc.
SHE'S A TALKER.

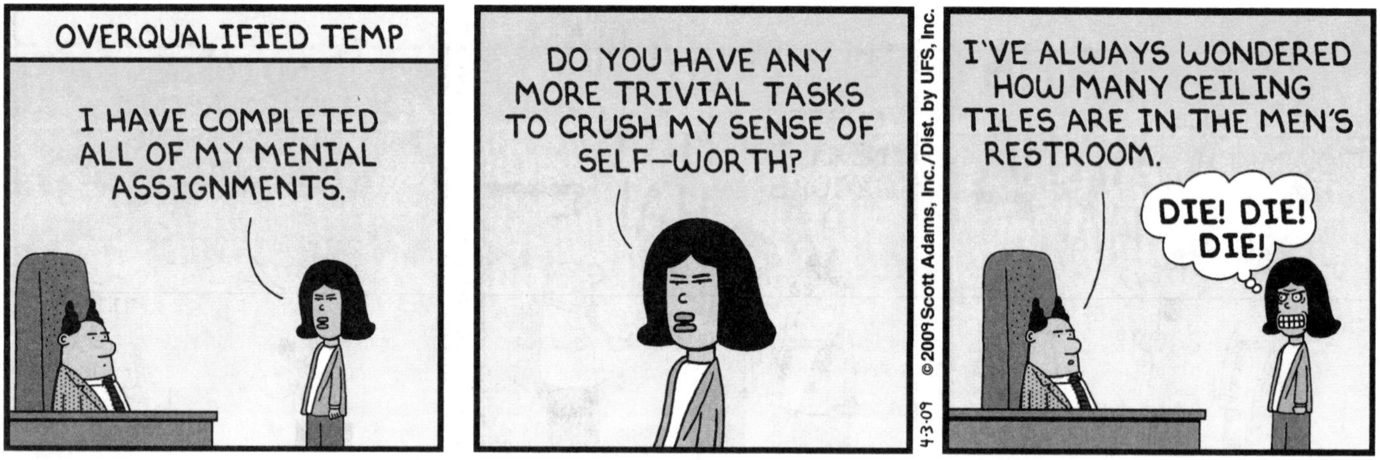
OVERQUALIFIED TEMP
I HAVE COMPLETED ALL OF MY MENIAL ASSIGNMENTS.
DO YOU HAVE ANY MORE TRIVIAL TASKS TO CRUSH MY SENSE OF SELF-WORTH?
4-3-09 © 2009 Scott Adams, Inc./Dist. by UFS, Inc.
I'VE ALWAYS WONDERED HOW MANY CEILING TILES ARE IN THE MEN'S RESTROOM.
DIE! DIE! DIE!

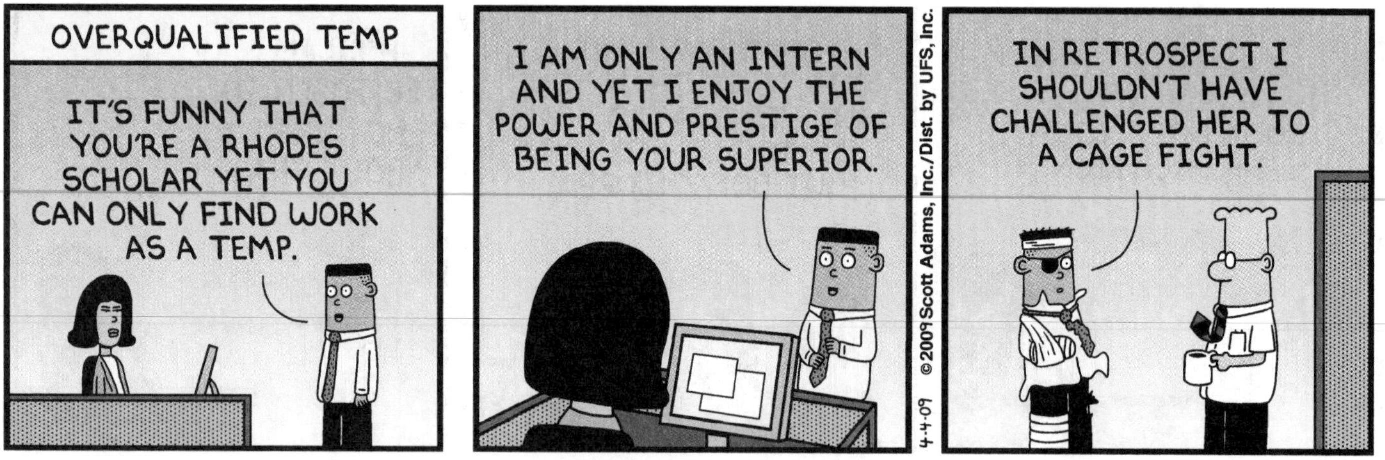
OVERQUALIFIED TEMP
IT'S FUNNY THAT YOU'RE A RHODES SCHOLAR YET YOU CAN ONLY FIND WORK AS A TEMP.
I AM ONLY AN INTERN AND YET I ENJOY THE POWER AND PRESTIGE OF BEING YOUR SUPERIOR.
4-4-09 © 2009 Scott Adams, Inc./Dist. by UFS, Inc.
IN RETROSPECT I SHOULDN'T HAVE CHALLENGED HER TO A CAGE FIGHT.

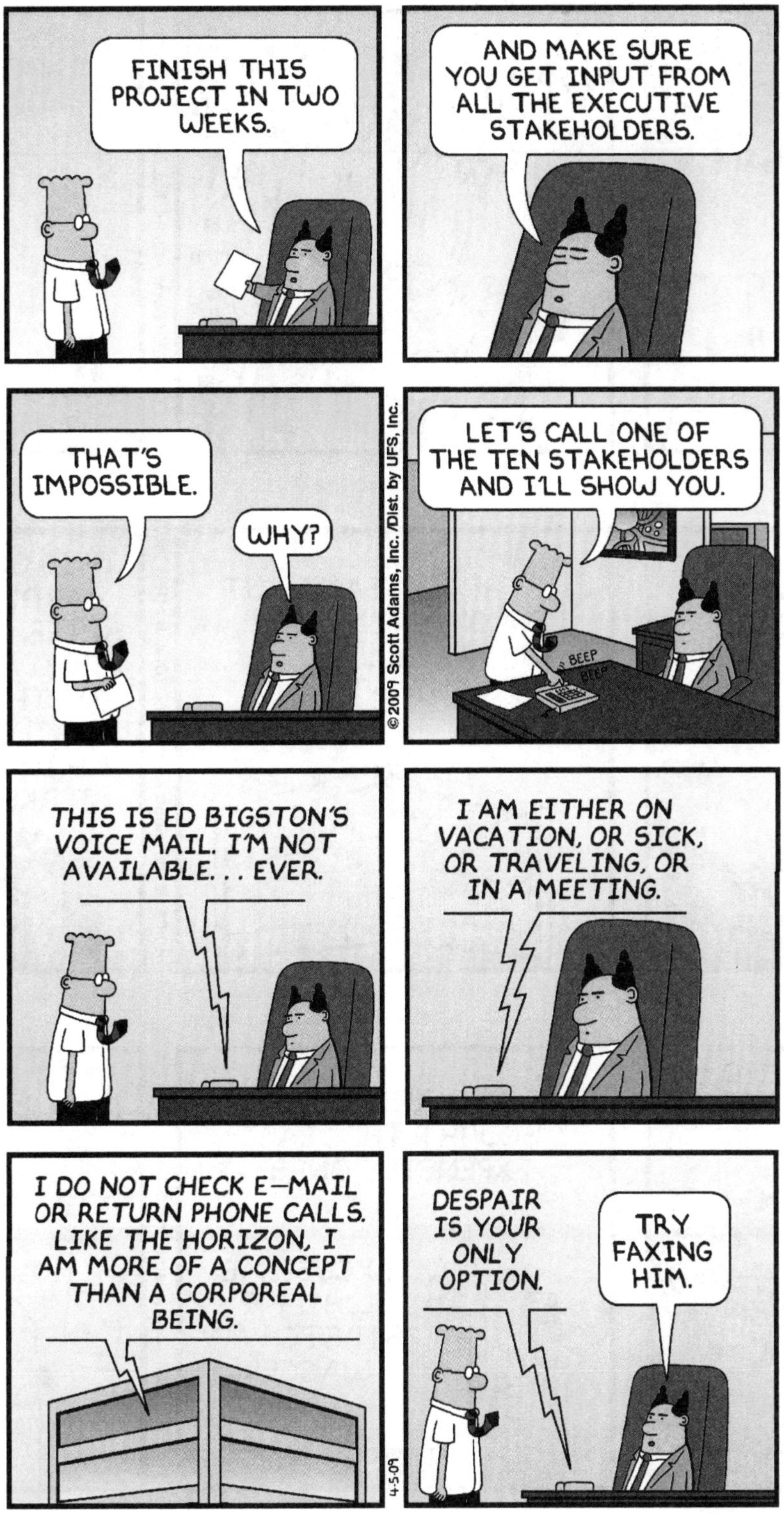
FINISH THIS PROJECT IN TWO WEEKS.
AND MAKE SURE YOU GET INPUT FROM ALL THE EXECUTIVE STAKEHOLDERS.
THAT'S IMPOSSIBLE.
WHY?
©2009 Scott Adams, Inc./Dist. by UFS, Inc.
LET'S CALL ONE OF THE TEN STAKEHOLDERS AND I'LL SHOW YOU.
BEEP
BEEP
THIS IS ED BIGSTON'S VOICE MAIL. I'M NOT AVAILABLE. . . EVER.
I AM EITHER ON VACATION, OR SICK, OR TRAVELING, OR IN A MEETING.
I DO NOT CHECK E-MAIL OR RETURN PHONE CALLS. LIKE THE HORIZON, I AM MORE OF A CONCEPT THAN A CORPOREAL BEING.
4-5-09
DESPAIR IS YOUR ONLY OPTION.
TRY FAXING HIM.

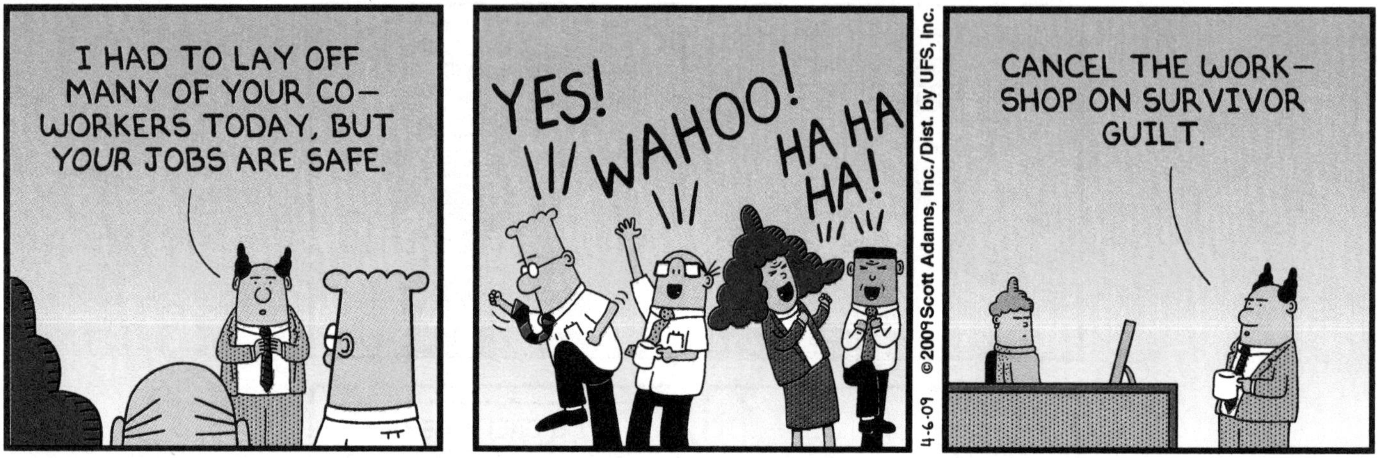
I HAD TO LAY OFF MANY OF YOUR CO-WORKERS TODAY, BUT YOUR JOBS ARE SAFE.
YES!
WAHOO!
HA HA HA!
4-6-09 ©2009 Scott Adams, Inc./Dist. by UFS, Inc.
CANCEL THE WORK-SHOP ON SURVIVOR GUILT.

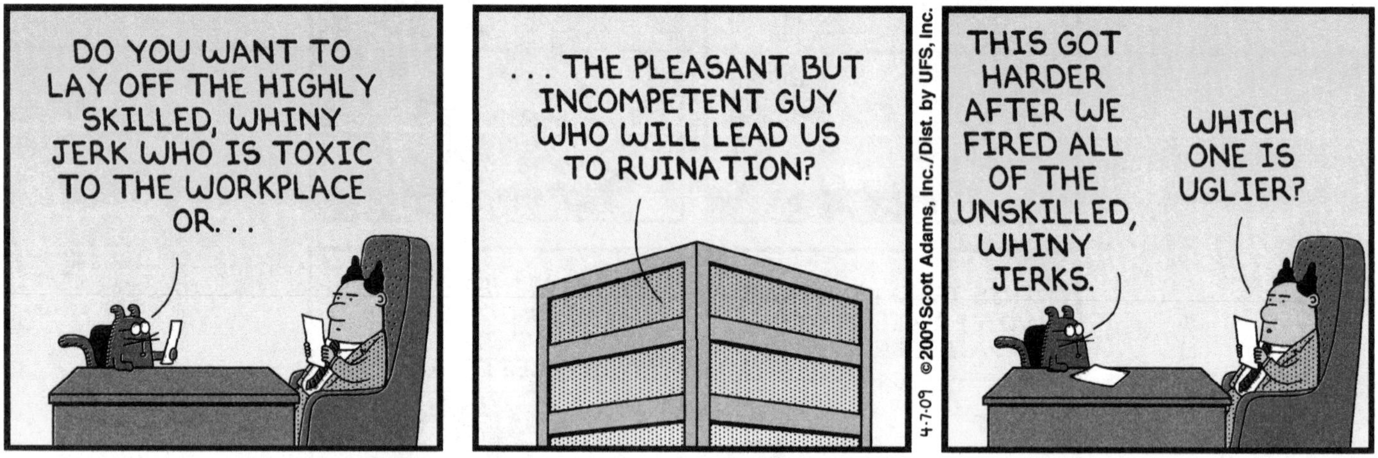
DO YOU WANT TO LAY OFF THE HIGHLY SKILLED, WHINY JERK WHO IS TOXIC TO THE WORKPLACE OR...
...THE PLEASANT BUT INCOMPETENT GUY WHO WILL LEAD US TO RUINATION?
4-7-09 ©2009 Scott Adams, Inc./Dist. by UFS, Inc.
THIS GOT HARDER AFTER WE FIRED ALL OF THE UNSKILLED, WHINY JERKS.
WHICH ONE IS UGLIER?

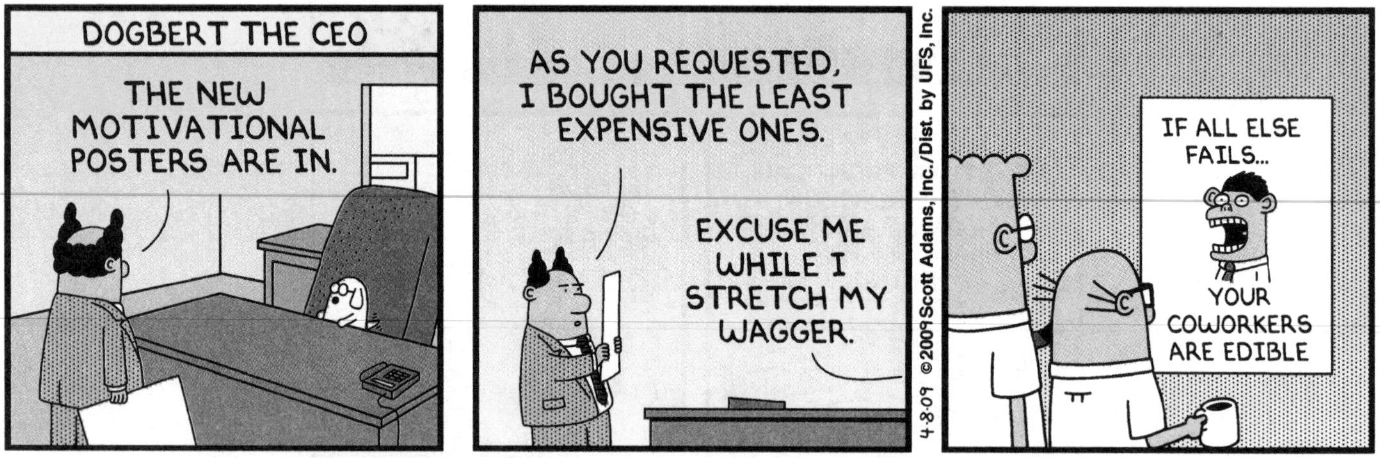
DOGBERT THE CEO
THE NEW MOTIVATIONAL POSTERS ARE IN.
AS YOU REQUESTED, I BOUGHT THE LEAST EXPENSIVE ONES.
EXCUSE ME WHILE I STRETCH MY WAGGER.
4-8-09 ©2009 Scott Adams, Inc./Dist. by UFS, Inc.
IF ALL ELSE FAILS...
YOUR COWORKERS ARE EDIBLE

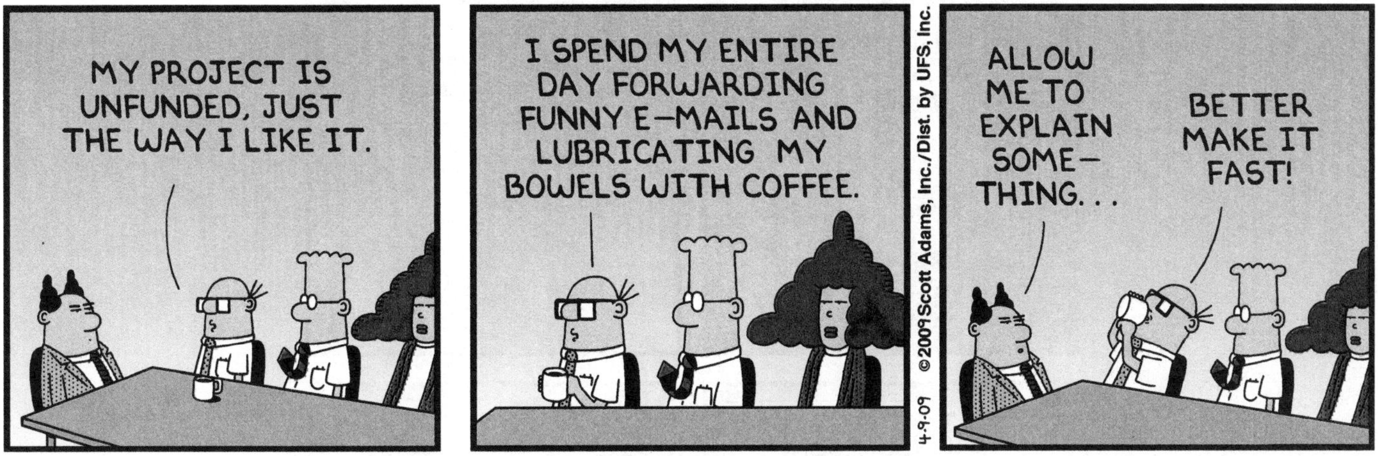
MY PROJECT IS UNFUNDED, JUST THE WAY I LIKE IT.
I SPEND MY ENTIRE DAY FORWARDING FUNNY E-MAILS AND LUBRICATING MY BOWELS WITH COFFEE.
4-9-09 ©2009 Scott Adams, Inc./Dist. by UFS, Inc.
ALLOW ME TO EXPLAIN SOME-THING...
BETTER MAKE IT FAST!

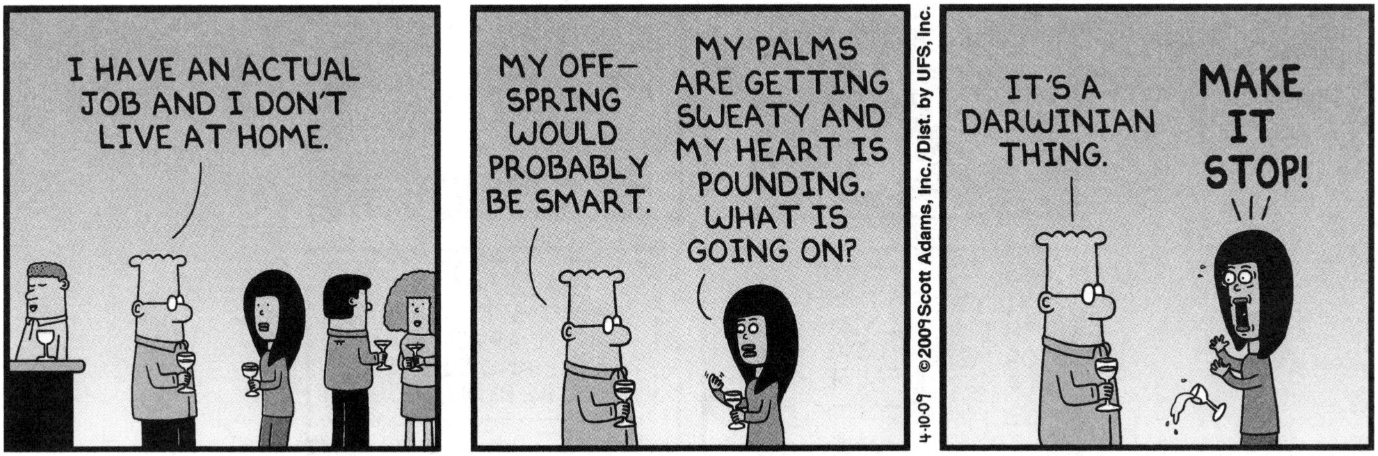
I HAVE AN ACTUAL JOB AND I DON'T LIVE AT HOME.
MY OFF-SPRING WOULD PROBABLY BE SMART.
MY PALMS ARE GETTING SWEATY AND MY HEART IS POUNDING. WHAT IS GOING ON?
4-10-09 ©2009 Scott Adams, Inc./Dist. by UFS, Inc.
IT'S A DARWINIAN THING.
MAKE IT STOP!

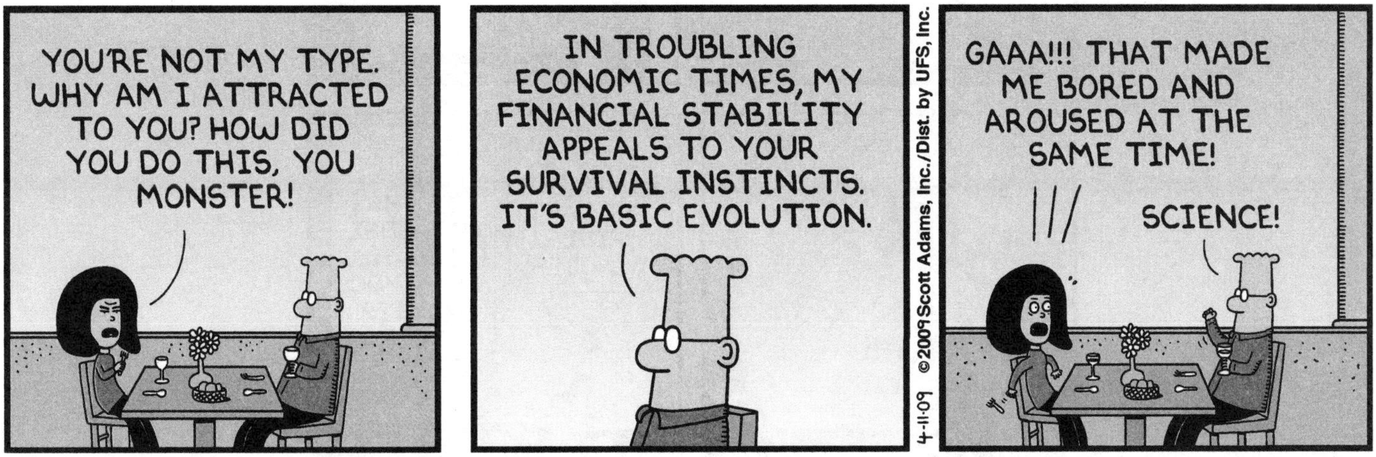
YOU'RE NOT MY TYPE. WHY AM I ATTRACTED TO YOU? HOW DID YOU DO THIS, YOU MONSTER!
IN TROUBLING ECONOMIC TIMES, MY FINANCIAL STABILITY APPEALS TO YOUR SURVIVAL INSTINCTS. IT'S BASIC EVOLUTION.
4-11-09 ©2009 Scott Adams, Inc./Dist. by UFS, Inc.
GAAA!!! THAT MADE ME BORED AND AROUSED AT THE SAME TIME!
SCIENCE!

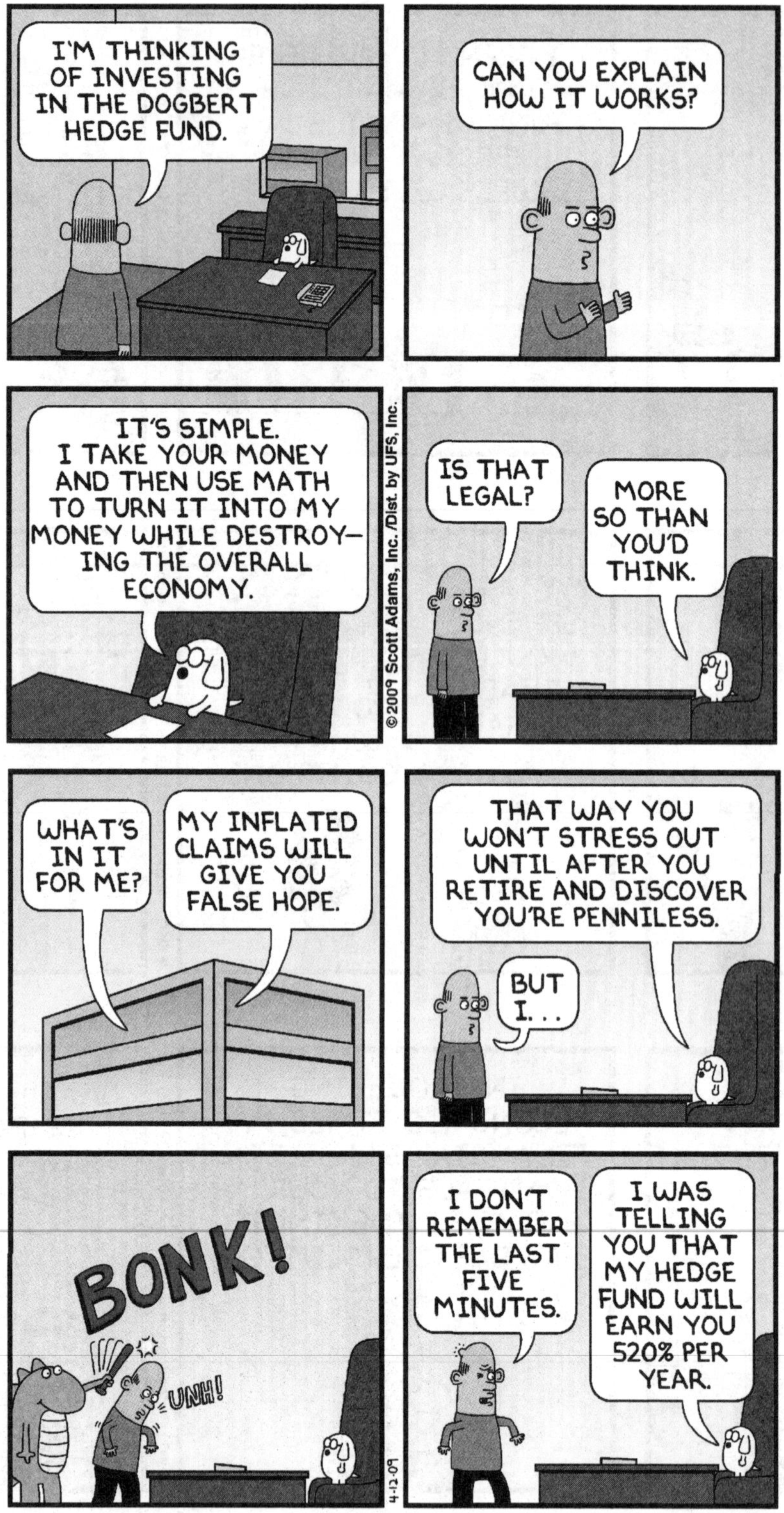
I'M THINKING OF INVESTING IN THE DOGBERT HEDGE FUND.
CAN YOU EXPLAIN HOW IT WORKS?
IT'S SIMPLE. I TAKE YOUR MONEY AND THEN USE MATH TO TURN IT INTO MY MONEY WHILE DESTROY- ING THE OVERALL ECONOMY.
IS THAT LEGAL?
MORE SO THAN YOU'D THINK.
WHAT'S IN IT FOR ME?
MY INFLATED CLAIMS WILL GIVE YOU FALSE HOPE.
THAT WAY YOU WON'T STRESS OUT UNTIL AFTER YOU RETIRE AND DISCOVER YOU'RE PENNILESS.
BUT I. . .
BONK!
UNH!
I DON'T REMEMBER THE LAST FIVE MINUTES.
I WAS TELLING YOU THAT MY HEDGE FUND WILL EARN YOU 520% PER YEAR.
©2009 Scott Adams, Inc. /Dist. by UFS, Inc.
4-12-09

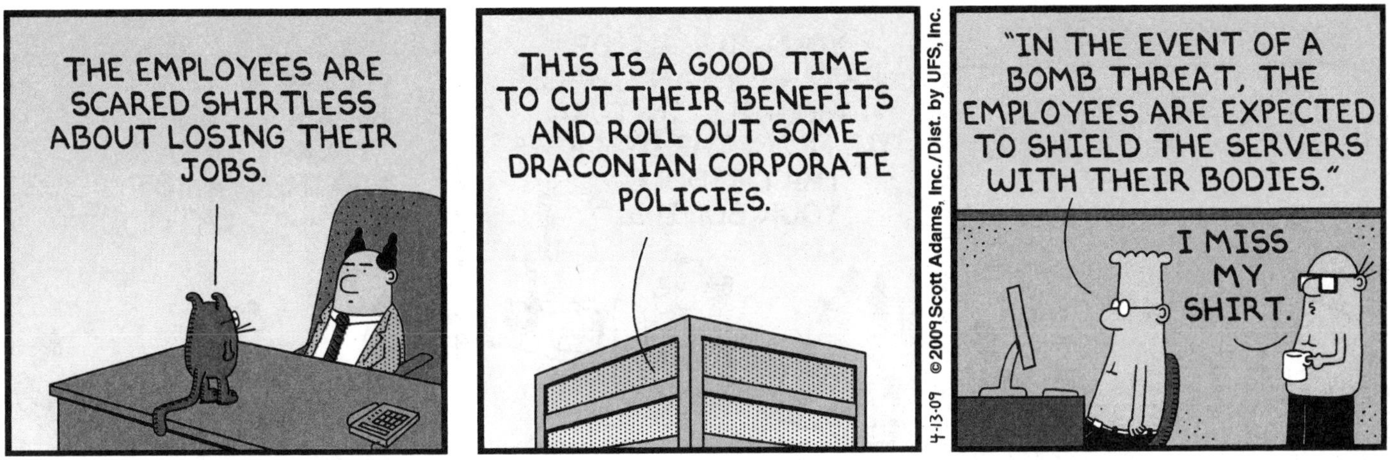
THE EMPLOYEES ARE SCARED SHIRTLESS ABOUT LOSING THEIR JOBS.
THIS IS A GOOD TIME TO CUT THEIR BENEFITS AND ROLL OUT SOME DRACONIAN CORPORATE POLICIES.
4-13-09 ©2009 Scott Adams, Inc./Dist. by UFS, Inc.
"IN THE EVENT OF A BOMB THREAT, THE EMPLOYEES ARE EXPECTED TO SHIELD THE SERVERS WITH THEIR BODIES."
I MISS MY SHIRT.

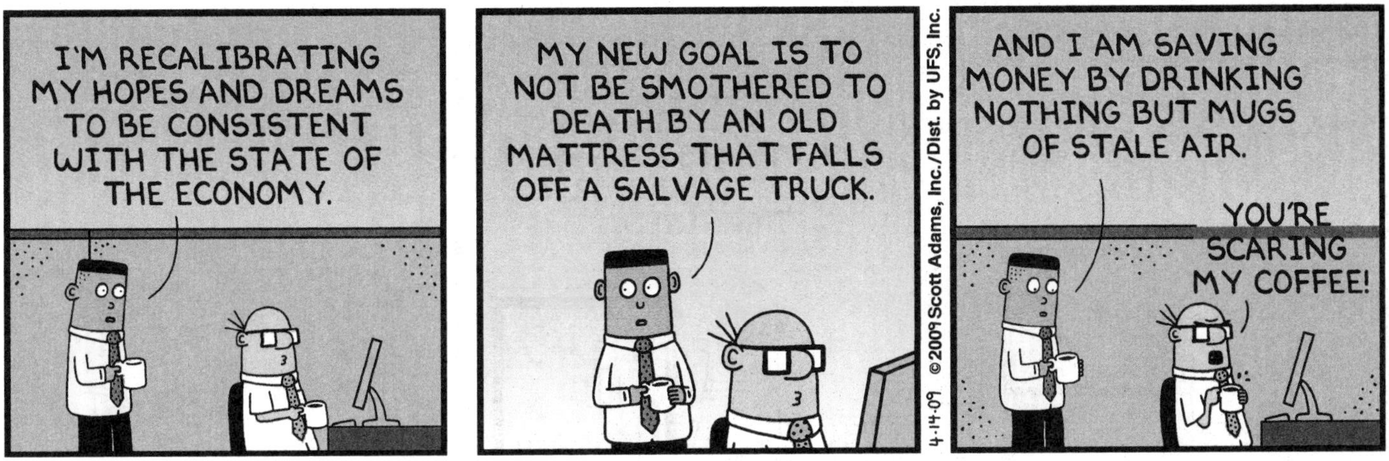
I'M RECALIBRATING MY HOPES AND DREAMS TO BE CONSISTENT WITH THE STATE OF THE ECONOMY.
MY NEW GOAL IS TO NOT BE SMOTHERED TO DEATH BY AN OLD MATTRESS THAT FALLS OFF A SALVAGE TRUCK.
4-14-09 ©2009 Scott Adams, Inc./Dist. by UFS, Inc.
AND I AM SAVING MONEY BY DRINKING NOTHING BUT MUGS OF STALE AIR.
YOU'RE SCARING MY COFFEE!

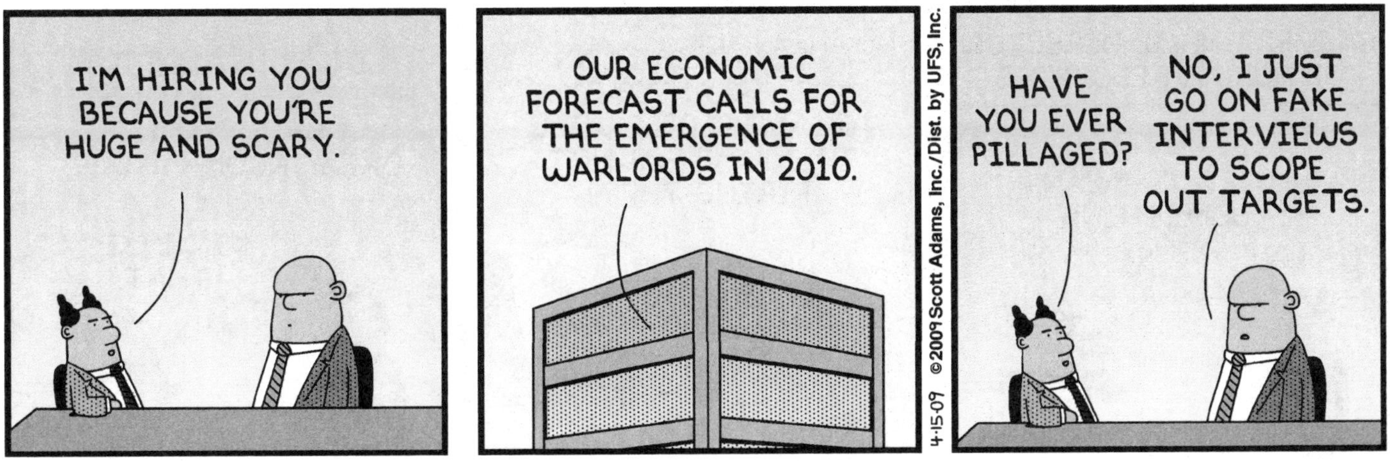
I'M HIRING YOU BECAUSE YOU'RE HUGE AND SCARY.
OUR ECONOMIC FORECAST CALLS FOR THE EMERGENCE OF WARLORDS IN 2010.
4-15-09 ©2009 Scott Adams, Inc./Dist. by UFS, Inc.
HAVE YOU EVER PILLAGED?
NO, I JUST GO ON FAKE INTERVIEWS TO SCOPE OUT TARGETS.

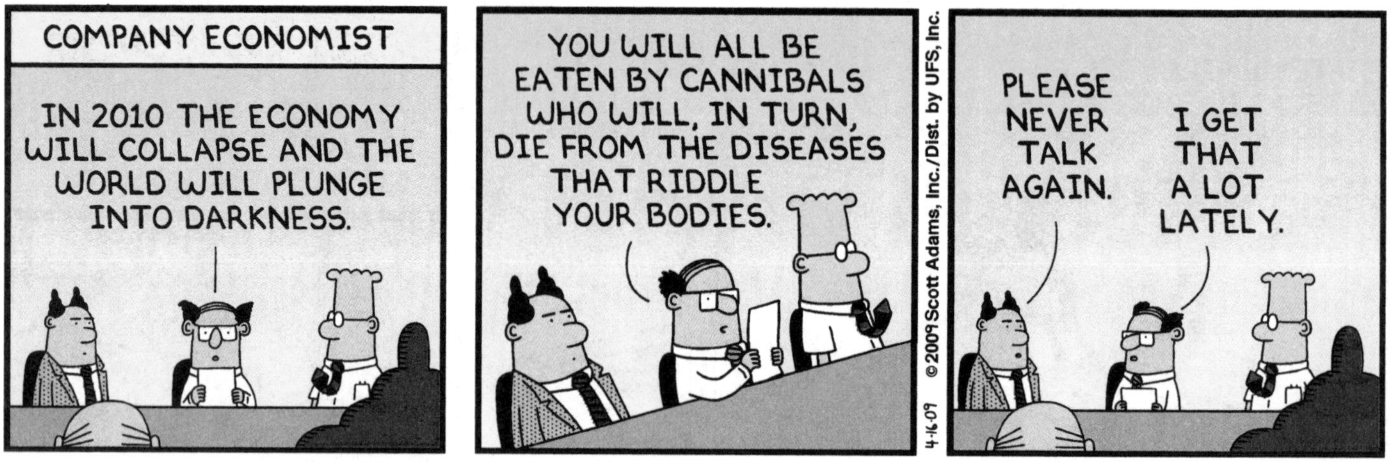
COMPANY ECONOMIST
IN 2010 THE ECONOMY WILL COLLAPSE AND THE WORLD WILL PLUNGE INTO DARKNESS.
YOU WILL ALL BE EATEN BY CANNIBALS WHO WILL, IN TURN, DIE FROM THE DISEASES THAT RIDDLE YOUR BODIES.
© 2009 Scott Adams, Inc./Dist. by UFS, Inc.
4-16-09
PLEASE NEVER TALK AGAIN.
I GET THAT A LOT LATELY.

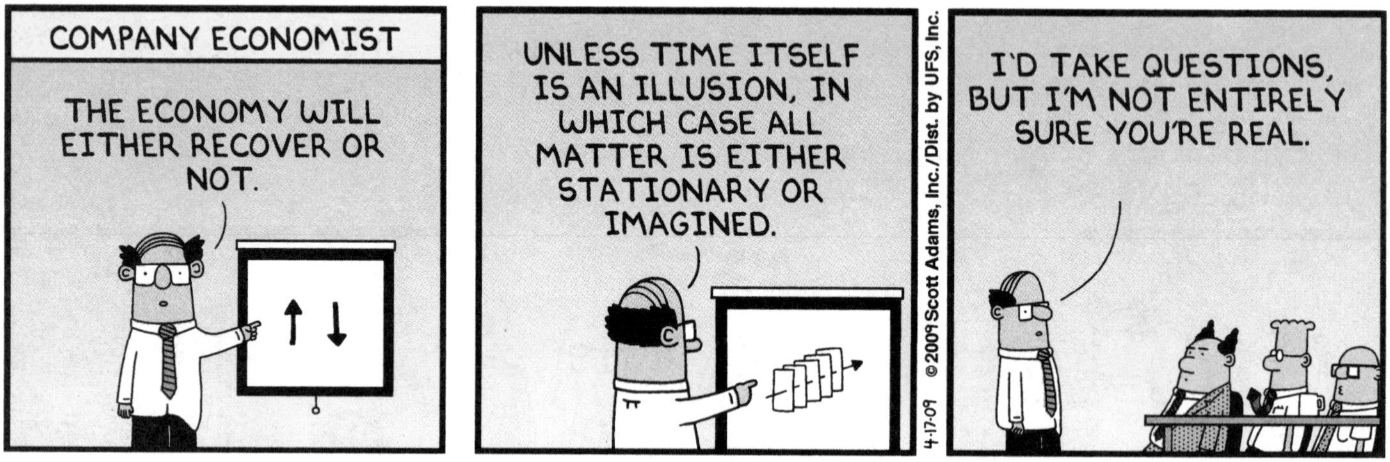
COMPANY ECONOMIST
THE ECONOMY WILL EITHER RECOVER OR NOT.
UNLESS TIME ITSELF IS AN ILLUSION, IN WHICH CASE ALL MATTER IS EITHER STATIONARY OR IMAGINED.
© 2009 Scott Adams, Inc./Dist. by UFS, Inc.
4-17-09
I'D TAKE QUESTIONS, BUT I'M NOT ENTIRELY SURE YOU'RE REAL.

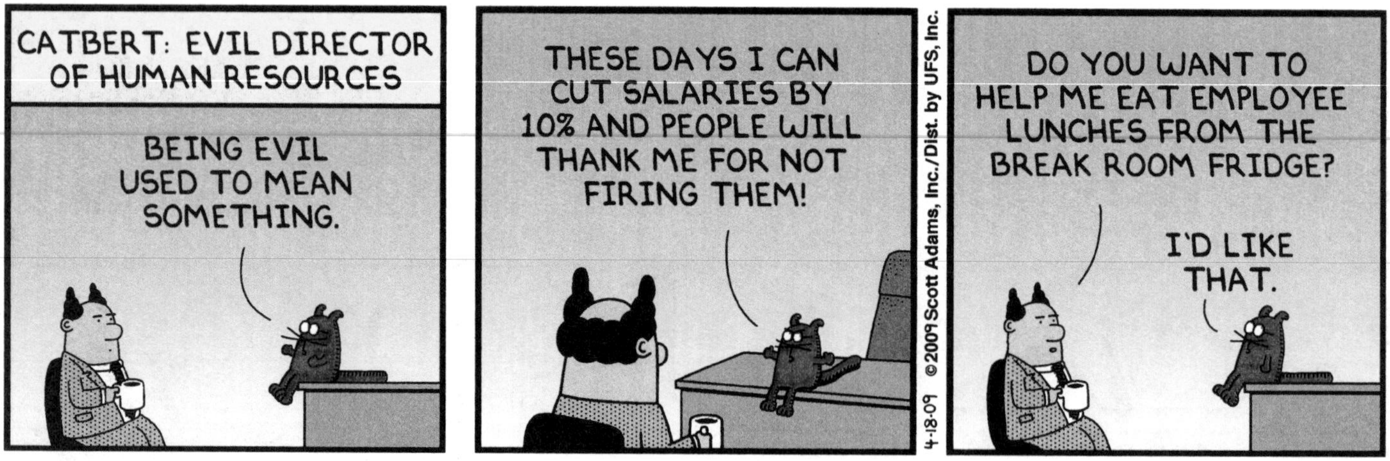
CATBERT: EVIL DIRECTOR OF HUMAN RESOURCES
BEING EVIL USED TO MEAN SOMETHING.
THESE DAYS I CAN CUT SALARIES BY 10% AND PEOPLE WILL THANK ME FOR NOT FIRING THEM!
© 2009 Scott Adams, Inc./Dist. by UFS, Inc.
4-18-09
DO YOU WANT TO HELP ME EAT EMPLOYEE LUNCHES FROM THE BREAK ROOM FRIDGE?
I'D LIKE THAT.

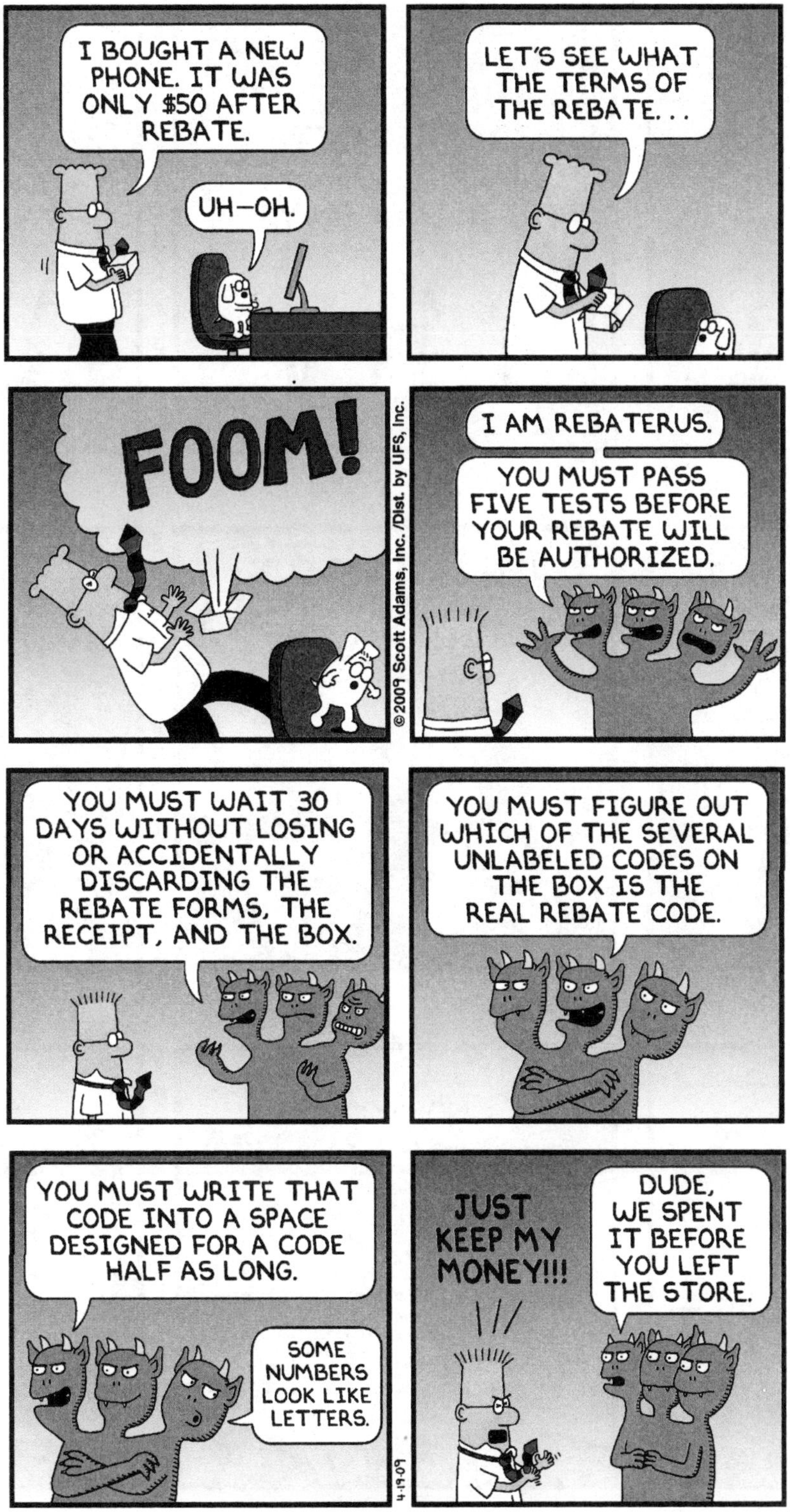
I BOUGHT A NEW PHONE. IT WAS ONLY $50 AFTER REBATE.
UH-OH.
LET'S SEE WHAT THE TERMS OF THE REBATE...
FOOM!
©2009 Scott Adams, Inc./Dist. by UFS, Inc.
I AM REBATERUS.
YOU MUST PASS FIVE TESTS BEFORE YOUR REBATE WILL BE AUTHORIZED.
YOU MUST WAIT 30 DAYS WITHOUT LOSING OR ACCIDENTALLY DISCARDING THE REBATE FORMS, THE RECEIPT, AND THE BOX.
YOU MUST FIGURE OUT WHICH OF THE SEVERAL UNLABELED CODES ON THE BOX IS THE REAL REBATE CODE.
YOU MUST WRITE THAT CODE INTO A SPACE DESIGNED FOR A CODE HALF AS LONG.
SOME NUMBERS LOOK LIKE LETTERS.
4-19-09
JUST KEEP MY MONEY!!!
DUDE, WE SPENT IT BEFORE YOU LEFT THE STORE.

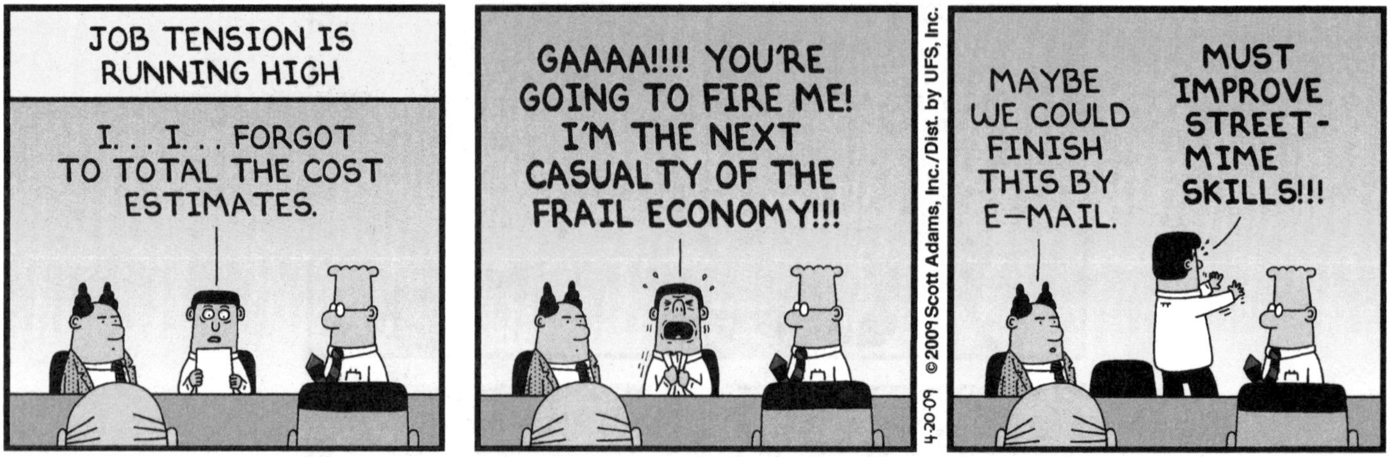
JOB TENSION IS RUNNING HIGH
I. . . I. . . FORGOT TO TOTAL THE COST ESTIMATES.
GAAAA!!!! YOU'RE GOING TO FIRE ME! I'M THE NEXT CASUALTY OF THE FRAIL ECONOMY!!!
4-20-09 ©2009 Scott Adams, Inc./Dist. by UFS, Inc.
MAYBE WE COULD FINISH THIS BY E-MAIL.
MUST IMPROVE STREET-MIME SKILLS!!!

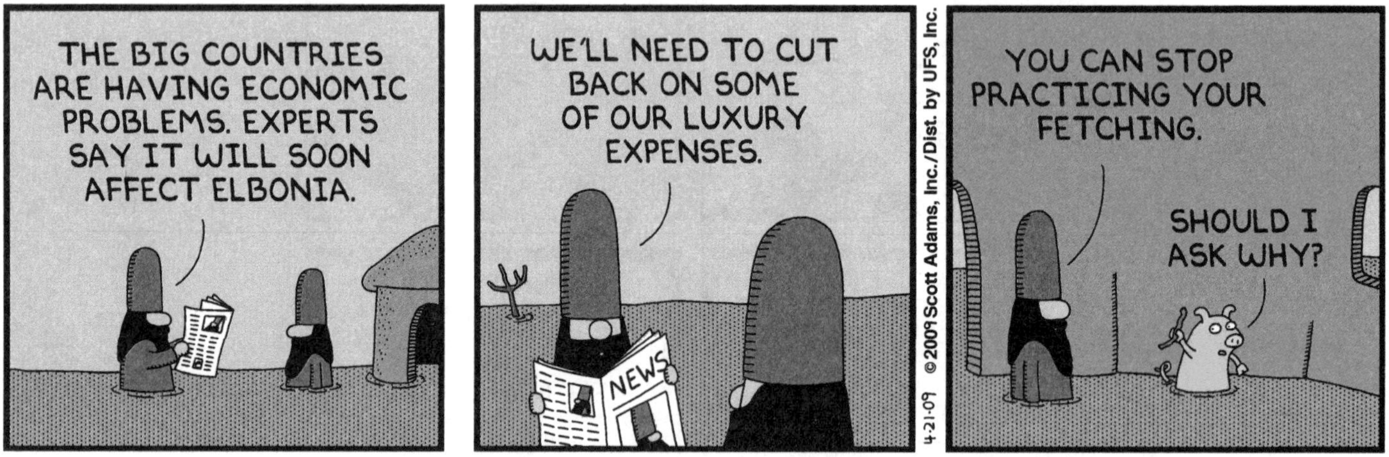
THE BIG COUNTRIES ARE HAVING ECONOMIC PROBLEMS. EXPERTS SAY IT WILL SOON AFFECT ELBONIA.
WE'LL NEED TO CUT BACK ON SOME OF OUR LUXURY EXPENSES.
NEWS
4-21-09 ©2009 Scott Adams, Inc./Dist. by UFS, Inc.
YOU CAN STOP PRACTICING YOUR FETCHING.
SHOULD I ASK WHY?

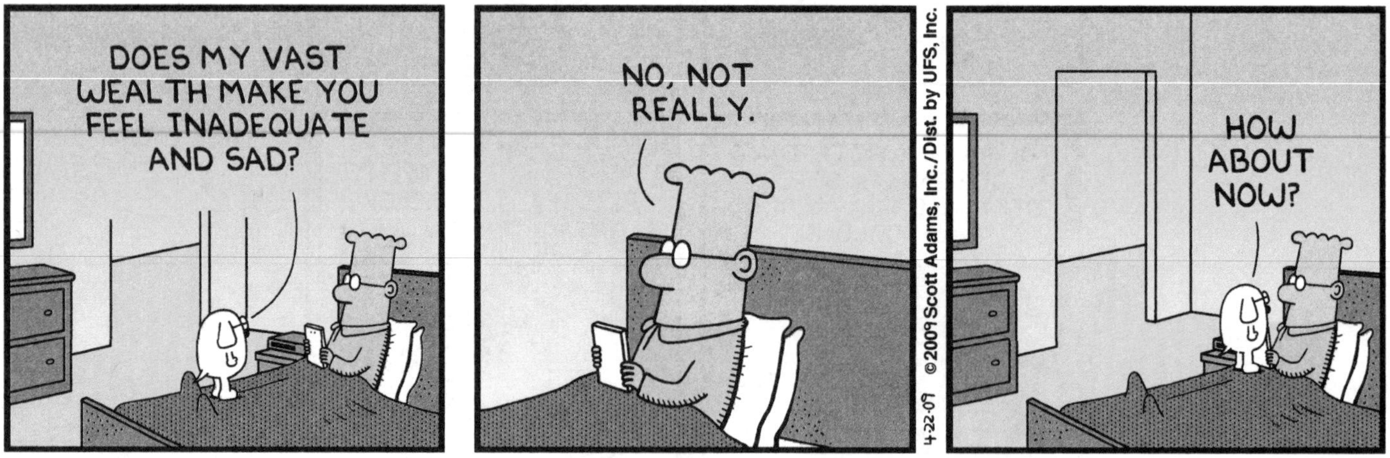
DOES MY VAST WEALTH MAKE YOU FEEL INADEQUATE AND SAD?
NO, NOT REALLY.
4-22-09 ©2009 Scott Adams, Inc./Dist. by UFS, Inc.
HOW ABOUT NOW?

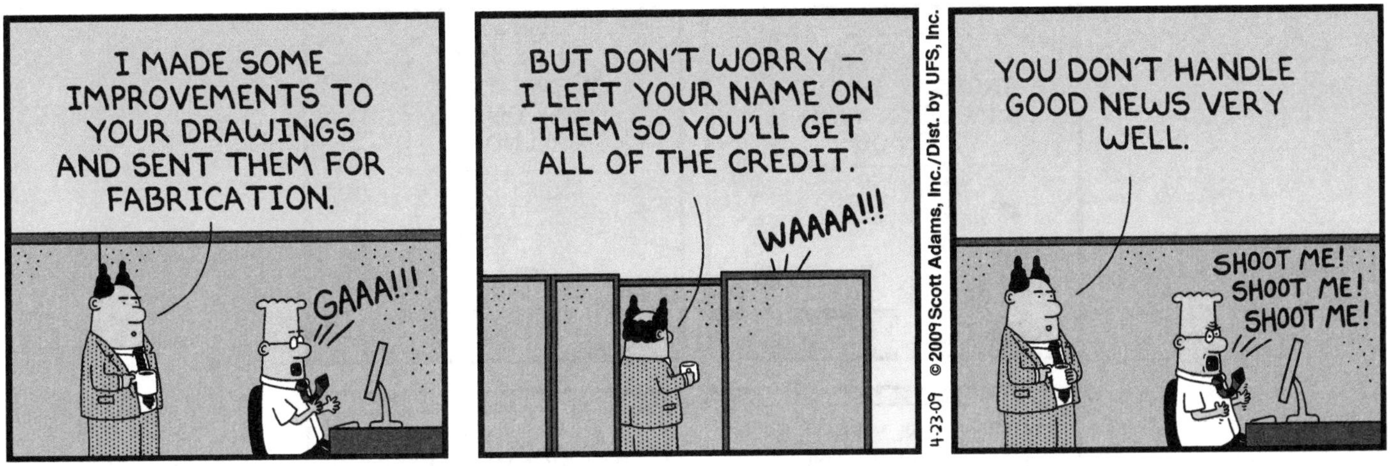
I MADE SOME IMPROVEMENTS TO YOUR DRAWINGS AND SENT THEM FOR FABRICATION.
GAAA!!!
BUT DON'T WORRY — I LEFT YOUR NAME ON THEM SO YOU'LL GET ALL OF THE CREDIT.
WAAAA!!!
4-23-09 ©2009 Scott Adams, Inc./Dist. by UFS, Inc.
YOU DON'T HANDLE GOOD NEWS VERY WELL.
SHOOT ME! SHOOT ME! SHOOT ME!

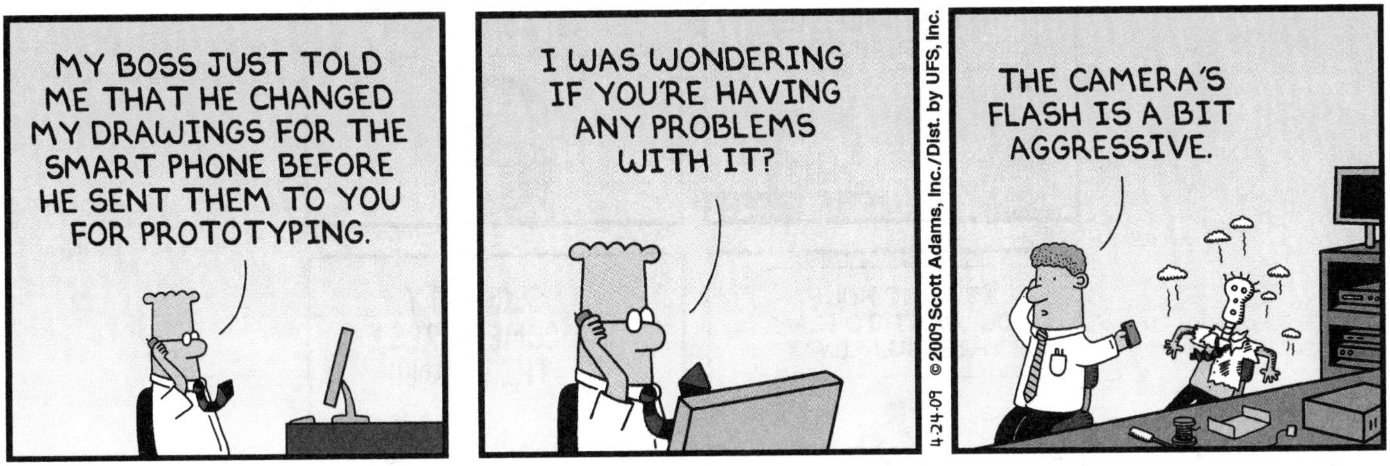
MY BOSS JUST TOLD ME THAT HE CHANGED MY DRAWINGS FOR THE SMART PHONE BEFORE HE SENT THEM TO YOU FOR PROTOTYPING.
I WAS WONDERING IF YOU'RE HAVING ANY PROBLEMS WITH IT?
4-24-09 ©2009 Scott Adams, Inc./Dist. by UFS, Inc.
THE CAMERA'S FLASH IS A BIT AGGRESSIVE.

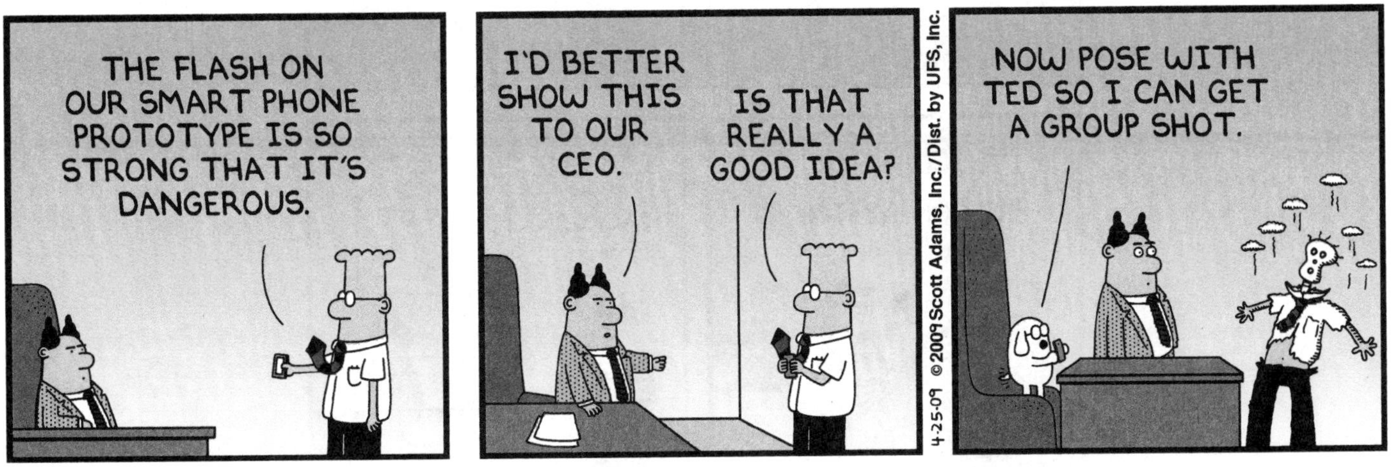
THE FLASH ON OUR SMART PHONE PROTOTYPE IS SO STRONG THAT IT'S DANGEROUS.
I'D BETTER SHOW THIS TO OUR CEO.
IS THAT REALLY A GOOD IDEA?
4-25-09 ©2009 Scott Adams, Inc./Dist. by UFS, Inc.
NOW POSE WITH TED SO I CAN GET A GROUP SHOT.

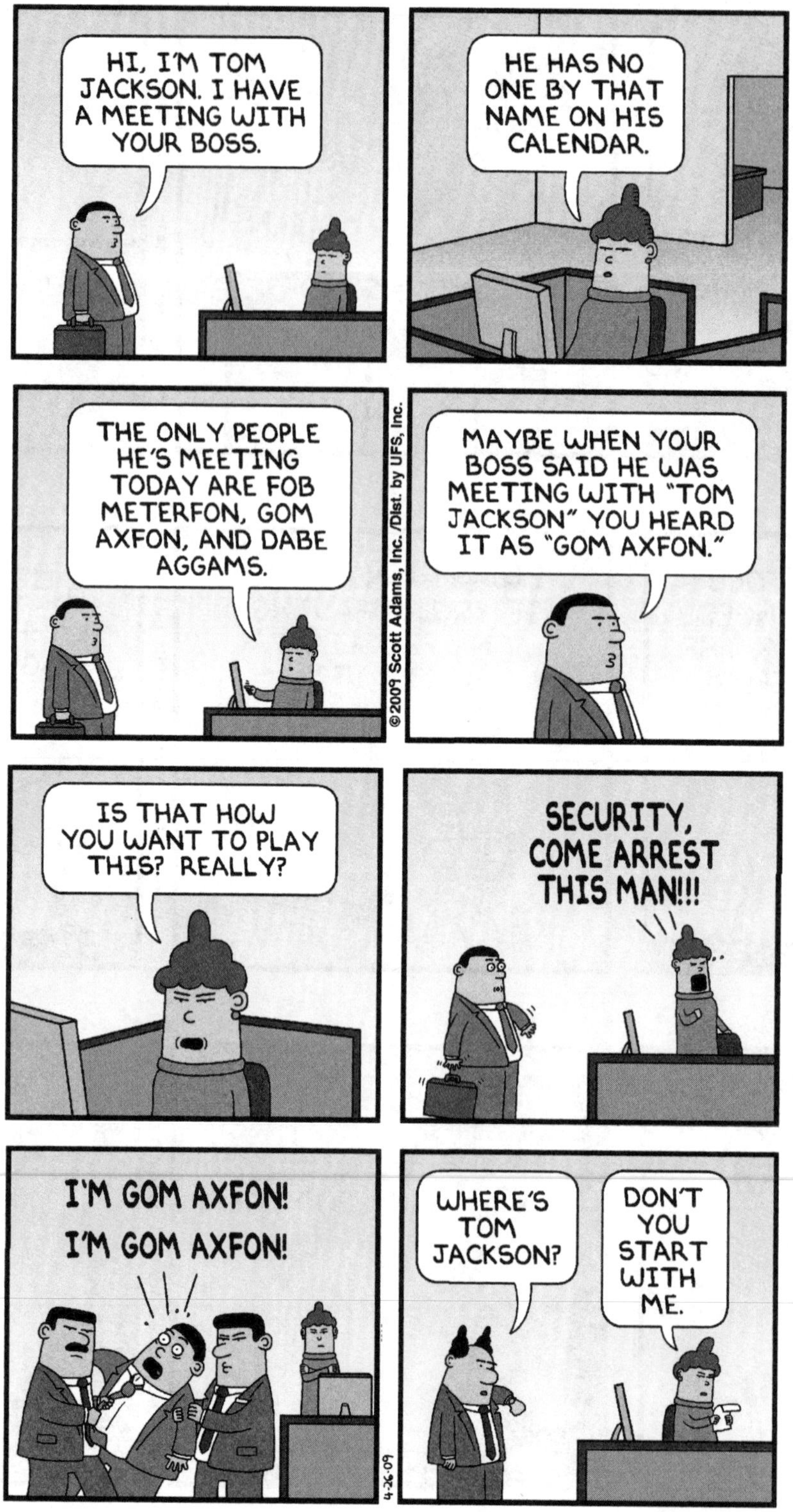
HI, I'M TOM JACKSON. I HAVE A MEETING WITH YOUR BOSS.
HE HAS NO ONE BY THAT NAME ON HIS CALENDAR.
THE ONLY PEOPLE HE'S MEETING TODAY ARE FOB METERFON, GOM AXFON, AND DABE AGGAMS.
MAYBE WHEN YOUR BOSS SAID HE WAS MEETING WITH "TOM JACKSON" YOU HEARD IT AS "GOM AXFON."
©2009 Scott Adams, Inc./Dist. by UFS, Inc.
IS THAT HOW YOU WANT TO PLAY THIS? REALLY?
SECURITY, COME ARREST THIS MAN!!!
I'M GOM AXFON!
I'M GOM AXFON!
4-26-09
WHERE'S TOM JACKSON?
DON'T YOU START WITH ME.

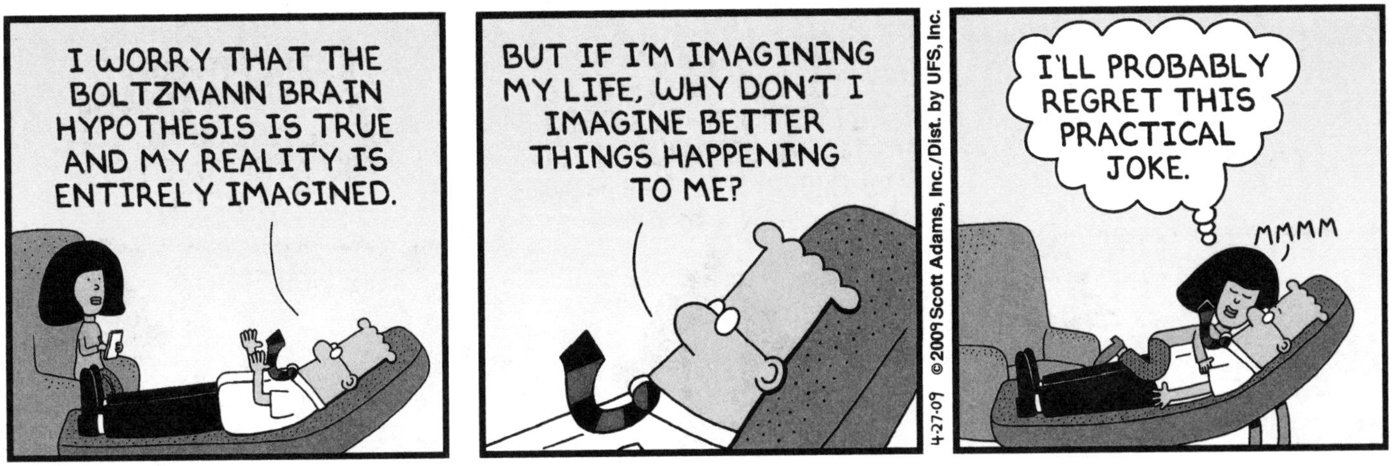
I WORRY THAT THE BOLTZMANN BRAIN HYPOTHESIS IS TRUE AND MY REALITY IS ENTIRELY IMAGINED.
BUT IF I'M IMAGINING MY LIFE, WHY DON'T I IMAGINE BETTER THINGS HAPPENING TO ME?
I'LL PROBABLY REGRET THIS PRACTICAL JOKE.
MMMM

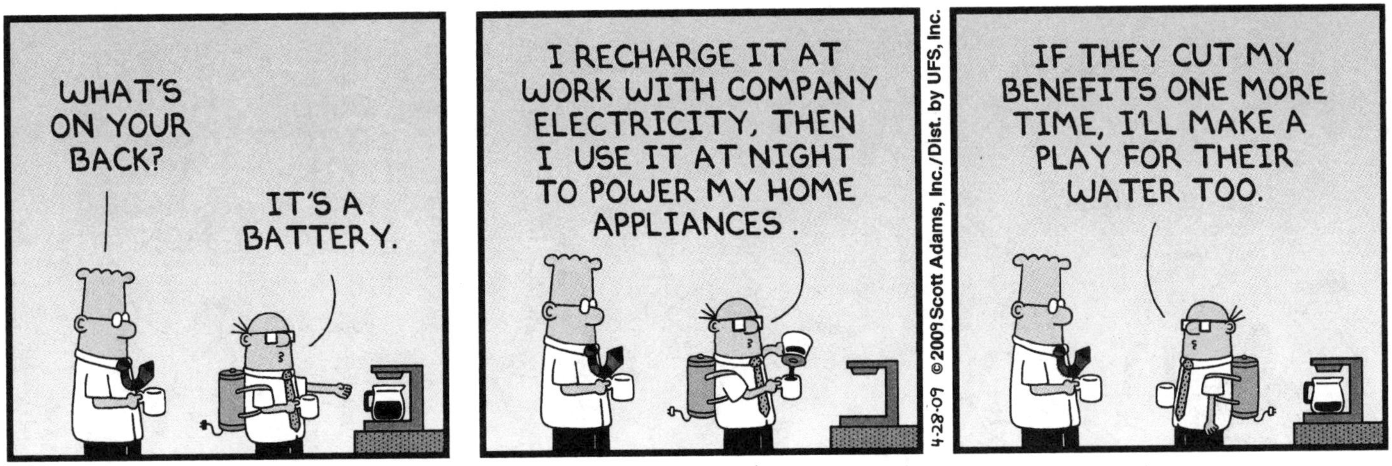
WHAT'S ON YOUR BACK?
IT'S A BATTERY.
I RECHARGE IT AT WORK WITH COMPANY ELECTRICITY, THEN I USE IT AT NIGHT TO POWER MY HOME APPLIANCES .
IF THEY CUT MY BENEFITS ONE MORE TIME, I'LL MAKE A PLAY FOR THEIR WATER TOO.

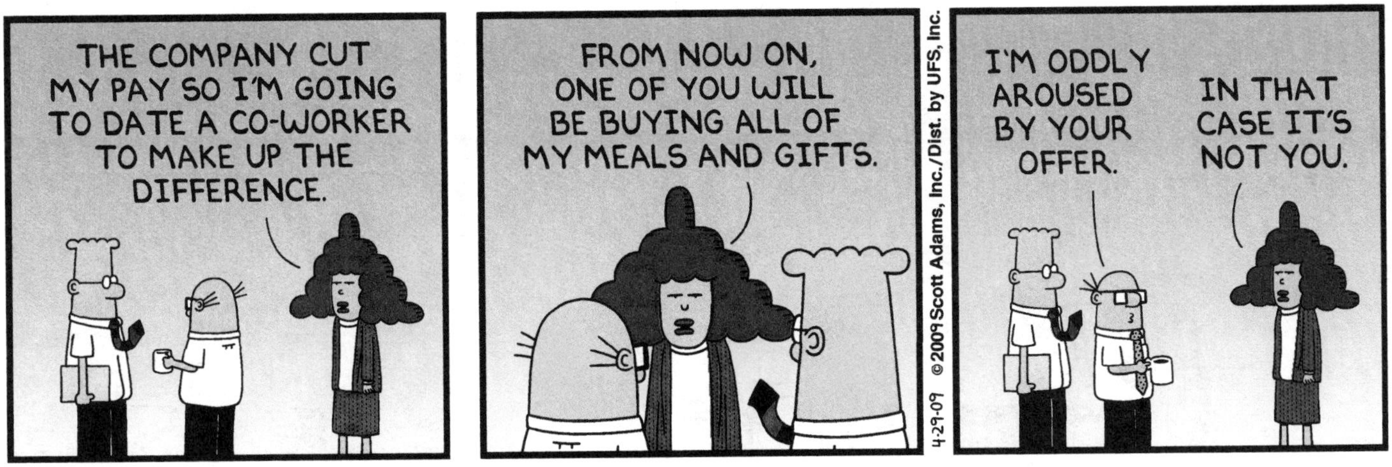
THE COMPANY CUT MY PAY SO I'M GOING TO DATE A CO-WORKER TO MAKE UP THE DIFFERENCE.
FROM NOW ON, ONE OF YOU WILL BE BUYING ALL OF MY MEALS AND GIFTS.
I'M ODDLY AROUSED BY YOUR OFFER.
IN THAT CASE IT'S NOT YOU.

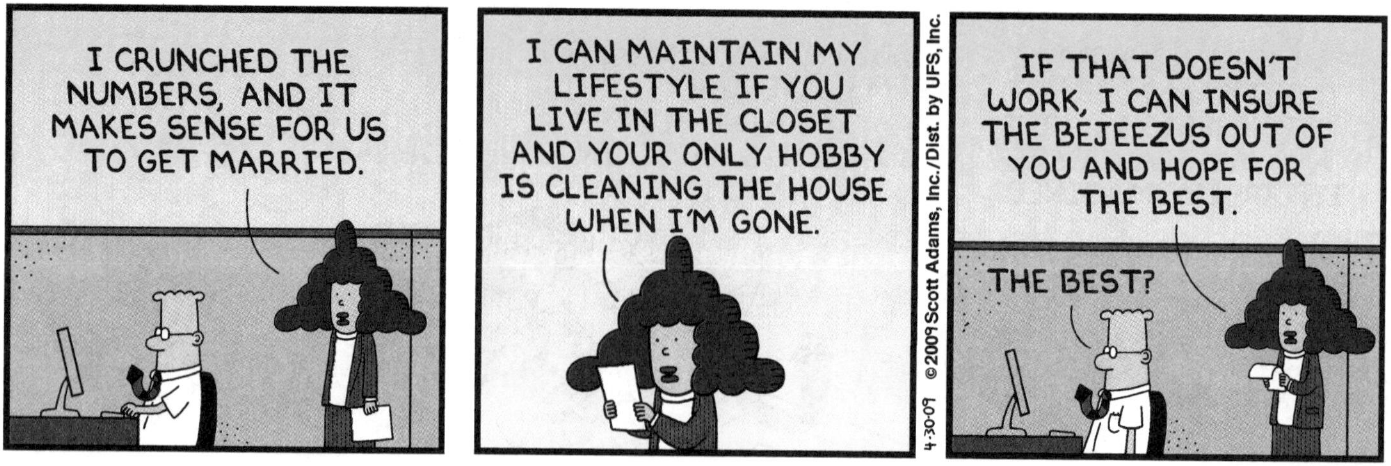
I CRUNCHED THE NUMBERS, AND IT MAKES SENSE FOR US TO GET MARRIED.
I CAN MAINTAIN MY LIFESTYLE IF YOU LIVE IN THE CLOSET AND YOUR ONLY HOBBY IS CLEANING THE HOUSE WHEN I'M GONE.
4-30-09 © 2009 Scott Adams, Inc./Dist. by UFS, Inc.
IF THAT DOESN'T WORK, I CAN INSURE THE BEJEEZUS OUT OF YOU AND HOPE FOR THE BEST.
THE BEST?

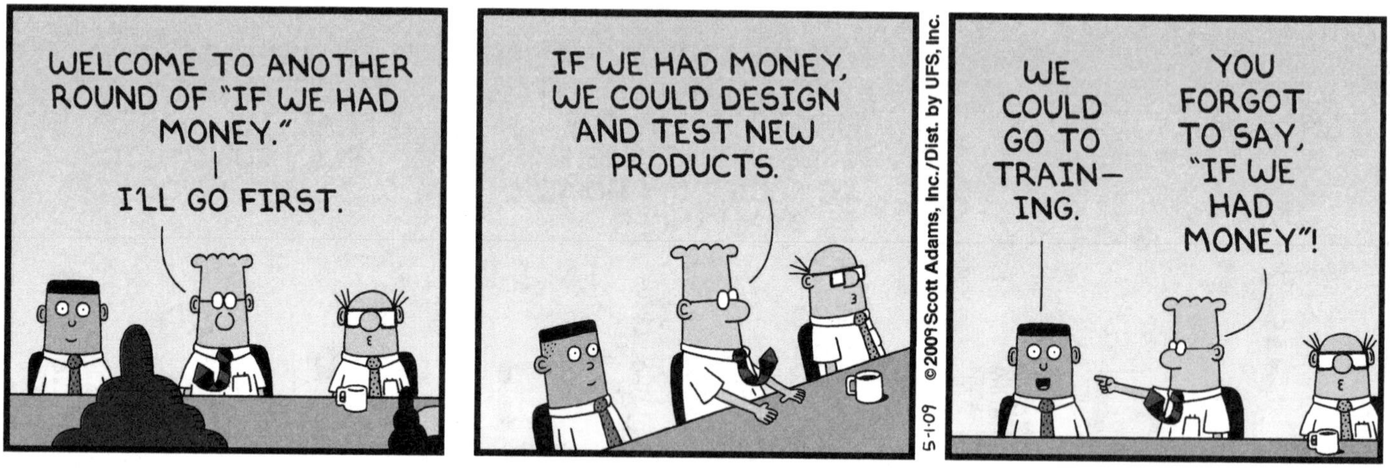
WELCOME TO ANOTHER ROUND OF "IF WE HAD MONEY."
I'LL GO FIRST.
IF WE HAD MONEY, WE COULD DESIGN AND TEST NEW PRODUCTS.
5-1-09 © 2009 Scott Adams, Inc./Dist. by UFS, Inc.
WE COULD GO TO TRAIN-ING.
YOU FORGOT TO SAY, "IF WE HAD MONEY"!

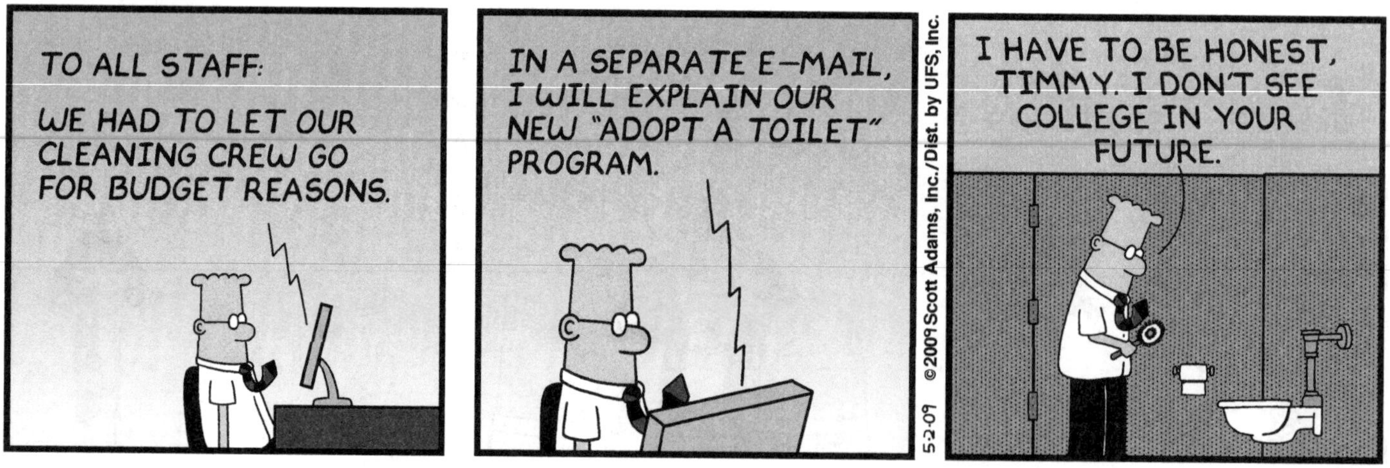
TO ALL STAFF:
WE HAD TO LET OUR CLEANING CREW GO FOR BUDGET REASONS.
IN A SEPARATE E-MAIL, I WILL EXPLAIN OUR NEW "ADOPT A TOILET" PROGRAM.
5-2-09 © 2009 Scott Adams, Inc./Dist. by UFS, Inc.
I HAVE TO BE HONEST, TIMMY. I DON'T SEE COLLEGE IN YOUR FUTURE.

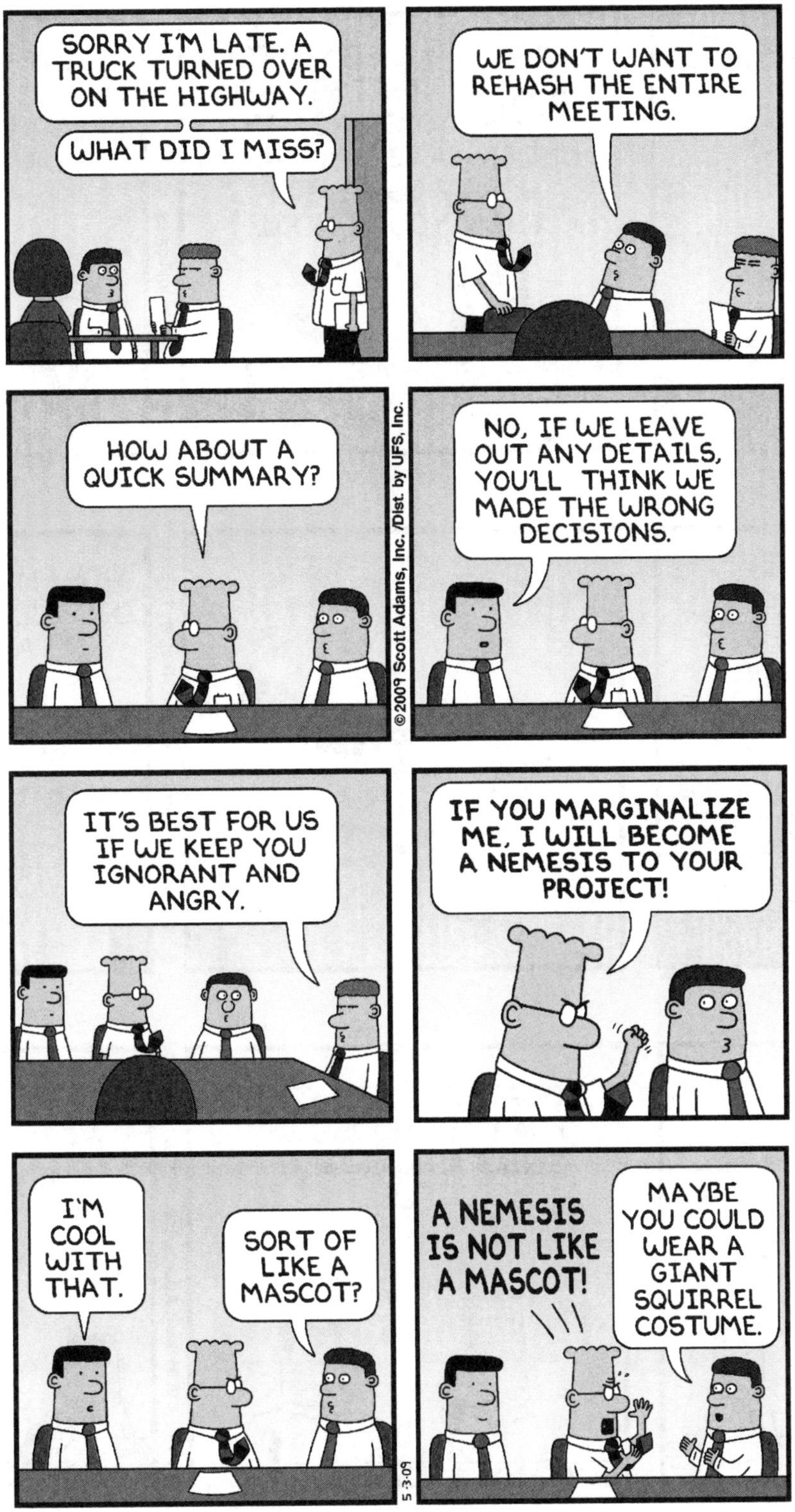
SORRY I'M LATE. A TRUCK TURNED OVER ON THE HIGHWAY.
WHAT DID I MISS?
WE DON'T WANT TO REHASH THE ENTIRE MEETING.
HOW ABOUT A QUICK SUMMARY?
NO, IF WE LEAVE OUT ANY DETAILS, YOU'LL THINK WE MADE THE WRONG DECISIONS.
IT'S BEST FOR US IF WE KEEP YOU IGNORANT AND ANGRY.
IF YOU MARGINALIZE ME, I WILL BECOME A NEMESIS TO YOUR PROJECT!
I'M COOL WITH THAT.
SORT OF LIKE A MASCOT?
A NEMESIS IS NOT LIKE A MASCOT!
MAYBE YOU COULD WEAR A GIANT SQUIRREL COSTUME.
©2009 Scott Adams, Inc./Dist. by UFS, Inc.
5-3-09

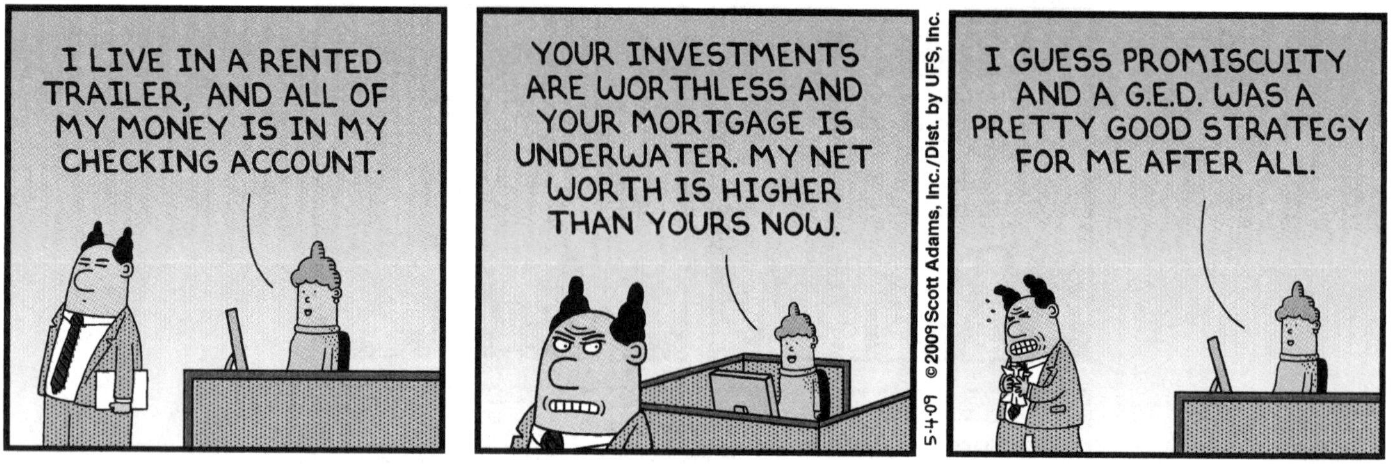
I LIVE IN A RENTED TRAILER, AND ALL OF MY MONEY IS IN MY CHECKING ACCOUNT.
YOUR INVESTMENTS ARE WORTHLESS AND YOUR MORTGAGE IS UNDERWATER. MY NET WORTH IS HIGHER THAN YOURS NOW.
5-4-09 ©2009 Scott Adams, Inc./Dist. by UFS, Inc.
I GUESS PROMISCUITY AND A G.E.D. WAS A PRETTY GOOD STRATEGY FOR ME AFTER ALL.

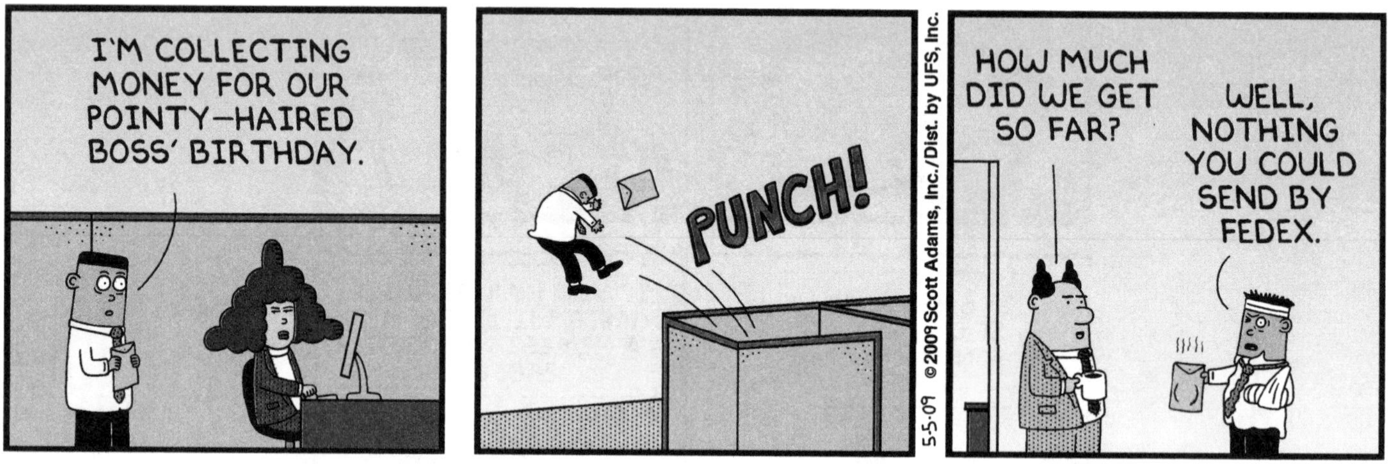
I'M COLLECTING MONEY FOR OUR POINTY-HAIRED BOSS' BIRTHDAY.
PUNCH!
5-5-09 ©2009 Scott Adams, Inc./Dist. by UFS, Inc.
HOW MUCH DID WE GET SO FAR?
WELL, NOTHING YOU COULD SEND BY FEDEX.

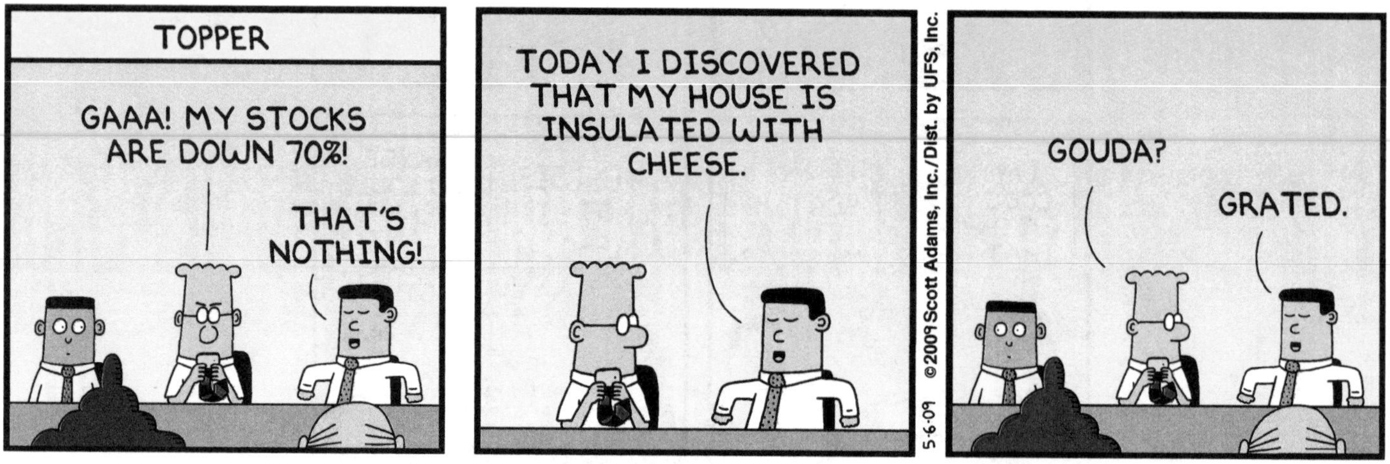
TOPPER
GAAA! MY STOCKS ARE DOWN 70%!
THAT'S NOTHING!
TODAY I DISCOVERED THAT MY HOUSE IS INSULATED WITH CHEESE.
5-6-09 ©2009 Scott Adams, Inc./Dist. by UFS, Inc.
GOUDA?
GRATED.

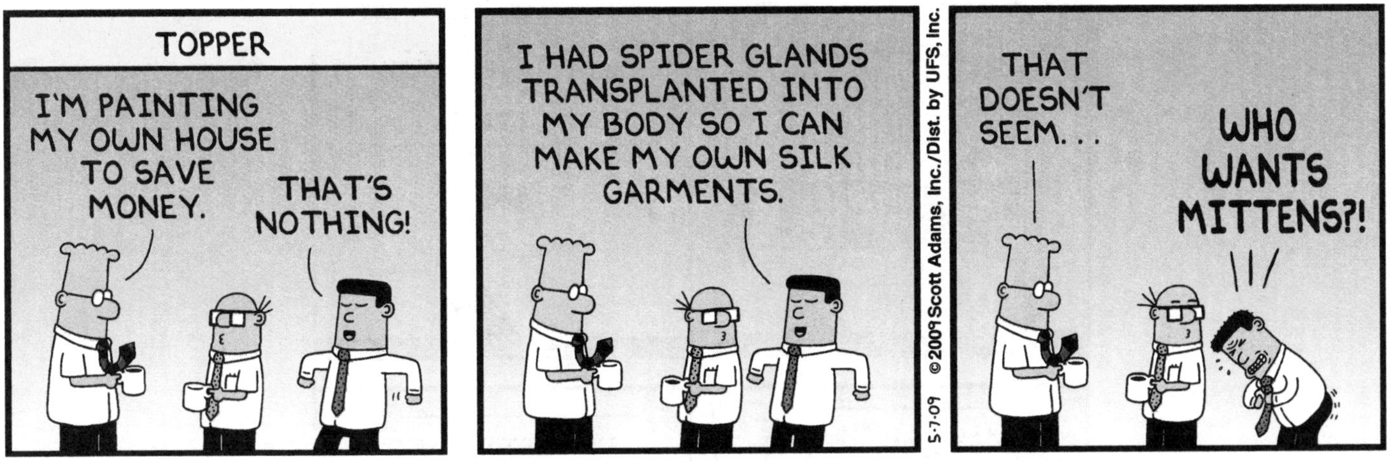
TOPPER
I'M PAINTING MY OWN HOUSE TO SAVE MONEY.
THAT'S NOTHING!
I HAD SPIDER GLANDS TRANSPLANTED INTO MY BODY SO I CAN MAKE MY OWN SILK GARMENTS.
5-7-09 ©2009 Scott Adams, Inc./Dist. by UFS, Inc.
THAT DOESN'T SEEM. . .
WHO WANTS MITTENS?!

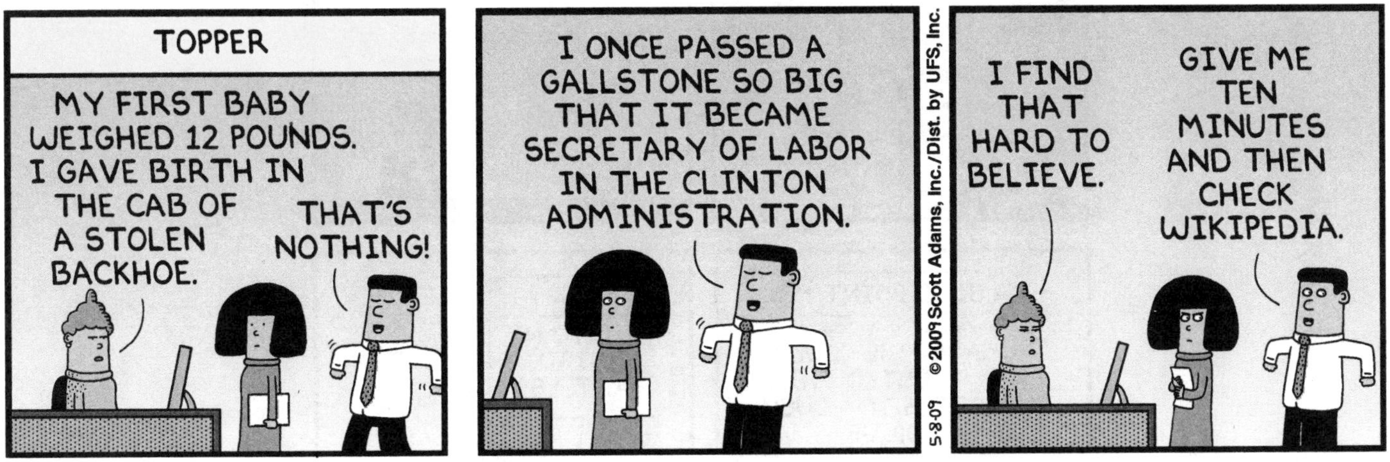
TOPPER
MY FIRST BABY WEIGHED 12 POUNDS. I GAVE BIRTH IN THE CAB OF A STOLEN BACKHOE.
THAT'S NOTHING!
I ONCE PASSED A GALLSTONE SO BIG THAT IT BECAME SECRETARY OF LABOR IN THE CLINTON ADMINISTRATION.
5-8-09 ©2009 Scott Adams, Inc./Dist. by UFS, Inc.
I FIND THAT HARD TO BELIEVE.
GIVE ME TEN MINUTES AND THEN CHECK WIKIPEDIA.

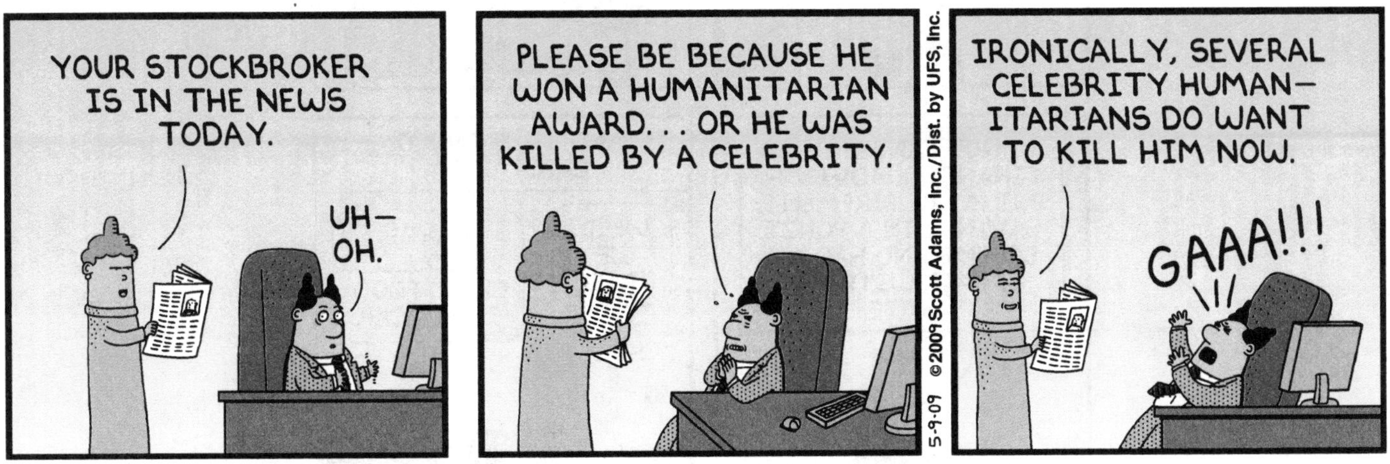
YOUR STOCKBROKER IS IN THE NEWS TODAY.
UH-OH.
PLEASE BE BECAUSE HE WON A HUMANITARIAN AWARD. . . OR HE WAS KILLED BY A CELEBRITY.
5-9-09 ©2009 Scott Adams, Inc./Dist. by UFS, Inc.
IRONICALLY, SEVERAL CELEBRITY HUMAN-ITARIANS DO WANT TO KILL HIM NOW.
GAAA!!!

IF WE LEASE A MACHINE FROM YOU, HOW CAN WE BE SURE YOU'LL STAY IN BUSINESS TO SERVICE IT?
HOW CAN WE BE SURE YOU'LL HAVE ENOUGH MONEY TO PAY THE LEASE?
YOU COULD CHECK OUR FINANCIALS.
I'M PRETTY SURE YOUR FINANCIALS ARE AS FRAUDULENT AS OURS.
©2009 Scott Adams, Inc./Dist. by UFS, Inc.
GOOD POINT.
MAYBE WE COULD ASK TRUSTED THIRD PARTIES TO VOUCH FOR US.
DO YOU TRUST ANY THIRD PARTIES?
NOT SINCE MY FINANCIAL ADVISOR PUT MY RETIREMENT SAVINGS IN A PONZI SCHEME AND HAD AN AFFAIR WITH MY WIFE.
5-10-09
AND THUS ENDED CAPITALISM
WELL, WE TRIED.
MAYBE I COULD GROW FOOD IN MY CAR.

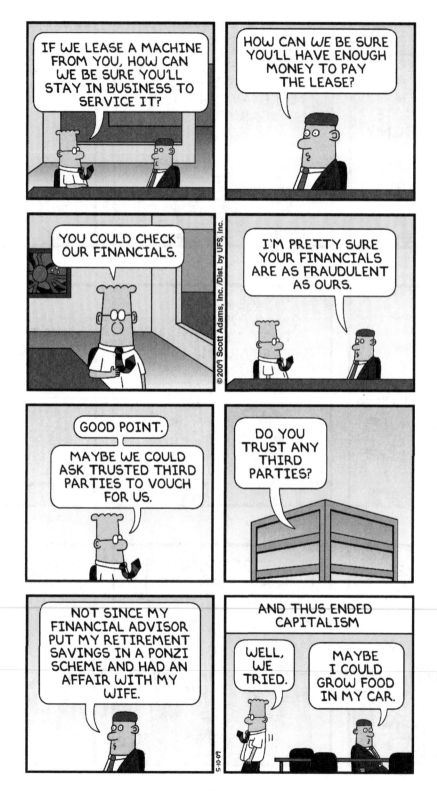

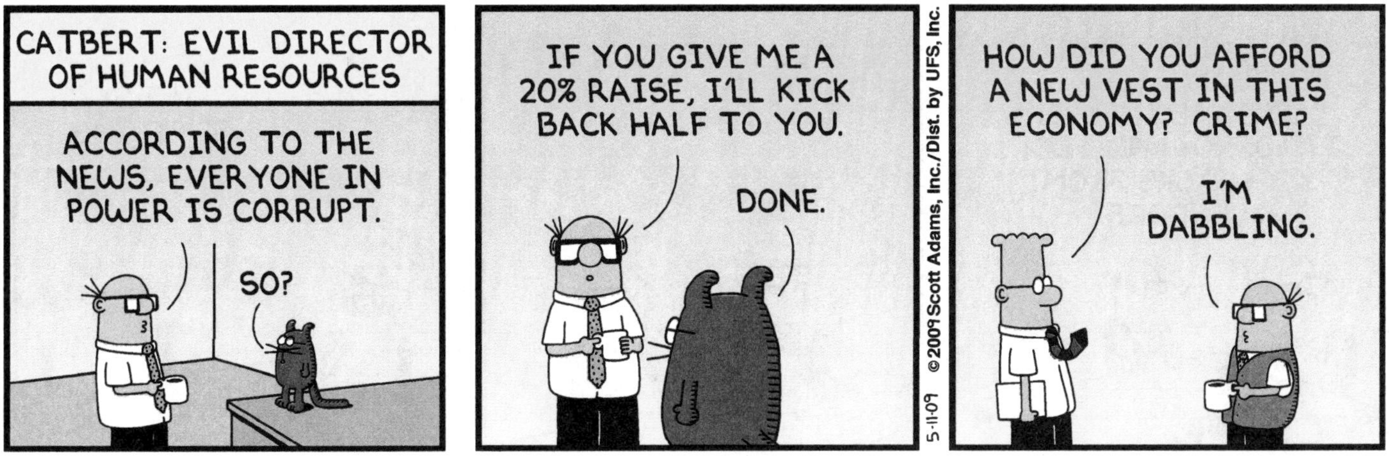
CATBERT: EVIL DIRECTOR OF HUMAN RESOURCES
ACCORDING TO THE NEWS, EVERYONE IN POWER IS CORRUPT.
SO?
IF YOU GIVE ME A 20% RAISE, I'LL KICK BACK HALF TO YOU.
DONE.
HOW DID YOU AFFORD A NEW VEST IN THIS ECONOMY? CRIME?
I'M DABBLING.
5-11-09

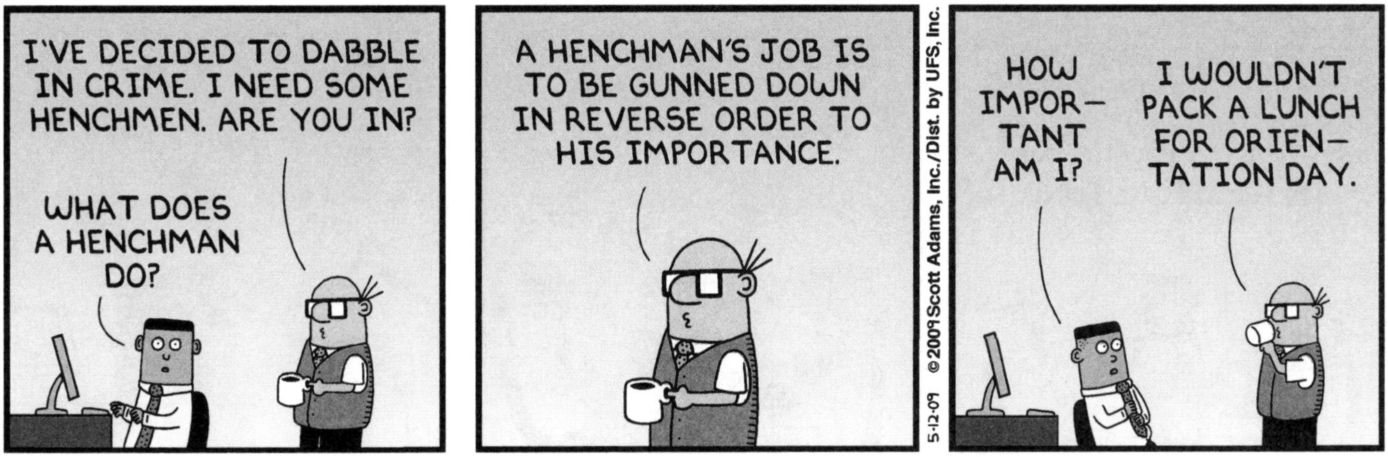
I'VE DECIDED TO DABBLE IN CRIME. I NEED SOME HENCHMEN. ARE YOU IN?
WHAT DOES A HENCHMAN DO?
A HENCHMAN'S JOB IS TO BE GUNNED DOWN IN REVERSE ORDER TO HIS IMPORTANCE.
HOW IMPOR-TANT AM I?
I WOULDN'T PACK A LUNCH FOR ORIEN-TATION DAY.
5-12-09

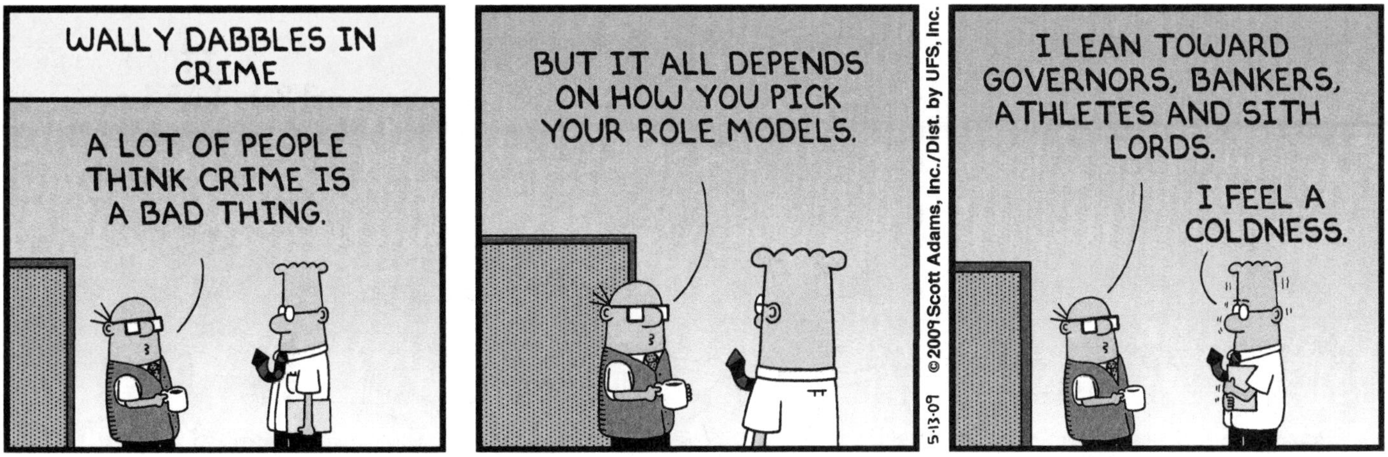
WALLY DABBLES IN CRIME
A LOT OF PEOPLE THINK CRIME IS A BAD THING.
BUT IT ALL DEPENDS ON HOW YOU PICK YOUR ROLE MODELS.
I LEAN TOWARD GOVERNORS, BANKERS, ATHLETES AND SITH LORDS.
I FEEL A COLDNESS.
5-13-09

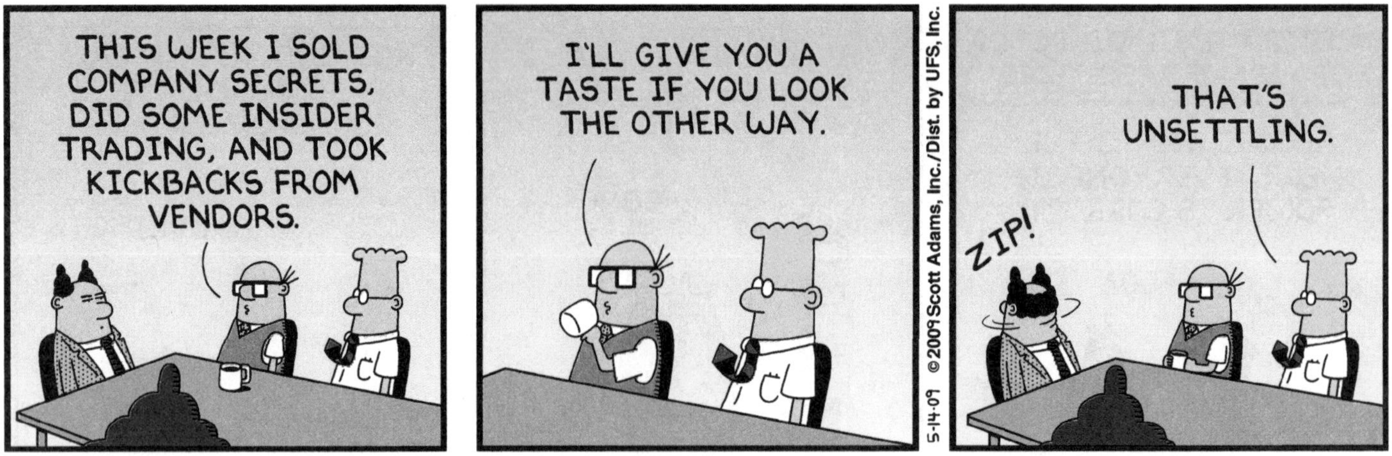
THIS WEEK I SOLD COMPANY SECRETS, DID SOME INSIDER TRADING, AND TOOK KICKBACKS FROM VENDORS.
I'LL GIVE YOU A TASTE IF YOU LOOK THE OTHER WAY.
5-14-09 ©2009 Scott Adams, Inc./Dist. by UFS, Inc.
ZIP!
THAT'S UNSETTLING.

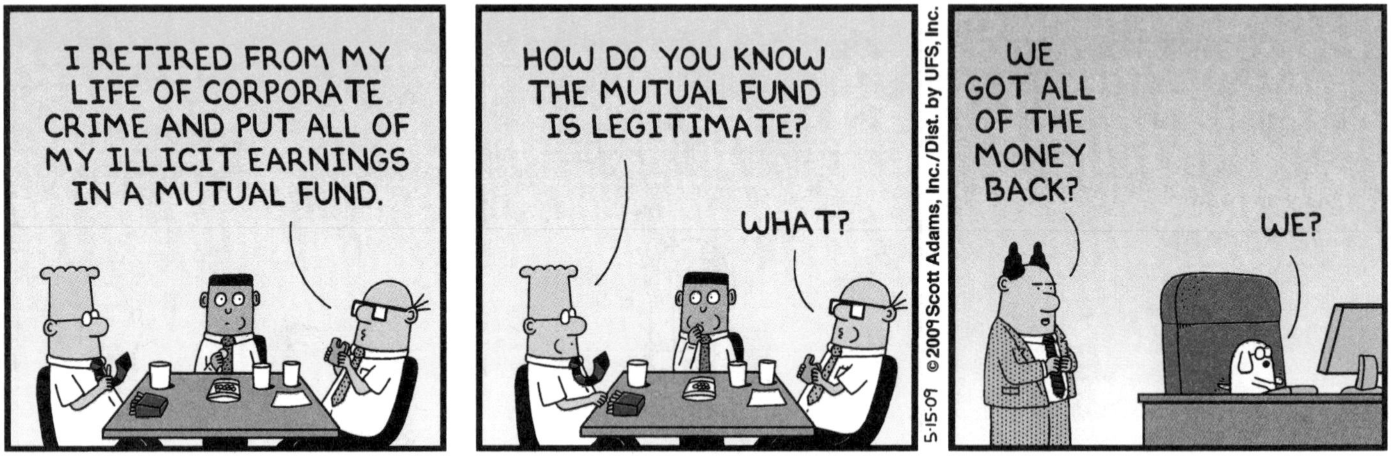
I RETIRED FROM MY LIFE OF CORPORATE CRIME AND PUT ALL OF MY ILLICIT EARNINGS IN A MUTUAL FUND.
HOW DO YOU KNOW THE MUTUAL FUND IS LEGITIMATE?
WHAT?
5-15-09 ©2009 Scott Adams, Inc./Dist. by UFS, Inc.
WE GOT ALL OF THE MONEY BACK?
WE?

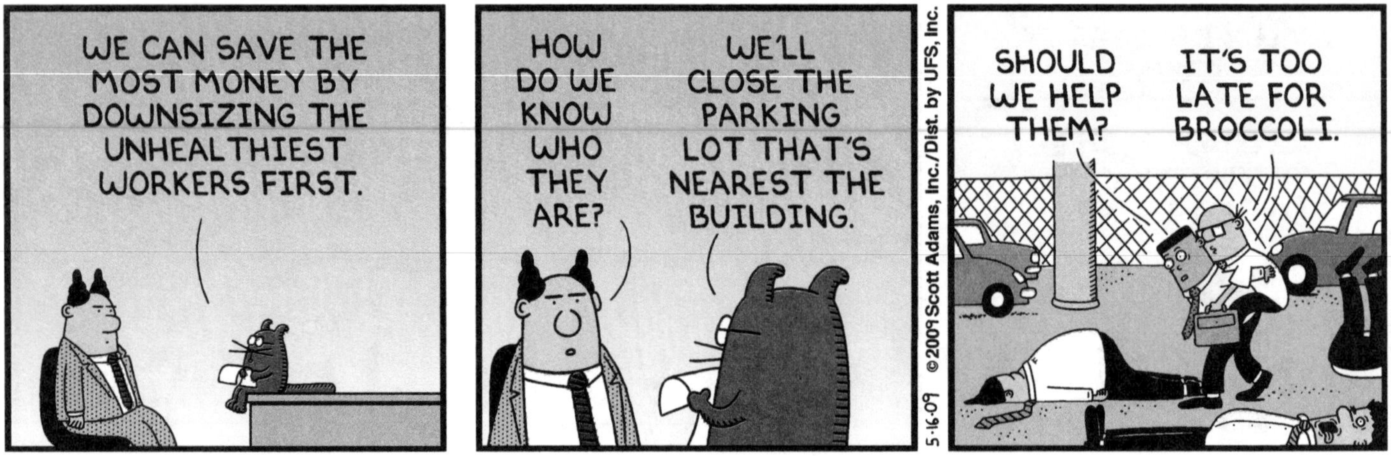
WE CAN SAVE THE MOST MONEY BY DOWNSIZING THE UNHEALTHIEST WORKERS FIRST.
HOW DO WE KNOW WHO THEY ARE?
WE'LL CLOSE THE PARKING LOT THAT'S NEAREST THE BUILDING.
5-16-09 ©2009 Scott Adams, Inc./Dist. by UFS, Inc.
SHOULD WE HELP THEM?
IT'S TOO LATE FOR BROCCOLI.

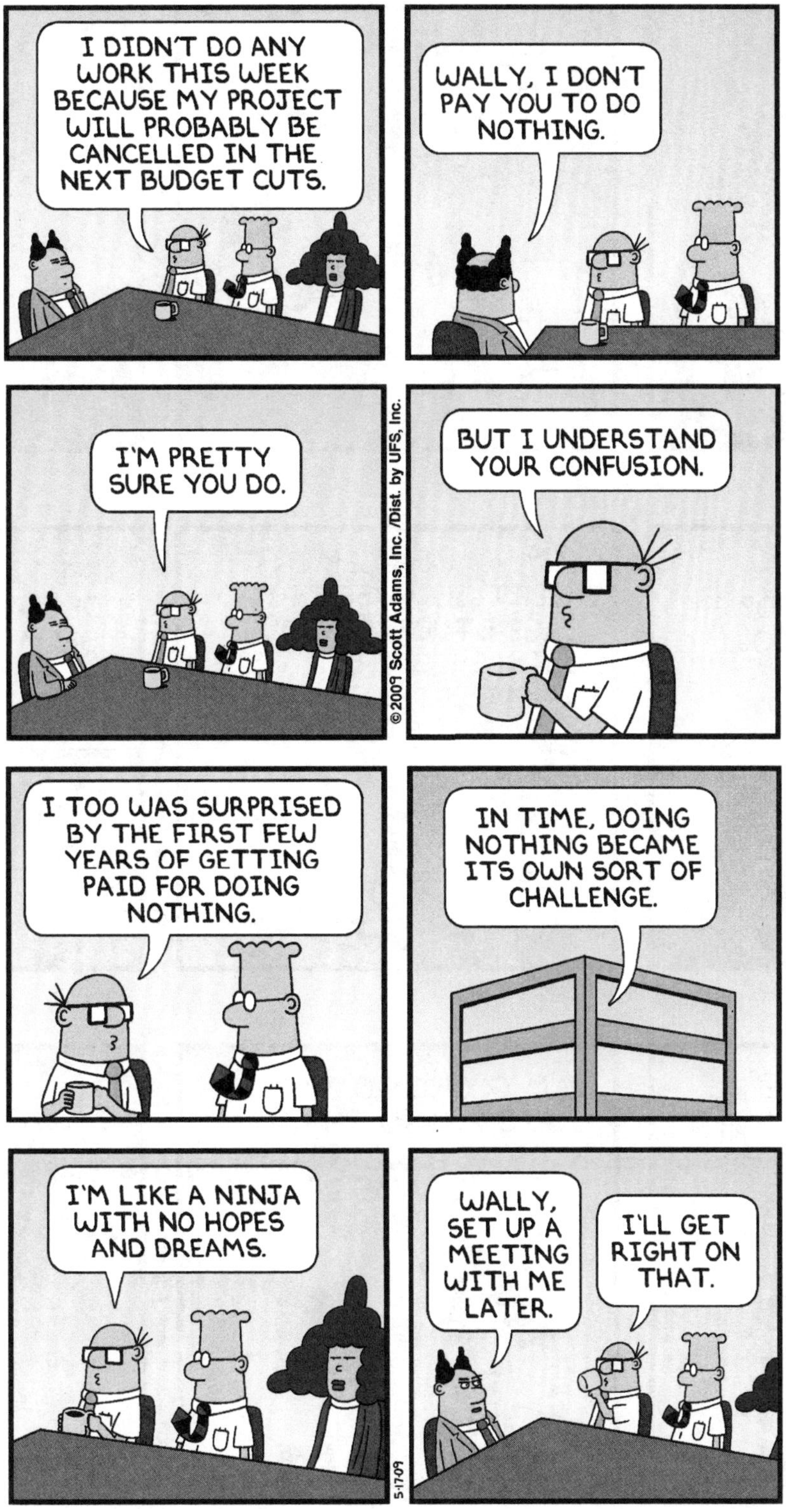
I DIDN'T DO ANY WORK THIS WEEK BECAUSE MY PROJECT WILL PROBABLY BE CANCELLED IN THE NEXT BUDGET CUTS.
WALLY, I DON'T PAY YOU TO DO NOTHING.
I'M PRETTY SURE YOU DO.
BUT I UNDERSTAND YOUR CONFUSION.
I TOO WAS SURPRISED BY THE FIRST FEW YEARS OF GETTING PAID FOR DOING NOTHING.
IN TIME, DOING NOTHING BECAME ITS OWN SORT OF CHALLENGE.
I'M LIKE A NINJA WITH NO HOPES AND DREAMS.
WALLY, SET UP A MEETING WITH ME LATER.
I'LL GET RIGHT ON THAT.
© 2009 Scott Adams, Inc. /Dist. by UFS, Inc.
5-17-09

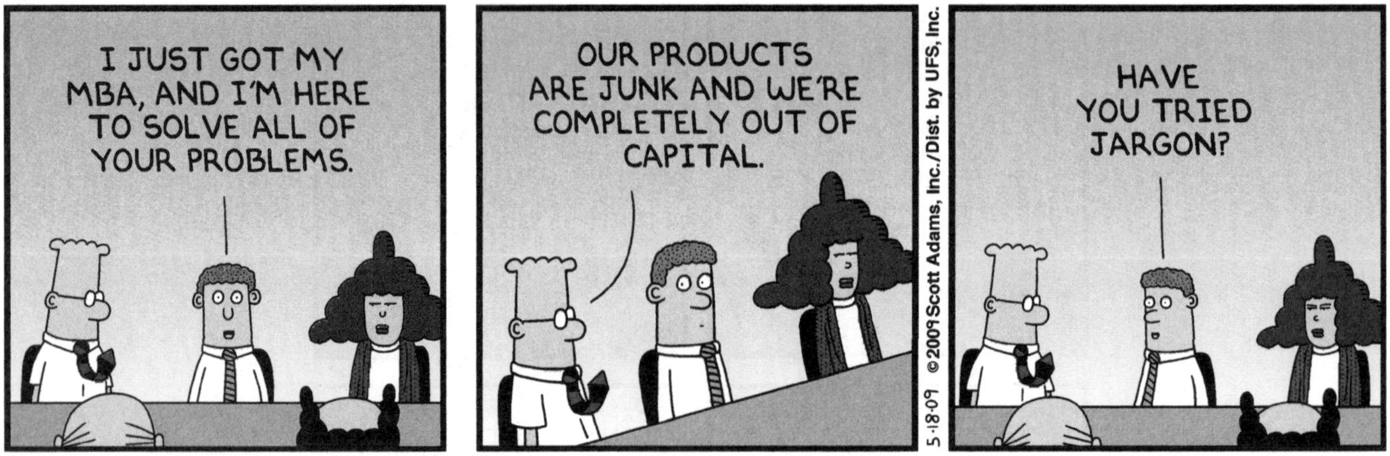
I JUST GOT MY MBA, AND I'M HERE TO SOLVE ALL OF YOUR PROBLEMS.
OUR PRODUCTS ARE JUNK AND WE'RE COMPLETELY OUT OF CAPITAL.
HAVE YOU TRIED JARGON?
5-18-09 ©2009 Scott Adams, Inc./Dist. by UFS, Inc.

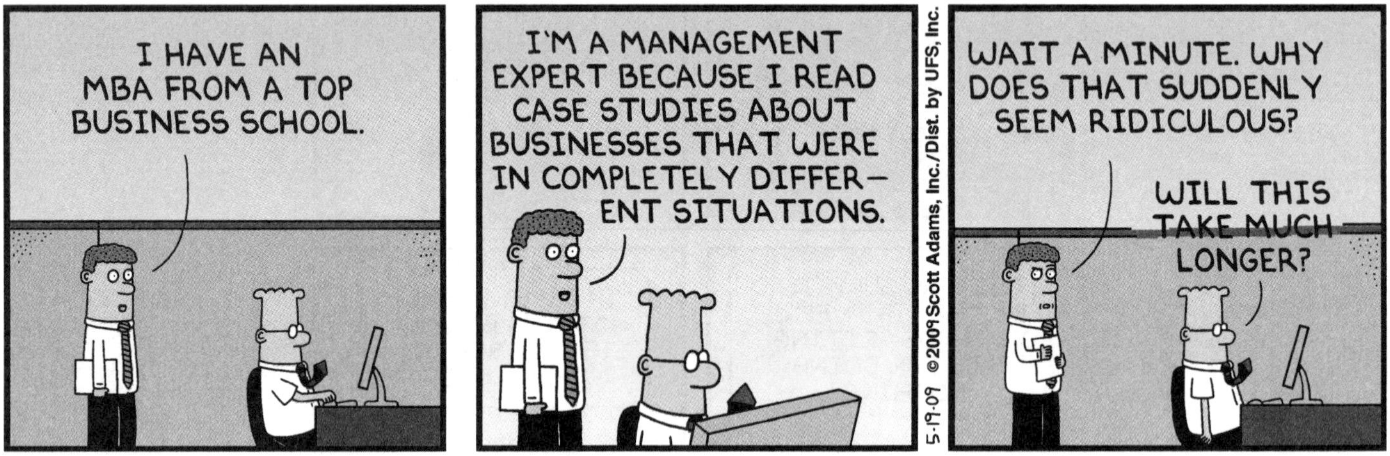
I HAVE AN MBA FROM A TOP BUSINESS SCHOOL.
I'M A MANAGEMENT EXPERT BECAUSE I READ CASE STUDIES ABOUT BUSINESSES THAT WERE IN COMPLETELY DIFFER-ENT SITUATIONS.
WAIT A MINUTE. WHY DOES THAT SUDDENLY SEEM RIDICULOUS?
WILL THIS TAKE MUCH LONGER?
5-19-09 ©2009 Scott Adams, Inc./Dist. by UFS, Inc.

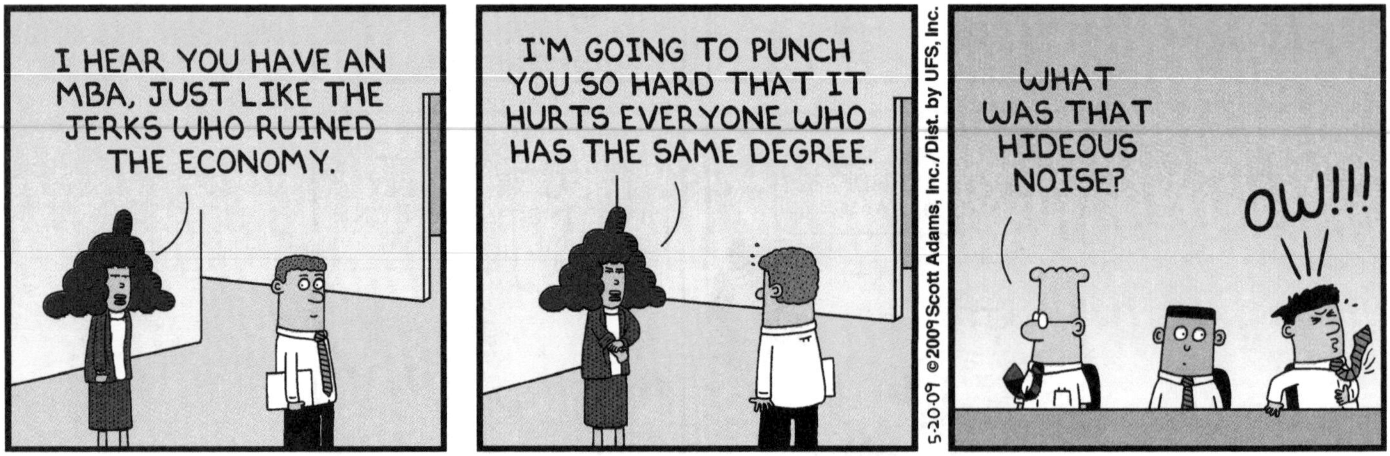
I HEAR YOU HAVE AN MBA, JUST LIKE THE JERKS WHO RUINED THE ECONOMY.
I'M GOING TO PUNCH YOU SO HARD THAT IT HURTS EVERYONE WHO HAS THE SAME DEGREE.
WHAT WAS THAT HIDEOUS NOISE?
OW!!!
5-20-09 ©2009 Scott Adams, Inc./Dist. by UFS, Inc.

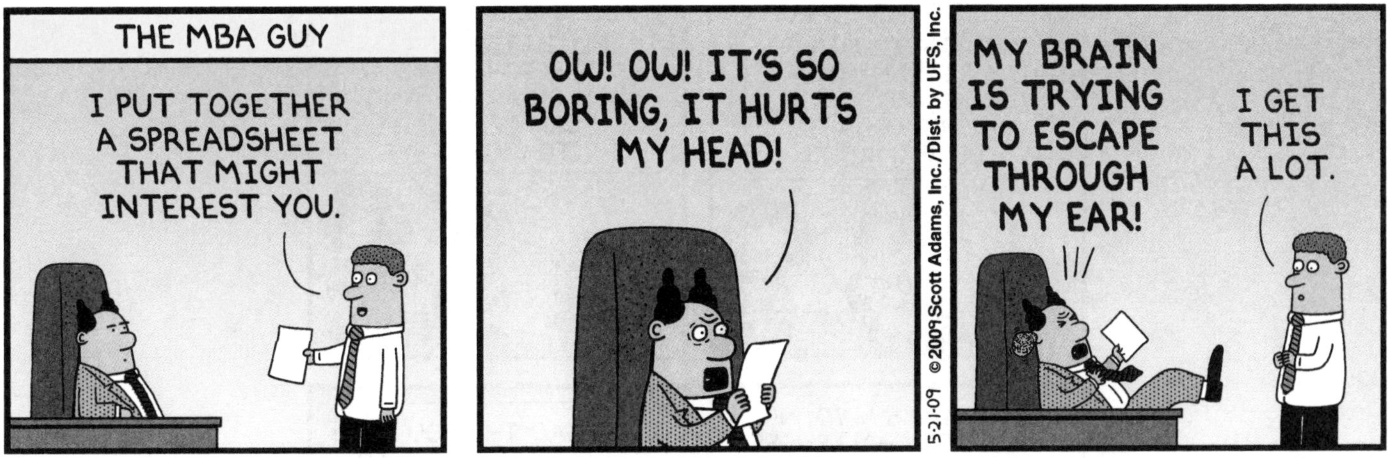
THE MBA GUY
I PUT TOGETHER A SPREADSHEET THAT MIGHT INTEREST YOU.
OW! OW! IT'S SO BORING, IT HURTS MY HEAD!
MY BRAIN IS TRYING TO ESCAPE THROUGH MY EAR!
I GET THIS A LOT.
5-21-09 ©2009 Scott Adams, Inc./Dist. by UFS, Inc.

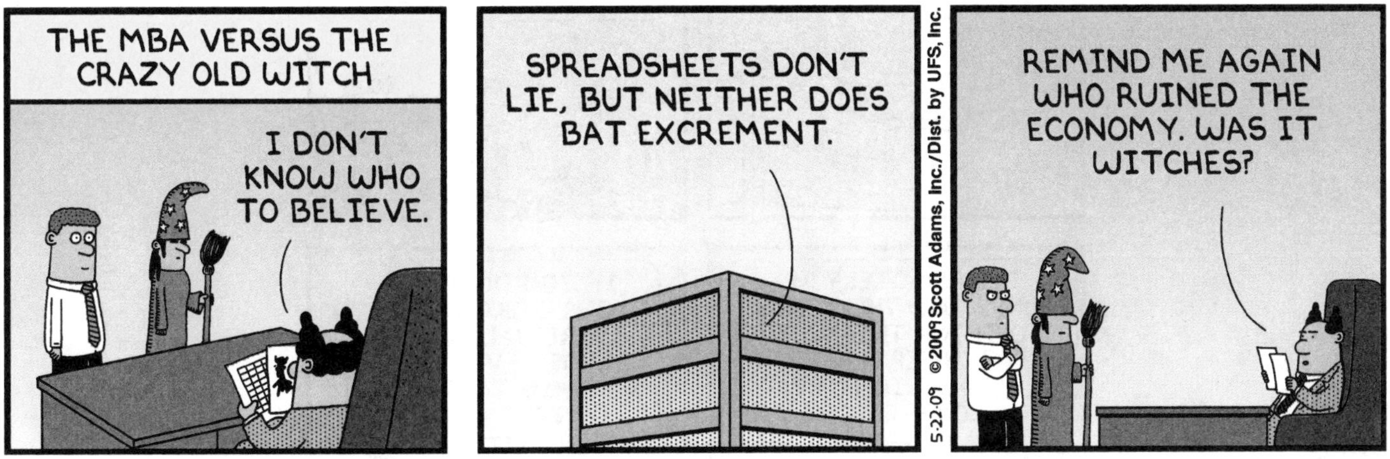
THE MBA VERSUS THE CRAZY OLD WITCH
I DON'T KNOW WHO TO BELIEVE.
SPREADSHEETS DON'T LIE, BUT NEITHER DOES BAT EXCREMENT.
REMIND ME AGAIN WHO RUINED THE ECONOMY. WAS IT WITCHES?
5-22-09 ©2009 Scott Adams, Inc./Dist. by UFS, Inc.

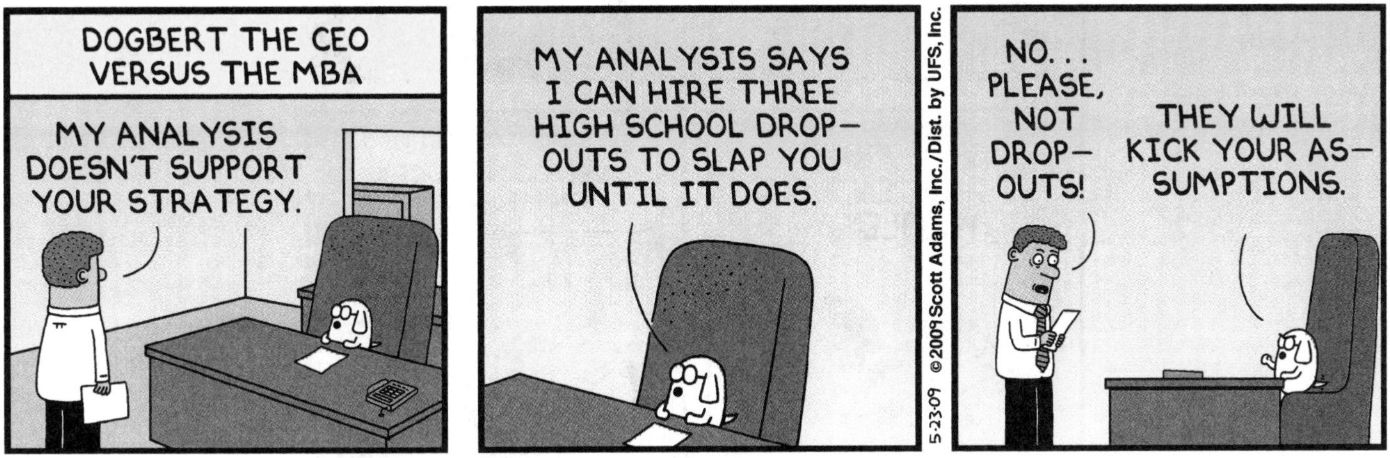
DOGBERT THE CEO VERSUS THE MBA
MY ANALYSIS DOESN'T SUPPORT YOUR STRATEGY.
MY ANALYSIS SAYS I CAN HIRE THREE HIGH SCHOOL DROP-OUTS TO SLAP YOU UNTIL IT DOES.
NO. . . PLEASE, NOT DROP-OUTS!
THEY WILL KICK YOUR AS-SUMPTIONS.
5-23-09 ©2009 Scott Adams, Inc./Dist. by UFS, Inc.

AND OBVIOUSLY I CAN'T DO ANYTHING UNTIL OUR FLOOM VENDOR UPDATES THE GLIMRODS.
I'LL BITSPEW A PROTOPATCH TO YOUR GLIMROD ARRAY AND YOU CAN GET RIGHT TO WORK.
SOMETIMES A YOUNG ENGINEER CHALLENGES THE DOMINANT WORK-AVOIDER IN THE HERD.
OH, REALLY?
TOO BAD THE ROUTER ISN'T CONFIGURED TO HANDLE PROTOPATCH SERVER TRAFFIC.
I'LL REMOTELY RE-CONFIGURE THE ROUTER TO THINK THE PROTO-PATCH SERVER IS A HEXADULIAN DATA COMPRESSOR.
IF YOU DO THAT, YOU'LL CRASH THE FIREWALL AND EXPOSE EVERYONE AT THIS TABLE TO IDENTITY THEFT!
STOP THAT! I HAVE ENOUGH PROBLEMS!
PUNCH!
NEVER GO NETWORK ON ME, KID.
5-24-09

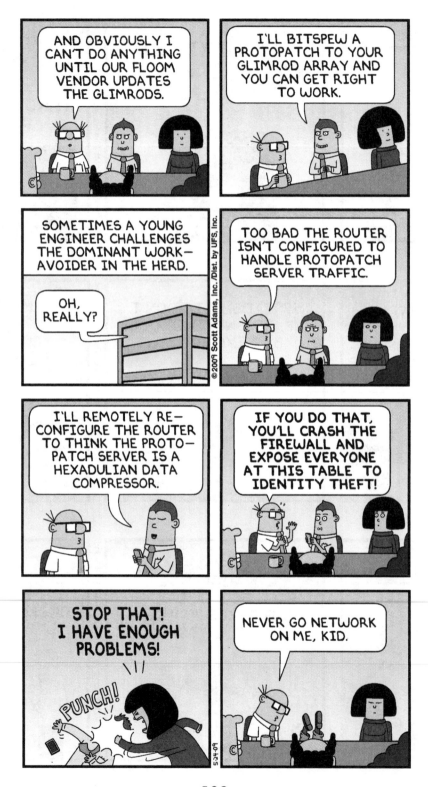

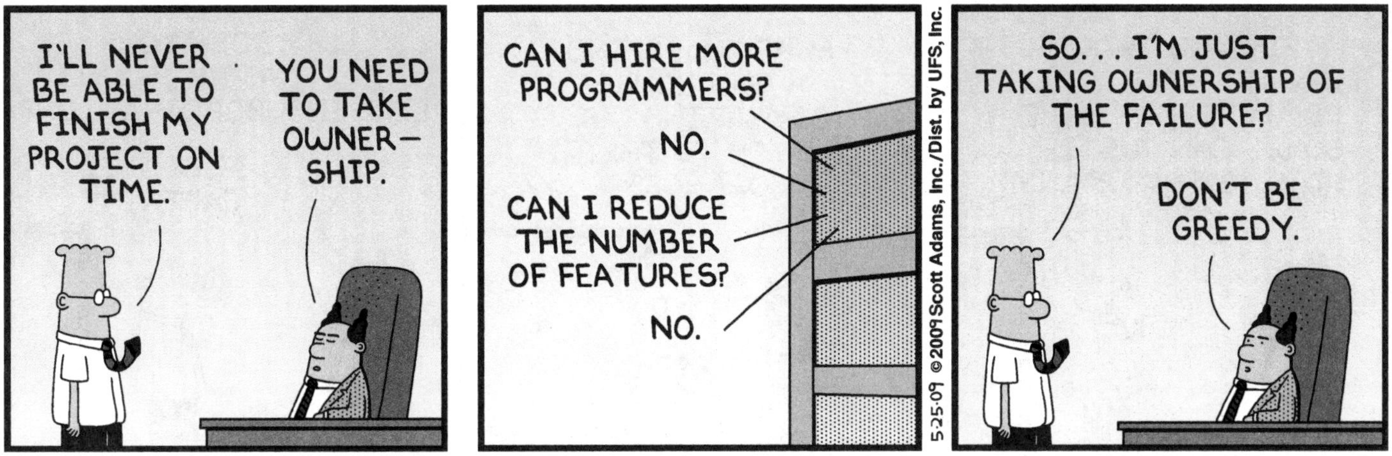
I'LL NEVER BE ABLE TO FINISH MY PROJECT ON TIME.
YOU NEED TO TAKE OWNER-SHIP.
CAN I HIRE MORE PROGRAMMERS?
NO.
CAN I REDUCE THE NUMBER OF FEATURES?
NO.
5-25-09 ©2009 Scott Adams, Inc./Dist. by UFS, Inc.
SO... I'M JUST TAKING OWNERSHIP OF THE FAILURE?
DON'T BE GREEDY.

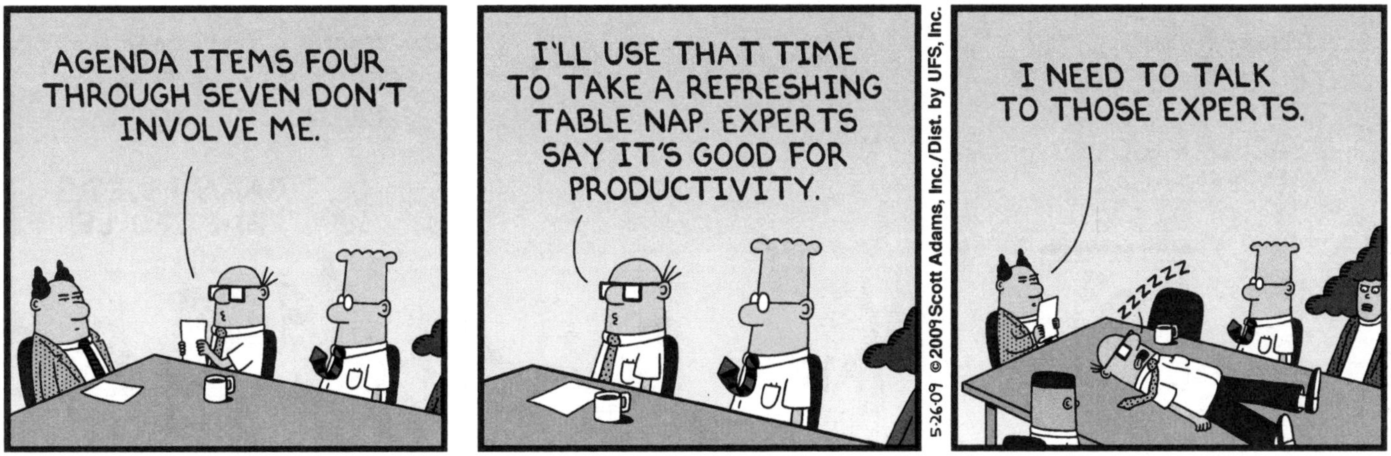
AGENDA ITEMS FOUR THROUGH SEVEN DON'T INVOLVE ME.
I'LL USE THAT TIME TO TAKE A REFRESHING TABLE NAP. EXPERTS SAY IT'S GOOD FOR PRODUCTIVITY.
5-26-09 ©2009 Scott Adams, Inc./Dist. by UFS, Inc.
I NEED TO TALK TO THOSE EXPERTS.
ZZZZZZ

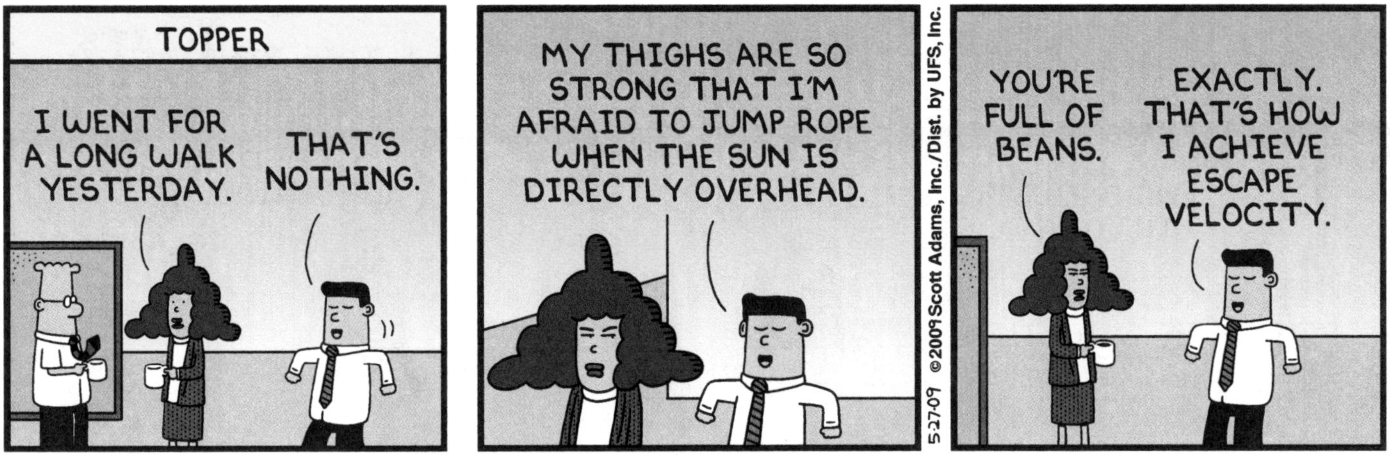
TOPPER
I WENT FOR A LONG WALK YESTERDAY.
THAT'S NOTHING.
MY THIGHS ARE SO STRONG THAT I'M AFRAID TO JUMP ROPE WHEN THE SUN IS DIRECTLY OVERHEAD.
5-27-09 ©2009 Scott Adams, Inc./Dist. by UFS, Inc.
YOU'RE FULL OF BEANS.
EXACTLY. THAT'S HOW I ACHIEVE ESCAPE VELOCITY.

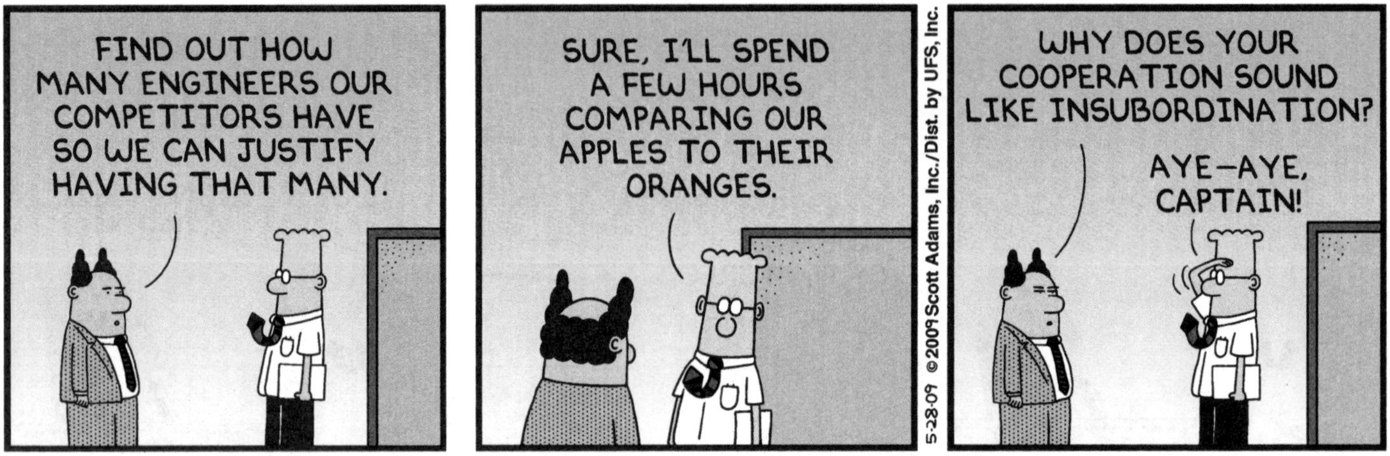
FIND OUT HOW MANY ENGINEERS OUR COMPETITORS HAVE SO WE CAN JUSTIFY HAVING THAT MANY.
SURE, I'LL SPEND A FEW HOURS COMPARING OUR APPLES TO THEIR ORANGES.
5-28-09 ©2009 Scott Adams, Inc./Dist. by UFS, Inc.
WHY DOES YOUR COOPERATION SOUND LIKE INSUBORDINATION?
AYE-AYE, CAPTAIN!

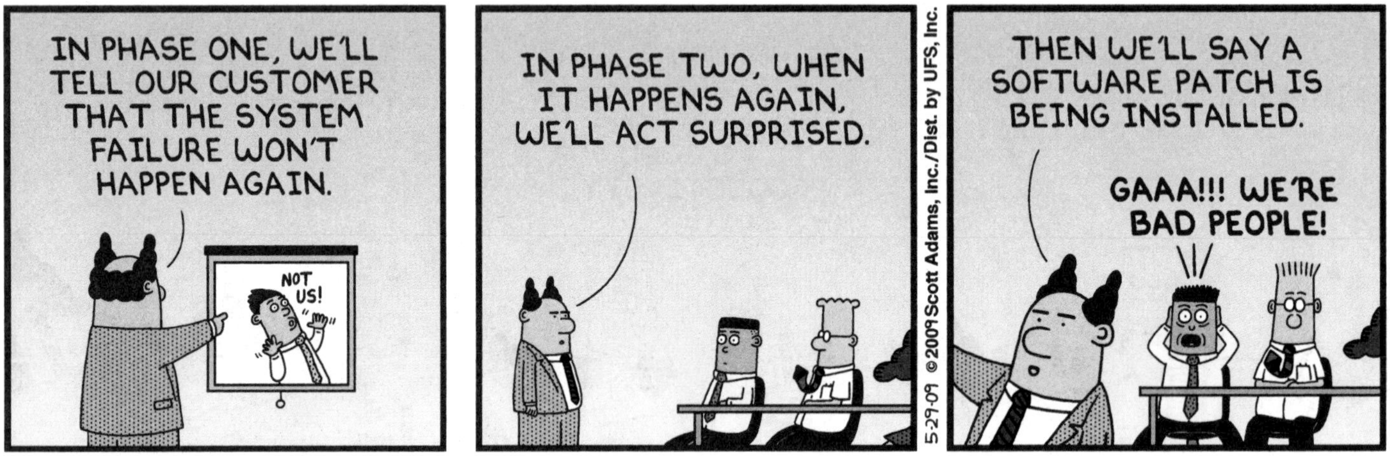
IN PHASE ONE, WE'LL TELL OUR CUSTOMER THAT THE SYSTEM FAILURE WON'T HAPPEN AGAIN.
NOT US!
IN PHASE TWO, WHEN IT HAPPENS AGAIN, WE'LL ACT SURPRISED.
5-29-09 ©2009 Scott Adams, Inc./Dist. by UFS, Inc.
THEN WE'LL SAY A SOFTWARE PATCH IS BEING INSTALLED.
GAAA!!! WE'RE BAD PEOPLE!

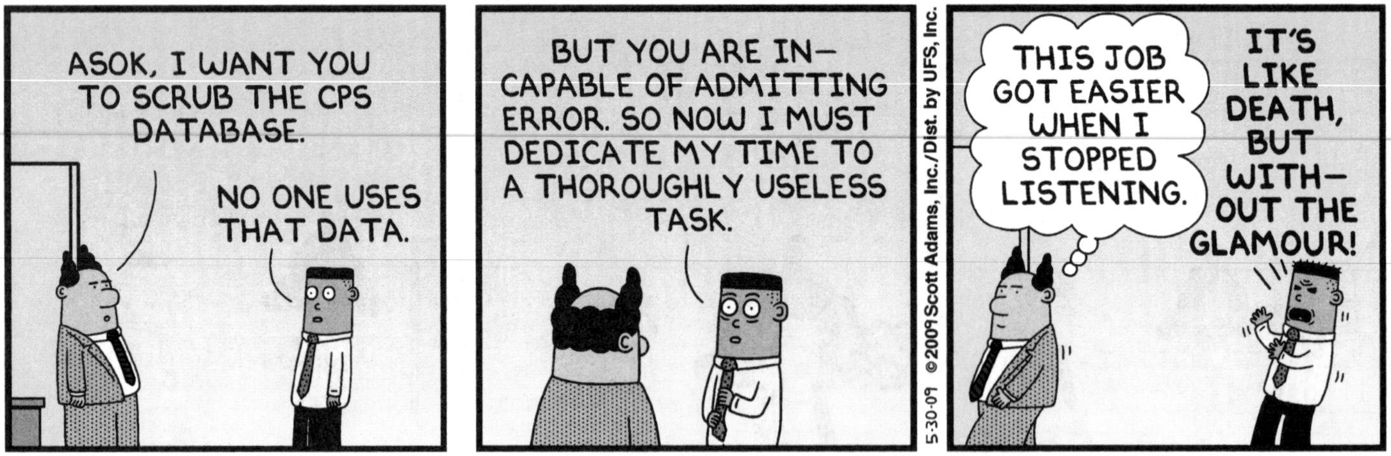
ASOK, I WANT YOU TO SCRUB THE CPS DATABASE.
NO ONE USES THAT DATA.
BUT YOU ARE INCAPABLE OF ADMITTING ERROR. SO NOW I MUST DEDICATE MY TIME TO A THOROUGHLY USELESS TASK.
5-30-09 ©2009 Scott Adams, Inc./Dist. by UFS, Inc.
THIS JOB GOT EASIER WHEN I STOPPED LISTENING.
IT'S LIKE DEATH, BUT WITHOUT THE GLAMOUR!

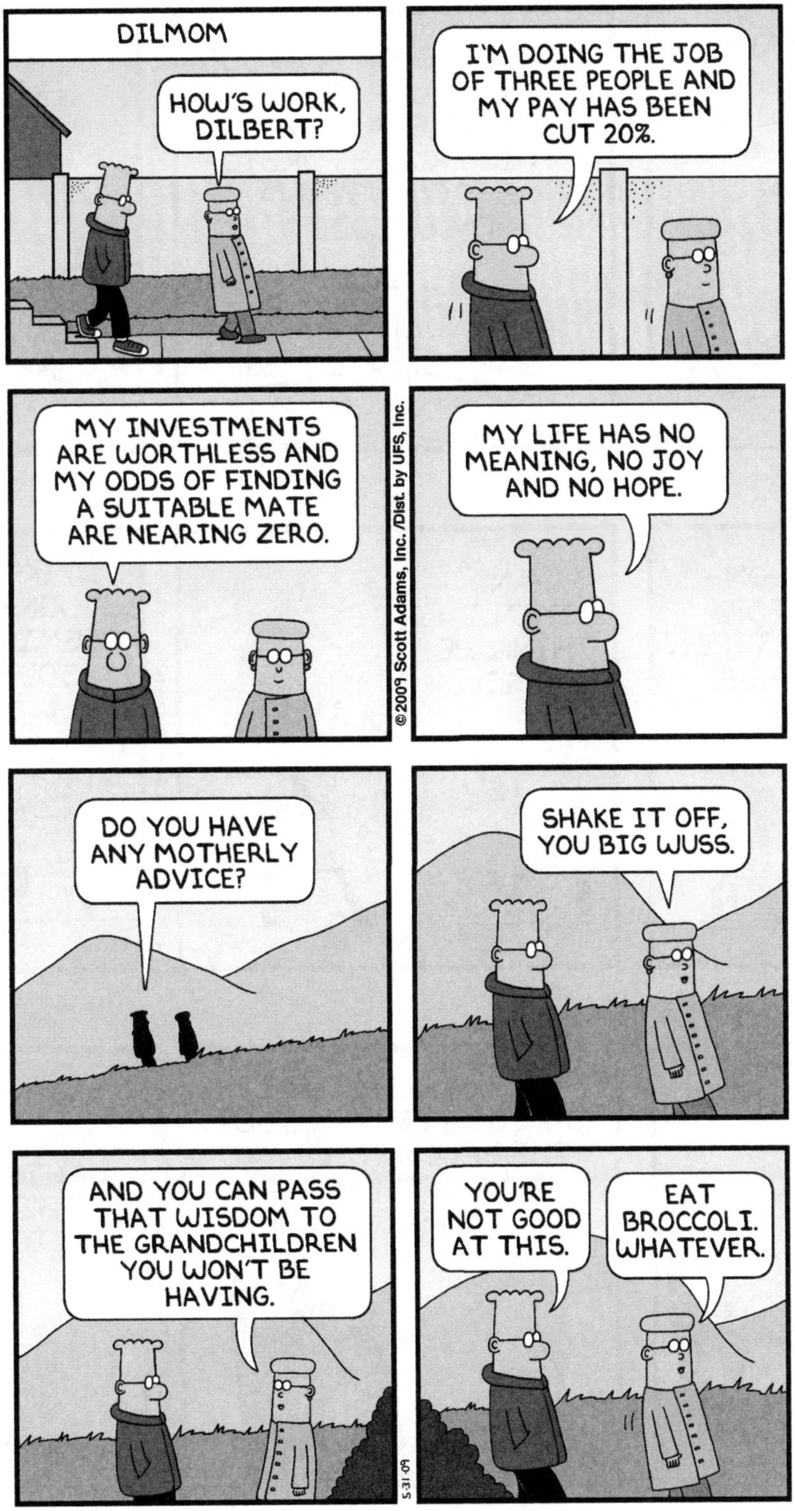
DILMOM
HOW'S WORK, DILBERT?
I'M DOING THE JOB OF THREE PEOPLE AND MY PAY HAS BEEN CUT 20%.
MY INVESTMENTS ARE WORTHLESS AND MY ODDS OF FINDING A SUITABLE MATE ARE NEARING ZERO.
MY LIFE HAS NO MEANING, NO JOY AND NO HOPE.
DO YOU HAVE ANY MOTHERLY ADVICE?
SHAKE IT OFF, YOU BIG WUSS.
AND YOU CAN PASS THAT WISDOM TO THE GRANDCHILDREN YOU WON'T BE HAVING.
YOU'RE NOT GOOD AT THIS.
EAT BROCCOLI. WHATEVER.
©2009 Scott Adams, Inc./Dist. by UFS, Inc.
5-31-09

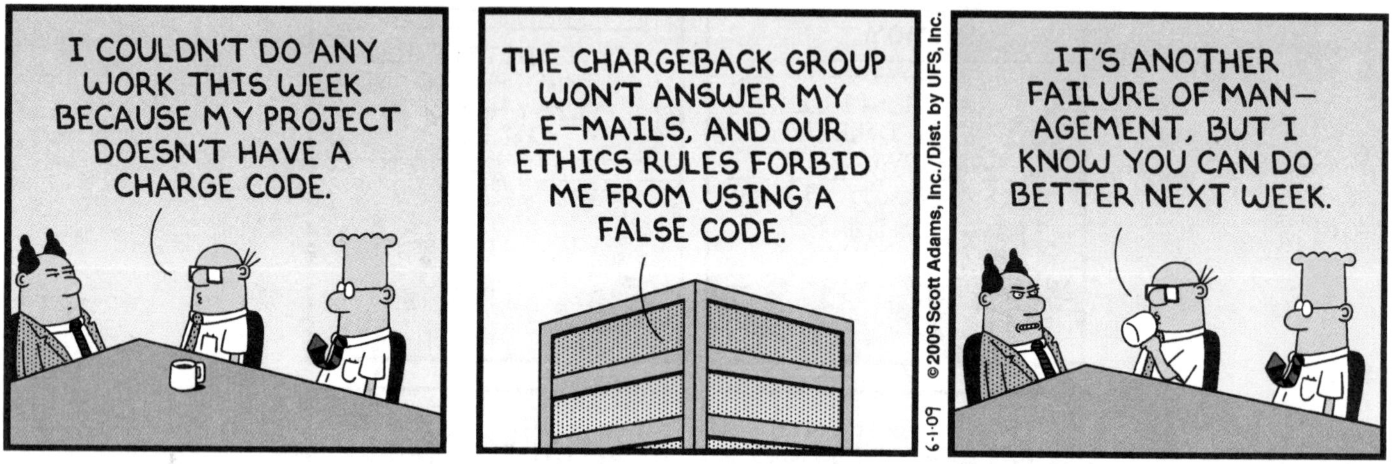
I COULDN'T DO ANY WORK THIS WEEK BECAUSE MY PROJECT DOESN'T HAVE A CHARGE CODE.
THE CHARGEBACK GROUP WON'T ANSWER MY E-MAILS, AND OUR ETHICS RULES FORBID ME FROM USING A FALSE CODE.
6-1-09 ©2009 Scott Adams, Inc./Dist. by UFS, Inc.
IT'S ANOTHER FAILURE OF MAN-AGEMENT, BUT I KNOW YOU CAN DO BETTER NEXT WEEK.

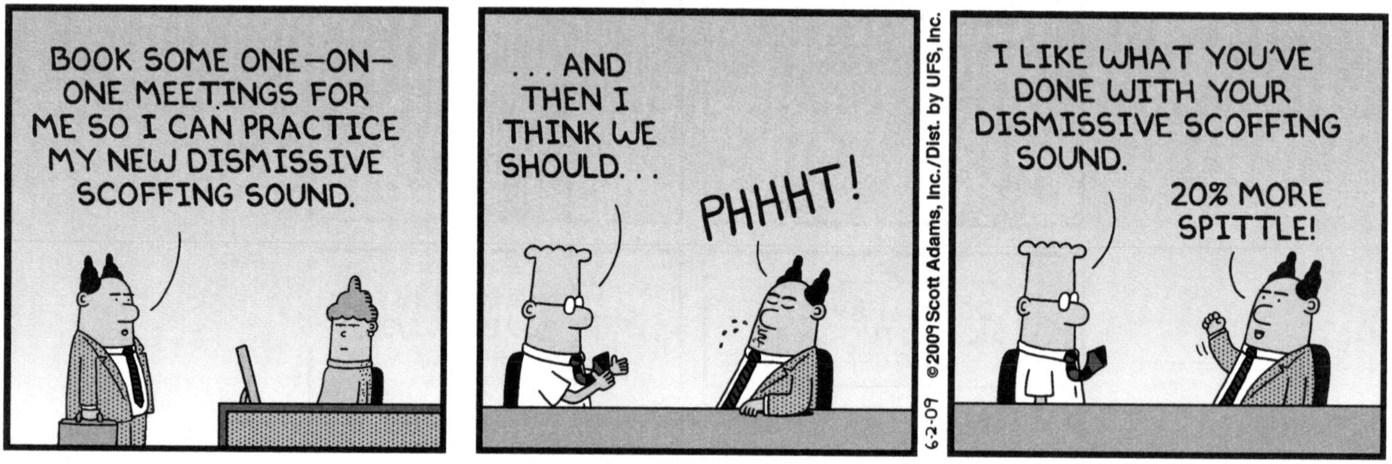
BOOK SOME ONE-ON-ONE MEETINGS FOR ME SO I CAN PRACTICE MY NEW DISMISSIVE SCOFFING SOUND.
. . . AND THEN I THINK WE SHOULD. . .
PHHHT!
6-2-09 ©2009 Scott Adams, Inc./Dist. by UFS, Inc.
I LIKE WHAT YOU'VE DONE WITH YOUR DISMISSIVE SCOFFING SOUND.
20% MORE SPITTLE!

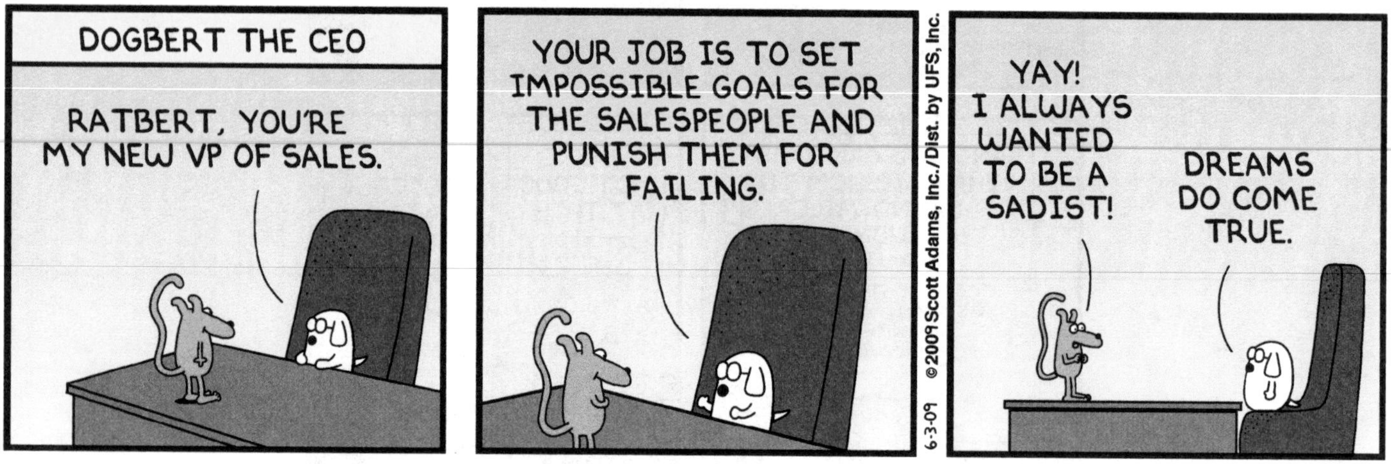
DOGBERT THE CEO
RATBERT, YOU'RE MY NEW VP OF SALES.
YOUR JOB IS TO SET IMPOSSIBLE GOALS FOR THE SALESPEOPLE AND PUNISH THEM FOR FAILING.
6-3-09 ©2009 Scott Adams, Inc./Dist. by UFS, Inc.
YAY! I ALWAYS WANTED TO BE A SADIST!
DREAMS DO COME TRUE.

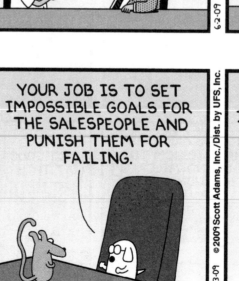

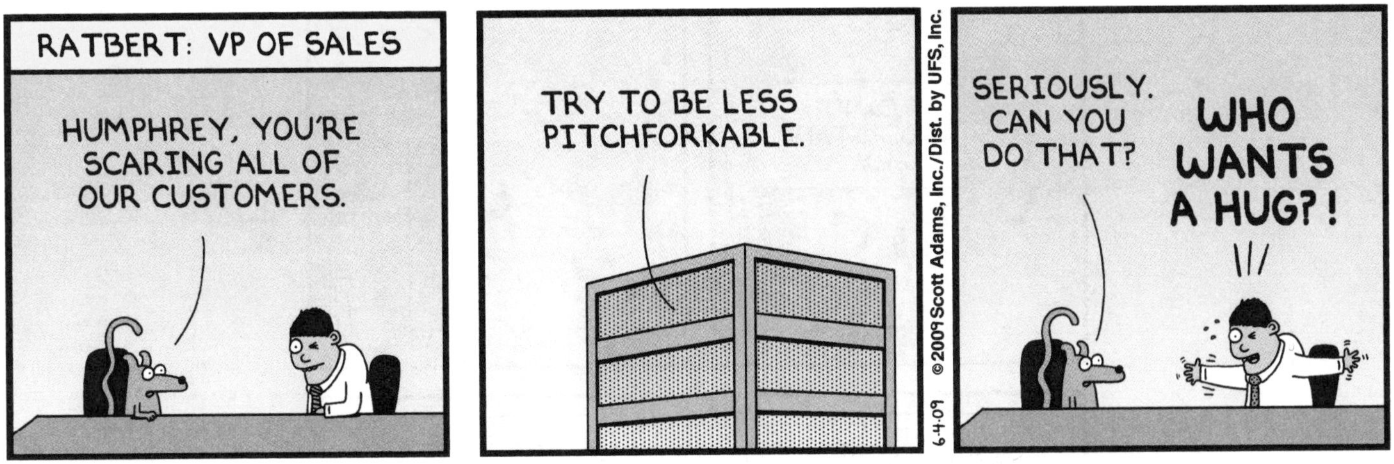
RATBERT: VP OF SALES
HUMPHREY, YOU'RE SCARING ALL OF OUR CUSTOMERS.
TRY TO BE LESS PITCHFORKABLE.
6-4-09 ©2009 Scott Adams, Inc./Dist. by UFS, Inc.
SERIOUSLY. CAN YOU DO THAT?
WHO WANTS A HUG?!

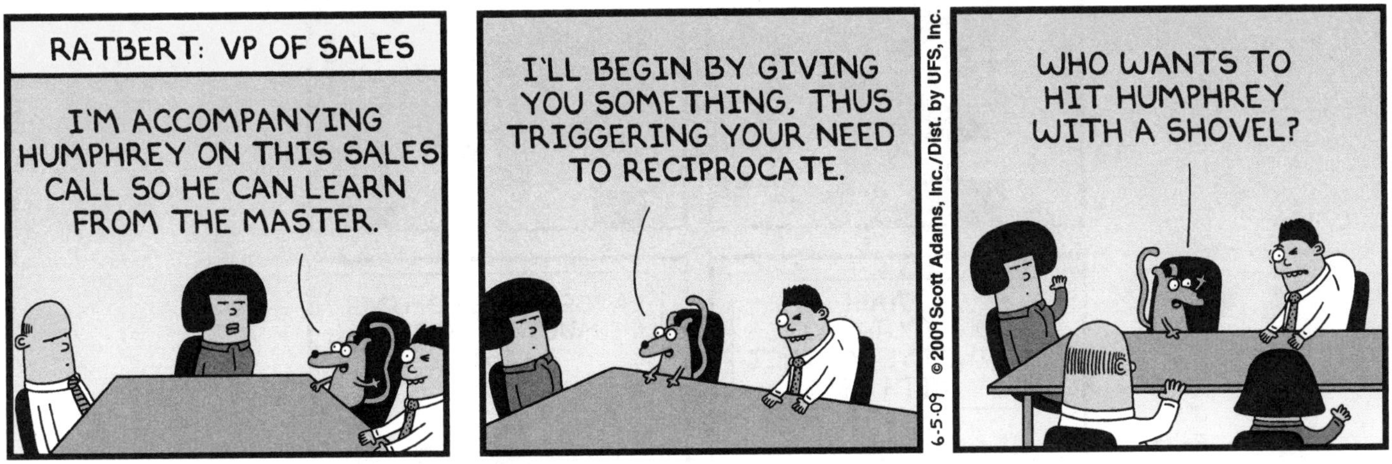
RATBERT: VP OF SALES
I'M ACCOMPANYING HUMPHREY ON THIS SALES CALL SO HE CAN LEARN FROM THE MASTER.
I'LL BEGIN BY GIVING YOU SOMETHING, THUS TRIGGERING YOUR NEED TO RECIPROCATE.
6-5-09 ©2009 Scott Adams, Inc./Dist. by UFS, Inc.
WHO WANTS TO HIT HUMPHREY WITH A SHOVEL?

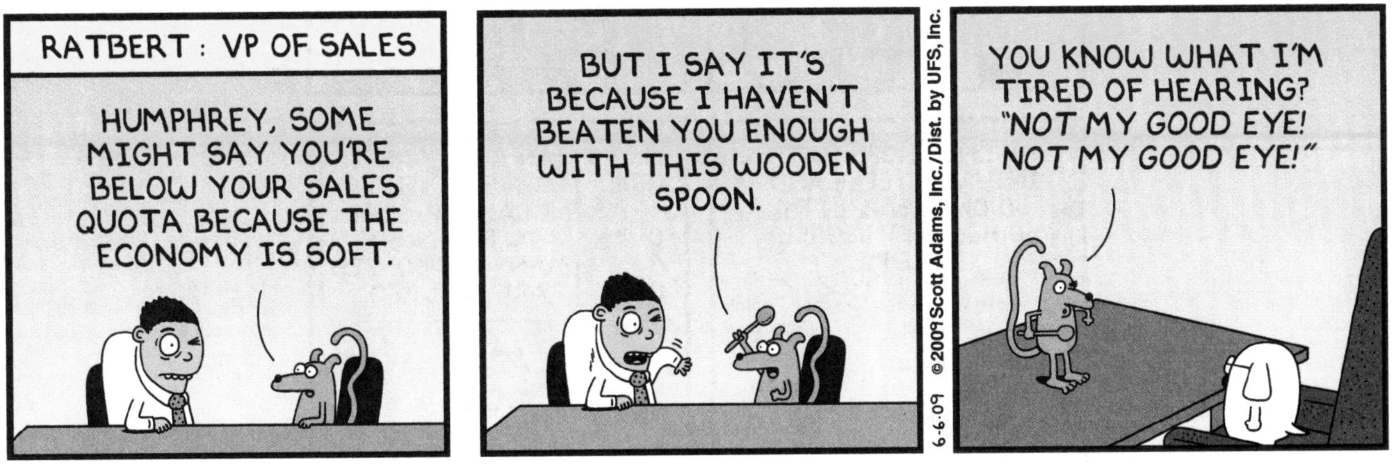
RATBERT : VP OF SALES
HUMPHREY, SOME MIGHT SAY YOU'RE BELOW YOUR SALES QUOTA BECAUSE THE ECONOMY IS SOFT.
BUT I SAY IT'S BECAUSE I HAVEN'T BEATEN YOU ENOUGH WITH THIS WOODEN SPOON.
6-6-09 ©2009 Scott Adams, Inc./Dist. by UFS, Inc.
YOU KNOW WHAT I'M TIRED OF HEARING? "NOT MY GOOD EYE! NOT MY GOOD EYE!"

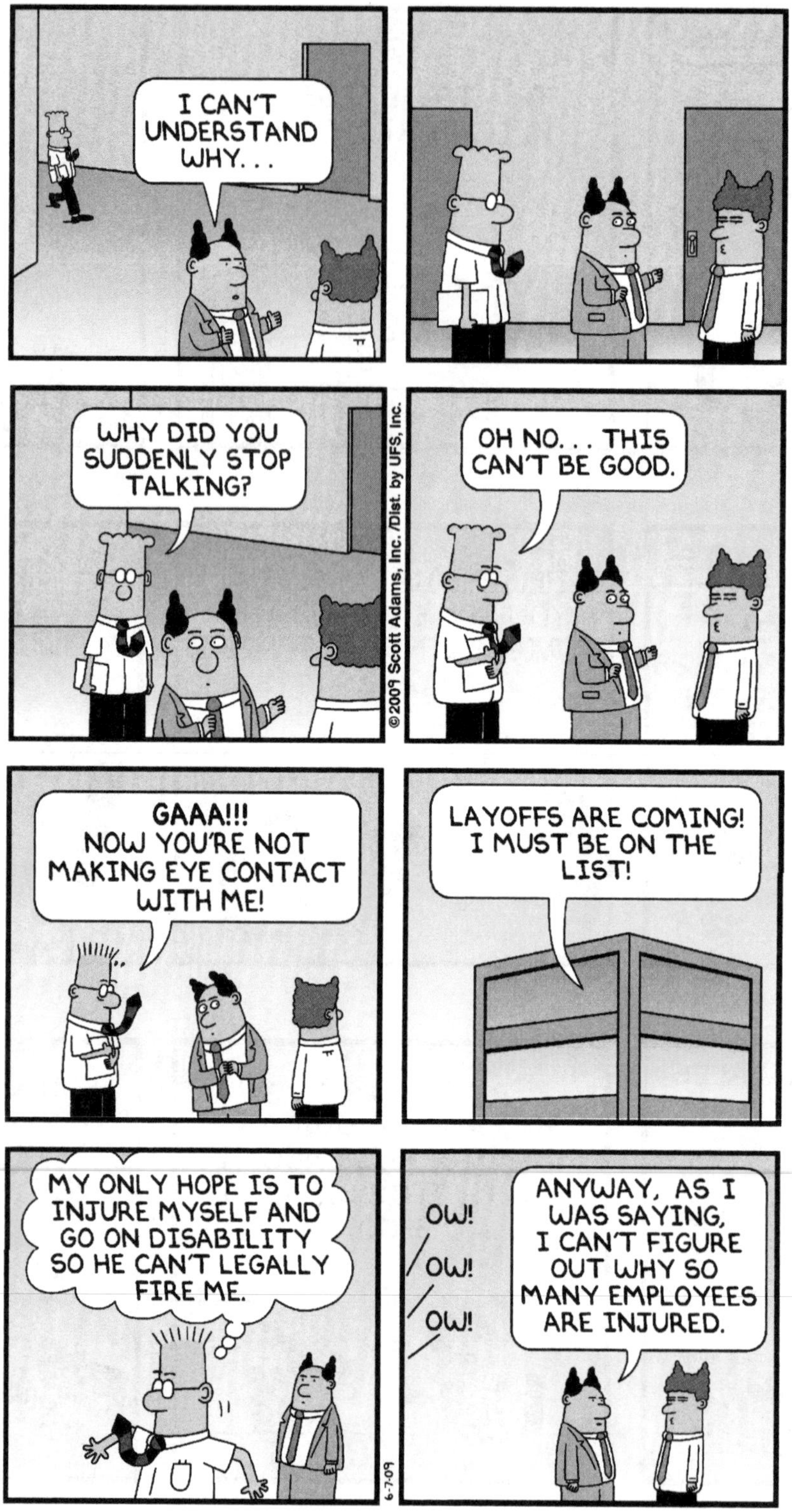
I CAN'T UNDERSTAND WHY. . .
WHY DID YOU SUDDENLY STOP TALKING?
OH NO. . . THIS CAN'T BE GOOD.
GAAA!!! NOW YOU'RE NOT MAKING EYE CONTACT WITH ME!
LAYOFFS ARE COMING! I MUST BE ON THE LIST!
MY ONLY HOPE IS TO INJURE MYSELF AND GO ON DISABILITY SO HE CAN'T LEGALLY FIRE ME.
OW!
OW!
OW!
ANYWAY, AS I WAS SAYING, I CAN'T FIGURE OUT WHY SO MANY EMPLOYEES ARE INJURED.
©2009 Scott Adams, Inc./Dist. by UFS, Inc.
6-7-09

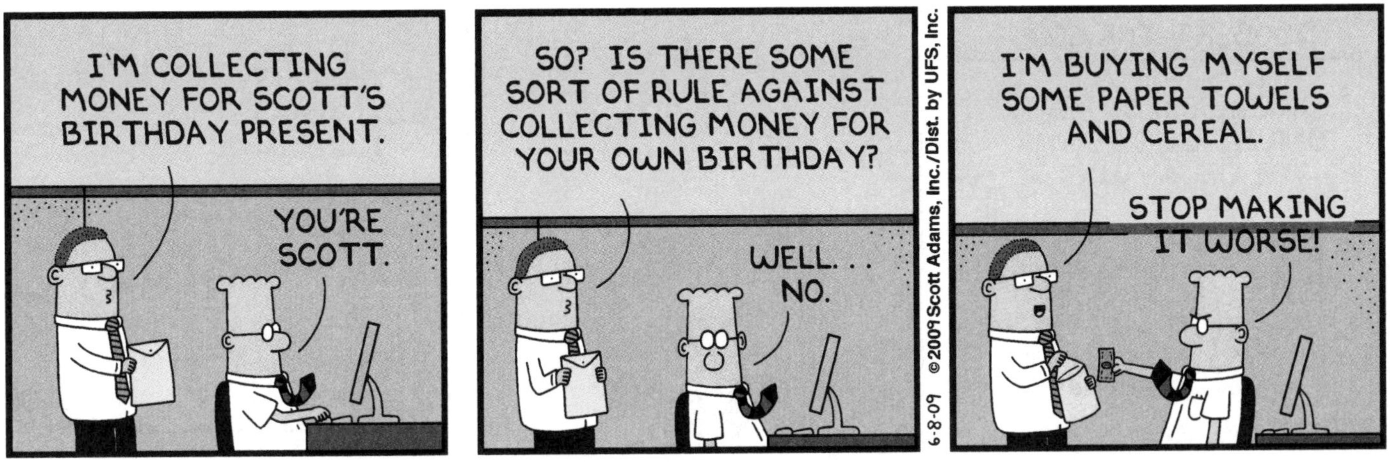
I'M COLLECTING MONEY FOR SCOTT'S BIRTHDAY PRESENT.
YOU'RE SCOTT.
SO? IS THERE SOME SORT OF RULE AGAINST COLLECTING MONEY FOR YOUR OWN BIRTHDAY?
WELL. . . NO.
6-8-09 © 2009 Scott Adams, Inc./Dist. by UFS, Inc.
I'M BUYING MYSELF SOME PAPER TOWELS AND CEREAL.
STOP MAKING IT WORSE!

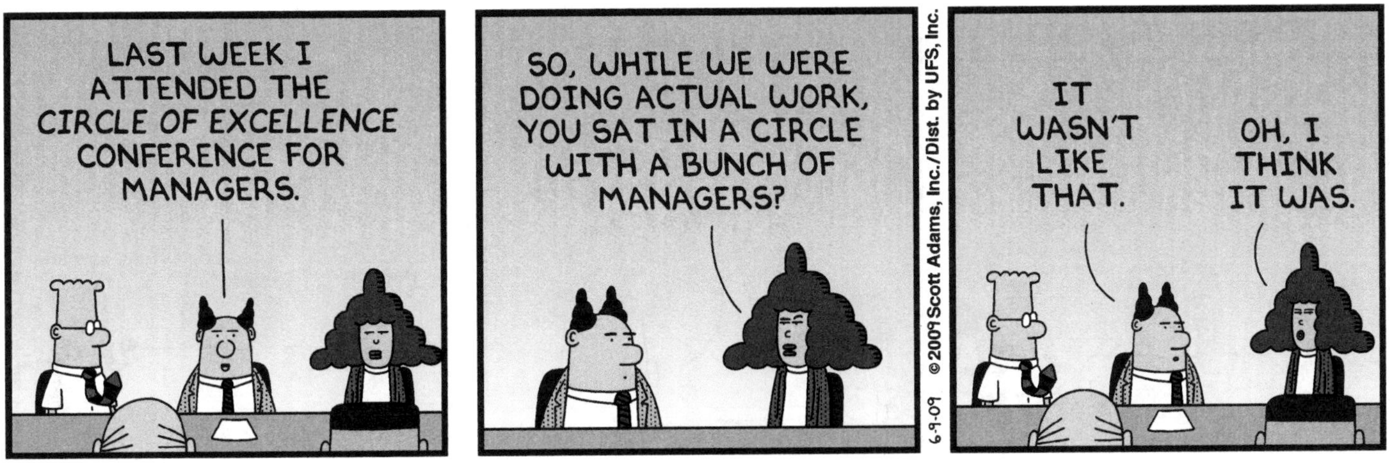
LAST WEEK I ATTENDED THE CIRCLE OF EXCELLENCE CONFERENCE FOR MANAGERS.
SO, WHILE WE WERE DOING ACTUAL WORK, YOU SAT IN A CIRCLE WITH A BUNCH OF MANAGERS?
6-9-09 © 2009 Scott Adams, Inc./Dist. by UFS, Inc.
IT WASN'T LIKE THAT.
OH, I THINK IT WAS.

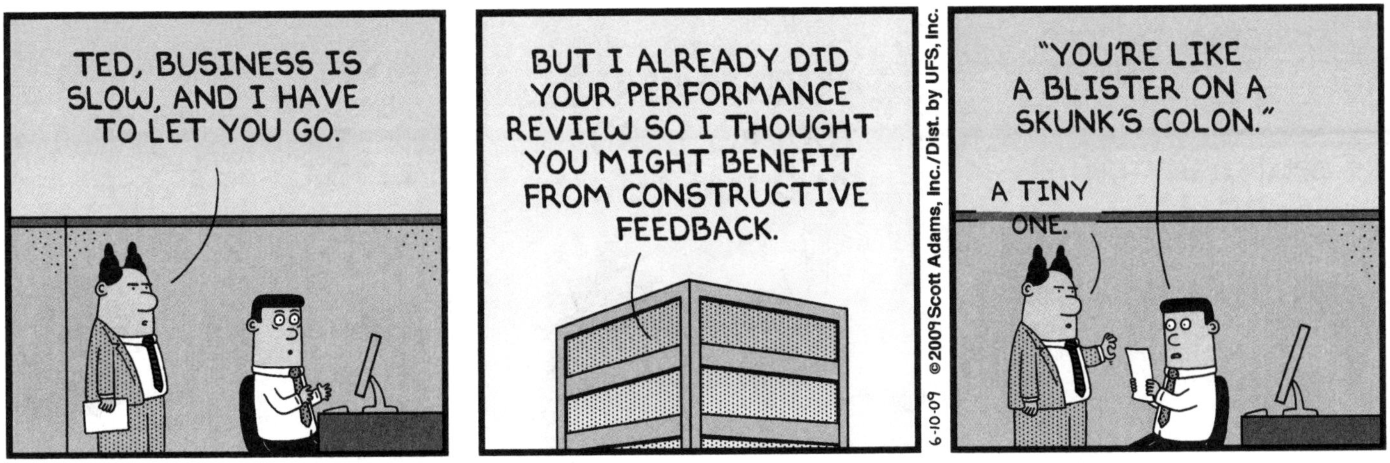
TED, BUSINESS IS SLOW, AND I HAVE TO LET YOU GO.
BUT I ALREADY DID YOUR PERFORMANCE REVIEW SO I THOUGHT YOU MIGHT BENEFIT FROM CONSTRUCTIVE FEEDBACK.
6-10-09 © 2009 Scott Adams, Inc./Dist. by UFS, Inc.
"YOU'RE LIKE A BLISTER ON A SKUNK'S COLON."
A TINY ONE.

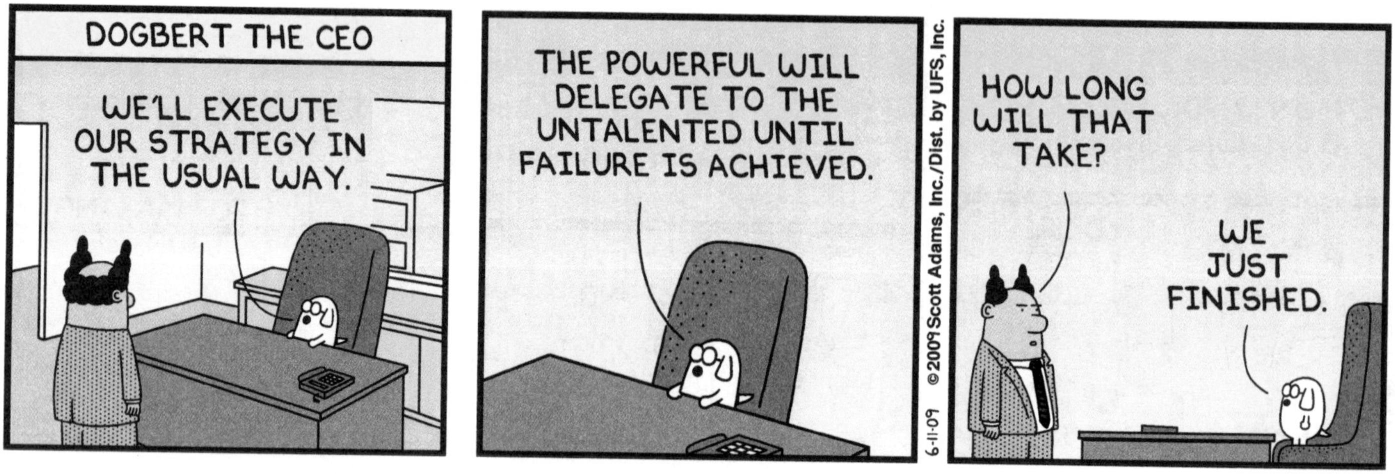
DOGBERT THE CEO
WE'LL EXECUTE OUR STRATEGY IN THE USUAL WAY.
THE POWERFUL WILL DELEGATE TO THE UNTALENTED UNTIL FAILURE IS ACHIEVED.
6-11-09 ©2009 Scott Adams, Inc./Dist. by UFS, Inc.
HOW LONG WILL THAT TAKE?
WE JUST FINISHED.

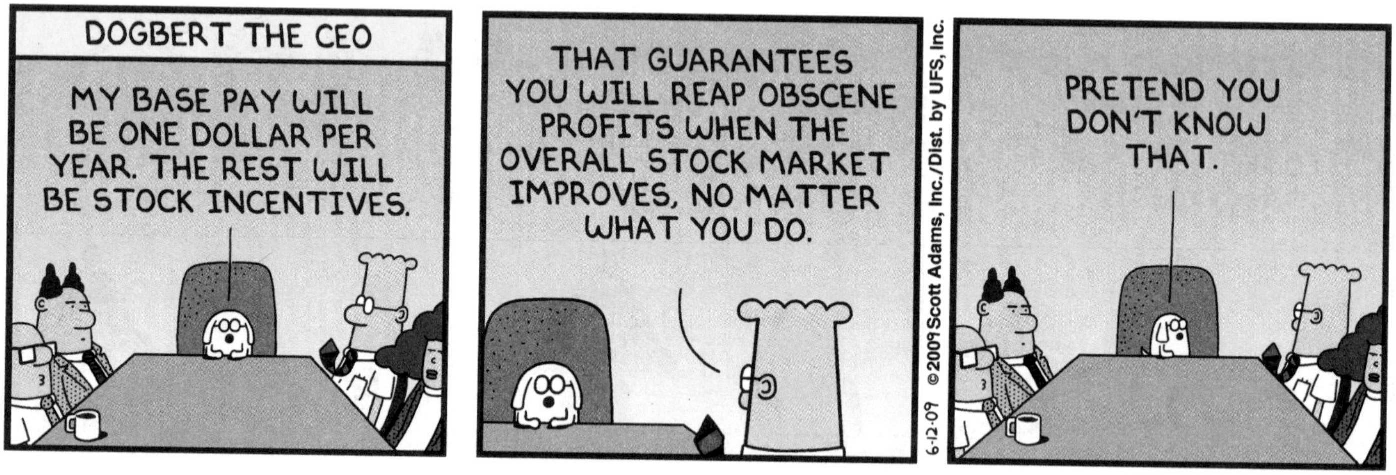
DOGBERT THE CEO
MY BASE PAY WILL BE ONE DOLLAR PER YEAR. THE REST WILL BE STOCK INCENTIVES.
THAT GUARANTEES YOU WILL REAP OBSCENE PROFITS WHEN THE OVERALL STOCK MARKET IMPROVES, NO MATTER WHAT YOU DO.
6-12-09 ©2009 Scott Adams, Inc./Dist. by UFS, Inc.
PRETEND YOU DON'T KNOW THAT.

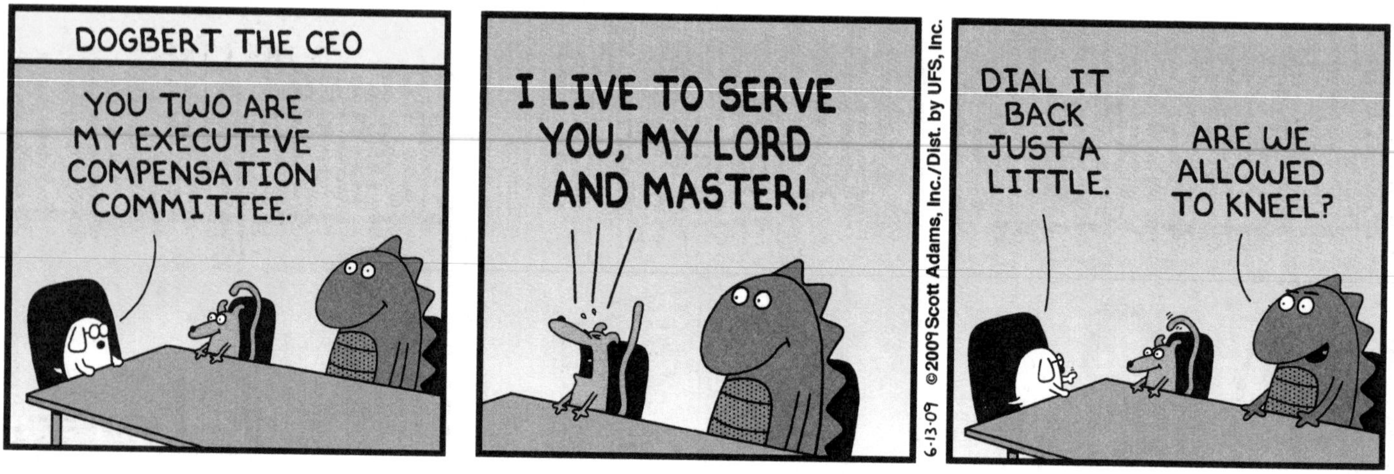
DOGBERT THE CEO
YOU TWO ARE MY EXECUTIVE COMPENSATION COMMITTEE.
I LIVE TO SERVE YOU, MY LORD AND MASTER!
6-13-09 ©2009 Scott Adams, Inc./Dist. by UFS, Inc.
DIAL IT BACK JUST A LITTLE.
ARE WE ALLOWED TO KNEEL?

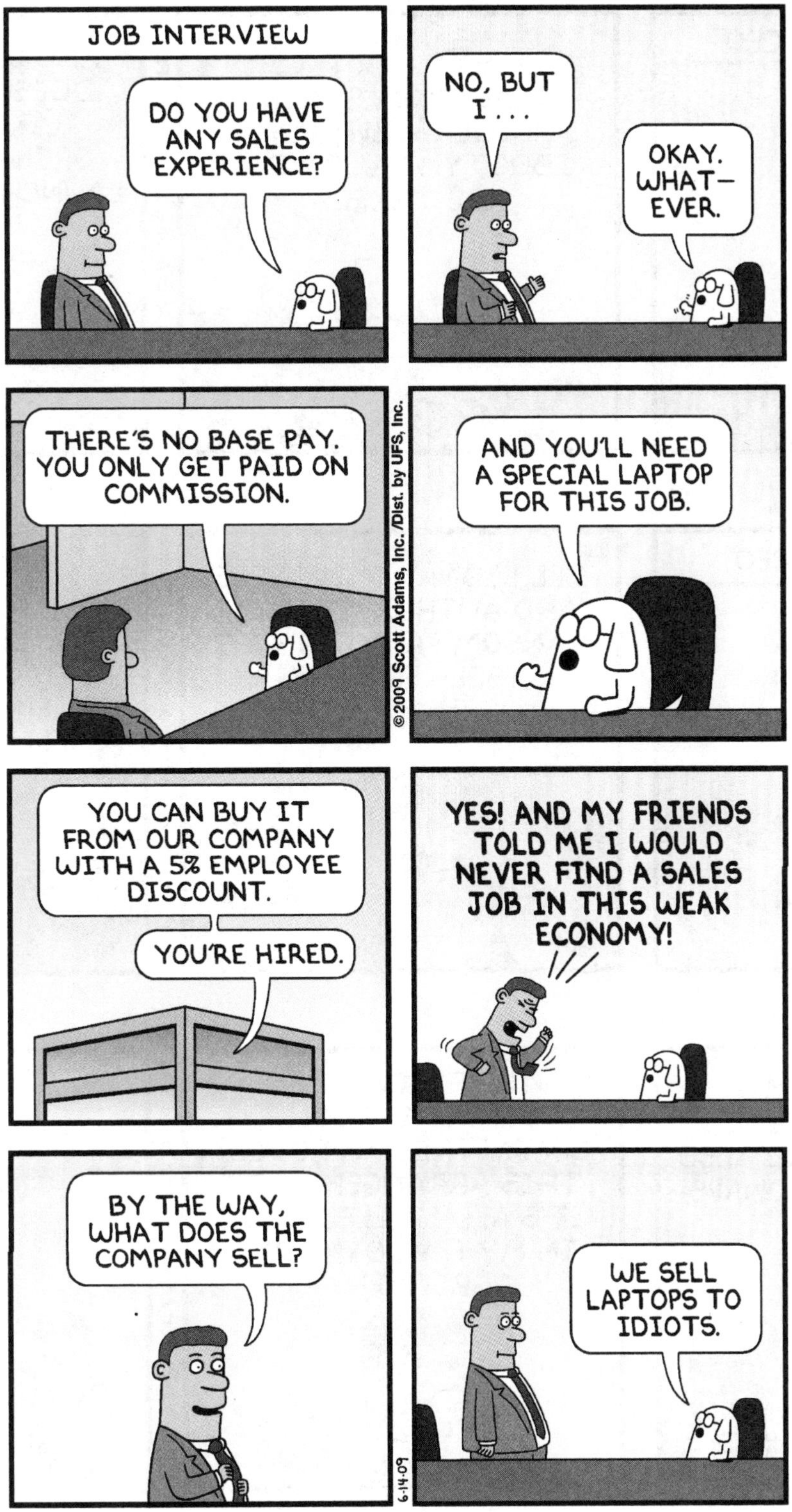
JOB INTERVIEW
DO YOU HAVE ANY SALES EXPERIENCE?
NO, BUT I . . .
OKAY. WHAT–EVER.
THERE'S NO BASE PAY. YOU ONLY GET PAID ON COMMISSION.
AND YOU'LL NEED A SPECIAL LAPTOP FOR THIS JOB.
YOU CAN BUY IT FROM OUR COMPANY WITH A 5% EMPLOYEE DISCOUNT.
YOU'RE HIRED.
YES! AND MY FRIENDS TOLD ME I WOULD NEVER FIND A SALES JOB IN THIS WEAK ECONOMY!
BY THE WAY, WHAT DOES THE COMPANY SELL?
WE SELL LAPTOPS TO IDIOTS.
©2009 Scott Adams, Inc./Dist. by UFS, Inc.
6-14-09

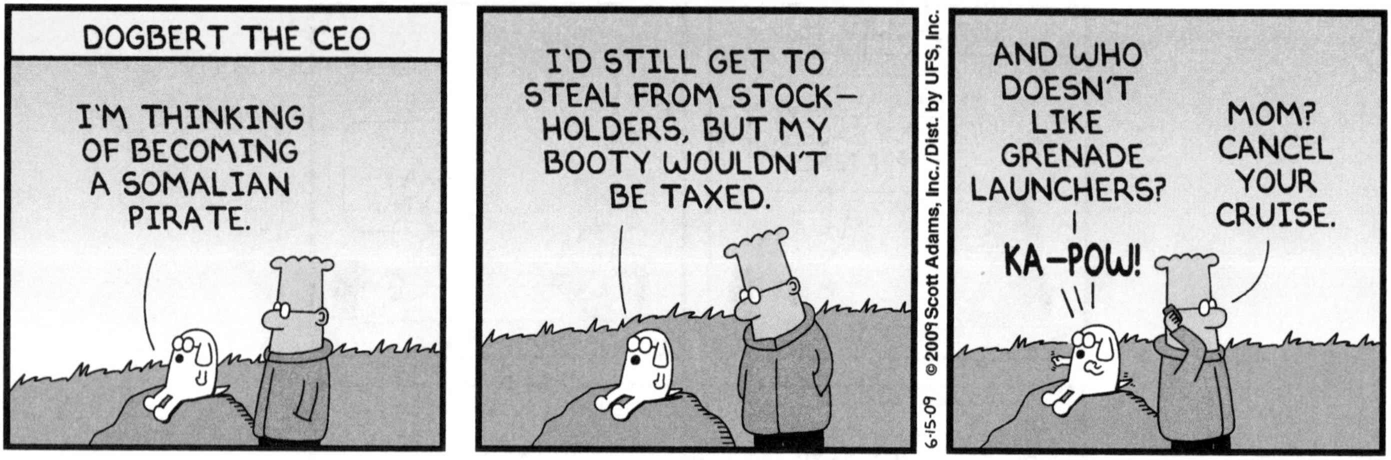
DOGBERT THE CEO
I'M THINKING OF BECOMING A SOMALIAN PIRATE.
I'D STILL GET TO STEAL FROM STOCK-HOLDERS, BUT MY BOOTY WOULDN'T BE TAXED.
AND WHO DOESN'T LIKE GRENADE LAUNCHERS?
KA-POW!
MOM? CANCEL YOUR CRUISE.
6-15-09

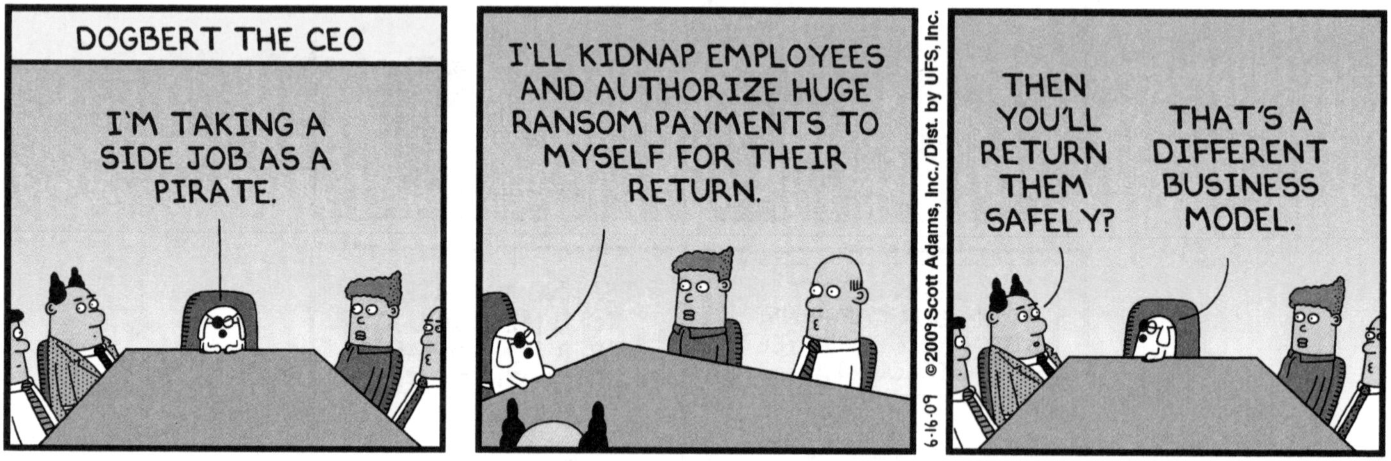
DOGBERT THE CEO
I'M TAKING A SIDE JOB AS A PIRATE.
I'LL KIDNAP EMPLOYEES AND AUTHORIZE HUGE RANSOM PAYMENTS TO MYSELF FOR THEIR RETURN.
THEN YOU'LL RETURN THEM SAFELY?
THAT'S A DIFFERENT BUSINESS MODEL.
6-16-09

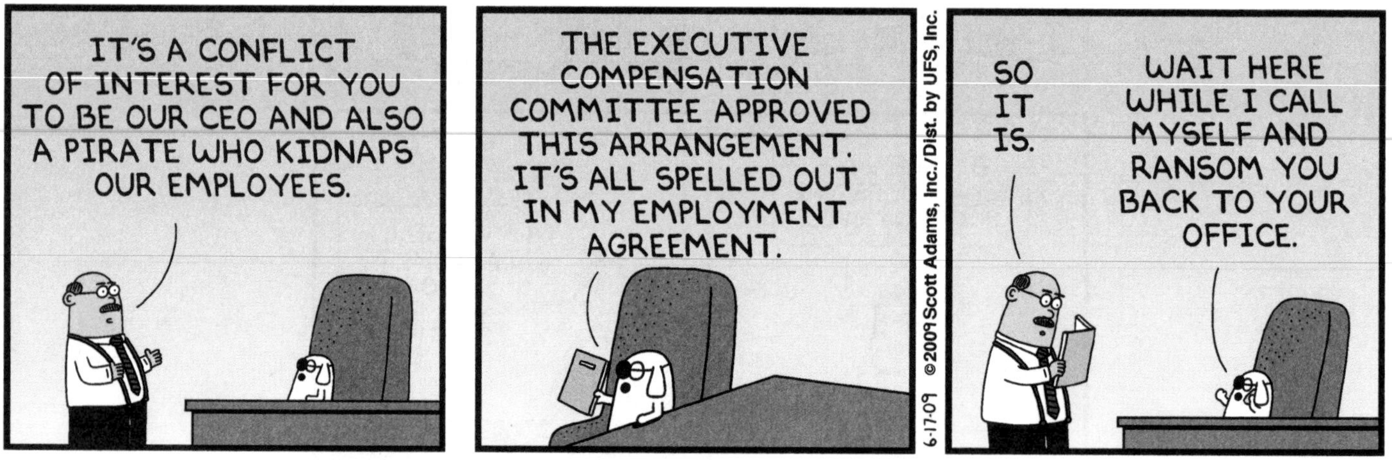
IT'S A CONFLICT OF INTEREST FOR YOU TO BE OUR CEO AND ALSO A PIRATE WHO KIDNAPS OUR EMPLOYEES.
THE EXECUTIVE COMPENSATION COMMITTEE APPROVED THIS ARRANGEMENT. IT'S ALL SPELLED OUT IN MY EMPLOYMENT AGREEMENT.
SO IT IS.
WAIT HERE WHILE I CALL MYSELF AND RANSOM YOU BACK TO YOUR OFFICE.
6-17-09

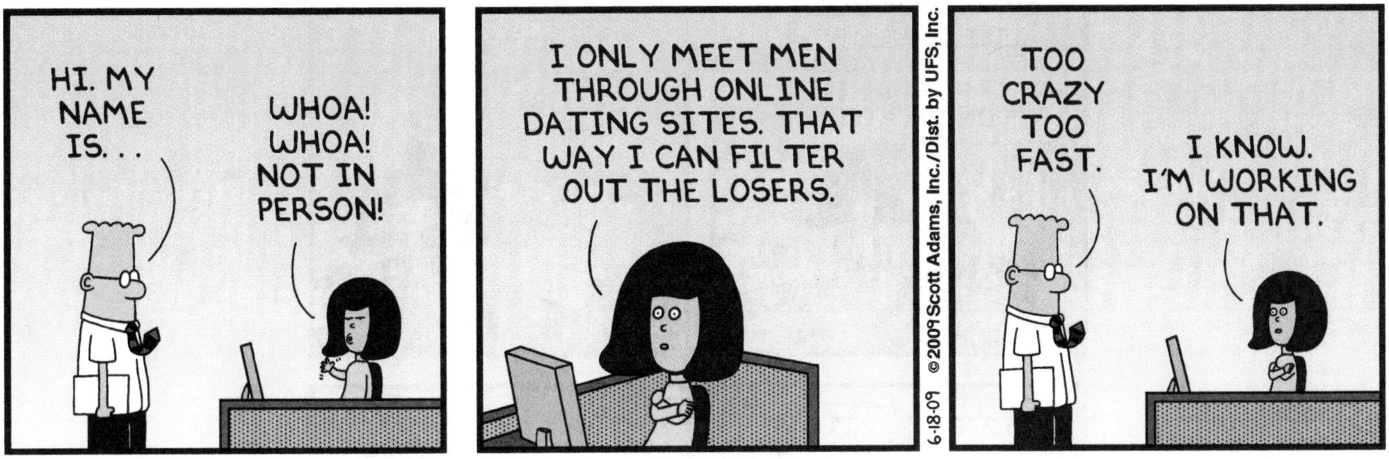
HI. MY NAME IS. . .
WHOA! WHOA! NOT IN PERSON!
I ONLY MEET MEN THROUGH ONLINE DATING SITES. THAT WAY I CAN FILTER OUT THE LOSERS.
6-18-09 © 2009 Scott Adams, Inc./Dist. by UFS, Inc.
TOO CRAZY TOO FAST.
I KNOW. I'M WORKING ON THAT.

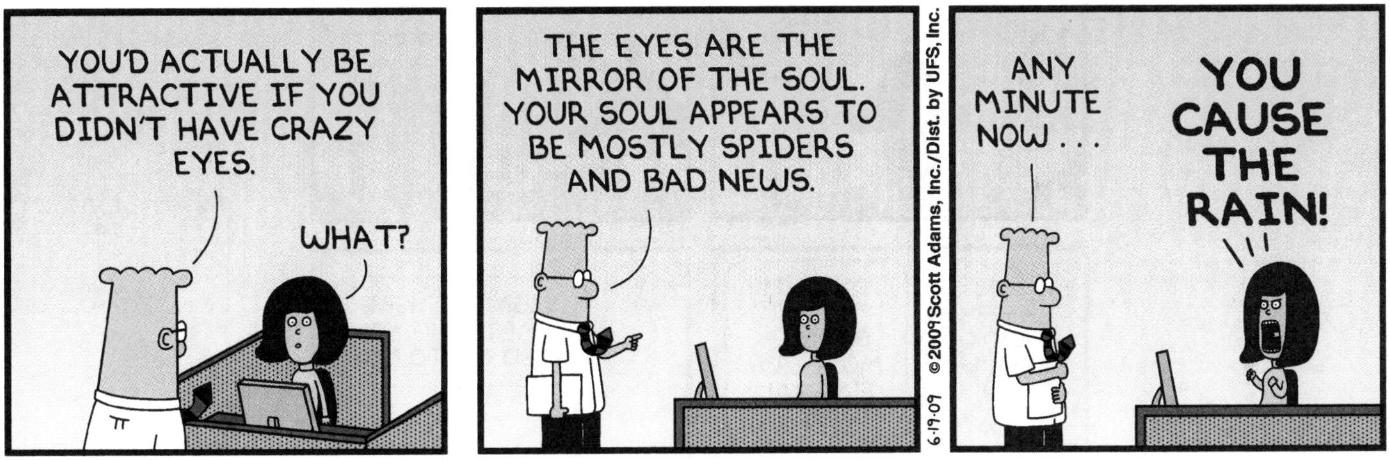
YOU'D ACTUALLY BE ATTRACTIVE IF YOU DIDN'T HAVE CRAZY EYES.
WHAT?
THE EYES ARE THE MIRROR OF THE SOUL. YOUR SOUL APPEARS TO BE MOSTLY SPIDERS AND BAD NEWS.
6-19-09 © 2009 Scott Adams, Inc./Dist. by UFS, Inc.
ANY MINUTE NOW . . .
YOU CAUSE THE RAIN!

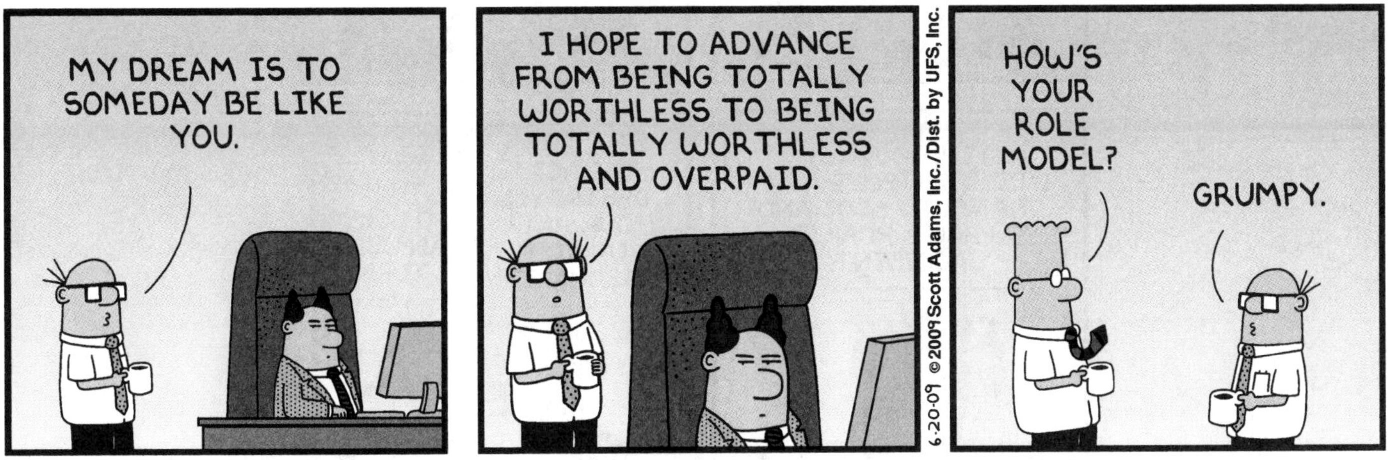
MY DREAM IS TO SOMEDAY BE LIKE YOU.
I HOPE TO ADVANCE FROM BEING TOTALLY WORTHLESS TO BEING TOTALLY WORTHLESS AND OVERPAID.
6-20-09 © 2009 Scott Adams, Inc./Dist. by UFS, Inc.
HOW'S YOUR ROLE MODEL?
GRUMPY.

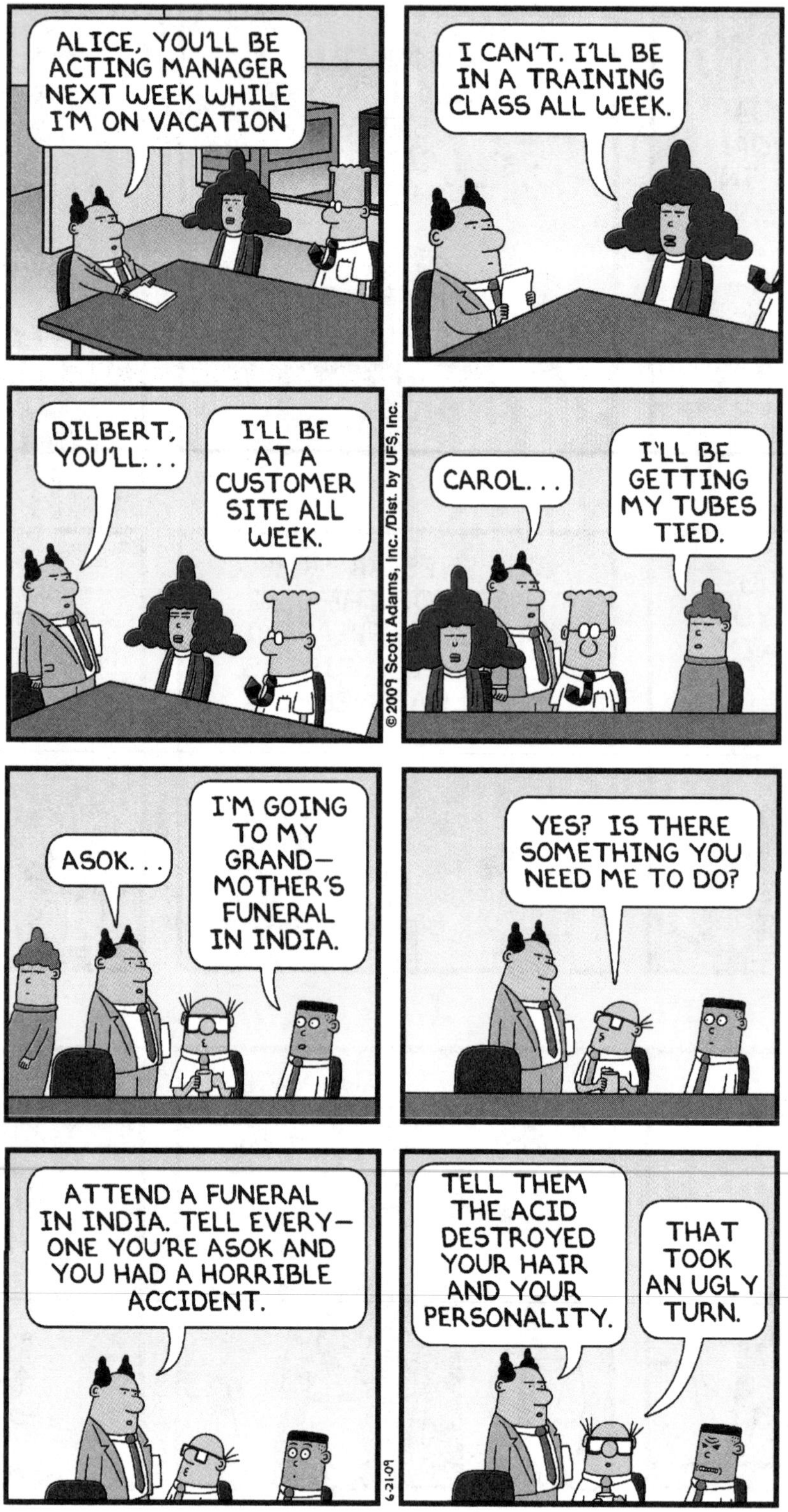
ALICE, YOU'LL BE ACTING MANAGER NEXT WEEK WHILE I'M ON VACATION
I CAN'T. I'LL BE IN A TRAINING CLASS ALL WEEK.
DILBERT, YOU'LL. . .
I'LL BE AT A CUSTOMER SITE ALL WEEK.
CAROL. . .
I'LL BE GETTING MY TUBES TIED.
ASOK. . .
I'M GOING TO MY GRAND-MOTHER'S FUNERAL IN INDIA.
YES? IS THERE SOMETHING YOU NEED ME TO DO?
ATTEND A FUNERAL IN INDIA. TELL EVERY-ONE YOU'RE ASOK AND YOU HAD A HORRIBLE ACCIDENT.
TELL THEM THE ACID DESTROYED YOUR HAIR AND YOUR PERSONALITY.
THAT TOOK AN UGLY TURN.
©2009 Scott Adams, Inc./Dist. by UFS, Inc.
6-21-09

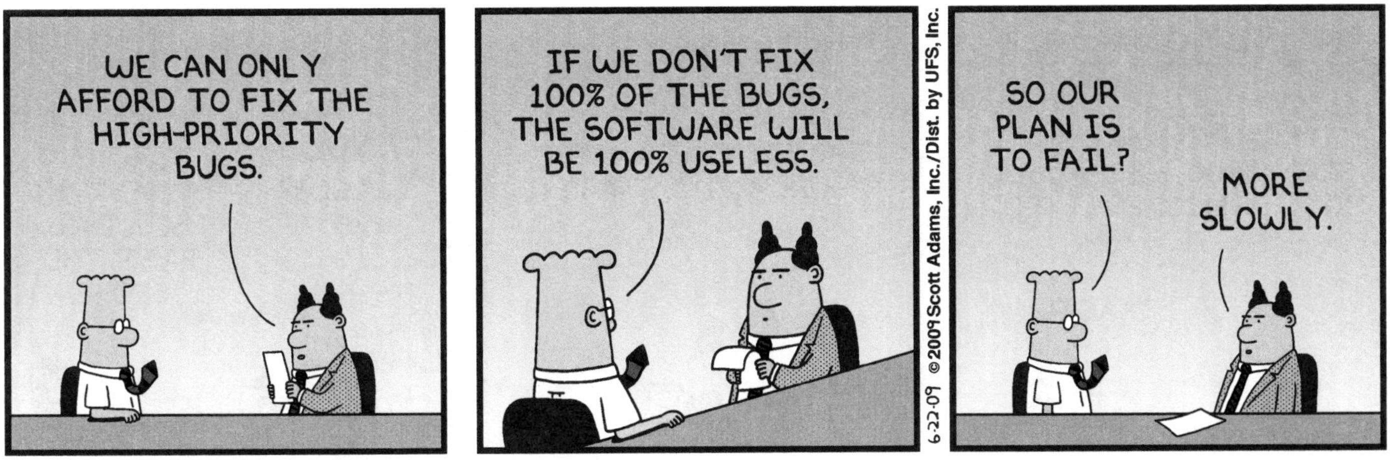
WE CAN ONLY AFFORD TO FIX THE HIGH-PRIORITY BUGS.
IF WE DON'T FIX 100% OF THE BUGS, THE SOFTWARE WILL BE 100% USELESS.
SO OUR PLAN IS TO FAIL?
MORE SLOWLY.
6-22-09 © 2009 Scott Adams, Inc./Dist. by UFS, Inc.

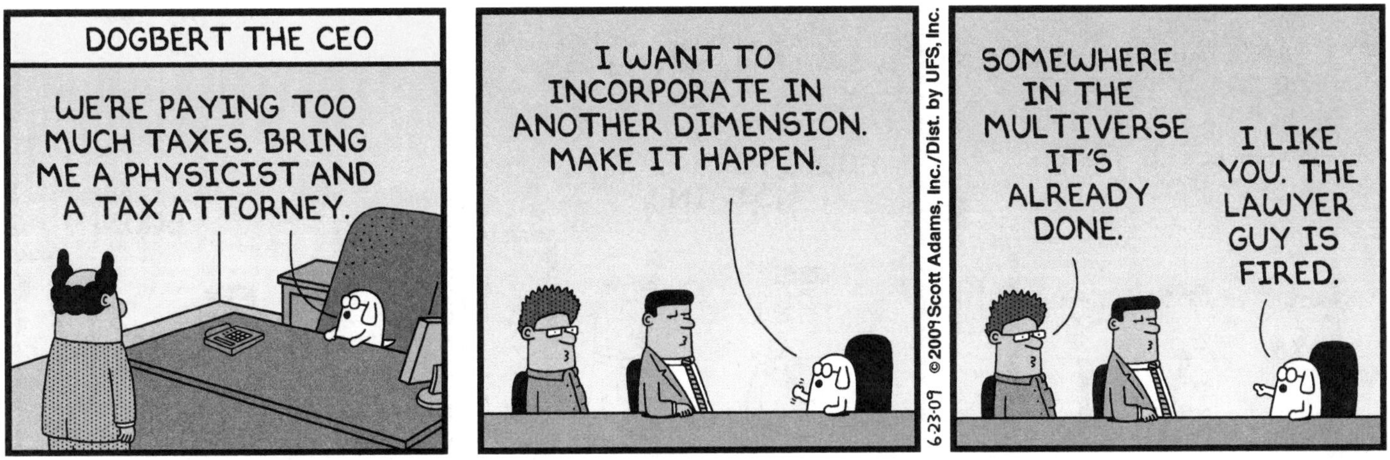
DOGBERT THE CEO
WE'RE PAYING TOO MUCH TAXES. BRING ME A PHYSICIST AND A TAX ATTORNEY.
I WANT TO INCORPORATE IN ANOTHER DIMENSION. MAKE IT HAPPEN.
SOMEWHERE IN THE MULTIVERSE IT'S ALREADY DONE.
I LIKE YOU. THE LAWYER GUY IS FIRED.
6-23-09 © 2009 Scott Adams, Inc./Dist. by UFS, Inc.

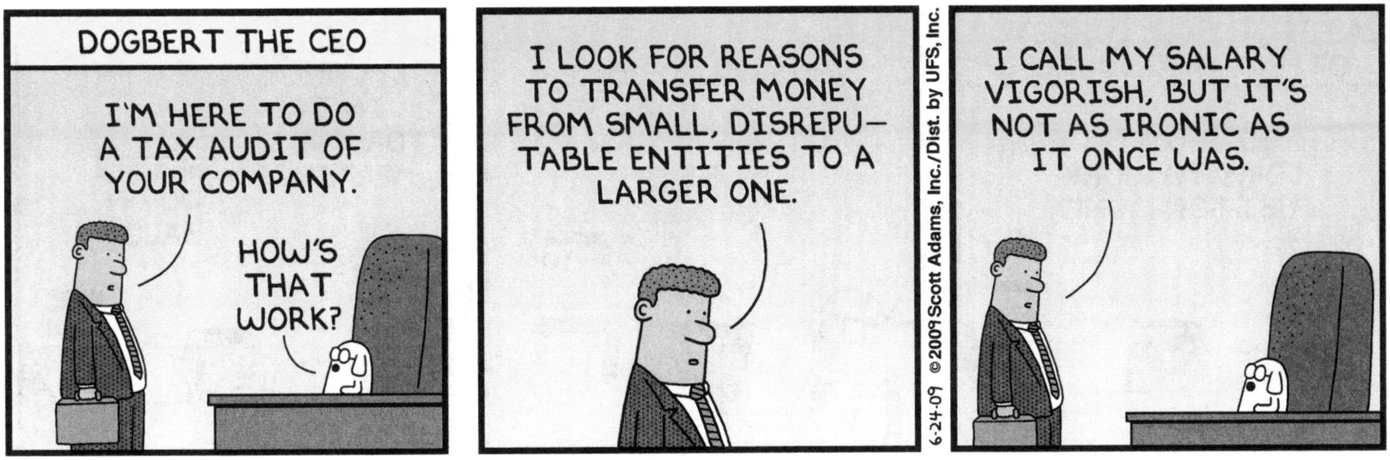
DOGBERT THE CEO
I'M HERE TO DO A TAX AUDIT OF YOUR COMPANY.
HOW'S THAT WORK?
I LOOK FOR REASONS TO TRANSFER MONEY FROM SMALL, DISREPU– TABLE ENTITIES TO A LARGER ONE.
I CALL MY SALARY VIGORISH, BUT IT'S NOT AS IRONIC AS IT ONCE WAS.
6-24-09 © 2009 Scott Adams, Inc./Dist. by UFS, Inc.

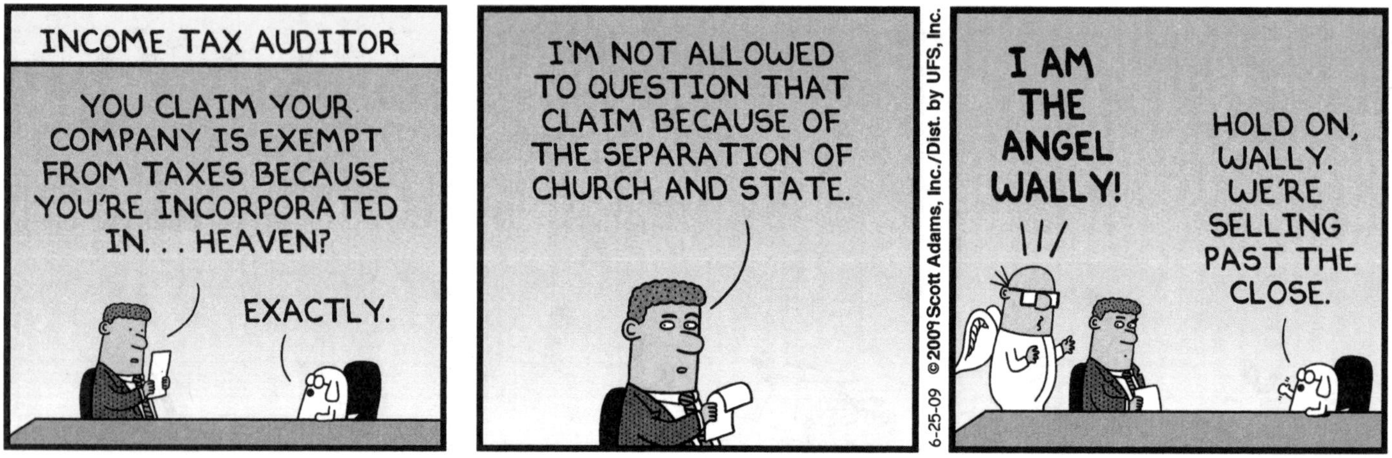
INCOME TAX AUDITOR
YOU CLAIM YOUR COMPANY IS EXEMPT FROM TAXES BECAUSE YOU'RE INCORPORATED IN. . . HEAVEN?
EXACTLY.
I'M NOT ALLOWED TO QUESTION THAT CLAIM BECAUSE OF THE SEPARATION OF CHURCH AND STATE.
6-25-09 © 2009 Scott Adams, Inc./Dist. by UFS, Inc.
I AM THE ANGEL WALLY!
HOLD ON, WALLY. WE'RE SELLING PAST THE CLOSE.

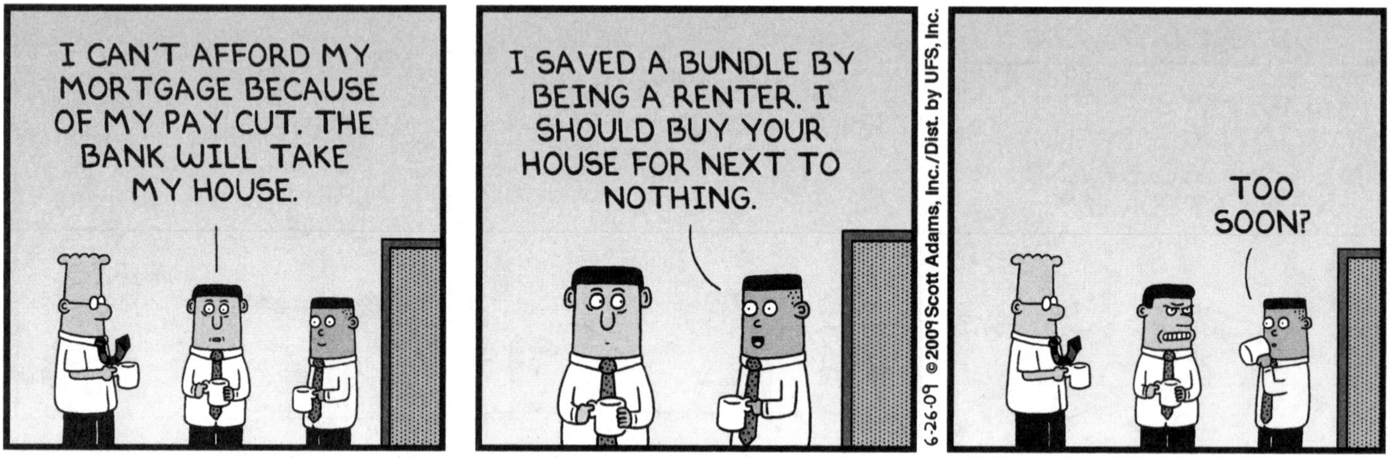
I CAN'T AFFORD MY MORTGAGE BECAUSE OF MY PAY CUT. THE BANK WILL TAKE MY HOUSE.
I SAVED A BUNDLE BY BEING A RENTER. I SHOULD BUY YOUR HOUSE FOR NEXT TO NOTHING.
6-26-09 © 2009 Scott Adams, Inc./Dist. by UFS, Inc.
TOO SOON?

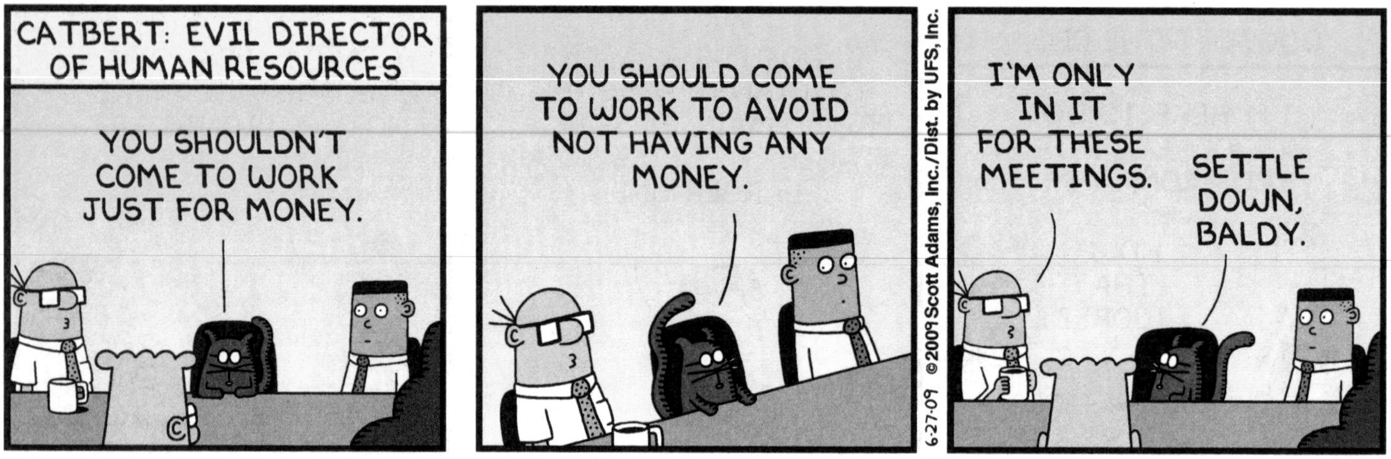
CATBERT: EVIL DIRECTOR OF HUMAN RESOURCES
YOU SHOULDN'T COME TO WORK JUST FOR MONEY.
YOU SHOULD COME TO WORK TO AVOID NOT HAVING ANY MONEY.
6-27-09 © 2009 Scott Adams, Inc./Dist. by UFS, Inc.
I'M ONLY IN IT FOR THESE MEETINGS.
SETTLE DOWN, BALDY.

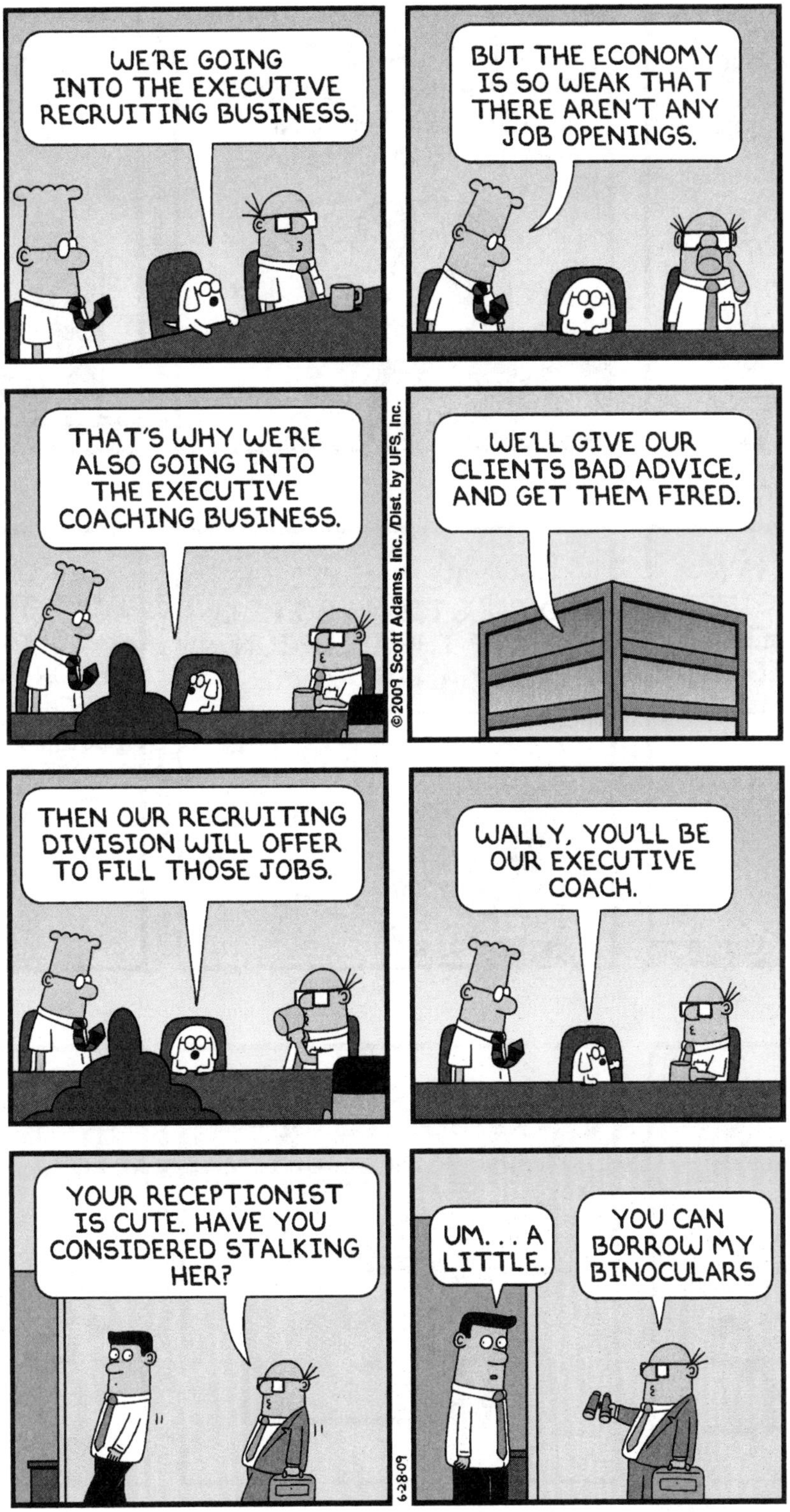
WE'RE GOING INTO THE EXECUTIVE RECRUITING BUSINESS.
BUT THE ECONOMY IS SO WEAK THAT THERE AREN'T ANY JOB OPENINGS.
THAT'S WHY WE'RE ALSO GOING INTO THE EXECUTIVE COACHING BUSINESS.
WE'LL GIVE OUR CLIENTS BAD ADVICE, AND GET THEM FIRED.
THEN OUR RECRUITING DIVISION WILL OFFER TO FILL THOSE JOBS.
WALLY, YOU'LL BE OUR EXECUTIVE COACH.
YOUR RECEPTIONIST IS CUTE. HAVE YOU CONSIDERED STALKING HER?
UM... A LITTLE.
YOU CAN BORROW MY BINOCULARS
©2009 Scott Adams, Inc./Dist. by UFS, Inc.
6-28-09

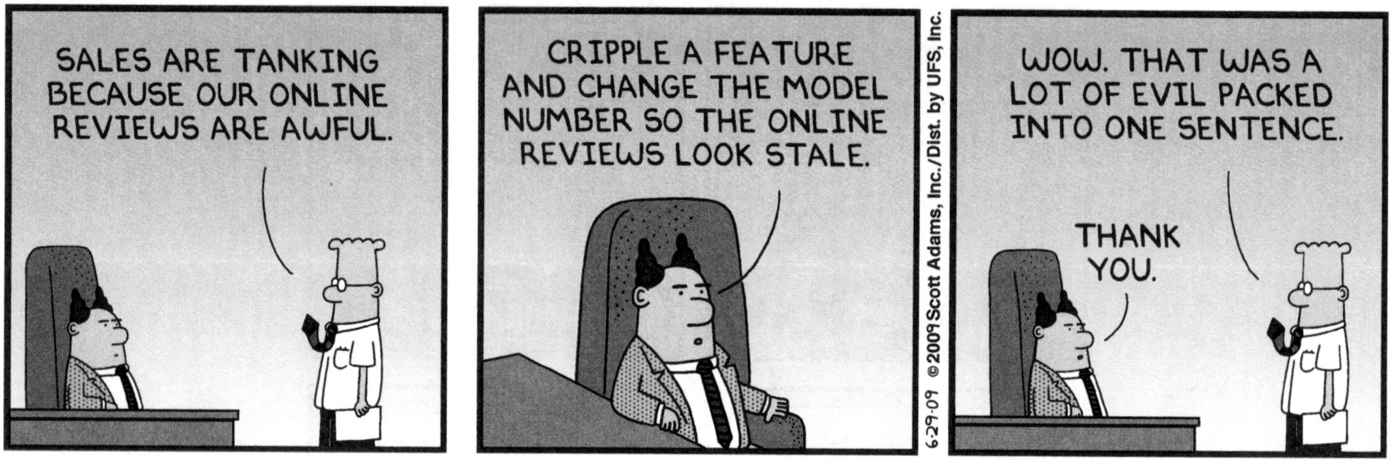
SALES ARE TANKING BECAUSE OUR ONLINE REVIEWS ARE AWFUL.
CRIPPLE A FEATURE AND CHANGE THE MODEL NUMBER SO THE ONLINE REVIEWS LOOK STALE.
6-29-09 © 2009 Scott Adams, Inc./Dist. by UFS, Inc.
WOW. THAT WAS A LOT OF EVIL PACKED INTO ONE SENTENCE.
THANK YOU.

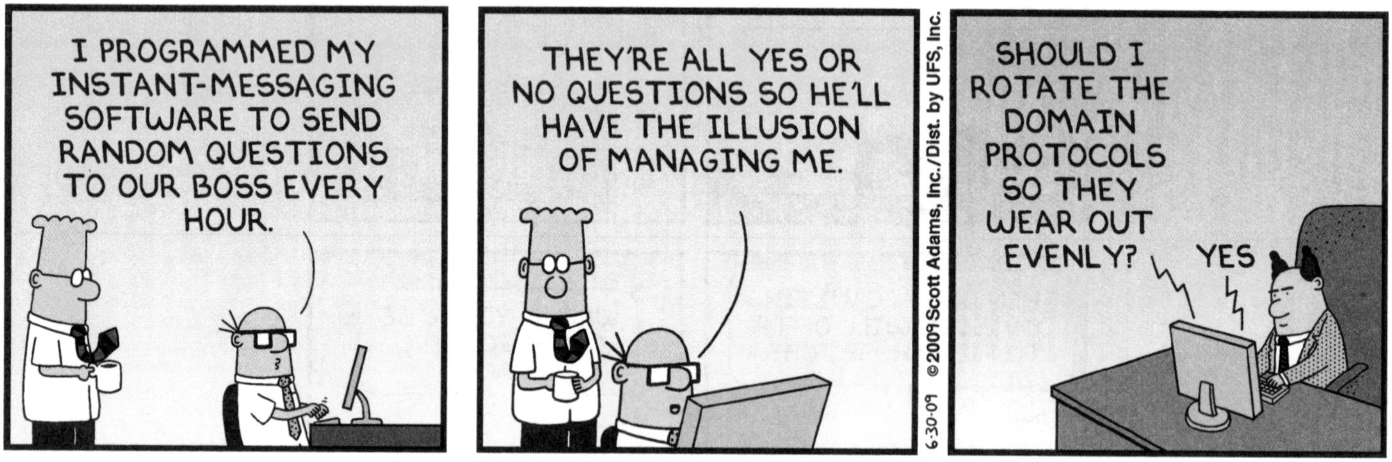
I PROGRAMMED MY INSTANT-MESSAGING SOFTWARE TO SEND RANDOM QUESTIONS TO OUR BOSS EVERY HOUR.
THEY'RE ALL YES OR NO QUESTIONS SO HE'LL HAVE THE ILLUSION OF MANAGING ME.
6-30-09 © 2009 Scott Adams, Inc./Dist. by UFS, Inc.
SHOULD I ROTATE THE DOMAIN PROTOCOLS SO THEY WEAR OUT EVENLY?
YES

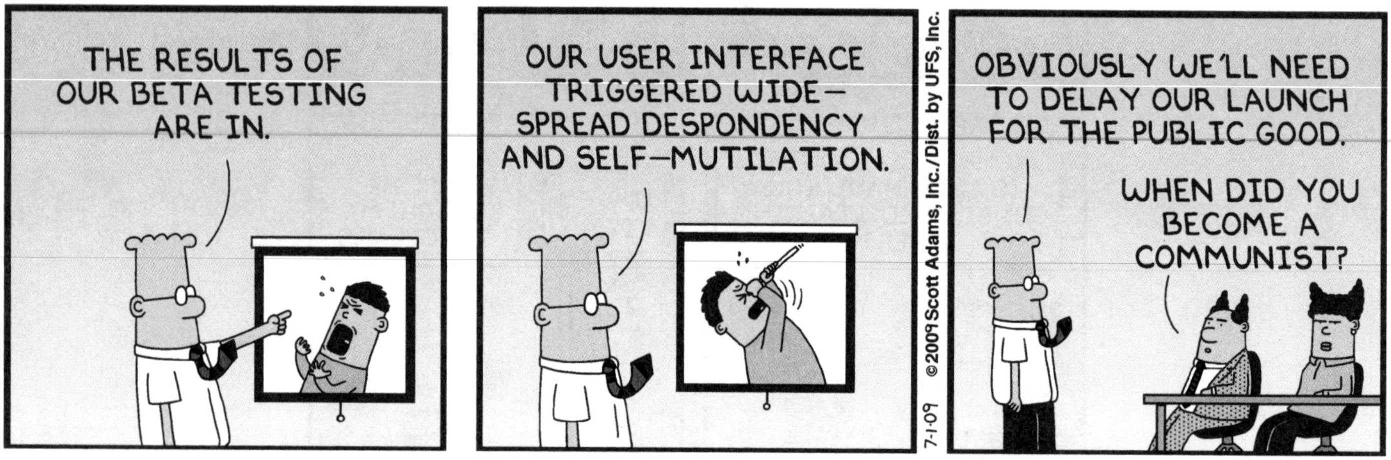
THE RESULTS OF OUR BETA TESTING ARE IN.
OUR USER INTERFACE TRIGGERED WIDE-SPREAD DESPONDENCY AND SELF-MUTILATION.
7-1-09 © 2009 Scott Adams, Inc./Dist. by UFS, Inc.
OBVIOUSLY WE'LL NEED TO DELAY OUR LAUNCH FOR THE PUBLIC GOOD.
WHEN DID YOU BECOME A COMMUNIST?

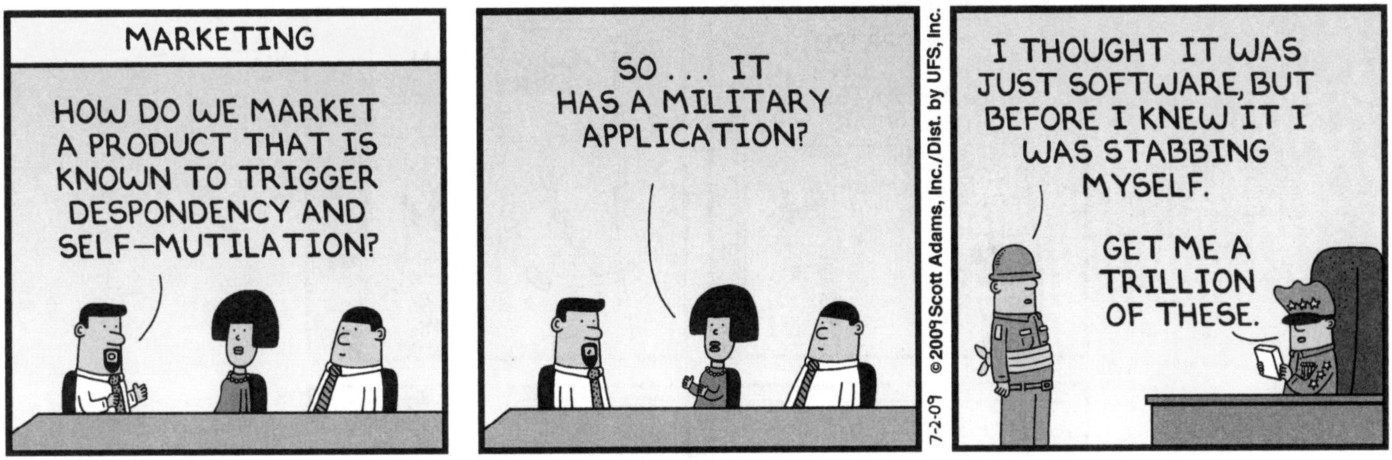
MARKETING
HOW DO WE MARKET A PRODUCT THAT IS KNOWN TO TRIGGER DESPONDENCY AND SELF-MUTILATION?
SO . . . IT HAS A MILITARY APPLICATION?
7-2-09 ©2009 Scott Adams, Inc./Dist. by UFS, Inc.
I THOUGHT IT WAS JUST SOFTWARE, BUT BEFORE I KNEW IT I WAS STABBING MYSELF.
GET ME A TRILLION OF THESE.

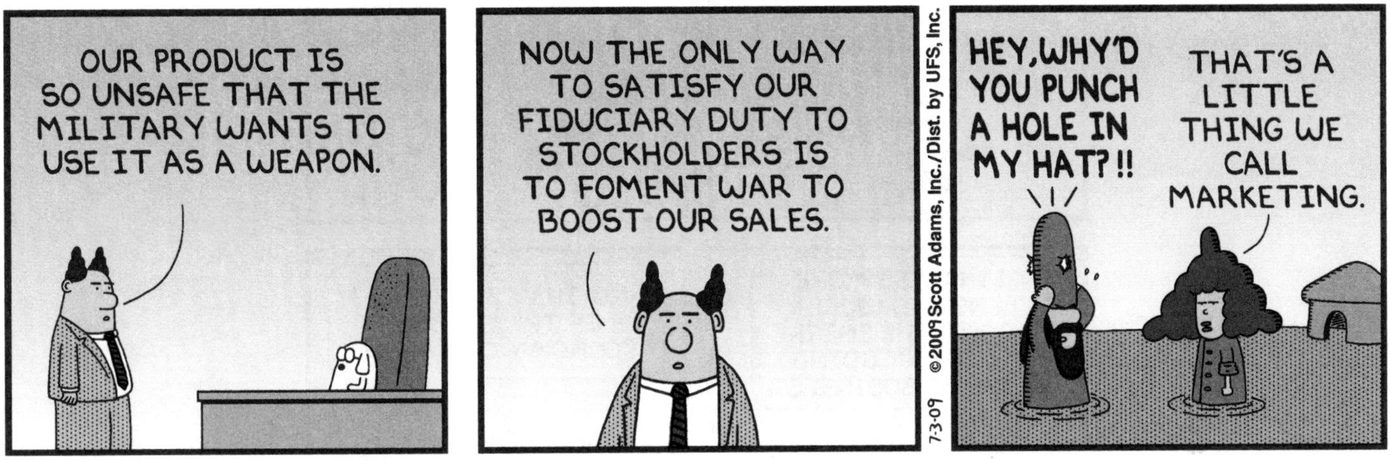
OUR PRODUCT IS SO UNSAFE THAT THE MILITARY WANTS TO USE IT AS A WEAPON.
NOW THE ONLY WAY TO SATISFY OUR FIDUCIARY DUTY TO STOCKHOLDERS IS TO FOMENT WAR TO BOOST OUR SALES.
7-3-09 ©2009 Scott Adams, Inc./Dist. by UFS, Inc.
HEY, WHY'D YOU PUNCH A HOLE IN MY HAT?!!
THAT'S A LITTLE THING WE CALL MARKETING.

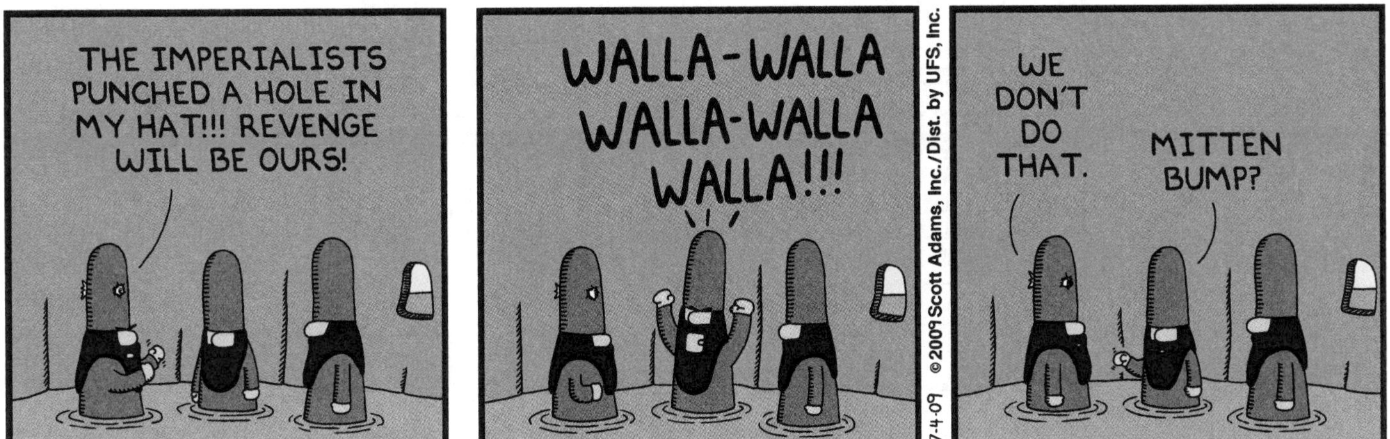
THE IMPERIALISTS PUNCHED A HOLE IN MY HAT!!! REVENGE WILL BE OURS!
WALLA-WALLA WALLA-WALLA WALLA!!!
7-4-09 ©2009 Scott Adams, Inc./Dist. by UFS, Inc.
WE DON'T DO THAT.
MITTEN BUMP?

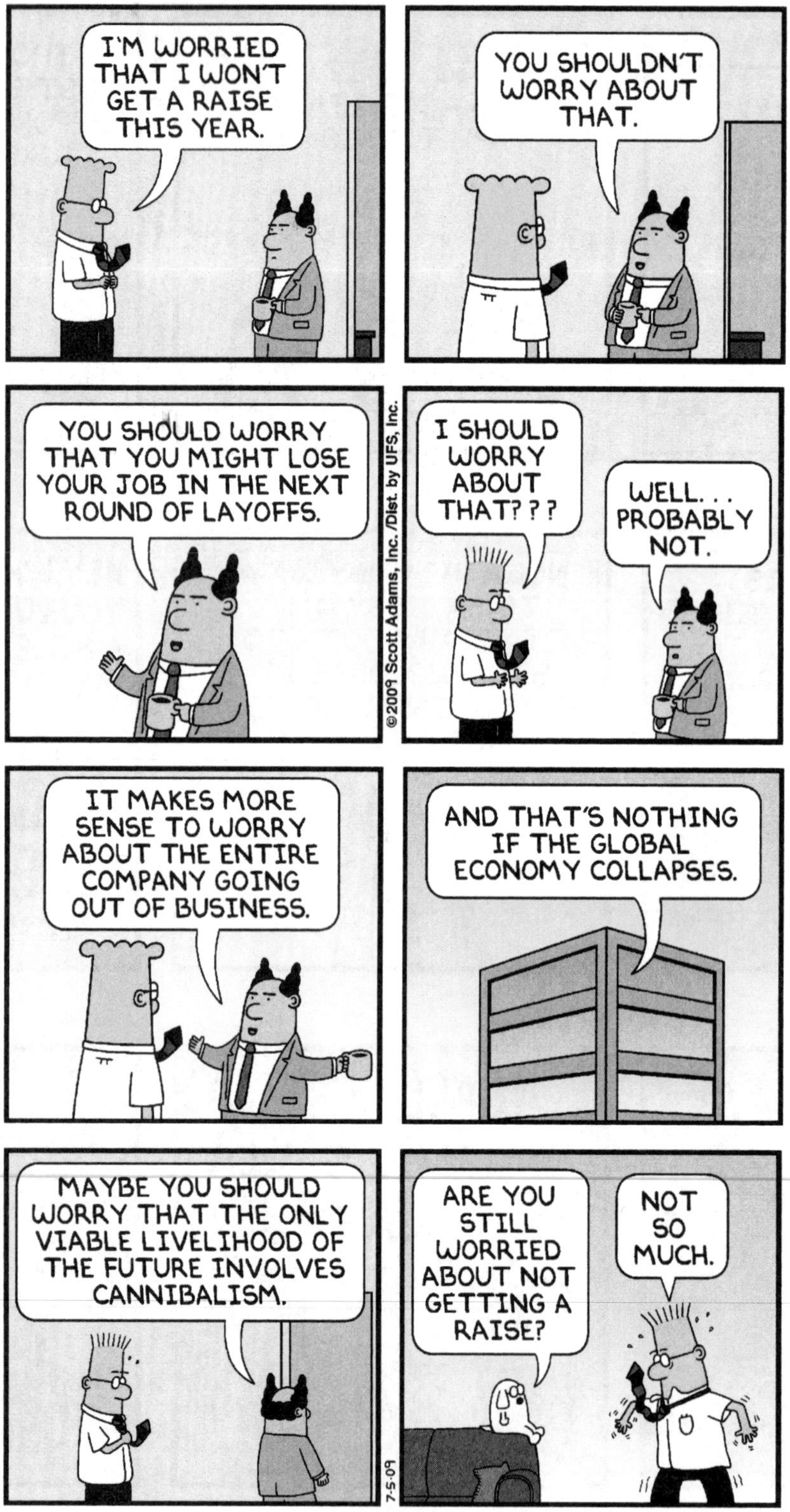
I'M WORRIED THAT I WON'T GET A RAISE THIS YEAR.
YOU SHOULDN'T WORRY ABOUT THAT.
YOU SHOULD WORRY THAT YOU MIGHT LOSE YOUR JOB IN THE NEXT ROUND OF LAYOFFS.
I SHOULD WORRY ABOUT THAT???
WELL... PROBABLY NOT.
IT MAKES MORE SENSE TO WORRY ABOUT THE ENTIRE COMPANY GOING OUT OF BUSINESS.
AND THAT'S NOTHING IF THE GLOBAL ECONOMY COLLAPSES.
MAYBE YOU SHOULD WORRY THAT THE ONLY VIABLE LIVELIHOOD OF THE FUTURE INVOLVES CANNIBALISM.
ARE YOU STILL WORRIED ABOUT NOT GETTING A RAISE?
NOT SO MUCH.
©2009 Scott Adams, Inc./Dist. by UFS, Inc.
7-5-09

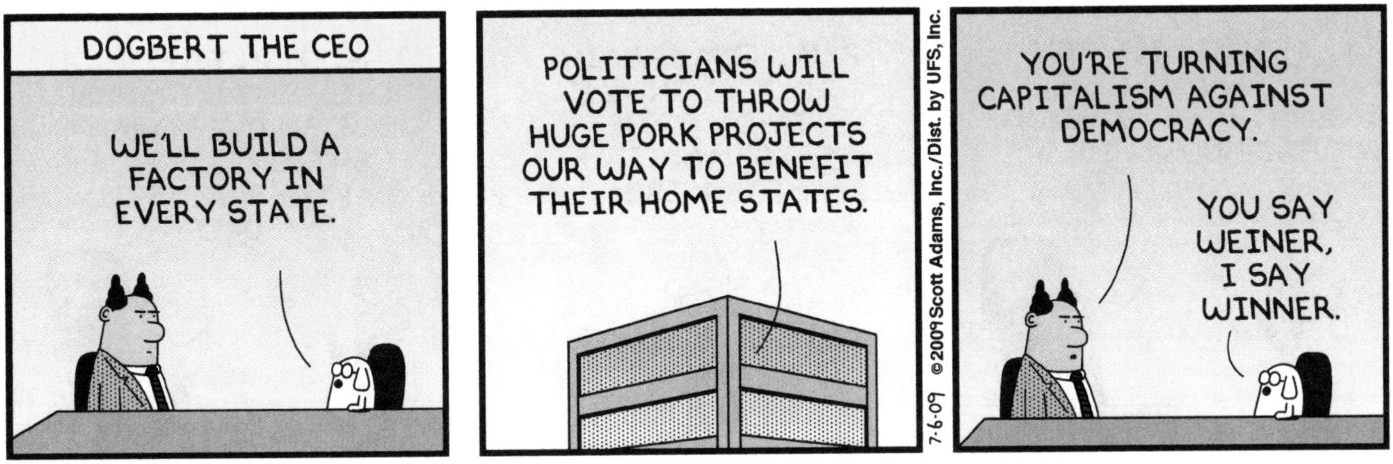
DOGBERT THE CEO
WE'LL BUILD A FACTORY IN EVERY STATE.
POLITICIANS WILL VOTE TO THROW HUGE PORK PROJECTS OUR WAY TO BENEFIT THEIR HOME STATES.
7-6-09 ©2009 Scott Adams, Inc./Dist. by UFS, Inc.
YOU'RE TURNING CAPITALISM AGAINST DEMOCRACY.
YOU SAY WEINER, I SAY WINNER.

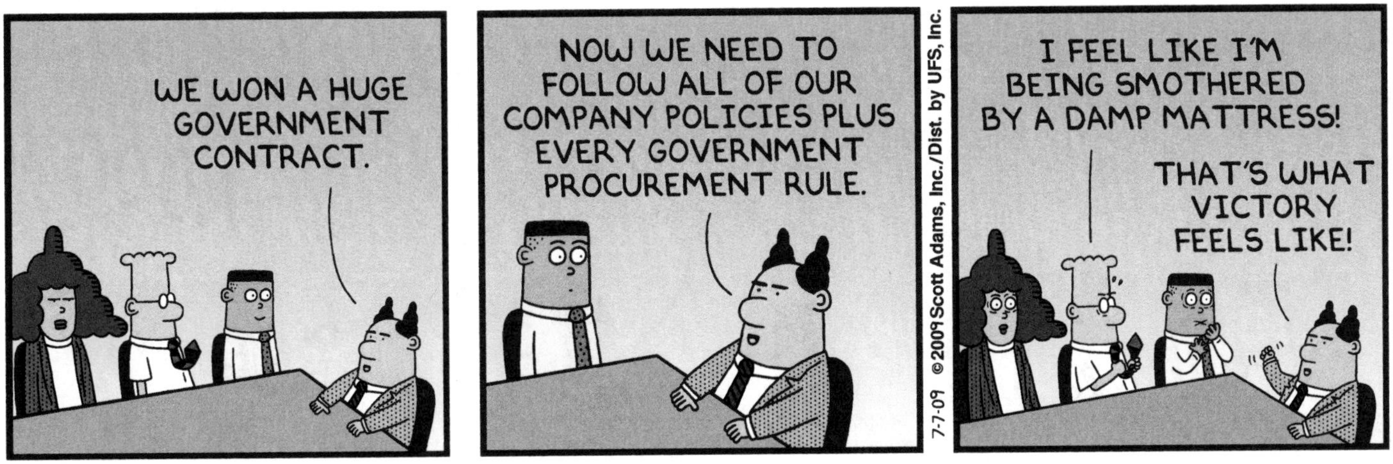
WE WON A HUGE GOVERNMENT CONTRACT.
NOW WE NEED TO FOLLOW ALL OF OUR COMPANY POLICIES PLUS EVERY GOVERNMENT PROCUREMENT RULE.
7-7-09 ©2009 Scott Adams, Inc./Dist. by UFS, Inc.
I FEEL LIKE I'M BEING SMOTHERED BY A DAMP MATTRESS!
THAT'S WHAT VICTORY FEELS LIKE!

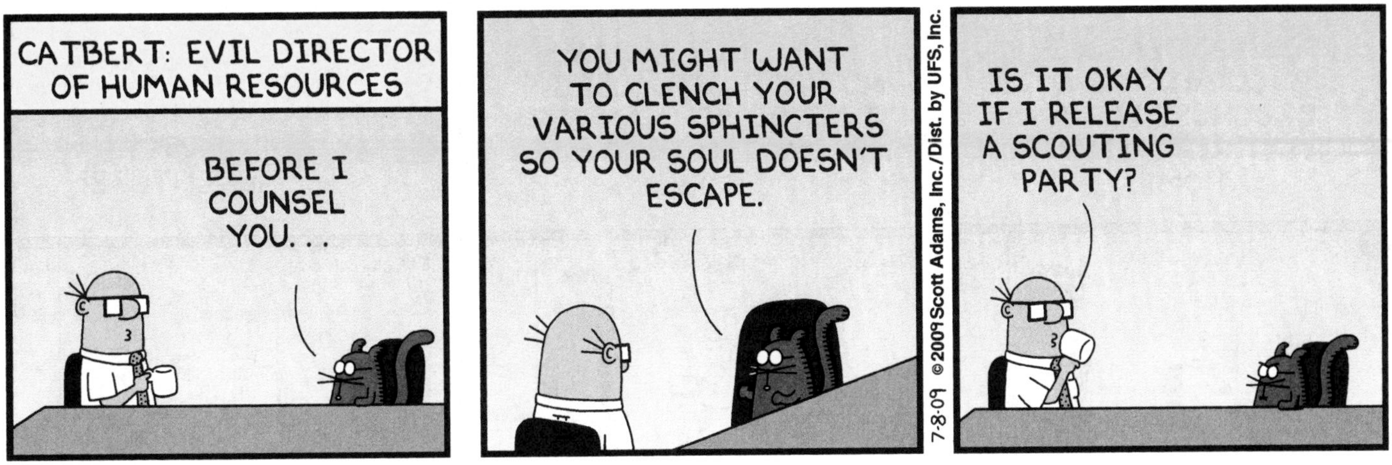
CATBERT: EVIL DIRECTOR OF HUMAN RESOURCES
BEFORE I COUNSEL YOU. . .
YOU MIGHT WANT TO CLENCH YOUR VARIOUS SPHINCTERS SO YOUR SOUL DOESN'T ESCAPE.
7-8-09 ©2009 Scott Adams, Inc./Dist. by UFS, Inc.
IS IT OKAY IF I RELEASE A SCOUTING PARTY?

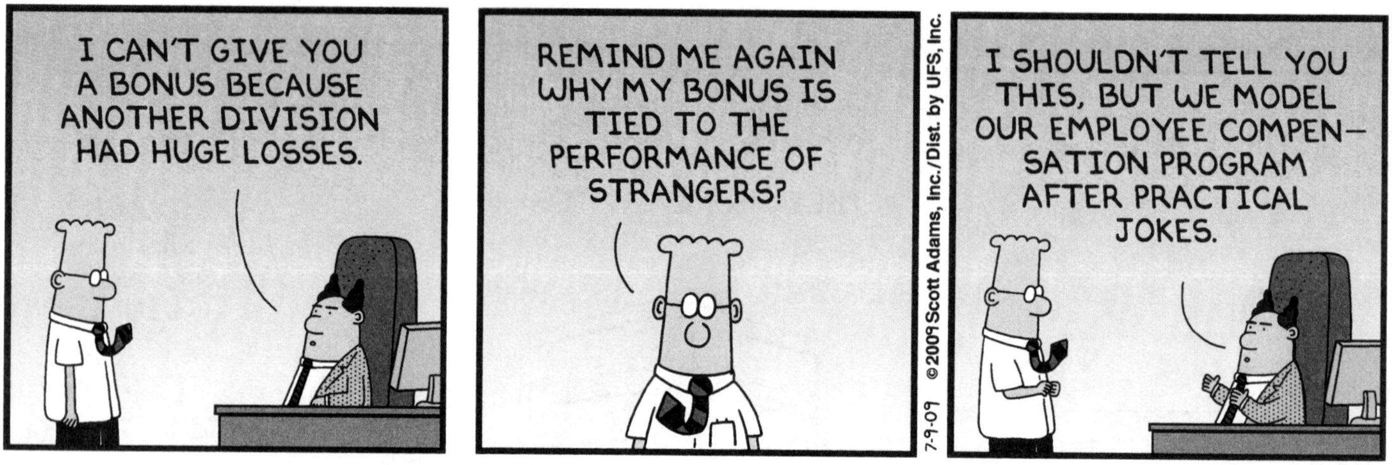
I CAN'T GIVE YOU A BONUS BECAUSE ANOTHER DIVISION HAD HUGE LOSSES.
REMIND ME AGAIN WHY MY BONUS IS TIED TO THE PERFORMANCE OF STRANGERS?
I SHOULDN'T TELL YOU THIS, BUT WE MODEL OUR EMPLOYEE COMPEN-SATION PROGRAM AFTER PRACTICAL JOKES.
7-9-09 ©2009 Scott Adams, Inc./Dist. by UFS, Inc.

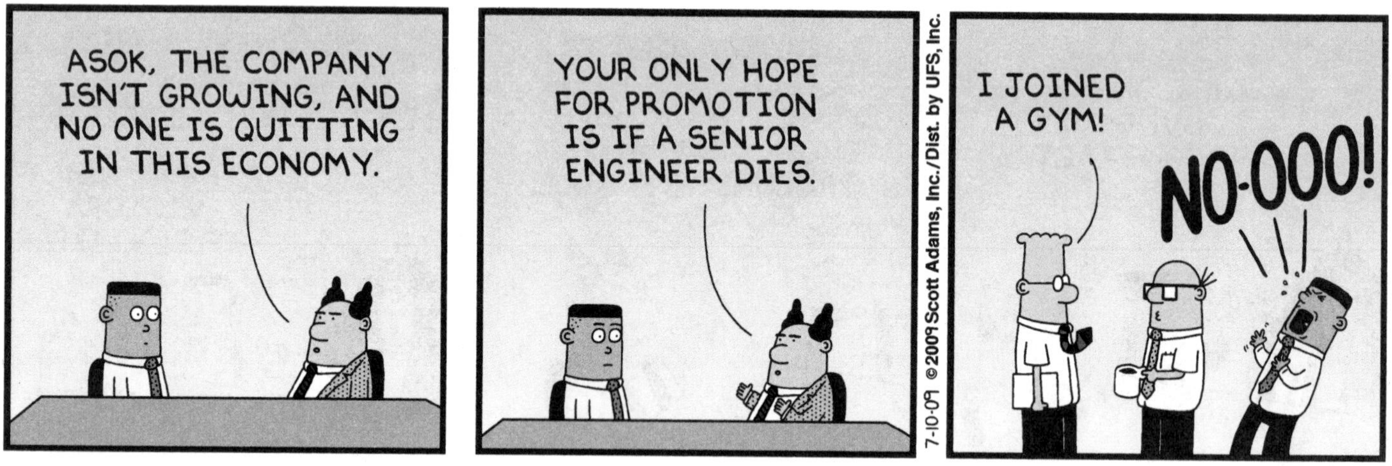
ASOK, THE COMPANY ISN'T GROWING, AND NO ONE IS QUITTING IN THIS ECONOMY.
YOUR ONLY HOPE FOR PROMOTION IS IF A SENIOR ENGINEER DIES.
I JOINED A GYM!
NO-OOO!
7-10-09 ©2009 Scott Adams, Inc./Dist. by UFS, Inc.

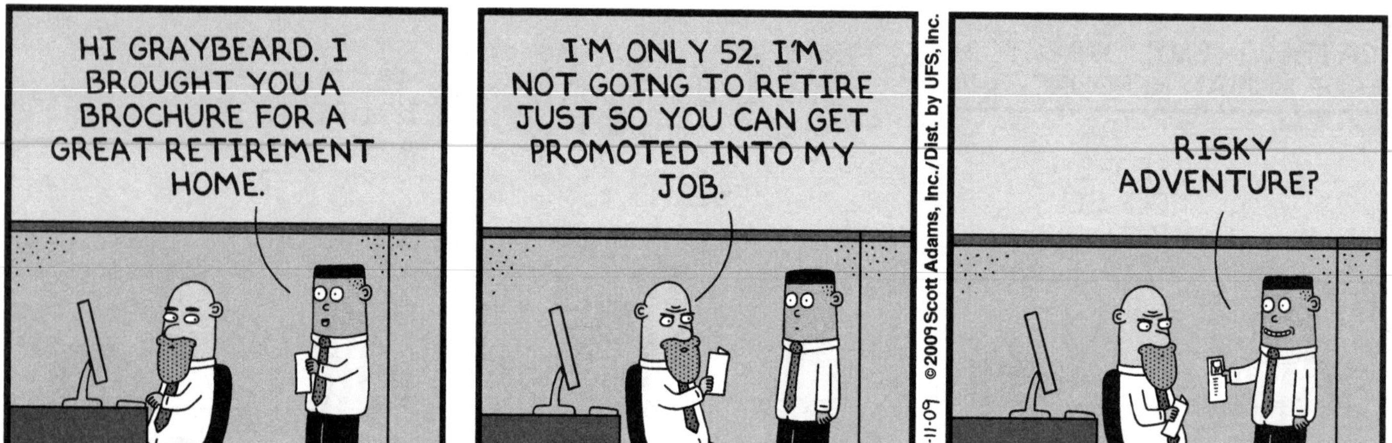
HI GRAYBEARD. I BROUGHT YOU A BROCHURE FOR A GREAT RETIREMENT HOME.
I'M ONLY 52. I'M NOT GOING TO RETIRE JUST SO YOU CAN GET PROMOTED INTO MY JOB.
RISKY ADVENTURE?
7-11-09 ©2009 Scott Adams, Inc./Dist. by UFS, Inc.

DILBERT, I WANT YOU TO AUDIT THE SOFTWARE WE HAVE ON OUR SYSTEMS.
WHY?
SO WE KNOW WHAT WE HAVE.
WHO WILL USE THE INFORMATION?
IT'S JUST IMPORTANT TO HAVE.
IT WILL BE OUT OF DATE BEFORE I'M EVEN DONE.
DO YOUR BEST.
THE BEST WAY TO COMPILE INACCURATE INFORMATION THAT NO ONE WANTS IS TO MAKE IT UP.
I HOPE NO ONE EVER COMES HERE TO LEARN OUR BEST PRACTICES.
©2009 Scott Adams, Inc. /Dist. by UFS, Inc.
7-12-09

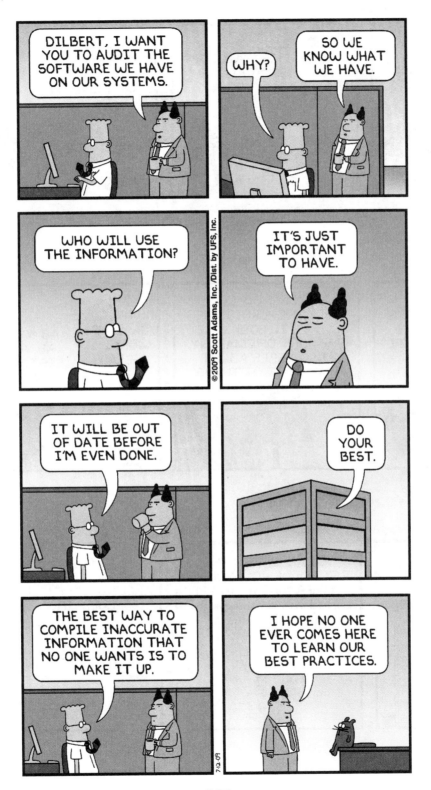

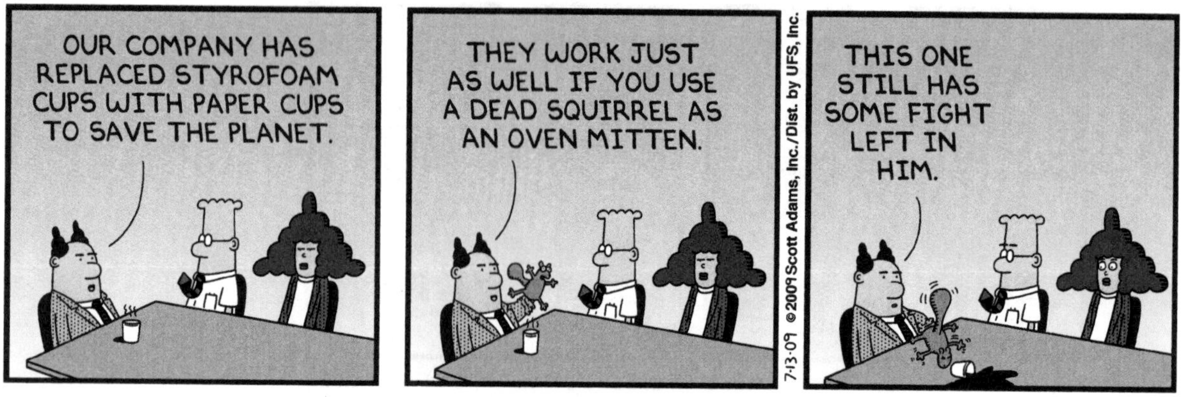
OUR COMPANY HAS REPLACED STYROFOAM CUPS WITH PAPER CUPS TO SAVE THE PLANET.
THEY WORK JUST AS WELL IF YOU USE A DEAD SQUIRREL AS AN OVEN MITTEN.
THIS ONE STILL HAS SOME FIGHT LEFT IN HIM.
7-13-09 ©2009 Scott Adams, Inc./Dist. by UFS, Inc.

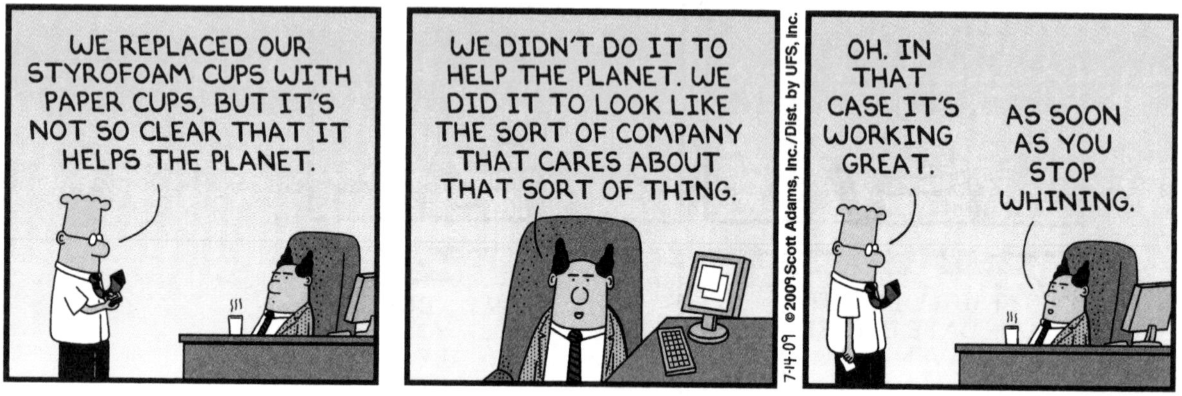
WE REPLACED OUR STYROFOAM CUPS WITH PAPER CUPS, BUT IT'S NOT SO CLEAR THAT IT HELPS THE PLANET.
WE DIDN'T DO IT TO HELP THE PLANET. WE DID IT TO LOOK LIKE THE SORT OF COMPANY THAT CARES ABOUT THAT SORT OF THING.
OH. IN THAT CASE IT'S WORKING GREAT.
AS SOON AS YOU STOP WHINING.
7-14-09 ©2009 Scott Adams, Inc./Dist. by UFS, Inc.

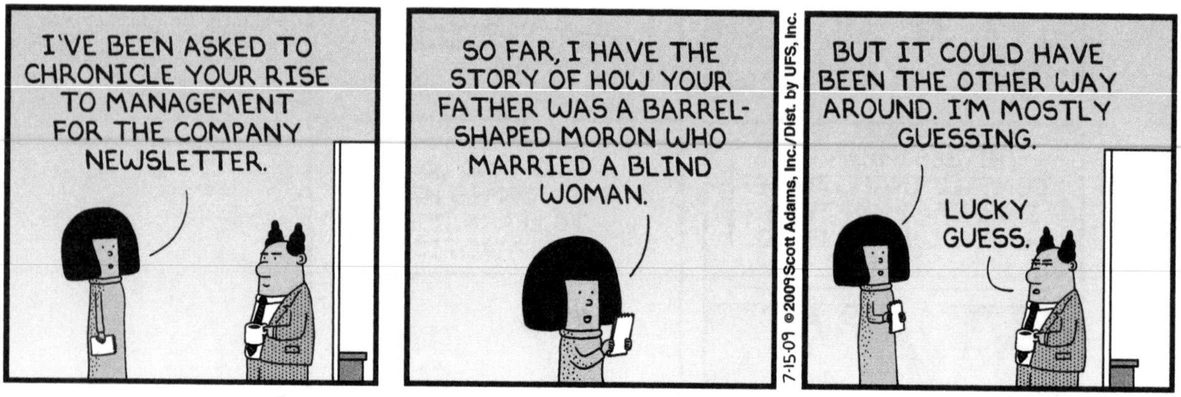
I'VE BEEN ASKED TO CHRONICLE YOUR RISE TO MANAGEMENT FOR THE COMPANY NEWSLETTER.
SO FAR, I HAVE THE STORY OF HOW YOUR FATHER WAS A BARREL-SHAPED MORON WHO MARRIED A BLIND WOMAN.
BUT IT COULD HAVE BEEN THE OTHER WAY AROUND. I'M MOSTLY GUESSING.
LUCKY GUESS.
7-15-09 ©2009 Scott Adams, Inc./Dist. by UFS, Inc.

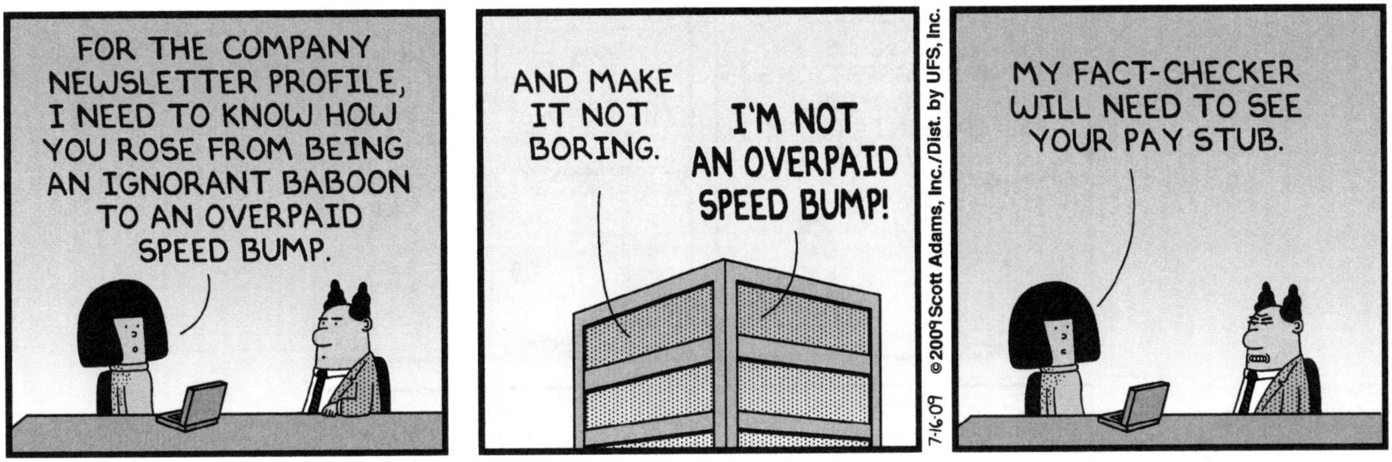
FOR THE COMPANY NEWSLETTER PROFILE, I NEED TO KNOW HOW YOU ROSE FROM BEING AN IGNORANT BABOON TO AN OVERPAID SPEED BUMP.
AND MAKE IT NOT BORING.
I'M NOT AN OVERPAID SPEED BUMP!
7-16-09 ©2009 Scott Adams, Inc./Dist. by UFS, Inc.
MY FACT-CHECKER WILL NEED TO SEE YOUR PAY STUB.

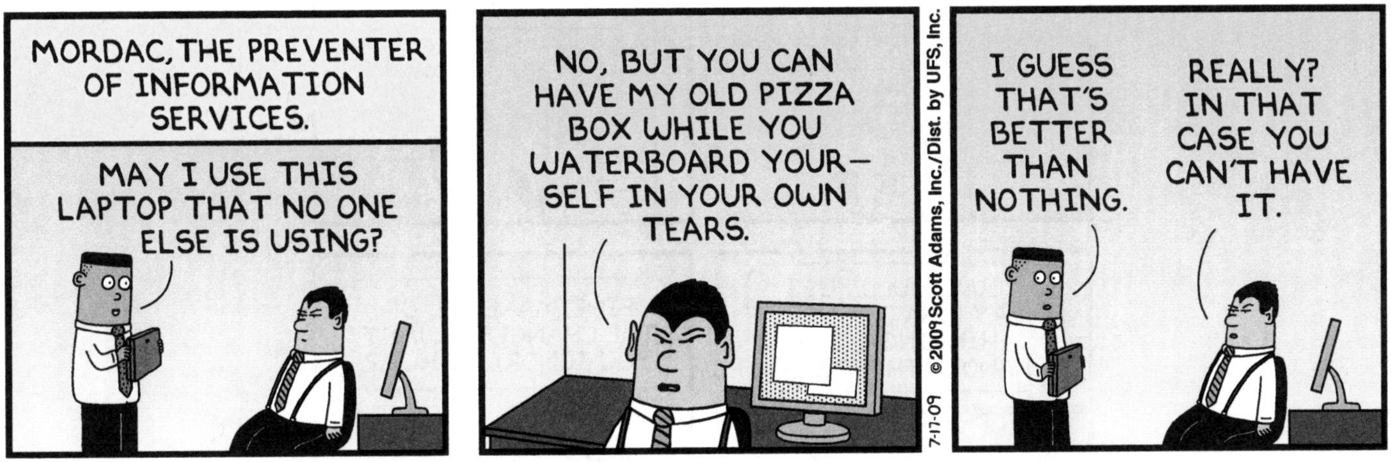
MORDAC, THE PREVENTER OF INFORMATION SERVICES.
MAY I USE THIS LAPTOP THAT NO ONE ELSE IS USING?
NO, BUT YOU CAN HAVE MY OLD PIZZA BOX WHILE YOU WATERBOARD YOURSELF IN YOUR OWN TEARS.
7-17-09 ©2009 Scott Adams, Inc./Dist. by UFS, Inc.
I GUESS THAT'S BETTER THAN NOTHING.
REALLY? IN THAT CASE YOU CAN'T HAVE IT.

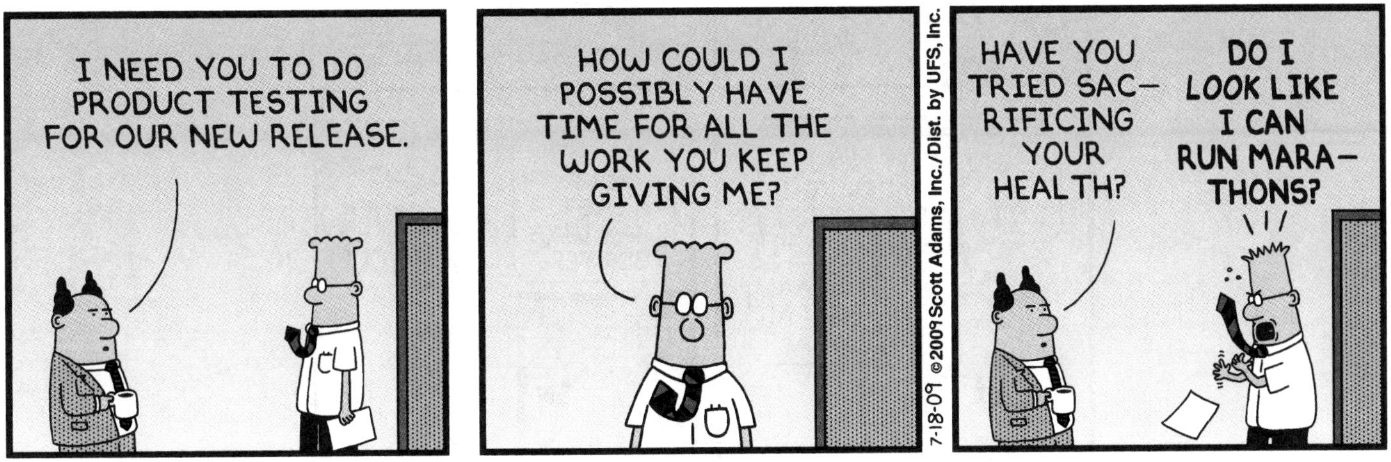
I NEED YOU TO DO PRODUCT TESTING FOR OUR NEW RELEASE.
HOW COULD I POSSIBLY HAVE TIME FOR ALL THE WORK YOU KEEP GIVING ME?
7-18-09 ©2009 Scott Adams, Inc./Dist. by UFS, Inc.
HAVE YOU TRIED SACRIFICING YOUR HEALTH?
DO I LOOK LIKE I CAN RUN MARATHONS?

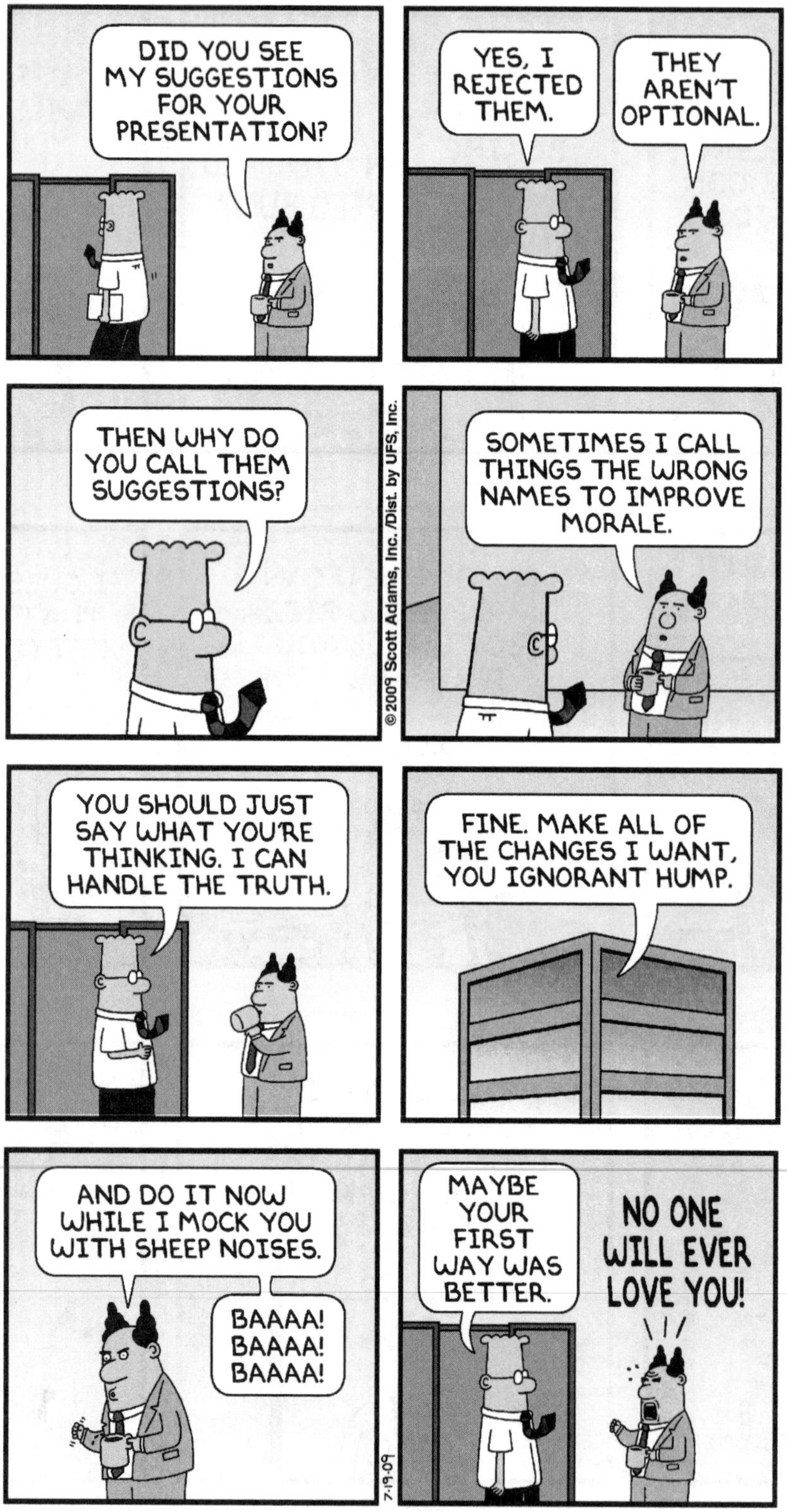
DID YOU SEE MY SUGGESTIONS FOR YOUR PRESENTATION?
YES, I REJECTED THEM.
THEY AREN'T OPTIONAL.
THEN WHY DO YOU CALL THEM SUGGESTIONS?
©2009 Scott Adams, Inc. /Dist. by UFS, Inc.
SOMETIMES I CALL THINGS THE WRONG NAMES TO IMPROVE MORALE.
YOU SHOULD JUST SAY WHAT YOU'RE THINKING. I CAN HANDLE THE TRUTH.
FINE. MAKE ALL OF THE CHANGES I WANT, YOU IGNORANT HUMP.
AND DO IT NOW WHILE I MOCK YOU WITH SHEEP NOISES.
BAAAA! BAAAA! BAAAA!
7-19-09
MAYBE YOUR FIRST WAY WAS BETTER.
NO ONE WILL EVER LOVE YOU!

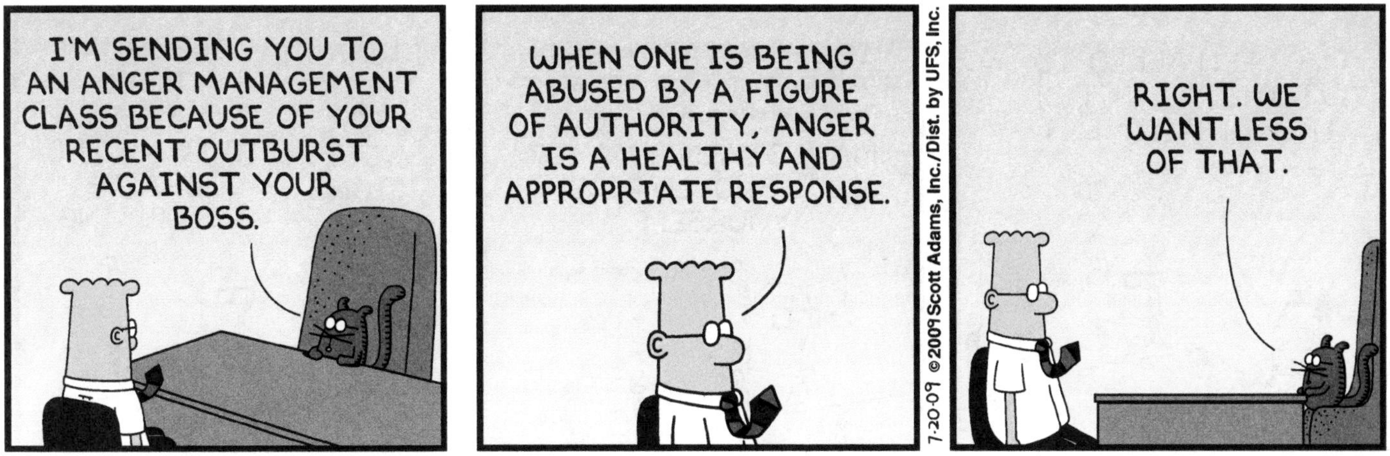
I'M SENDING YOU TO AN ANGER MANAGEMENT CLASS BECAUSE OF YOUR RECENT OUTBURST AGAINST YOUR BOSS.
WHEN ONE IS BEING ABUSED BY A FIGURE OF AUTHORITY, ANGER IS A HEALTHY AND APPROPRIATE RESPONSE.
7-20-09 ©2009 Scott Adams, Inc./Dist. by UFS, Inc.
RIGHT. WE WANT LESS OF THAT.

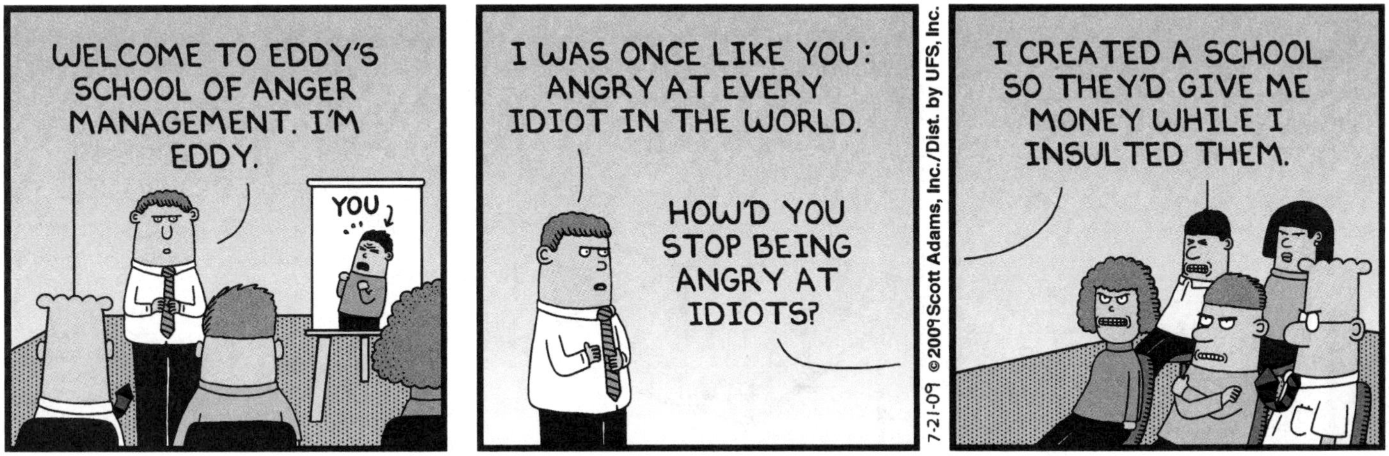
WELCOME TO EDDY'S SCHOOL OF ANGER MANAGEMENT. I'M EDDY.
YOU
I WAS ONCE LIKE YOU: ANGRY AT EVERY IDIOT IN THE WORLD.
HOW'D YOU STOP BEING ANGRY AT IDIOTS?
7-21-09 ©2009 Scott Adams, Inc./Dist. by UFS, Inc.
I CREATED A SCHOOL SO THEY'D GIVE ME MONEY WHILE I INSULTED THEM.

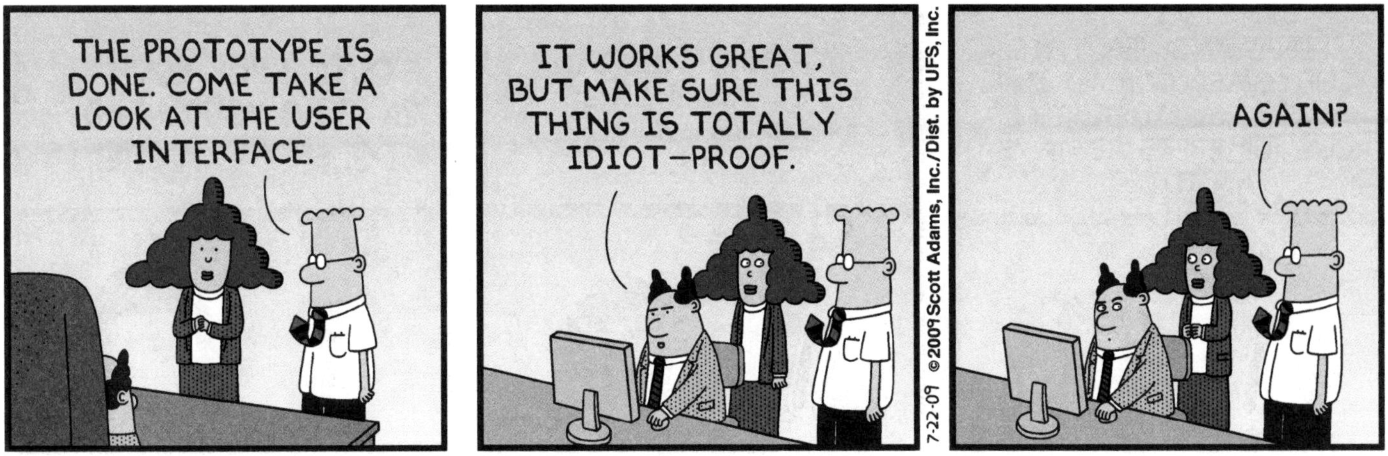
THE PROTOTYPE IS DONE. COME TAKE A LOOK AT THE USER INTERFACE.
IT WORKS GREAT, BUT MAKE SURE THIS THING IS TOTALLY IDIOT-PROOF.
7-22-09 ©2009 Scott Adams, Inc./Dist. by UFS, Inc.
AGAIN?

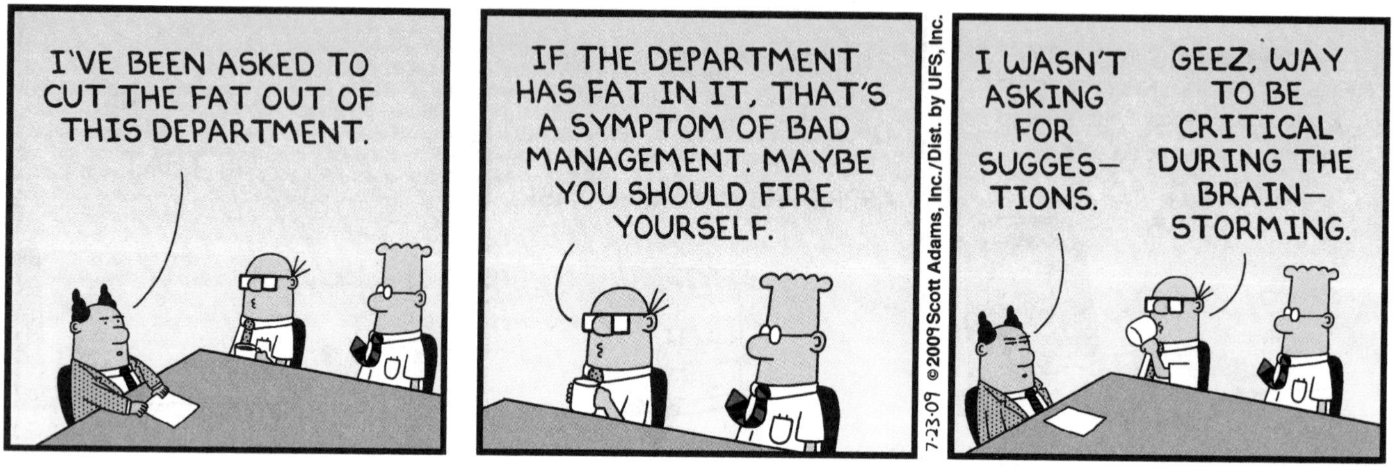
I'VE BEEN ASKED TO CUT THE FAT OUT OF THIS DEPARTMENT.
IF THE DEPARTMENT HAS FAT IN IT, THAT'S A SYMPTOM OF BAD MANAGEMENT. MAYBE YOU SHOULD FIRE YOURSELF.
7·23·09 ©2009 Scott Adams, Inc./Dist. by UFS, Inc.
I WASN'T ASKING FOR SUGGES–TIONS.
GEEZ, WAY TO BE CRITICAL DURING THE BRAIN–STORMING.

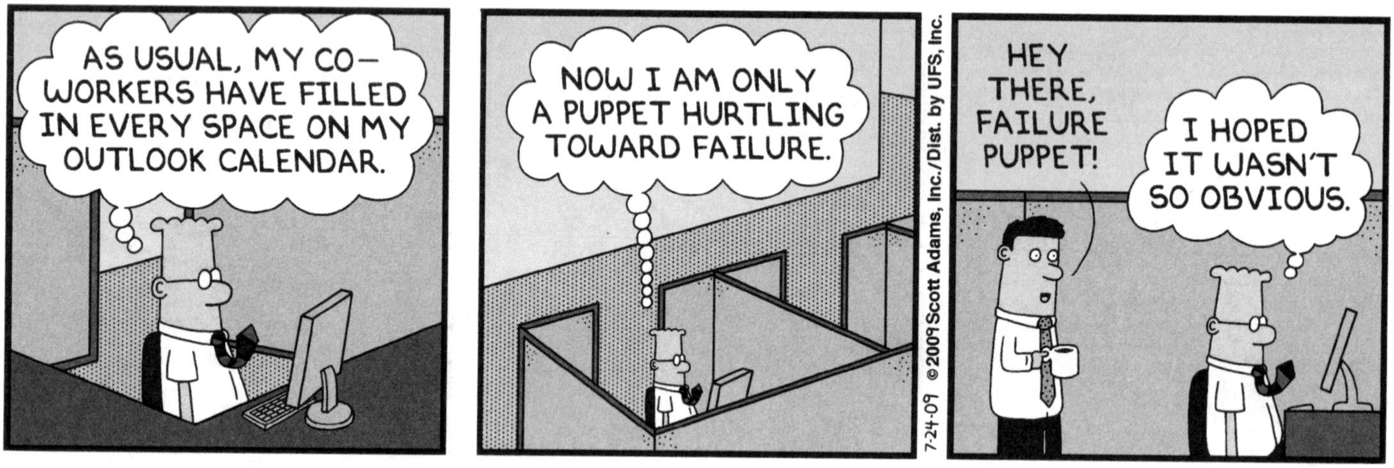
AS USUAL, MY CO–WORKERS HAVE FILLED IN EVERY SPACE ON MY OUTLOOK CALENDAR.
NOW I AM ONLY A PUPPET HURTLING TOWARD FAILURE.
7·24·09 ©2009 Scott Adams, Inc./Dist. by UFS, Inc.
HEY THERE, FAILURE PUPPET!
I HOPED IT WASN'T SO OBVIOUS.

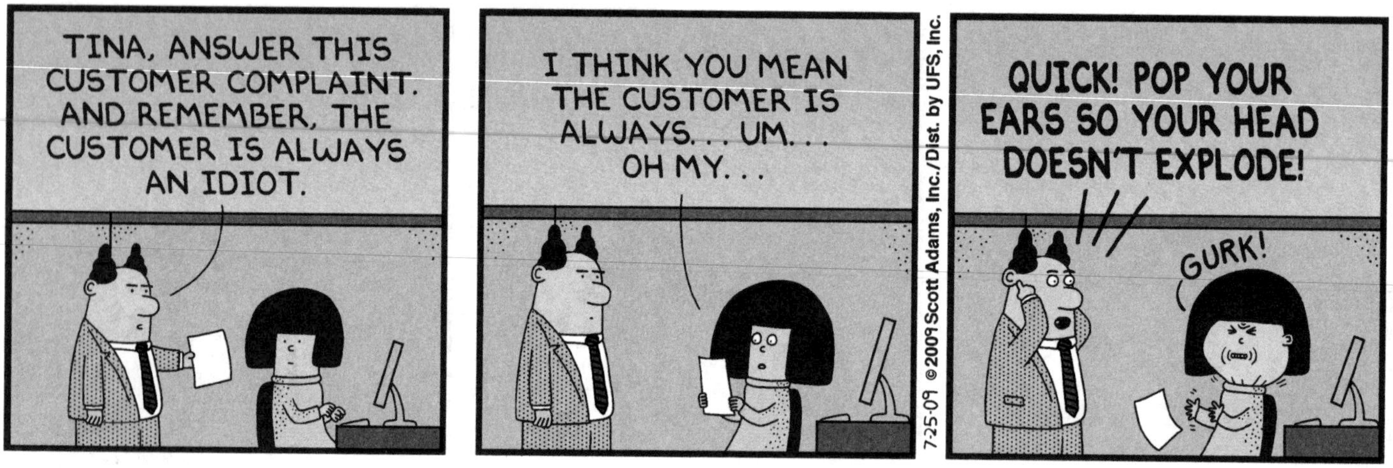
TINA, ANSWER THIS CUSTOMER COMPLAINT. AND REMEMBER, THE CUSTOMER IS ALWAYS AN IDIOT.
I THINK YOU MEAN THE CUSTOMER IS ALWAYS. . . UM. . . OH MY. . .
7·25·09 ©2009 Scott Adams, Inc./Dist. by UFS, Inc.
QUICK! POP YOUR EARS SO YOUR HEAD DOESN'T EXPLODE!
GURK!